Bastards in Egypt
Social and Legal Illegitimacy in the Roman Era

The Journal of Juristic Papyrology
Supplement XXXVII

UNIVERSITY OF WARSAW
FACULTY OF LAW AND ADMINISTRATION
CHAIR OF ROMAN AND ANTIQUE LAW

UNIVERSITY OF WARSAW
INSTITUTE OF ARCHAEOLOGY
DEPARTMENT OF PAPYROLOGY

THE RAPHAEL TAUBENSCHLAG
FOUNDATION

The Journal of Juristic Papyrology

Supplements

SERIES EDITORS
TOMASZ DERDA
ADAM ŁAJTAR
JAKUB URBANIK

VOLUME XXXVII

The Journal of Juristic Papyrology
Supplement XXXVII

Bastards in Egypt
Social and Legal Illegitimacy in the Roman Era

Maria Nowak

PEETERS
LEUVEN – PARIS – BRISTOL, CT
2020

Supplements to The Journal of Juristic Papyrology are jointly published by the Faculty of Law and Administration of the University of Warsaw, the Institute of Archaeology of the University of Warsaw, and the Raphael Taubenschlag Foundation, Krakowskie Przedmieście 26/28, 00–927 Warszawa 64
tel.: (+4822) 55 22 815 and (+4822) 55 20 384, fax: (+4822) 55 24 319
e-mails: t.derda@uw.edu.pl, kuba@adm.uw.edu.pl
a.lajtar@uw.edu.pl, g.ochala@uw.edu.pl
books@taubenschlagfoundation.pl
web-page: http://www.taubenschlagfoundation.pl

Reviewed by Maria Zabłocka

Cover design by Maryna Wiśniewska

Editing and proofreading by Tomasz Płóciennik
English proofreading by Jesse Simon
Computer design and DTP by Antoni Grabowski

The present book was published thanks
to the National Science Centre grant no. 2015/17/D/HS3/00376.

Cover photos
papyrus: © Staatliche Museen zu Berlin – Ägyptisches Museum und Papyrussammlung, Berliner Papyrusdatenbank, P 11656 B (Ausschnitt)
gold glass medallion with a mother and child:
© The Metropolitan Museum of Art
inscription: https://edh-www.adw.uni-heidelberg.de/edh/foto/F024293
(© F. Feraudi-Gruénais)

A catalogue record for this book is available from the Library of Congress.

ISBN 978-90-429-4268-4
eISBN 978-90-429-4269-1
D/2020/0602/68

In Memory
of Józef Mélèze Modrzejewski

TABLE OF CONTENTS

ACKNOWLEDGMENTS

IN THE COURSE OF WRITING this book I have benefited from the input and advice of numerous colleagues and friends, to whom I would like now to express my immense gratitude.

This book would not have been written without the support of Agnieszka Kacprzak, whom I am fortunate to count not only as an esteemed colleague but also a dear friend; in addition to reading the entire manuscript – some parts more than once – she was also willing to spend long hours discussing with me various possible interpretations of sources. Jakub Urbanik, my mentor and now a fellow papyrologist, offered valuable comments on the manuscript and engaged in many discussions regarding certain positions adopted in the book. My colleagues Adam Łajtar and Tomasz Derda from the Faculty of History at the University of Warsaw also provided much insightful commentary, and while writing the initial manuscript I benefited from the corrections and remarks of Ewa Wipszycka and Adam Ziółkowski.

I am grateful to Professor Andrea Jördens, who hosted me in Heidelberg for the two years of my Humboldt fellowship, during which much of the final manuscript was written; in addition to discussing aspects of my research, she also provided me the opportunity to present different stages of my work at her seminar. I should also wish to express my gratitude to the participants of these seminars, as well as to the colleagues with whom I became acquainted at the Institute of Papyrology at the Ruprecht Karl University of Heidelberg, including Rodney Ast, Julia Lougovaya-Ast, James Cowey, Giuditta Mirizio, and Mario Varvaro who spent a semester in 2018 in Heidelberg. My work benefited from their comments during the seminars, and they were patient enough to answer numerous questions pertaining to their areas of expertise. This book profited also from the discussions carried out in the framework of the project financed by the Spanish Ministerio de Economía y Competitividad (DER 2015-67052-P).

Special gratitude is owed to Małgorzata Krawczyk, who collected the Latin epigraphical sources used in this book, and made my work much easier. Sandra Lippert and David Lewis provided me with much literature on illegitimacy in Egypt and slave-free unions in the Greek world, respectively, and I am grateful for these important sources. As a non-native English speaker I have benefited from the assistance of Jesse Simon throughout my academic career; this book was no exception and I am grateful for his proofreading. Tomasz Płóciennik assisted in giving the final shape to this book; Konstantinos Balamoshev kindly proofread the translations from the Greek which appear in the book. Medha Chaturvedi contributed various linguistic improvements, making the text more accessible (and perhaps even a bit more enjoyable to read).

Last but not least, I owe my deepest gratitude to my husband, Grzegorz Ochała, who has been a constant source of support for me.

The publication, research and proofreading of this book was financed by the National Science Centre (grant no. UMO-2015/17/D/HS3/00376).

The Journal of Juristic Papyrology
Supplement XXXVII

Bastards in Egypt

Social and Legal Illegitimacy in the Roman Era

INTRODUCTION

History of bastards is a mixed bag: from stigmatization so entrenched in the language that we reserve the denomination for certain persons of reduced kindness, to the flair and panache of famous bastards like William the Conqueror and Cesare Borgia. Like other people not really fitting in with the social systems, which preferred that such people did not exist in the first place, they were at the same time discriminated and recognized – a situation perhaps more depicted, or rather blazoned, by batons sinister: negatively distinguishing the bearers but still allowing them to display the coat of arms.

Dropping some of the more appealing cultural depictions of bastardy, like a jocular reference to the almost historical film by Quentin Tarantino, we should indulge in real-life examples. For this purpose, I have chosen legal examples attesting to discrimination of bastards but, also, painting their picture more nuanced than the popular culture would prompt.

An exemplary passage in this respect is excerpted from a decision by the Massachusetts Supreme Judicial Court in the case Goodridge v. Department of Public Health.

> Goodridge v. Dep't of Pub. Health, 798 N.E.2d 941, 957 (Mass. 2003):[1] Where a married couple has children, their children are also directly or indirectly, but no less auspiciously, the recipients of the special legal and economic protections obtained by civil marriage. Notwithstanding the Commonwealth's strong public policy to abolish legal distinctions between marital and nonmarital children in providing for the support and care of minors (see Department of Revenue v. Mason M., 439 Mass. 665 [2003]; Woodward v. Commissioner of Social Sec., 435 Mass. 536, 546 [2002]), the

[1] Full text of the decision is available on http://masscases.com/cases/sjc/440/440mass309.html.

> fact remains that marital children reap a measure of family stability and economic security based on their parents' legally privileged status that is largely inaccessible, or not as readily accessible, to nonmarital children. Some of these benefits are social, such as the enhanced approval that still attends the status of being a marital child. Others are material, such as the greater ease of access to family-based State and Federal benefits that attend the presumptions of one's parentage.

It was the first decision by the U.S. state's highest court that same-sex couples had the right to marry. The case was brought by seven same-sex couples against the Massachusetts Department of Health, which had refused to issue marriage certificates to these couples. One of arguments in favour of same-sex marriages concerned the offspring: according to the Court the couples should be allowed to marry so that their children had the opportunity to become marital offspring in the same way as children of heterosexual couples, underlining the fact that legitimacy is still a factor in the social and legal standing of children.

An even more telling example is an amendment to the Civil Code of Malta introduced ony in 2004, which eliminated the term 'illegitimate' and the prerogative distinction between children were eliminated. It also altered the procedure of child's recognition by its father by making a consent of mother necessary for his acknowledgment of fatherhood. Before this amendment took place, the father was allowed to acknowledge his children by his unilateral declaration with the omission of both the mother and the children.

Examples like these, which are by no means unique in the contemporary world, clearly illustrate that being an out-of-wedlock child can still be a matter of controversy. This negative perception of bastardy is evidently rooted in the history of Western civilization, where numerous analogous examples can be traced. Among them we find, for instance, the *Edictum Rothari* enacted in AD 643 by the assembly of the Longobard army. The edict is considered primitive compared with other codes of the so-called *leges barbarorum*, and is believed to be a collection of old tribal customs of the Lombards supplemented with Biblical texts and laws from Roman and Germanic sources.[2] In regard to those born out of wedlock it remains

[2] N. Everett, 'Literacy and the law in Lombard government', *Early Medieval Europe* 9 (2000), pp. 93–127, p. 96.

ambiguous: such individuals could obtain much less than marital offspring, but they are still allowed to a meager part of the paternal inheritance, which could be interpreted as both a repression and a favour.

> *Edictum Rothari*, c. 154–155 (in: *Leges Langobardorum*, *MGH Leges* 4, pp. 35–36):[3] De filiûs legetimûs et naturalis. Si quis dereliquerit filium legitimum unum, quod est fulboran, et filiûs naturalis unum aut plures, filius legitimus tollat duas portiones de patris substantia, naturalis tertiam. Si duo fuerint legitimi, habeant naturales quintam partem, quanticumque fuerent; si tres fuerent legitimi, habeant naturales septimam partem (...). 155. Nulli sit licentia, naturales filiûs aequales aut consemelis facere legetimis filiis, nisi si filii legetimi post conpletam legetimam aetatem patri consenserint. Legitima aetas est, postquam filii duodicem annûs habuerint.
>
> On legitimate and natural sons. If someone leaves a legitimate son, who is well-born, and a natural son or a few, the legitimate son takes two parts of the paternal property, the natural one-third. If legitimate sons are two, natural ones have one-fifth, no matter how many they are; if legitimate sons are three, natural ones have one-seventh (...). 155. No one has the liberty to make natural sons equal or similar to legitimate sons, except for if legitimate sons having reached the legitimate age consent. The legitimate age is this after which sons are twelve years old.

Another passage comes from *The Third Statute of Lithuania* issued in AD 1588 in the early modern Polish-Lithuanian Commonwealth. This was the last of three codifications prepared and issued in the sixteenth century in order to unify Lithuanian law. All three Statutes contained private and public regulations and were based on local laws and customs as well as the Roman law taught in the universities of sixteenth-century Europe. *The Third Statute*, which remained in force until the nineteenth century, is considered a masterpiece of legislation for its time.[4] It ostensibly illustrates the lower position of bastards, who, having been murdered, were always treated as commoners no matter who their parents were.

[3] Another edition: 'Edictum Rothari', [in:] C. Azzara & S. Gasparri (eds.), *Le leggi dei Longobardi. Storia, memoria e diritto di un popolo germanico*, Milan 1992.

[4] On the statute, see: J. Bardach, 'Les statuts lituaniens – codifications de l'époque de la Renaissance', [in:] B. Geremek & A. Mączak (eds.), *Poland at the 14th International Congress of Historical Sciences in San Francisco. Studies in Comparative History*, Wrocław – Warsaw – Kraków – Gdańsk 1975, pp. 45–65.

The Third Statute of Lithuania (ed. 1786), 14.32: Ktoby Bękarta zabił, taki od gardła wolny bydź ma. Wszakże jeśliby Matka żywa była onego Bękarta, wolno iey będzie głowszczyzny dochodzić. A głowszczyzna takowemu Synowi, by go też miała nie wiedzieć z jak zacnym Człowiekiem, nie ma bydź płacona, iedno jak za prostego stanu Człowieka.

Whoever would kill a bastard shall not be beheaded. Yet, if a mother of such a bastard lives, she shall be allowed to seek weregild. The weregild for such a son, even if she had him with the most illustrious man, shall be paid as for a commoner.

The third quotation has its origin in the Napoleonic Code, one of the first modern codifications, designed to both replace old feudal laws and reinforce the principles of the French Revolution. It is a famous passage forbidding any search for fathers of children born out of marriage, a regulation that automatically deprived the children of any rights deriving from their fathers.

Code civil §340: La recherche de la paternité est interdite. Dans le cas d'enlèvement, lorsque l'époque de cet enlèvement se rapportera à celle de la conception, le ravisseur pourra être, sur la demande des parties intéressées, déclaré père de l'enfant.

Scrutiny as to paternity is forbidden. In the case of rape, when the period of such rape shall refer to that of conception, the ravisher may be declared, on the petition of the parties interested, the father of the child.[5]

The above examples, which originated in disparate legal and cultural realities, serve to illustrate an obvious truth: throughout the course of Western history, children born out of wedlock enjoyed neither the social nor legal standing of marital children. Of course, there were exceptions, especially among the elite, who enjoyed good lives despite being born out of wedlock, or means to make illegitimate children legitimate. For instance, John of the Lithuanian Dukes, from the time of the Lithuanian Statute, was the natural son of the Polish king Sigismund I the Old and Katarzyna Telniczanka. He was granted the bishopric of Vilnius, and later

[5] Tr. *The French Civil Code. Literally Translated from the Original and Official Edition. Published at Paris, in 1804*, translation attributed to G. Spence, London 1827.

of Posen, but even he, the king's son, could not have achieved his noble title or position of bishop without a papal dispensation.[6] The case of John of the Lithuanian Dukes illustrates that even royal bastards needed to be freed from the stigma to achieve dignities and honours. Being born out of wedlock caused complications in the lives of not only commoners, but even the elite. The question is whether these attitudes developed independently or if they had a common root.

1. COMMON ROOT?

In modern scholarship, especially comparative legal studies, there is a strong tendency to look for the common root. In branches of law regulating the relationships within a family, Roman law is the usual suspect. In the introductions to many books discussing modern legal institutions, 'Roman law' is presented as a kind of 'ideal law',[7] which may be understood as a model for modern practices, not only in the scholarship, but even in judicial decisions. A recent example is the dissenting opinion of judges Pejchal and Wojtyczek in the case *Orlandi and Others v. Italy* brought to the European Court of Human Rights by six same-sex couples who tried to register their legal marriages contracted outside of Italy, but whose applications were rejected. While the Court decided that the rejections violated the right of protection and recognition for same-sex unions, judges Pejchal and Wojtyczek expressed a contrary opinion. One of their arguments referred to the definition of marriage by Modestinus and Justinian.

> Pejchal and Wojtyczek's dissenting opinion in Judgment of the European Court of Human Rights of 14.12.2017, Orlandi and Others v. Italy,

[6] A. Theiner, *Vetera monumenta Poloniae et Lithuaniae gentiumque finitimarum historiam illustrantia maximam partem nondum edita ex tabulariis Vaticanis deprompta collecta ac serie chronologica disposita*, vol. II, Rome 1861, pp. 334–336 & 366.

[7] This phenomenon developed in modern studies on Roman and comparative laws was discussed in regard to Roman marriage by J. Urbanik, 'On the uselessness of it all: the Roman law of marriage and modern times', *Fundamina* 20.1 = *Editio specialis: Meditationes de iure et historia. Essays in honour of Laurens Winkel* (2014), pp. 937–951, p. 937. The author convincingly demonstrated that Roman categories should not be translated into modern ones due to, among other, very different meaning of modern and Roman institutions.

> no. 26431/12: In this context we note firstly that the terms 'to marry' and 'marriage' have become polysemes. Marriage in its initial meaning presupposes the community of lives between a man and a woman. We note in this context the following definitions of marriage: 'Nuptiae sunt coniunctio maris et feminae et consortium omnis vitae, divini et humani iuriscommunicatio' (Modestinus, *Digesta Iustiniani* 23.2.1); 'Nuptiae autem sive matrimonium est viri et mulieris coniunctio, individuam consuetudinem vitae continens' (*Institutiones Iustiniani*, 1.10). The complementariness of the biological sexes of the two spouses is a constitutive element of marriage. Moreover, marriage in this meaning is – by definition – a social institution open to procreation. The fact that certain married couples may suffer from infertility does not affect its social function.

This opinion illustrates the presumption that modern legal institutions should resemble, at least to some extent, the Roman ones, that Roman institutions can be a landmark for reconstructing natural law, and that modern institutions have evolved directly from the Roman ones.[8]

The issue is even more complicated when it comes to the notion of illegitimacy. In the modern world, whether in a local court of law or in the European Court of Human Rights, it would be unthinkable to argue that a daughter or son born out of wedlock should not be granted succession after their father simply because this was how the things worked for the Romans. Indeed, such an opinion might provoke surprised reactions among academics, lawyers and perhaps even the public. In popular perception, the stigmatization of children born out of wedlock was connected less to Roman law than to changes introduced by the spread of Christianity either in late Antiquity or in the Middle Ages. This opinion can be found in a study on the legal position of illegitimate children issued by the League of Nations in 1939:

> In the Roman Empire, for example, the conception of the family introduced by the Christian Church completely transformed the legal and social position of illegitimate children. Concubinage was disavowed and, to bring about its disappearance, the emperors introduced various restrictive measures preventing illegitimate and legitimate children from being placed on

[8] That this is not true in regard to the Roman marriage and that the Roman marriage was a product of its epoch, not a universal concept, has been demonstrated in Urbanik, 'On the uselessness of it all' (cit. n. 7).

> the same footing. Thus the children were made to suffer as a means of indirectly penalising extra-marital relations (p. 8).

or even in a more recent legal study:

> Roman law was not originally quite so harsh, requiring mothers who kept their illegitimate children to support them, but the later Christian emperors denied certain classes of illegitimate children all support.[9]

or:

> This *ius commune* took shape within the framework of the first attempt to unify family law which occurred in Europe. This unification represented the final point in the gradual replacement of the wide spectrum of pre-Christian marriage and divorce law, characterised by its informal rules as to the formation of marriage, easy divorce, tolerance towards concubinage and the acceptance of illegitimate children, by an entirely new set of uniform canon law rules.[10]

2. AIMS AND QUESTIONS

But was Christianity responsible for shaping the ways that non-marital children were perceived and treated in late Roman law? While the changes themselves may have come from Christianity, it was Roman law which provided the framework for their emergence. The primary aim of this book is, therefore, to reconstruct the Roman concept of bastardy and how that concept evolved between the imperial and late Roman periods in Roman Egypt. An important question to address is whether the 'illegitimate' or 'extramarital' children in the Roman era formed a homogenous group, or whether they were subdivided into classes of individuals born of various situations, which then resulted in different legal standings.

[9] R.F. Storrow, 'The phantom children of the Republic: international surrogacy and the new illegitimacy', *American University Journal of Gender Social Policy and Law* 20. 3 (2012), pp. 561–609, p. 568.

[10] M. Antokolskaia, ' The harmonisation of family law: old and new dilemmas', *European Review of Private Law* 1 (2003), pp. 28–49, p. 39.

My reconstruction will be based on individual studies of terminology, descriptions, rules concerning status acquisition, and laws of succession. In examining the question of illegitimacy I may also be able to shed some light on the wider problem of status acquisition in Roman Egypt. Yet, I will not provide the readers with detailed studies on the succession by and from persons born out of wedlock, neither will I study particular problems, such as adoption. There are two reasons for this. First, I do not aim to provide with this book a companion of illegitimacy in Roman law or Roman Empire, but to comprehend what illegitimacy meant in both legal thought and practice. Some of these issues – and that is the other reasons – I discuss in a number of shorter studies, such as succession or adoption or access to corn dole, that came to light as offshoots of this mongraph.[11]

3. SCHOLARSHIP

A monograph explaining who children born out of wedlock were in Roman Egypt is in demand, because this issue has never been studied as a whole: only a few rather brief (but important) articles devoted mostly to the terminology are available. Aristide Calderini was the first to approach the problem of descriptions relating to illegitimacy and drew conclusions on social status of people described with them.[12] Perhaps the best known work devoted to illegitimate children in Roman Egypt is an article by Her-

[11] A. Kacprzak & M. Nowak, 'Foundlings in the Greco-Roman world: Status and the (im)possibility of adoption', *Tijdschrift voor Rechtsgeschiedenis* 86 (2018), pp. 13–54; M. Nowak, 'The hereditary rights of the extramarital children in light of the law of papyri', [in:] B. Caseau & S.R. Huebner (eds.), *Inheritance, Law and Religions in the Ancient and Mediaeval Worlds* [= *Monographies du Centre de Recherche d'Histoire et Civilisation de Byzance – Collège de France* XLV], Paris 2014, pp 11–24; eadem, 'The fatherless and family structure in Roman Egypt', [in:] D. Leão & G. Thür (eds.), *Symposion 2015, Vorträge zur griechischen und hellenistischen Rechtsgeschichte (Coimbra 1–4 Setembro 2015)* [= *Akten der Gesellschaft für Griechische und Hellenistische Rechtsgeschichte* XXV], Vienna 2016, pp. 100–114; eadem, 'Get your free corn: The fatherless in the corn-dole archive from Oxyrhynchos', [in:] M. Nowak, A. Łajtar & J. Urbanik (eds.), *Tell Me Who You Are. Labelling Status in the Graeco-Roman World*, Warsaw 2018, pp. 215–228; eadem, 'Fatherless among *οἱ ἀπὸ τῆς μητροπόλεως* – a revision', *Zeitschrift für Papyrologie und Epigraphik* 208 (2018), pp. 213–225.

[12] A. Calderini, '*Ἀπάτορες*', *Aegyptus* 33 (1953), pp. 358–369.

bert Youtie, where he concluded that children born out of wedlock were not socially stigmatized in Roman Egypt.[13] Relatively recently the problem gained more attention in studies by Myrto Malouta,[14] Roger Bagnall,[15] Yanne Broux,[16] Uri Yiftach[17] and myself. The results of these investigations and my take on them are discussed in detail in chapter 1. Obviously, questions related to being born out of wedlock also occur in scholarship on family or army, referred to and discussed in various places in this book.

4. SOURCES AND SCOPE OF RESEARCH

Although the conclusions reached in this book – especially those in the first and last chapters – are relevant to the whole of the Roman empire, the present work is focused on Roman Egypt. This geographical limitation is dictated for the most part by the sources available for the period. Much of our information on families, children, and familial status within the Roman Empire comes from texts of Roman law. Yet, the problem with constructing a picture of illegitimacy based solely on Roman law is that the sources represent an idea *sensu stricto* of what the Roman family should be. In practical terms, this means that non-Romans are mentioned only

[13] H. Youtie, '*Ἀπάτορες*. Law vs. custom in Roman Egypt', [in:] J. Bingen, G. Cambier & G. Nachtergael (eds.), *Le monde grec : pensée, littérature, histoire, documents. Hommages à Claire Préaux*, Brussels 1975, pp. 723–740 (reprinted in: H. Youtie, *Scriptiunculae posteriores*, vol. I, Bonn 1981, pp. 17–35).

[14] M. Malouta, 'The terminology of fatherlessness in Roman Egypt: ἀπάτωρ and χρηματίζων μητρός', [in:] J. Frösén, T. Purola & E. Salmenkivi (eds.), *Proceedings of the 24th International Congress of Papyrology, Helsinki, 1–7 August, 2004* [= *Commentationes Humanarum Litterarum* CXXII], Helsinki 2007, vol. II, pp. 615–623; eadem, 'Fatherlessness and formal identification in Roman Egypt', [in:] S.R. Huebner & D. M. Ratzan (eds.), *Growing up Fatherless in Antiquity*, Cambridge 2009, pp. 120–138.

[15] R.S. Bagnall, 'Illegitimacy in Roman and late antique Egypt', [in:] T. Derda, A. Łajtar, & J. Urbanik (eds.), in collaboration with A. Mirończuk & G. Ochała, *Proceedings of the 27th International Congress of Papyrology, Warsaw 29.07–3.08 2013* [= *The Journal of Juristic Papyrology Supplement* XXVII], Warsaw, vol. I, pp. 5–17.

[16] Y. Broux, 'Re: Apatores. Identification issues and loss of status in Roman Egypt', *Zeitschrift für Papyrologie und Epigraphik* 2015 (194), pp. 212–214.

[17] U. Yiftach, '*Apator metros*: The rise of a formula in bureaucratic perspective. Response to Maria Nowak', [in:] D. Leão & G. Thür (eds.), *Symposion 2015* (cit. n. 11), pp. 115–120.

when they interact with Roman citizens or once they acquire citizenship. Some exceptions exist, such as the *Gnomon of idios logos*, but they are few.

Some practical issues were simply not discussed in the corpus of Roman law, and some were mentioned only in passing. One example is a mysterious law stating that children born to a woman who knew that her partner was someone else's slave were to be considered slaves (G. 1.86). The law is mentioned only once in the entire corpus of dogmatic Roman law and remains largely incomprehensible (a full discussion follows in Chapter 2).

An additional but crucial problem with legal sources is that they do not represent 'real' reality. Although imperial laws and jurisprudence often refer to real-life cases, they do not provide us with enough information to understand how the law was applied in practice. A reconstruction based solely on the theoretic corpus of Roman law would give us only a picture of an 'ideal' or 'intended' reality. Thus, if we are to understand legal phenomena beyond their theoretical application, we must examine not only the laws themselves, but also the legal practices that shed light on the actual legal and social phenomena described in legal codes and handbooks.

Within the Empire as the whole, inscriptions are the principal source for such information. For the Roman family, epitaphs are the most informative, although the details they provide are highly limited: name, age, occasionally an indication of the relationship between the commemorated and the commemorating individuals, or hints regarding his/her personal status (e.g. *l(ibertus)* or *Sp(urii) f(ilius)*). Even this data, however, does not offer a full picture of legal history, as the vocabulary of familial relationships refers not to legal definitions but to simple facts. The label *uxor*, for example, designates both female life-partners and legally wedded wives. Constructing a model of illegitimacy from such material is risky.

Only in Egyptian papyri do we find abundant information regarding the actual standing of persons born out of wedlock. Such individuals occur in all types of documents: texts concerning personal status (birth registrations, scrutinies, census returns), fiscal documents, and deeds of private law. The pieces of information that we find in them not only provide us with the raw data from which we can reconstruct familial structures, but also allow us to compare positive law with the actual legal practice. Many a time, the data gathered from papyri can be examined against the laws preserved in 'books' and inscriptions. In some cases, the conclusions drawn from this material are clearly limited to the Egyptian province, but in other ones, pan-imperial generalisations are possible.

5. CHRONOLOGY

The 'Roman era' that forms the chronological scope of this book begins with the Roman conquest of Egypt and extends to the end of Constantine's reign. Although our discussion formally begins in 30 BC, material dated to the first century of the Roman rule in Egypt occurs rarely. This is due to the chronological distribution of the material: considerably fewer papyri date from the beginnig of the Roman era than from the later period;[18] as a result, texts that refer, be it directly or indirectly, to extramarital status are almost non-existent before the late first century AD. There may also be another reason for the imbalance: the 'Romanisation' of legal and administrative practices most probably was not immediate, but rather took place over the span of several decades or even a century. Even if the Romans had started enforcing their rules in Egypt immediately, it would certainly take time for legal practices to adapt to the new laws.

Occasionally, I refer to the material predating the Roman rule, thus providing an interpretive context and a possible source of comparative data. This is, for instance, necessary for the reconstruction of the rules governing status acquisition by individuals born to parents of different civic or freedom standing. Such cases are identifiable in the source material, which makes the comparison possible.[19] Unfortunately, this kind of comparative argument could not fill in all lacunae in our knowledge. For example, we cannot compare the situation of fatherless individuals, because such special terms as ἀπάτωρ or *spurius* indicating the fatherlessness known from

[18] W. HABERMANN, 'Zur chronologischen Verteilung der papyrologischen Zeugnisse', *Zeitschrift für Papyrologie und Epigraphik* 122 (1998), pp. 144–160, p. 147, fig. 1.

[19] They are based on works of excellent experts in Ptolemaic law, especially Józef Mélèze Modrzejewski. See J. MÉLÈZE MODRZEJEWSKI, *Statut personnel et liens de famille dans les droits de l'Antiquité*, Aldershot 1993; IDEM, *Droit et justice dans le monde grec et hellénistique* [= *The Journal of Juristic Papyrology Supplement* X], Warsaw 2010; IDEM, *Loi et coutume dans l'Égypte grecque et romaine* [= *The Journal of Juristic Papyrology Supplement* XXI], Warsaw 2014.

the Roman era are not attested in sources from Hellenistic Egypt. The same concerns false filiations: even if they did exist, they would be difficult to trace, because we do not have a text similar to Plutarch's *Moralia* 288 E–F, which explains the false filiation *Spurii filius*. There can be no doubt that fatherless individuals were present in the social landscape of Ptolemaic Egypt, but our inability to identify them naturally limits the research to the Roman period.

The reign of Constantine offers a natural ending point for this book, as the laws issued by Constantine near the end of his life changed the standing of individuals born out of wedlock and shaped legal definitions of illegitimacy for the centuries to come.[20] The final chapter explains these changes and proposes an explanation for their occurrence.

6. ROMAN BASTARDS DATABASE

The present study is a part of a larger project that also includes the *Roman Bastards Database* (www.romanbastards.wpia.uw.edu.pl), an online reference containing data on more than 1,800 individuals known or believed to have been born out of wedlock. The entries, collected by Małgorzata Krawczyk (University of Warsaw) and myself, are drawn from papyri and inscriptions and contain basic information on both the individual (names, sex, *status libertatis* and *civitatis*, provenance, parents, siblings, children, and spouses) and the text from which the entry was extracted (language, date, edition[s], basic literature and links to other papyrological or epigraphical databases with digital editions). Entries from outside Egypt were added by Krawczyk, and those from Egyptian texts were introduced by me.

The selection of the material for Egypt has been based on my research presented in the book. The database obviously includes individuals described with direct labels, such as ἀπάτωρ or *spurius*. Metronyms are more problematic, because the sources usually do not provide enough information on whether the metronym was used because a person did not have a father or for other reasons. Similarly, the presence of maternal

[20] J. Tate, 'Inheritance rights of nonmarital children in late Roman law', *Roman Legal Tradition* 4 (2008), pp. 1–36.

onomastics in the names and descriptions of Roman children does not necessarily imply that they were born outside of *iustae nuptiae*. Only the descriptor χρηματίζων / χρηματίζουσα μητρός always appears as a sign of fatherlessness. Therefore, all the individuals described in this way have been entered into the database, contrariwise, persons for whom the metronym replaces the patronym, or with maternal *gentilicia*, have only been added if their fatherless status is confirmed by other sources.

The research was not limited to papyri.info, and also drew upon both the latest volumes of papyrus editions and the most recent issues of papyrological journals, some individuals may still be missing or have been entered in error. The database, however, is editable and it will be possible to introduce ameliorations and corrections even long after this book has been published.

The records have been collected on tha basis of papyri.info and then checked against printed editions and subsequent corrections. In this way, it was possible to eliminate certain texts in which readings that included terms indicating fatherlessness were later amended, but the corrections have not been introduced online so far. One such example is *P. Mich.* XVIII 792 (Oxyrhynchos, AD 221), a receipt of payment in advance for lease. Both the *editio princeps* and the digital edition provide the reading [Αὐρήλιο]ς Φιλώτας̣ ἀπά[τ]ω̣ρ̣ μ̣[ητρὸς] | Ταηρ[ακλ]είδου in lines 1–2. Peter van Minnen, however, published a duplicate of the document (P. Mich. inv. 379), where he reads: [Αὐρήλιος Φιλ]ώτας Πετεμούνιος μ̣ητρὸς | [Ταηρακλείδου].[21] This would have been the only certain case of an individuals described once with a patronym and once with its substitution, ἀπάτωρ. Yet, having checked the images of *P. Mich.* XVIII 792, van Minnen also corrected his reading of ἀπά[τ]ω̣ρ̣ in line 1 to Πετεμού[νιος]. Obviously, Aurelius Philotas was not entered into the database.

Another example is *P. Fay.* 319 *descr.* = *SB* XX 14111, an *epikrisis* to the group of *katoikoi* (Ptolemais Euergetis, AD 160/1 or later). Among the people listed in one of the census returns attached to the application we find ἀπάτ⟨ο⟩ρα̣ Ἡρωίδα̣ ἀδελφὴν ὁ̣μ̣ο̣μ̣[ήτριον - *ca.* ? -] listed in line 18. Orsolina

[21] P. van Minnen, 'Another copy of *P. Mich.* XVIII 792', *Zeitschrift für Papyrologie und Epigraphik* 191 (2014), pp. 251–252.

Montevecchi read ἀπάτωρ as the label of Herois.[22] Yet, if this were correct, it would be the only known attestation of the term applied to an individual whose father was known (except for *P. Lond.* II 324, p. 63 = *W. Chr.* 208, which receives a different explanation in Chapter 1). Roger Bagnall, however, found the reading ἀπάτ⟨ο⟩ρα̣ both paleographically and syntactically implausible, and read ραπτS instead, which he interpreted as ῥάπτης.[23] Examples such as these are worth highlighting because, if the first readings had been accepted, they would have created artificial interpretative problems and perhaps even changed conclusions regarding ἀπάτορες.

We should also note that, in many cases, both ἀπάτωρ and χρηματίζων / χρηματίζουσα μητρός occur in an abbreviated form,[24] and the readings of these abbreviations are often far from secure; this is the case of two ostraca from Elephantine, *O. Eleph. DAIK* 47 (Elephantine, AD 185) and *O. Bodl.* II 832, discussed in Chapter 1. In some cases, highly conjectural readings had to be left aside. In line 99 of *P. Stras.* IX 829 (Theadelphia, AD 138–161), the reading: υἱὸς ̣ιλκ( ) ἀ̣π(άτορος) διε̣ ̣ ̣ , was proposed; although the text comes from second-century Theadelphia, where one may indeed expect to find ἀπάτωρ, the grounds for such a reading are far too meager to include it in the database.[25]

Cases in which the terms indicating that a person was born out of wedlock were plausibly, but not certainly reconstructed were generally entered into the database, but marked as problematic and annotated with further explanation. One example is *SB* VI 9069 (Arsinoite nome, 3rd c. AD), a registration of land sale submitted to the ***bibliotheke enkteseon***. One of the buyers was Agathos Daimon, whose patronym did not survive. The editor reconstructed it with ἀπάτωρ, ll. 15–16: Ἀγαθοῦ Δα̣ί̣[μονος | ἀπάτ(ορος) μητ(ρὸς)] Εὐ̣δα̣ι̣μονίδος ἀπελευθέρας Ἀντ[ωνίου (?)], but did not explain it

[22] O. Montevecchi, 'Epikrisis e dichiarazioni di censimento di cateci arsinoiti', *Aegyptus* 70 (1990), pp. 27–31.

[23] R.S. Bagnall, 'Notes on Egyptian census declarations V', *The Bulletin of the American Society of Papyrologists* 30 (1993), pp. 35–56, p. 39.

[24] M. Nowak, 'Ways of describing illegitimate children vs. their legal situation', *Zeitschrift für Papyrologie und Epigraphik* 193 (2015), pp. 207–219, pp. 207–208.

[25] The text contains no other ἀπάτορες, but it does list ἀπελευθέροι abbreviated to ἀπελ().

in the commentary.[26] The reconstruction is certainly possible, although a short patronym without papponym could also have been written in the lacuna. That the mother was a freedwoman is not at all proof that the man was born out of wedlock, as freedwomen are frequently attested as mothers of individuals described with petronyms. The numbers accompanying names refer to their records at the publicly available database at www.romanbastards.wpia.uw.edu.pl.

[26] A. Leeman-De Ridder, 'Requête concernant une vente de terrains. Papyrus de Leyde', [in:] *Symbolae ad jus et historiam antiquitatis pertinentes Julio Christiano van Oven dedicatae*, Leiden 1946, pp. 122–128.

CHAPTER ONE

TERMINOLOGY

INTRODUCTION

THE TERMS RECOGNISED in the literature as referring to illegitimacy will be analysed in this chapter. In ancient Greek and Latin, there were several words used to refer to a child born out of wedlock. Aristide Calderini listed: *νόθοι, νοθογέννητοι, παρθένιοι, κύρνοι, κοριναῖοι, ματρόξενοι, σκοτίοι, ὄθνιοι, σπούριοι, ἀπάτορες*[1] and *χρηματίζοντες μητρός*.[2] In the following chapter, I discuss only the terms attested in Egyptian material. The majority of terms in Calderini's list do not appear in Roman Egypt, although we do find the term *φυσικοί* which Calderini did not include. The first question we must ask is whether those terms were indeed used to mean 'born out of wedlock' in sources dating from before the early fourth century AD. If they were, we must establish their specific meaning and determine their function within the context of Egyptian social and legal practices and even wider in the Roman Empire.

1. NOTHOI

The word *νόθος* is attested already in the Iliad: *νόθος υἱός* as opposition to *γνήσιος*, but its etymology is unknown. In attic Greek, it also meant some-

[1] A. CALDERINI, '*Ἀπάτορες*', *Aegyptus* 33 (1953), pp. 358–369, p. 358.

[2] CALDERINI, '*Ἀπάτορες*' (cit. n. 1), p. 362, n. 3.

thing unauthentic, false.[3] Although *νόθος* is attested as meaning 'bastard'[4] in Byzantine Egypt,[5] we cannot be certain that it served the same function in Hellenistic and Roman documents. Hellenistic and Roman examples of *νόθος* in papyri are rather obscure, and the word is not applied in ways that allow for a simple translation; nor does it appear to have had the same meaning it did in inscriptions from other parts of the Hellenistic world, where it was usually used to describe an individual whose parents were both known and married, but whose civic status was problematic because the mother held a different status from the father.[6]

In Ptolemaic Egypt, *νόθοι* occur mostly in the context of the temple and were interpreted either as children born as a result of temple prostitution or as the illegitimate offspring of priests, temple slaves, *etc.*[7] There are two *testimonia* from the Roman period, but these are not related (at least not directly) to the temple context, and the information they provide is insufficient to help us determine whether *νόθος* was used to describe

[3] See P. CHANTRAINE, *Dictionnaire étymologique de la langue grecque. Histoire des mots*, Paris 1968, *s.v.* '*νόθος*'; F. De DECKER, 'Etymological and methodological observations on the "PG" and "PG?" vocabulary in Robert Beekes's *Etymological Dictionary of Greek*: N', *Studia Linguistica Universitatis Iagellonicae Cracoviensis* 133.3 (2016), pp. 149–169, p. 159.

[4] Cynthia Patterson claimed that *νόθοι* were children born of a concubine and acknowledged by their father: C. PATTERSON, 'Those Athenian bastards', *Classical Antiquity* 9.1 (1990), pp. 40–73. Yet, Ogden argued that in the classical Athenian sources the term applied to all children born out of wedlock. D. OGDEN, *Greek Bastardy in the Classical and Hellenistic Periods*, Oxford 1996, pp. 15–17.

[5] *P. Cair. Masp.* II 67151 (Antinoopolis, AD 570), ll. 205–207; copy 67152; *P. Cair. Masp.* III 67353 R (Antinoopolis, AD 569), ll. 16–18: reconstructed; perhaps influenced by the Greek *Novellae*. H.J. WOLFF, 'The background of the postclassical legislation on illegitimacy', *Seminar* 3 (1945), pp. 21–45, p. 31.

[6] J. VÉLISSAROPOULOS-KARAKOSTAS, 'Les nothoi hellénistiques', [in:] E. HARRIS & G. THÜR (eds.), *Symposion* 2007. *Vorträge zur griechischen und hellenistischen Rechtsgeschichte (Durham, 2.–6. September 2007)* [= *Akten der Gesellschaft für griechische und hellenistische Rechtsgeschichte* XX], Vienna 2008, pp. 253–274.

[7] *BGU* X 1937, l. 1 (provenance unknown, 3rd c. BC): a list related to a temple; *P. Count* 16 = *P. Petr.* III 59 = *W. Chr.* 66, l. 6 (Arsinoite, 243–217 BC): record of tax exemption; *P. Tor. Amen.* 6 = *UPZ* II 194 = *P. Tor.* 9 = *C. Ptol. Sklav.* I 97a, l. 14 (Thebes, 119 BC): record of proceedings; *P. Tebt.* II 302 = *W. Chr.* 368, l. 24 (Tebtynis, AD 71/2): petition to *praefectus Aegypti*. On the interpretations, see W. CLARYSSE & D.J. THOMPSON, *Counting the People in Hellenistic Egypt. Volume 2: Historical Studies* [= *Cambridge Classical Studies*], Cambridge 2006, pp. 179–180.

a person born out of wedlock. The first is a petition which describes the petitioner as Arthonis son of Arthonis with *νόθος* in genetive (*PSI* XIII 1356 [Oxyrhynchos, 1st c. AD], l. 2: *παρὰ Ἀρθοώνιος τοῦ Ἀρθοώνιος Νόθου*); in this instance the editor recognised *νόθος* as a part of the paternal name.[8] Although the name seems awkward, the interpretation is still possible: compound names consisting of the element *nothos* – *e.g.* Aristonothos or Nothokrates – were known to be used by Greeks since the archaic period and are also attested in Graeco-Roman Egypt.[9] It seems probable that Nothos, in this case, was simply a name and one can hardly agree with the opinion of Peter Sijpesteijn that 'the son or (more likely) the father was known in his village as "the bastard"',[10] as there are no other attestations of this meaning of *νόθος* in Roman Egypt.

The other document is *SB* XVI 12334 (Philadelphia, 2nd c. AD), a marriage agreement listing the goods belonging to the various parties. Among them, a slave is mentioned: [*τὴν ὑπάρχουσαν α*]*ὐτῇ παιδίσκην δούλην νόθον Εὐθηνίαν* (l. 13). In an article published in 2015 I interpreted this passage to mean 'the young slave Euthenia, whose father is unknown', but I am now of the opinion that the description must have been applied here as it was applied to live-stock where it signified 'cross-bred'.[11]

On the strength of this evidence we are justified in proposing that the term *νόθος* was not used to describe a 'bastard' or a child born of parents belonging to two different civic bodies either in Ptolemaic or Roman Egypt. The former meaning of the word was brought to Egypt only with the codifications of late antiquity.

[8] See *Onomasticon*, *s.v.* '*νόθος*'.

[9] *E.g.* *Νόθιππος*, 'Bastard Horse', appears once in a letter belonging to Zenon's archive (*P. Cair. Zen.* IV 59588, l. 2 [Philadelphia, 263–229 BC]) and once in a dated to the 2nd c. BC list of names to which numbers of arourae were prescribed (*P. Heid.* III 233, l. 5 [provenance unknown]). Full list of compound names consisting of the element *nothos*, see OGDEN, *Greek Bastardy* (cit. n. 4), pp. 26–27.

[10] P.J. SIJPESTEIJN, 'Short remarks on some papyri. V', *Aegyptus* 71 (1991), pp. 43–51, p. 48.

[11] As in *P. Hib.* I 32 = *M. Chr.* 37, l. 15 (Oxyrhynchite nome, 245 BC): *νόθα* describes *πρόβατα*. See *LSJ*, *s.v.* '*νόθος*'.

M. NOWAK, 'Ways of describing illegitimate children vs. their legal situation', *Zeitschrift für Papyrologie und Epigraphik* 193 (2015), pp. 207–219, p. 210.

2. PARTHENIOI

Even as early as the *Iliad*, we find the substantive παρθένιος used to mean 'the son of an unmarried woman'; the reference is to Eudoros, the son of Polymene by the god Hermes.[12] The famous Partheniai of Tarentum – the sons of Spartan women conceived when the Spartans fought the Messanians – clearly have the same root.[13] According to Calderini, παρθένιοι appears once in the papyri to denote children out of wedlock, *P. Ryl.* II 435 *descr.* (provenance unknown), a second-century fragmentary letter written in highly corrupted Greek:[14]

> ll. 1–3: *Σαραπάμμωνει χέρειν* (l. *χαίρειν*). *Παρήγκελκά συ* (l. *παρήγγελκά σοι*)
> *ἄλλα* (*BL* I 389) *ἄπαξ ὅτι ἆρẹν* (l. *ἆρον*) *τὰ παρθένειά* (or l. *παρθένια*)
> *σου τέκνα, ἆρεν* (l. *ἆρον* [?]) *αὐτὰ ἀπὸ σοῦ.*
> *ἤρκεις μὲν αὐτὰ ἀπὸ σοῦ, ἀλλὰ* [- *ca.* ? -]

The letter, addressed to a certain Sarapammon, says that the sender already (ἄλλα ἄπαξ) passed a message to Sarapammon that he should take τὰ παρθένειά σου τέκνα. The word, in this case, could refer either to children born to an unmarried woman or to children who are virgins, *i.e.* unmarried daughters, which is the primary meaning of παρθένιος.[15] As Sarapammon is clearly a male name and the children are his, the latter meaning seems most probable.

3. OTHNEIOS

The term ὀθνεῖος cannot be recognised as a *terminus technicus* for 'extramarital child'.[16] It is attested only once in the context of illegitimacy, in the famous *Papyrus Cattaoui* (Alexandria [?], after AD 142). The *verso* of the papyrus

[12] Ogden, *Greek Bastardy* (cit. n. 4), pp. 21 & 25; M. Ebbott, *Imagining Illegitimacy in Classical Greek Literature*, Lanham – Boulder – New York – Oxford 2003, pp. 17–21.

[13] D. Ogden, *The Crooked Kings of Ancient Greece*, London 1997, pp. 73–74.

[14] Calderini, 'Ἀπάτορες' (cit. n. 1), p. 358, n. 4.

[15] Cf. *LSJ*, *s.vv.* 'παρθένειος' and 'παρθένιος'. Yet, the *LSJ* gives *P. Ryl.* II 435 as the only attestation of παρθένειος as describing extramarital children.

[16] Calderini recognised it as synonymous to *spurius*: Calderini, 'Ἀπάτορες' (cit. n. 1), p. 361.

belongs to the archive of Iulius Agrippinus and consists of documents concerning a dispute between Tertia Drusilla and C. Iulius Agrippinus (*M. Chr.* 88). The *recto* collects seven precedents dealing with the (il)legality of marriages contracted by soldiers and the (il)legitimacy of their children;[17] the cases listed were tried by officials in charge of recognising the status of an individual, either the prefect, his *iudex datus*, or the procurator of the *idios logos*. The decisions collected to support C. Iulius Agrippus' claims against Drusilla state consistently that children born to soldiers during their time of service could not be counted as legitimate offspring, as the laws forbade it.

The case where the term *ὀθνεῖος* appears concerned the sons born to an Alexandrian woman and a soldier Octavius Valens who was also an Alexandrian citizen. It was brought before the prefect (col. IV, l. 16 – col. V, l. 26) because Octavius Valens wanted one of the children to be scrutinised as an Alexandrian citizen. The prefect, however, denied Alexandrian citizenship to the soldier's son explaining that, because Octavius served in the army, he could not have legitimate children and, furthermore, as his son was not recognised as the legitimate son of an Alexandrian he could not be recognised as an Alexandrian. Octavius Valens' sons would have been scrutinised as Alexandrian if not for the interference of Roman law, specifically the marriage ban for Roman soldiers, thus the prefect's decision may not have been comprehensible, which is discussed in detail later in this book (*infra*, pp. 145–147). This is perhaps why the prefect explained his decision in detail:

> *P. Catt.*, col. V, ll. 4–11: *Ἐξερχομέ|νου εἴτε ἐν τάξει εἴτε ἐν σπείρᾳ εἴτε [ἐ]ν εἴλῃ ὁ γεννη|θεὶς οὐ δύναται εἶναι νόμιμος υἱός. ⟦μη⟧ μὴ ὢν δὲ | νόμιμος υἱὸς τοῦ πατρὸς ὄντος Ἀλεξανδρέως Ἀλε|ξανδρεὺς οὐ δύναται εἶναι. ὁ παῖς [ο]ὗτος γεγέννη|ται τῷ Οὐάλεντι στρατευομένου* (l. *στρατευομένῳ*) *ἐ[ν] σπείρᾳ ὀθνεῖος | αὐτοῦ ἐστιν εἰσαχθῆναι ἰς* (l. *εἰς*) *τὴν πολειτείαν* (l. *πολιτείαν*) *τὴν Ἀλεξαν|δρέων οὐ δύναται.*

> One begotten of a man serving either in a legion or a cohort or an ala cannot be a legitimate son. And since he is not a legitimate son, if his father is an Alexandrian, he cannot be an Alexandrian. Such a boy was born to Valens when he served in the cohort – he is alien to him (Valens) and he cannot be enrolled in the citizen body of Alexandrians.

[17] Referred as *P. Catt.*, yet, consisting of *P. Catt.* and *BGU* I 114, was published several times entirely or in parts as *M. Chr.* 372, *FIRA* III 19, *Jur. Pap.* 22 a *&* b.

In this example, ὀθνεῖος served as a counterpart to the Latin *extraneus*, the opposite of *suus* being under the *patria potestas* as *legitimus* (νόμιμος υἱός).[18] The term was used to explain that the boy, despite being his father's son, was not legally related to the father. The explanation was based on Roman law, where an illegitimate child is *extraneus*[19] to his father, because he neither belongs to the family, nor follows the paternal status. When such children were appointed as heirs, it was as *heredes extranei*, not *sui*.

4. NATURALES

Another important term is *naturalis* (and φυσικός, its Greek counterpart). In the following section, I argue that *naturalis* / φυσικός was used to underline the bond between a father and his child as well as the descendents of the child and the antecedents of the father; this is not a bond based on law, but biology. The term was especially important in defining the relationship between children born out of wedlock and their fathers; although fathers and their extramarital children shared only this natural bond, *naturalis* was also used to describe the relationship between fathers and legitimate children.

4.1. *Roman law*

As Jean Baptiste Mispoulet observed, the meaning of *naturalis* in the jurisprudential sources is one and implies the existence of a blood bond between relatives;[20] although the adjective was applied in various specific contexts.[21]

[18] The association of the term *liber* in general with *suus* is expressed in D. 50.16.220 pr. (Callis. *quaes.* 2) or in G. 3.2.

[19] In fact, extraneous is one of the meanings of ὀθνεῖος in: F. Montanari, *The Brill Dictionary of Ancient Greek*, M. Goh & C. Schroeder (eng. ed.), Leiden 2015, *s.v.* 'ὀθνεῖος'.

[20] J.B. Mispoulet, 'Du nom et de la condicion de l'enfant naturel romain', *Nouvelle revue historique de droit français et étranger* 9 (1885), pp. 15–63.

[21] According to Wolff, the term *naturalis* had two meanings before the fourth century: it referred both to marital children and to extramarital children of slave status: Wolff, 'The background' (cit. n. 5), pp. 24 & 31. He also claimed that in 'classical' Roman legal sources

Giovanni Luchetti offered the following list of possible uses:[22]

1. children and antecedents born of *iustae nuptiae*:

a) born under the power of their *pater familias* (the term is used here as an antithesis to adoptive children), *e.g.*:[23]

> G. 1.104: Feminae vero nullo modo adoptare possunt, quia ne quidem **naturales liberos** in potestate habent.
>
> Women, however, cannot adopt in any way, because they do not even have their natural children under their power.

b) born under *patria potestas*, but later emancipated or given up for adoption, *e.g.*:[24]

> G. 3.41: (...) Prosunt autem liberto ad excludendum patronum **naturales liberi**, non solum quos in potestate mortis tempore habet, sed etiam emancipati et in adoptionem dati (...).
>
> On the other hand, natural children, not only such that he has under his power at the moment of his death, but also (children) emancipated and given into adoption, permit the freedman to exclude (his) patron.

the terms *naturalis* and *spurius* had separate meanings: *naturalis* could be applied to a slave son who belonged to the *familia* of his father in a broader sense, while *spurius* referred to one who did not belong to any family: *ibidem*, pp. 35–36. Niziołek and Evans-Grubbs followed this opinion. The latter noted that the legal status of the child at the birth, rather than the relationship between the parents, was the decisive factor: J. Evans-Grubbs, 'Making the private public: Illegitimacy and incest in Roman law', [in:] C. Ando & J. Rüpke (eds.) *Public and Private in Ancient Mediterranean Law and Religion* [= *Religionsgeschichtliche Versuche und Vorarbeiten* LXV], Berlin 2015, pp. 115–141, p. 119. See also M. Niziołek, 'Meaning of the phrase *liberi naturales* in Roman law sources up to Constantine's reign', *Revue internationale des droits de l'antiquité* 22 (1975), pp. 317–344. Beryl Rawson, however, noted that Wolff's definition is too narrow: B. Rawson, 'Spurii and the Roman view of illegitimacy', *Antichthon* 23 (1989), pp. 10–41, p. 15, n. 14.

22 G. Luchetti, *La legittimazione dei figli naturali nelle fonti tardo imperiali e giustinianee*, Milan 1990, p. 6.

23 Luchetti, *La legittimazione* (cit. n. 22), p. 8, sources listed in n. 10.

24 *Ibidem*, p. 9, sources in n. 11.

2. extramarital children:
a) born of two slaves, *e.g.*:[25]

D. 23.2.14.2 (Paul. *ad ed.* 35): Serviles quoque cognationes in hoc iure observandae sunt. Igitur suam matrem manumissus non ducet uxorem: tantundem iuris est et in sorore et sororis filia. Idem e contrario dicendum est, ut pater filiam non possit ducere, si ex servitute manumissi sint, etsi dubitetur patrem eum esse. Unde nec **volgo quaesitam filiam pater naturalis** potest uxorem ducere, quoniam in contrahendis matrimoniis naturale ius et pudor inspiciendus est: contra pudorem est autem filiam uxorem suam ducere.

In this law, even blood bonds between slaves should be recognised. Therefore, a freedman will not bring his mother home as a wife – just as much the same applies to the sister and sister's daughter according to this law. The same should be said of the contrary – a father cannot bring his daughter home as a wife, if they are freed from slavery, even if there is a doubt that he is (her) father. Whence, natural father cannot bring his bastard daughter home as a wife, since in contracting marriages natural law and decency should be observed, and then it is against decency to bring one's own daughter home as a wife.

b) born to a slave mother and free father, *e.g.*:[26]

G. 1.19: Iusta autem causa manumissionis est veluti si quis **filium filiamve aut fratrem sororemve naturalem** aut alumnum aut paedagogum aut servum procuratoris habendi gratia aut ancillam matrimonii causa apud consilium manumittat.

A just reason for manumission is that someone manumits before the council, for instance, a natural son or daughter or brother or sister or (his) *alumnus* or teacher or a slave for the reason of having him as procurator or a slave woman for marriage.

c) extramarital children in general, including those born to two free partners, *e.g.*:[27]

[25] *Ibidem*, p. 9, sources in n. 12.

[26] *Ibidem*, p. 9, sources in n. 13.

[27] *Ibidem*, p. 9, sources in n. 14. D. 38.10.4.2 (Mod. *pand.* 12) devoted to natural and civil *cognationes* defines *naturalis cognatio* as independent from civil kinship; rather it refers to the

D. 28.6.45 pr. (Paul. *resp.* 12): Lucius Titius legitimum filium et alterum naturalem heredes instituit eosque invicem substituit (...).

Lucius Titius appointed his legitimate son and another (being) natural as his heirs and he substituted one for another.

4.2. *Inscriptions*

In his monograph on the Roman concubinate, Raimund Friedl has noted that the same uses of *naturalis* are found in the epigraphic sources, where it refers to children born of legitimate marriages, as well as *contubernia*, clear or possible concubinates, and relationships difficult to identify.[28] The problem, however, is that only a few status identifications are secure. We can be certain that the term does not refer to a legitimate child: if a child is mentioned to be either a slave or freedman; if their mother is described as a slave or if we are certain that a child was born before her manumission; if their father is described as a slave or if it is known that he was manumitted only after this child was born.[29] Cases such as these were covered by a clear rule regulating the civic and familial status of children born of slaves.[30]

relationship between mothers and their children *vulgo* begotten as an example of *naturalis cognatio*. Wolff claimed that this part of the passage was a postclassical gloss intended to elaborate the meaning to a reader no longer aware of the difference between *cognatio* and *agnatio*. This suggestion, however, is not supported by sufficient arguments. Wolff made similar claims for other passages which did not fit with his theory (D. 23.2.14.2: Paul. *ad ed.* 35, quoted as D. 32.2.14.2, C. 9.9.3 and D. 36.1.17.4: Ulp. *fideicom.* 4). *E.g.* on C. 9.9.3 he commented only: 'The almost unintelligible text of Cod. Ius. 9.9.3 is obviously an unsuccessful abridgement of the original rescript (AD 213). Even if the words *non naturalis* (*viz. patris mulieris*) *sed iusti dumtaxat* do have some foundation in the original text and are not a mere gloss, they cannot prove anything for the classical terminology': Wolff, 'The background' (cit. n. 5), pp. 25–27.

[28] R. Friedl, *Der Konkubinat im kaiserzeitlichen Rom. Von Augustus bis Septimius Severus* [= *Historia – Einzelschriften* XCVIII], Stuttgart 1996, pp. 146–147.

[29] Cases which Friedl recognised or suggested as belonging to those categories were listed in: Friedl, *Der Konkubinat im kaiserzeitlichen Rom* (cit. n. 28), p. 372.

[30] Yet, the rule that the child would be born free was modified by a *lex* from the time of perhaps Augustus and the *senatus consultum Claudianum* on which see p. 45–48 & 104–108.

This would be the case for Capriolus who, together with his mother, an imperial slave, founded an epitaph for his father (*CIL* IX 888 = no. 1730 [Luceria in Apulia, 3rd c.]).[31] No matter whether the boy was free or a slave at the moment when the inscription was created, the fact that he was born of a slave mother excluded him from the *agnatio*, even having been freed he did not enter the *potestas* of his father. The same conclusion can be drawn in cases where the father was a slave: a child could be free if conceived by a free woman, but they would remain extramarital, because a slave could not be a father. This is the case of Marcus Cocceius Martialis who founded an epitaph for his natural father, Martialis, *Caesaris servus* (*CIL* X.2 7822 = no. 30 [Pirri in Sardinia, 2nd–3rd c.]).

The familial status of *naturales* born to free or freed parents, however, depended on many circumstances which are rarely revealed in inscriptions. Sometimes, children had the *nomina gentilicia* of their fathers which might constitute grounds for assuming that they were legitimate. Yet even in these cases the identification of familial status is not obvious. The problems of making a certain identification is illustrated in an epitaph of Otacilia Serana (no. 29):

> ALFÖLDY, *ZPE* 54 (1984), pp. 235–237 (Jérica in Hispania, 2nd c.): D(is) Ṃ(anibus). / Otacil(iae) Seṛan(a)e / ann(orum) XVIII / Otacil(ius) Seranus / filiae naturali / et Otac(ilia) Chryso/polis filiae / pientissimae / h(ic) s(itae).
>
> To the spirits departed. For Otacilia Serana, 18 years old, Otacilius Seranus (had this made) for his natural daughter, and Otacilia Chrysopolis for the most devoted daughter laid here.

All three family members have the same *gentilicium*,[32] and the father and his daughter also share the *cognomen*; the mother, moreover, has a Greek *cognomen*. Based on the onomastics, Géza Alföldy suggested the follow-

[31] Nos. after www.romanbastards.wpia.uw.edu.pl.

[32] As in the following texts: Rome: *CIL* VI.2 10707a (2nd c. AD) = nos. 1721–1722; Lambaesis in Numidia: *CIL* VIII.1 3909 = *CIL* VIII *Suppl.* 2 18201 *descr.* (AD 50–300) = no. 1720; 3910 (AD 50–300) = no. 40; Narbo in Gallia Narbonensis: *CIL* XII 5194 = *CAG* XI.1, p. 427 (AD 50–300) = nos. 1723–1725; Jerica in Hispania citerior: ALFÖLDY, *ZPE* 54 (1984), pp. 235–237, pl. 12b. (2nd c. AD) = no. 29.

ing interpretation: the mother was a freedwoman of Otacilius Seranus, as she had a Greek name and the *gentilicium* Otacilia which she would have acquired together with her freedom, and Serana was her daughter born out of wedlock.[33] Such a scenario is indeed possible, yet it is not the only one. Another option is that the girl was born in slavery and only after freed by her father.

The practice of giving paternal *cognomina* to children, whose parents were not married but lived together, is indeed well-attested, at least in Rome[34] and supports Alföldy's interpretation. A legitimate child, however, could also bear the paternal *cognomen.* That Otacilia Serana have both names from her father could mean that she was indeed his daughter-freedwoman born when her mother was still a slave or a free-born child or even his legitimate daughter. As there are several possible interpretations of the *status familiae* and *liberartis*, it would appear that Alföldy's interpretation is based on his understanding of the term *naturalis* as a mark of illegitimacy.

Would the case of Otacilia Serana have been so different from other cases in which *naturales* had *gentilicia* after their fathers? For instance in an epitaph from Lambaesis in Numidia, we read:

> *CIL* VIII.1 3909 = *CIL* VIII *Suppl.* 2 18201 (Lambaesis in Numidia, AD 50–300): D(is) M(anibus) s(acrum) / Memmia Iu/liosa vix(it) an(nos) VI / mens(es) II C(aius) Mem/mius Fortunat(us) / filiae natura/li fecit.
>
> To the memory of spirits departed. Memmia Iuliosa lived 6 years and 2 months. Caius Memmius Fortunatus has made for his natural daughter.

In this case the commemorated girl, Memmia Iuliosa (no. 1720), has the same *gentilicium* as her father, but a different *cognomen.* The father's *cognomen* is Fortunatus, a name often given to slaves, which might suggest that

[33] G. Alföldy, 'Epigraphica Hispanica V. Inschriften aus Jérica und Umgebung', *Zeitschrift für Papyrologie und Epigraphik* 54 (1984), pp. 221–245, p. 236.

[34] See M. Krawczyk, 'Paternal onomastical legacy vs. illegitimacy in Roman epitaphs', [in:] M. Nowak, A. Łajtar & J. Urbanik (eds.), *Tell Me Who You Are. Labelling Status in the Graeco-Roman World*, Warsaw 2018, pp. 107–128 with further literature.

he was a freedman.[35] If this were the case, would it mean that the daughter was born in slavery and freed later – which would explain the common *gentilicium* of both, father and daughter – or was she born after her father had been granted his freedom, which would also explain their common *gentilicium*? Can we interpret the lack of a common *cognomen* as an argument for the latter hypothesis; as a legitimate daughter she would have not needed an additional marker of her bond with the father?[36] Yet it is also possible that the girl was born to a free female member of the family to which Fortunatus belonged, which would explain the *gentilicium* as well, as extramarital children were often given their maternal *gentilicia*.[37] Other cases in which children are described as *naturales* but have the *gentilicia* of their fathers can be questioned in the same way.[38]

Interpretations of the term *naturalis* in inscriptions are especially difficult as the data is limited when compared either to Roman law sources or papyri. Inscriptions mention the name and age of a commemorated person, and usually also the name or names of those who founded the inscription, but there is little else that allows us to establish personal status.

> *CIL* X 1138 (Abellinum in Campania, 2nd c.): D(is) M(anibus) / C(aio) Mamercio Sp(uri) f(ilio) / Ianuario q(uaestori) aed(ili) praet(ori) / IIvir(o) q(uaestori) alimentor(um) et / Pacciae Lucretianae / P(ublius) Paccius Ianuarius / filio naturali et Ma/mercia Grapte mater / infelicissimi filio et / cognatae piissimis / fecerunt.
>
> To the spirits departed. To Caius Mamercius Ianuarius son of Spurius, quaestor, aedile, praetor, IIvir, quaestor of provisions, and to Paccia Lucretiana. Publius Paccius Ianuarius, to his natural son, and his mother Mamercia Grapte, most unhappy parents made this to their son and to their kinswoman who both were devout.[39]

[35] I. Kajanto, *The Latin Cognomina* [= *Commentationes Humanarum Litterarum* XXXVI 2], Helsinki 1965, p. 273.

[36] B. Rawson, rev. of I. Kajanto, *The Latin Cognomina* [= *Commentationes Humanarum Litterarum* XXXVI 2], Helsinki 1965, *Classical Philology* 63 (1968), pp. 154–159, p. 158.

[37] Krawczyk, 'Paternal onomastical legacy' (cit. n. 34), p. 117; T. Nuorluoto, 'Emphasising matrilineal ancestry in a patrilineal system: Maternal name preference in the Roman world', [in:] *Tell Me Who You Are* (cit. n. 34), pp. 257–281, pp. 257–264.

[38] Friedl, *Der Konkubinat im kaiserzeitlichen Rom* (cit. n. 28), p. 371.

[39] Tr. by Nuorluoto, 'Emphasising matrilineal ancestry' (cit. n. 37), p. 259.

As Tuomo Nuorluoto has pointed out, the extramarital status of Caius Mamercius Ianuarius (no. 26) is almost certain thanks to the false filiation expressed with the abbreviation *Sp() f()* and the fact that he had a maternal *gentilicium* and paternal *cognomen*.[40] The Greek *cognomen* of the mother suggests that she might have been a freedwoman, but her son was born free as he hold some high offices inaccessible to freedmen. However, another scenario is that P(ublius) Paccius Ianuarius gave his son into adoption to Spurius Mamericius, which would explain both the term *filius naturalis* and filiation *Sp(urii) f(ilius)*. It is impossible to decide which interpretation is more likely.

It is always possible to suggest that *naturales* with different *gentilicia* than their fathers were born out of wedlock.[41] Yet, this is rarely the only possible explanation. A child could have been given up for adoption and later commemorated by their natural father. A child of legitimate marriage might have taken the maternal *gentilicium* for reasons not mentioned in the epitaph, but not connected to illegitimacy.[42] Therefore, the interpretation is never secure unless there is additional information in the text itself or outside of it.

The principal conclusion we can draw regarding *naturales* in inscriptions is that, as Friedl observed, the terminology is not coherent. The term was used to denote a relationship between a father and his child based on procreation rather than *agnatio*. (But it does not always exclude *agnatio*.) Moreover, *naturalis* served as a description for both those born free and as slaves. The number of epigraphic sources attesting the word is, however, limited: we know of fewer than 40 examples in total, the majority of which come either from Italy or the city of Rome itself. Two come from Gallia

[40] Nuorluoto, 'Emphasising matrilineal ancestry' (cit. n. 37), p. 261.

[41] Friedl, *Der Konkubinat im kaiserzeitlichen Rom* (cit. n. 28), p. 371: child(ren) with maternal *gentilicium*, free mother: *CIL* VI.2 14217 = nos. 1708–1711 (Rome, 2nd c. AD): here children have single names, and no further status indication; VI.3 18658 = no. 1712 (Rome, AD 50–300); 18837 = no. 1713 (Rome, AD 50–300); VI.4.2 34048 a = no. 1715 (Rome, AD 50–300); IX 1887 = no. 1716 (Beneventum, 2nd c. AD); *CIL* XIV *Suppl. Ost.*1 4791 = no. 27 (Ostia, 2nd–3rd c. AD): no mother indicated at all; *CIL* VI.2 8098 = no. 1717 (Rome, 1st–3rd c. AD); V.1 3417 = no. 1718 (Verona, AD 50–300); military milieu: *CIL* V.2 5268 = no. 28 (Comum in Transpadana, AD 1–50).

[42] Nuorluoto, 'Emphasising matrilineal ancestry' (cit. n. 37).

Narbonensis, two from Numidia, two from Pannonia inferior, one from Hispania, one from Gallia Lugdunensis, one from Baetica. The examples are therefore not representative of the provinces and especially not of the East.[43] When compared with the number of inscriptions attesting the term *Sp0 f0*, the epigraphic material suggests that *naturalis* was not widely used.

4.3. *Papyri*

Although attestations in papyri are less numerous, they are usually easier to interpret. The first document is a papyrus dated to the second century, *Ch. L. A.* X 427 (provenance unknown) containing a fragmentary Latin copy of a will[44] made for a certain Caius Hostilius Clemens; the surviving text includes an introductory formula with full *tria nomina* of the testator, a fragmentary *heredis institutio*, part of the disinheritance clause and short fragments from other provisions, such as the *cretio* (ll. 6–7). In lines 3 and 4, we find an appointment of the testator's children as heirs, a son and daughter:

> C̣(aius) Hostili⟦s⟧ụṣ Clemens fil[ius (?) - *ca.* ? -]
> tilia Gaia liberi mei na[turales (?) - *ca.* ? -]

Liberi mei na[*turales*] is indeed a possible reconstruction, but it is hardly plausible that the children were extramarital. The son bears not only the *praenomen* and *nomen* of his father, Caius Hostilius, but also his *cognomen*, Clemens, which in this case suggests the status of a first-born son: within formal families the first-born son was usually given the father's *cognomen* so that he could have the same *tria nomina* as his father.[45] Furthermore, *na*[*turales*] is not the only way the lacuna could be filled: *na*[*ti in*] followed

[43] See www.romanbastards.wpia.uw.edu.pl, *s.v.* '*naturalis*'.

[44] On copies of Roman wills, see M. Nowak, *Wills in the Roman Empire: A Documentary Approach* [= *The Journal of Juristic Papyrology Supplement* XXIII], Warsaw 2015, pp. 97–98.

[45] See B. Salway, 'What's in a name? A survey of Roman onomastic practice from c. 700 bc to ad 700', *The Journal of Roman Studies* 84 (1994), pp. 124–145, p. 127.

by the place where the children were born is well attested in Latin inscriptions, and is a possible alternative to *na*[*turales*].

Another example is provided by *P. Diog.* 1 = *CPL* 159 (Contrapollonopolis, AD 127), a *testatio* of a soldier's son. The document belongs to the archive of Marcus Lucretius Diogenes, but predates him: it was written for Marcus Lucretius Clemens, the great grand-father of the archive's owner, to confirm the birth of his son Serenus, Diogenes' great uncle (no. 112). As Paul Schubert, the editor of the archive, has pointed out, Marcus Lucretius Clemens was a soldier serving in *auxilia* when the *testatio* was written, as Serenus is said to be *in militia natus* (l. 7).[46] As an auxiliary soldier, Marcus Lucretius Clemens was not a Roman, and could neither marry nor produce legitimate children before the end of his service.[47]

Yet by AD 140 auxiliary soldiers were granted Roman citizenship together with their children at the time of their discharge.[48] The *testatio* must, therefore, have been composed in order to serve as proof for the further claim of citizenship rights for the son.[49] The text says that Marcus Lucretius Clemens made the *testatio*, ll. 11–13: *ut possit post honestam missionem suam* | *ad epicrisin suam adprobare filium suum* | *naturalem esse*, 'so that after his *honesta missio* he could prove at his scrutiny that he (Serenus) is his

[46] Commentary to *P. Diog.* 1.

[47] *P. Diog.*, pp. 41–42; C. Sánchez-Moreno Ellart, 'Notes on some new issues concerning the birth certificates of Roman citizens', *The Journal of Juristic Papyrology* 34 (2004), pp. 107–119, pp. 108–109. Before *P. Diog.* 5 was published, scholars had been of the opinion that Marcus Lucretius Clemens was a Roman. For an overview of the scholarly discussion, including arguments that he was a peregrine, see idem, '*Ipsis liberis posterisque eorum*. Die Bedeutung der Geburtsurkunden von Soldaten der Auxiliareinheiten und der Wandel im Formular von *diplomata militaria* im Jahre 140 n. Chr. ausweislich RMD I 39 und RMD IV 266', *Zeitschrift der Savigny-Stiftung für Rechtsgeschichte RA* 125 (2008), pp. 348–374, pp. 359–362.

[48] As C. Sánchez-Moreno Ellart pointed out, *testationes* by auxiliary soldiers were by no means obligatory. They served purely probatory aims at the scrutiny of veterans' children: Sánchez-Moreno Ellart, '*Ipsis liberis*' (cit. n. 47), p. 356. Yet, as Michael Speidel observed, they had to be controlled by the army, as they were a proof for further privilege of the *civitas*: M.A. Speidel, 'Les femmes et la bureaucratie. Quelques réflexions sur l'interdiction du mariage dans l'armée romaine', *Cahiers Glotz* 24 (2013), pp. 205–215, p. 213.

[49] That Marcus Lucretius Clemens completed this *testatio* speaks against Roman status of the boy's mother. If she had been a Roman, she would have declared her son securing his citizenship already from the moment of his birth: Sánchez-Moreno Ellart, '*Ipsis liberis*' (cit. n. 47), p. 369.

natural son'. We know that these claims were upheld, as copies of both the father's and son's *epikrisis* are preserved in the archive (*P. Diog.* 5 [Arsinoite nome, after AD 138]).[50]

There is still the question of whether the term *naturalis* was used in this text to signify a child born out of wedlock.[51] In my opinion, it was not. The term as it appears in *P. Diog.* 1 has the wider meaning of 'flesh of my flesh', not specifically a 'child born out of *iustae nuptiae*'.[52] Serenus was indeed born out of wedlock, but the aim of the text is not to indicate his illegitimate birth, but the fact that that he was the biological son of his father.[53] There are several arguments to support the claim that *naturalis* was used in this sense. The text specifies that the *testatio* (*P. Diog.* 1) was prepared for the *epikrisis* in order to prove that Serenus was the *filius naturalis* of Marcus Lucretius Clemens; the *epikrisis* (*P. Diog.* 5), in turn, was made according to *diploma militaris*[54] which granted citizenship to auxiliary soldiers and their children. The basis for *liberorum civitas* was that the children belonged to a soldier who had been dismissed from military service. *Civitas* was granted to the children of auxiliary soldiers because they were children of their fathers born during their military service.[55] These documents were focussed solely on the issue of paternity,[56] consequently the term *naturalis* in the *testatio* was to underline this bond between the child declared and the auxiliary soldier who declared them.

[50] On scrutiny of auxiliary soldiers, see S. Waebens, 'Reflecting the "change in AD 140": the veteran categories of the *epikrisis* documents revisited', *Zeitschrift für Papyrologie und Epigraphik* 180 (2012), pp. 267–277, pp. 267–270.

[51] Wolff clearly understood here *naturalis* as illegitimate: Wolff, 'The background' (cit. n. 5), p. 24.

[52] As Bell already observed. Yet, he interpreted *naturalis* as antithesis for *adoptivus*: 'no doubt "by birth" as opposed to *adoptivus*': H.I. Bell, 'A Latin registration of birth', *The Journal of Roman Studies* 27.1 [= *Papers Presented to Sir Henry Stuart Jones*] (1937), pp. 30–36, p. 35.

[53] Luchetti, *La legittimazione* (cit. n. 22), p. 7.

[54] *P. Diog.* 5, ll. 6–8: ἐπέδε̣ι̣|[ξεν ὁ Κλήμης δέλτον χαλ]κῆν ἐ̣κ̣σφράγισμα στή[λ]ης̣ χαλ̣κῆς ἀνα|[κειμένης ἐν Ῥώμῃ δι' ἧ]ς̣ ἐδηλο[ῦ]τ̣ο – 'Clemens showed a bronze tablet being an official copy of a bronze stele settled in Rome by which he proved...'.

[55] See Speidel, 'Les femmes et la bureaucratie' (cit. n. 48), p. 212: he discussed soldiers of praetorian fleet, but concludes that in general the grant was given only to children born during the service.

[56] Sánchez-Moreno Ellart, '*Ipsis liberis*' (cit. n. 47), p. 369.

Two further documents attesting the Greek equivalent of *naturalis*, *φυσικός*, belong to the same category of deeds as *P. Diog.* 1, registrations of children. Both, however, are much later and were composed in a civilian milieu: *P. Oxy.* XLIII 3136 (Oxyrhynchos, AD 295) and XLIV 3183 (Oxyrhynchos, AD 292). In both texts *φυσικός* is part of the description of registered children; it does not appear as an independent description, but occurs with the nouns *θυγάτηρ* (*P. Oxy.* XLIII 3136, ll. 19–21) and *υἱοί* (*P. Oxy.* XLIV 3183, ll. 22–25), *i.e. filii naturales*. The two papyri belong to the group of late third-century Oxyrhynchite applications made by parents of gymnasial status requesting to register their children in the *γραφὴ ἀφηλίκων* for their future *epikrisis*.[57] These requests for registration were addressed to *systates* – the clerks responsible for, *inter alia*, keeping the records (including those concerning status) of a *phyle* – or to the *koinon* of those responsible for taxes.[58] The requests contained a genealogical description of the child, information regarding the *amphodon* to which they should be registered, and an indication of their gymnasial status – (*δωδεκάδραχμος*) *ἀπὸ γυμνασίου*. The request was to have a child placed (*ταγῆναι*) in a list of minors recorded by this official in the category of their peers (*διὰ τῆς καταχωριζομένης ὑφ' ὑμῶν γραφῆς ἀφηλίκων ἐν τῇ τῶν ὁμηλίκων τάξει*; or simply: *εἰς τὴν τῶν ὁμηλίκων τάξιν*).

In the two Oxyrhynchite papyri mentioned above, the meaning of *φυσικός* is reasonably certain. As the editors noticed, it served to underline that a child was not adoptive (*μὴ θέσει*).[59] Further support for this observation can be found in the documents of *epikrisis* to the gymnasial status, which contained an oath that a child aspiring to the group of *οἱ ἀπὸ τοῦ γυμνασίου* was by no means adoptive, as in *P. Oxy.* X 1266, ll. 32–37 (Oxyrhynchos, AD 98): *εἶναι δ' ἐμοῦ καὶ τῆς | Θερμουθίου φύσ̣[ει υἱὸν τὸ]ν̣ Πλου|τίωνα καὶ μὴ θέ[σει μηδὲ ὑπ]όβλη|τον μηδ' ἀλλοτρίαις [ἀσφαλ]ε̣ί̣αις ἢ |*

[57] *P. Ups. Frid.* 6 (AD 273); *P. Oxy.* XXXVIII 2855 (AD 291): *γραφὴ ἀφηλίκων* not mentioned specifically; XLVI 3295 (AD 285); XLIII 3136 (AD 295): *γραφὴ ἀφηλίκων* not mentioned specifically, too fragmentary; 3137 (AD 295); LXV 4489 (AD 297).

[58] N. Lewis, 'Notationes legentis', *The Bulletin of the American Society of Papyrologists* 29 (1992), pp. 127–133, p. 129.

[59] Commentary to *P. Oxy.* XLIII 3136.

ὁμωνυμίᾳ κεχρῆ[σθαι], ἢ ἔνοχος | εἴην τῷ ὅρκῳ.[60] A child admitted to the οἱ ἀπὸ τοῦ γυμνασίου in Oxyrhynchos had to have been born of their parents, not adopted (*infra*, pp. 226–228).

All the evidence found in the papyri, the inscriptions, and the Roman legal sources suggest that *naturalis* was used in the broader sense of 'natural', and denoted a biological, rather than a legal, relationship between usually father and child. The term is applied to children born both within a marriage and out of wedlock. In cases where the children were born out of wedlock, the biological bond was the only one, and the use of *naturalis* in such instances could lead to the impression that the word carried a narrower meaning. Yet in none of our sources do we find even a single example of *naturalis* or its Greek counterpart used to mean specifically 'extramarital' or 'out of wedlock'.

5. SPURII FILII

Among the terms used to describe extramarital children, Calderini listed σπούριος. Both σπούριος or *spurius*, and false filiation (*Spurii filius* or Σπουρίου υἱός) are well-attested in the papyri, in Roman legal sources and, above all, in inscriptions. Yet, the origin and precise meaning of this term are not fully clear.

Spurius was originally a *praenomen*, but it also functioned as a *nomen gentilicium* and to a limited extent as a *cognomen*;[61] it developed into a substantive meaning 'extramarital child'.[62] It is not clear why this happened, but two explanations have been offered for this phenomenon: 1. Spurius would have been a name given to children born out of wedlock and the name

[60] Other documents attesting this clause: *P. Oxy.* II 257, ll. 40–44 (Oxyrhynchos, AD 94–95); *SB* XIV 11271, ll. 6–8 (Oxyrhynchos, AD 117); *P. Oxy.* XVIII 2186, l. 10 (Oxyrhynchos, AD 260); *PSI* V 457, ll. 19–21 (Oxyrhynchos, AD 268); *P. Mich.* XIV 676, ll. 20–22 (Oxyrhynchos, AD 272).

[61] Y. Broux, 'Ancient profiles exploited. First results of Named Entity Recognition applied to Latin inscriptions', *Tell Me Who You Are* (cit. n. 34), pp. 11–33, p. 17.

[62] O. Salomies, *Die römischen Vornamen. Studien zur römischen Namengebung* [= *Commentationes Humanarum Litterarum* LXXXII], Helsinki 1987, p. 51; Friedl, *Der Konkubinat im kaiserzeitlichen Rom* (cit. n. 28), p. 143.

thus developed into the term 'bastard'.[63] 2. The name Spurius was abbreviated to *sp()* the same way as *s(ine) p(atre)*, description given to children born out of wedlock. Both *s(ine) p(atre) f(ilius)* and *Sp(urii) f(ilius)* were abbreviated as *spf*;[64] *Spurii filius* developed into a false filiation as the result of confusion between two identical abbreviations signifying different things: *sine patre filius* became *Spurii filius* and the basis for the substantive *spurius*, meaning *vulgo quaesitus*. As Olli Salomies noted, this is the explanation given by Plutarch and Gaius (discussed *infra*, pp. 50–52 and 81–83).[65]

Spurius as term had to be relatively late, as it was still unknown to Quintilian, who wrote that the Latin did not have a counterpart for *nothus* (*Inst.* 3.6.97). Indeed, *spurius* is attested only in first-century sources such as Plutarch and Verrius.[66] Salomies' hypothesis about the first-century origin of the word seems to be further supported by the fact that the popularity of the *praenomen* decreased significantly in the last years of the Republic; the name, having become a compound of false filiation, would have taken on an unpleasant[67] or, more likely, ambiguous meaning, and people may have stopped giving their sons the *praenomen* Spurius in order to avoid future confusion.

5.1. *Inscriptions*

Spurii filius, the expression recognised as the source of the term *spurius* and independent label of illegitimacy, is well attested in the epigraphic record, with over 600 individuals described in this way.[68] The exact formula is usually *spf*, but one will occasionally find the longer abbreviations *Spurii*

[63] Brunt explains that in some republican families *praenomen* Spurius came into hereditary use, as a first holder of the name was indeed a bastard: P.A. Brunt, *Italian Manpower: 225 BC – AD 14*, Oxford 1971, p. 150.

[64] Further literature given in Salomies, *Die römischen Vornamen* (cit. n. 62), p. 51.

[65] *Ibidem.*

[66] Salomies, *Die römischen Vornamen* (cit. n. 62), pp. 51–52.

[67] Salomies, *Die römischen Vornamen* (cit. n. 62), p. 52.

[68] Over 600 on www.romanbastards.wpia.uw.edu.pl; Rawson mentioned 184, but she counted for the city of Rome (now certainly over 200 from Rome on www.romanbastards.wpia.uw.edu.pl): Rawson, 'Spurii' (cit. n. 21), p. 29.

f() or *sp() filius*. In Greek inscriptions, the expression is written out in full: *Σπουρίου υἱός / θυγάτηρ*. As Yanne Broux has observed, the term appears far more frequently in Italy – and, specifically, in Rome – although it was certainly not absent from the provinces.[69] In the literature it was claimed that *Spurii filius* or, rather, the abbreviation *spf* played a double role:

1. From the late first century BC,[70] the description became a mark of **illegitimacy**,[71]
2. It was also the mark of **free born Roman** children who had no legal father and took *status civitatis* after their mother.[72]

1. As far as the first point is concerned, it is obvious that not every child born out of *iustae nuptiae* was described as the son or daughter of Spurius.[73] It is less easy to determine whether only illegitimate children were described as *Spurii filii* and if this in turn caused the name Spurius to become a marker of illegitimacy. In my opinion this was not the case.

Although Spurius survived as a *nomen gentilicium*,[74] this is not necessarily evidence for the name's perception, as the *nomen* was not, in principle, a matter of an individual choice. The *cognomen* Spurius is far more interesting. It is attested in the imperial period to a limited extent and scholars have suggested that it might have been a status marker, a 'birth name',[75] which seems a natural suggestion if we also believe that the decrease of the *praenomen* Spurius was caused by the increase of the false filiation, *Spurii filius*, and by the moral opprobrium connected with the name Spurius. The question is whether this hypothesis can be confirmed by the sources.

Yanne Broux came to the conclusion that the hypothesis was essentially correct. Her reasoning was supported by two texts. The first was *ILAfrique*

[69] Broux, 'Ancient profiles exploited' (cit. n. 61), p. 26, fig. 6.

[70] Until the end of the second century / beginning of the third century, which is discussed in the last chapter of this book, pp. 262.

[71] Salomies, *Die römischen Vornamen* (cit. n. 62), p. 51.

[72] Rawson, 'Spurii' (cit. n. 21), p. 29.

[73] Rawson, 'Spurii' (cit. n. 21), p. 30.

[74] Broux, 'Ancient profiles exploited' (cit. n. 61), p. 19, fig. 3.

[75] Kajanto, *Latin Cognomina* (cit. n. 35), p. 73.

173 (Sidi Ali Ben Brahim in Africa, 1st–3rd c.), an inscription founded for a daughter (no. 1505) by her mother, Aelia Victorina.

[---] IV
RIA VI
TA FINI
VIT R
MISER
RIMIS
PATRI
N . SVO
ET AELIA
VICTORINA
MATRE
QVI HOC
PII D . F[76]

The main problem with using this text as evidence for the *cognomen* Spurius and Spuria as a marker of illegitimacy is that we cannot be certain that the commemorated woman was in fact named Spuria. Although the beginning of the inscription was not preserved, the text legible in lines 1 and 2 is ////// IV / RIA, according to the diplomatic transcription; this was interpreted by the editors as [*Sp(urii) f(ilia) S*]*puria*.[77] However, it is only one of several possible reconstructions of the *cognomen*. The decision to read the *cognomen* as Spuria was influenced by the reading of *naturalis pater* in the text and the interpretation of the *cognomen* Spurius as a name given to children born out of wedlock.[78]

The text mentions that the dead girl or woman left her mother, Aelia Victorina, and father in misery: the father is indicated as PATRI / N SVO

[76] Reading proposed in A. Piganiol & R. Laurent-Vibert, 'Recherches archéologiques à Ammaedara (Haïdra)', *Mélanges d'archéologie et d'histoire* 32 (1912), pp. 69–229, p. 181: [*S*]*puria vita(m) finivit r(elictis) miserrimis patr*[*e*] *n(aturali) suo et Aelia Victorina matre qui hoc pii d(ederunt) f(ecerunt)*.

[77] Piganiol & Laurent-Vibert, 'Recherches (Haïdra)' (cit. n. 76), p. 181.

[78] Piganiol & Laurent-Vibert, 'Recherches (Haïdra)' (cit. n. 76), p. 182.

– which the editors interpreted as *patri n(aturali) suo* for *patre n(aturali) suo*[79] – but his name is not given. Broux has suggested that his absence means that he did not want to be known, or that his identity was unimportant from a legal point of view.[80] It was, however, the mother who founded the inscriptions, and it is obvious that her name would be inscribed on the stone; it seems equally probable that the father's name could have been omitted if there was not enough space on the stone for both names, which seems to have been the case here.

The other text analysed by Broux is no less problematic. The funerary inscription *CIL* IX 2696 (Aesernia in Samnium, 1st c. AD) reads: *Ç(aio) Afinio* | *Ṣpuri f(ilio)* | *Ṣpurio* (no. 1531). The commemorated person had the *cognomen* Spurius and the filiation *Spurii filius*. Even if the filiation is false,[81] we cannot assume that the *cognomen* Spurius was an indicator of illegitimacy in general or was used as such in this case only, or simply the *cognomen* did not point out the family status.

The above texts cannot offer any definitive proof regarding the *cognomen*. In other sources attesting Spurius as a *cognomen*, there is no additional information that might lead us to assume that the individual in question was born out of wedlock, or disprove it.[82]

In the filiation *Spurii filius*, Spurius acts as the *praenomen*. Although it is generally accepted that the use of Spurius as a *praenomen* decreased significantly during the course of the imperial period, it did not die out completely.[83] There must therefore have been *Spurii filii* who were simply children of men bearing the *praenomen* Spurius,[84] and it is doubtful that they would

[79] *Ibidem*.

[80] Broux, 'Ancient profiles exploited' (cit. n. 61), pp. 23–24.

[81] Broux, 'Ancient profiles exploited' (cit. n. 61), p. 24.

[82] *E.g. To archaiologiko ergo ste Makedonia kai Thrake* 17 (2003), p. 418 [b] (Dion in Macedonia, 1st–2nd c. AD) = no. 1536; *CIL* XI.2.1 5662 (Nuceria Camellaria in Umbria, 1st–3rd c. AD) = no. 1534; Notizie dal Chiostro del Monastero Maggiore 63–64 (1999), p. 154, no. 8 (Vimercate in Transpadana, AD 50–200) = no. 1533; *CIL* IX 4139 (Nersae in Samnium, 1st–3rd c. AD) = no. 1532; and two ostraca from Egypt: *O. Bodl.* II 1619 (Thebes, AD 200 or 229) and 1686 (Thebes, 3rd c. AD) = no. 23.

[83] See fig. 4 in Broux, 'Ancient profiles exploited' (cit. n. 61), p. 21.

[84] Salomies, *Die römischen Vornamen* (cit. n. 62), p. 52.

have taken a different false filiation to avoid confusion with children born out of wedlock.

The most obvious example is *CIL* VI.2 7593 (Rome, AD 1–30) erected in the first century AD by Sp(urius) Carvilius Sp(uri) l(ibertus) Eros (no. 1643), a freedman of *gens Carvilia*. Eros not only bore the *praenomen* Spurius, but also was a freedman of Spurius Carvilius. Children of the manumittor, as well as those of his freedmen, would have had the filiation *Sp() f()*, which was not a false filiation; the same filiation appears in the name of Carvilia Sp(urii) f(ilia) Bassa (no. 1075), the co-founder of the epitaph. Interestingly, the plebeian *gens Carvilia*, who held some of the highest offices in Republican times, favoured the *praenomen* Spurius. The *gens* is well attested in the third and second centuries BC, and the name re-appeared toward the end of the Republican period.[85] If the *gens* is the same, there can be no doubt that Spurius served as a proper *praenomen* with no connection to bastardy.

A further possible example comes from *CIL* V.2 7535 (Forum Fulvii in Liguria, AD 1–50) and reads:

> Calpurniae P(ubli) f(iliae) Ruf() / matri / L(ucius) Curtius Sp(uri) f(ilius) / Salvius / loc(us) in front(e) p(edes) XII.
>
> To Calpurnia daughter of Pulius Ruf(), mother, Lucius Curtius son of Spurius Salvius (founded) place 12 feet broad.

In the inscription, L. Curtius Salvius (no. 1203), described as *Sp() f()*, commemorates his mother Calpurnia daughter of Publius; as the son and his mother have different *nomina*, Lucius Curtius Salvius was probably the son of a certain Spurius Curtius. A similar example is found in a first-century epitaph also from Liguria, *Sup. It.* XXV (AS) 23, in which a mother of the *gens Didia*,[86] daughter of Caius, commemorates her son M(arcus) Terentius Sp. f. (no. 1283). There is no convincing evidence that Spurius as *praenomen* or *cognomen* was given specifically to those born out of wedlock.

[85] K.-L. Elvers, 'Carvilius', [in:] H. Cancik & H. Schneider (eds.), *Der Neue Pauly. Enzyklopädie der Antike*, vol. II, Stuttgart – Weimar 1997, coll. 1000–1001.

[86] C. Didius was a legate of Caesar who took part in the campaign against Pompeius. Of course, the identification is not certain: K.-L. Elvers, 'Didius', [in:] *Der Neue Pauly* (cit. n. 85), vol. III, Stuttgart – Weimar 1997, coll. 540–541.

Spurius, therefore, does not seem to be a telling name in any sense. It cannot be compared to Aurelius,[87] for new citizens of AD 212 were Aurelii because they were enrolled to the *gens Aurelia*, and they acquired the *nomen* Aurelius by the law because Marcus Aurelius Severus Antoninus Augustus made them citizens. Spurius as both *cognomen* and *praenomen* was a name of individual choice. It cannot be compared to meaningful names, as copronyms, although this comparison only illustrates that taking names at face value can be dangerous.[88]
2. Beryl Rawson observed that many *Spurii filii* came from families whose members were freedmen. The label *Spurii filius* would have highlighted the social promotion of an individual (and their family): it would mean that a person was born free, and not a slave as their parents had been.[89] In other words, *Spurii filii* would have been first-generation freeborn Romans. According to this hypothesis, an individual born in slavery and later freed would not have the false filiation *Spurii filius*, but the description *libertus/-a*; furthermore, an individual born of free-born parents would prefer not to have this designation, as it would not be a marker of social promotion, but only of extramarital birth.

Spurii filii, thus, would be reserved for first generation of free-born children of freedmen. If someone was born of a free mother, but had no father in the legal and/or social sense, is likely to be *Spurii filius*; the alternative would have been to give no filiation or a different filiation (*e.g.* maternal

[87] Broux, 'Ancient profiles exploited' (cit. n. 61), p. 24.

[88] Paul Perdrizet introduced the hypothesis that individuals bearing copronyms – Kopres, Kopreus, *etc.* – were foundlings raised for slaves (P. Perdrizet, 'Copria', *Revue de l'Égypte ancienne* 23 [1921], pp. 85–94). Yet Sarah Pomeroy, who collected papyrological attestations of copronyms, concluded that there are no grounds to claim that they were foundlings, as very few among them were slaves, and the majority had patronyms and even matronyms; children who were undoubtedly *expositi* have various names, but not copronyms (S. Pomeroy, 'Copronyms and the exposure of infants in Egypt', [in:] R.S. Bagnall & W.V. Harris (eds.), *Studies in Roman Law in Memory of A. Arthur Schiller* [= *Columbia Studies in the Classical Tradition* XIII], Leiden 1986, pp. 147–162). Deborah Hobson offered an interpretation of copronyms based on comparative anthropological studies. She noticed that names of unpleasant meaning – such as 'dunghill', 'flea' or others containing elements denoting 'death' – appear in different cultures and are given to children whose mothers had difficulties with conceiving or whose previous children died immediately after birth or were stillborn (D.W. Hobson, 'Naming practices in Roman Egypt', *The Bulletin of the American Society of Papyrologists* 26 (1989), pp. 157–174, pp. 162–164).

[89] Rawson, 'Spurii' (cit. n. 21), p. 31; Broux, 'Ancient profiles exploited' (cit. n. 61), pp. 27–28.

grandfather's *praenomen*). Individuals who have the same *nomina* as their mothers and nothing to suggest that their mothers were freedwomen are traceable among *Spurii filii*, for instance M. Lucilius Sp. f. Maximus (no. 1275) and his mother Lucilla Sp. f. Secunda (no. 1176); Ocia Sp. f. Procula and her mother Ocia Trophime (no. 1303); or P. Cornelius Sp. f. Ianuarius and his mother Cornelia P. f. (no. 1330).[90] Additional four examples of *Spurii filii* born of free-born women with no traces of slaves or freedmen involved as fathers – nos. 843 (*BGU* IV 1032), nos. 844–845 (*P. Oxy.* XII 1451), nos. 851–852 (*P. Mich.* III 169), no. 86 (*PSI* XVII 1691) – are discussed in the last section of this sub-chapter.

In fact, in many cases nothing suggests the presence of *liberti*, but as in numerous inscriptions fathers were freedmen, the same is often assumed for those texts in which the data is insufficient. Yet a group of four inscriptions, discussed by Rawson, offers proof that such generalisations are potentially misleading:

a) *CIL* VI.2 8148 (Rome, 1st c. AD): L. Abbucius Onesimus + ? = L. Abbucius Sp. f. Onesimus (no. 846);

b) *CIL* VI.2 15007 (Rome, 1st c. AD): Ti. Claudius Dius + ? = Ti. Claudius Sp. f. Quir. Dius (no. 1427);

c) *CIL* VI.3 20171 (Rome, 3rd c. AD): C. Iulius C. l. Palleus + ? = C. Iulius Sp. f. Col. Phalleus (no. 1053);[91]

d) *CIL* VI.2 14310 (Rome, 1st–3rd c. AD): T. Camurenus Eros + Camurena Tyche lib. = T. Camurenus Sp. filius Celer (no. 1450).

In analysing these cases, Rawson wrote: 'In a number of cases, where the father has the same *nomen* as a spurious child but no status formula, this combination (same *nomen* although child illegitimate, thus same *nomen* also as

[90] No. 1176: DUNCAN, *PBSR* 26 (1958), pp. 72–73, no. 2 (Sutrium in Etruria, 2nd–3rd c. AD); no. 1303: SIJPESTEIJN, *ZPE* 111 (1996), pp. 285–286, no. 6 (Ostia, 2nd–3rd c. AD); no. 1330: *CIL* VI.3 16337 (Rome, 1st–3rd c. AD). In the last inscription, Publius Fannius, husband, is also mentioned, but he was not the father of Publius Cornelius. Publius Cornelius was described *suus* by Cornelia which suggests that there was a relationship between them, but not between Publius Fanius and Publius Cornelius.

[91] These three discussed also by KRAWCZYK, 'Paternal onomastical legacy' (cit. n. 34), pp. 124–125.

mother, plus contrast in status formulae) strongly suggests that the father is a *libertus*. The child's use of Sp.f. marks an improvement in status in the next generation'.[92] In *CIL* VI.2 14310 and *CIL* VI.3 20171 the families are indeed composed of freedmen. In *CIL* VI.2 14310, the father, mother and son have the same *nomen*, and it is likely that Camurena Tyche was a freedwoman of T. Camurenus Eros, as only she is described as *liberta*. Alternatively, all three (or just the parents) could have been freed by the same patron. In *CIL* VI.3 20171, the mother is absent, the father is *libertus*, and the son has both the *nomen gentilicium* and *cognomen* of his father. The mother could thus have been a freedwoman of the same patron as her partner, or could have belonged to the patron's *gens*: this would explain the *gentilicium* 'Iulius' for her son.[93]

In both *CIL* VI.2 8148 and 15007, however, there is little to suggest the freed status of the parents. Indeed, both of the *Spurii filii*, L. Abbucius Sp. f. Onesimus and Ti. Claudius Sp. f. Dius, have the *nomina* of their fathers. Because of the onomastics and analogy with the two other texts, Rawson believed that the fathers were freedmen who had belonged to the same *familia* as the absent mothers, who would have been freedwomen. Yet this is far from certain. It is well attested in the Egyptian material that children born out of wedlock, but of stable unions could have the *nomina* of their fathers (*infra*, p. 126). Furthermore, both the fathers and sons have Greek *cognomina*, Dius and Onesimus. Ti. Claudius Sp. f. Dius belonged to the tribus Quirina; he and his father have the *nomen* Claudius and *praenomen* Tiberius. Finally, as the inscription is dated to the first century, it could be proposed that Ti. Claudii Dii were new citizens who took their *praenomina*, *nomina* and *tribus* from the emperor Claudius or Nero.[94] If they were indeed new Romans, the son would not be subject to paternal power, which would explain the false filiation (G. 1.93). Certainly, neither the son nor his father were imperial freedmen, because they would carry a label of *libertus Augusti*, but they could be descendants of such a freedman, which would also illustrate that the description of *Spurii filii* was used by offspring of free-born parents.

[92] Rawson, 'Spurii' (cit. n. 21), p. 31.

[93] Krawczyk, 'Paternal onomastical legacy' (cit. n. 34), p. 125.

[94] R. Stewart, 'Tribus', [in:] R.S. Bagnall *et al.* (eds.), *The Encyclopedia of Ancient History*, online edition, doi:10.1002/9781444338386.wbeah20132.

The question remains whether only free-born individuals used this filiation. *Prima facie*, this is not an unreasonable assumption. In the early imperial Roman nomenclature,[95] freeborn people were described with filiations – *f(ilius)* / *f(ilia)* + father's *praenomen* in the genitive – while freedmen were described as *l(ibertus)* / *l(iberta)* + their patron's *praenomen* in the genitive[96] (or sometimes their cognomen or even their full name).[97] If this was the rule obeyed without exceptions, we would not expect to find freedmen and slaves among the *Spurii filii*; if they had no filiation, they would not have required a false one. However the epitaphs which provide the majority of attestations of *Spurii filii* are not official texts; rather the person or persons who funded the inscription could decide how they described both themselves and the person they wished to commemorate. It is also worth noting that, from the mid-first century onward, freedmen, except for *Augusti liberti*, omitted their status identification.[98] Moreover, Heikki Solin observed that the filiation was not always a clear sign that an individual was born free.[99] Among his examples, he listed *CIL* VI.3 20040 = no. 59 (Rome, 1st–3rd c. AD), questioning whether all *Spurii filii* should indeed be interpreted as freeborn.[100] The inscription is an epitaph funded by a certain C. Iulius Primus for his *verna*, C. Iulius Sp. f. Hedynon (no. 59); Solin proposed that the child was a slave born to a free mother and a slave of C. Iulius Primus, and interpreted it as an illustration of how the *senatus consultum Claudianum* worked in practice.[101]

[95] H. Solin, *Beiträge zur Kenntnis der griechischen Personennamen in Rom*, vol. I [= *Commentationes Humanarum Litterarum* XLVIII], Helsinki 1971, p. 36.

[96] L.R. Taylor, 'Freedmen and freeborn in the epitaphs of imperial Rome', *American Journal of Philology* 82.2 (1961), pp. 113–132, p. 123.

[97] P.R.C. Weaver, *Familia Caesaris. A Social Study of the Emperor's Freedmen and Slaves*, Cambridge 1972, p. 42.

[98] Weaver, *Familia Caesaris* (cit. n. 97), p. 43.

[99] See freedmen with filiations in: H. Solin, 'Name', [in:] G. Schöllgen, H. Brakmann, S. de Blaauw, T. Fuhrer *et al.* (eds.), *Reallexikon für Antike und Christentum. Sachwörterbuch zur Auseinandersetzung des Christentums mit der antiken Welt*, vol. XXV, Stuttgart 2013, coll. 723–795, col. 766.

[100] This case was brought to my attention by Małgorzata Krawczyk.

[101] Solin, *Beiträge zur Kenntnis* (cit. n. 95), p. 125; E. Herrmann-Otto, *Ex ancilla natus: Untersuchungen zu den „hausgeborenen" Sklaven und Sklavinnen im Westen des Römischen Kaiserreiches* [= *Forschungen zur antiken Sklaverei* XXIV], Mainz 1993, p. 44.

Originally, under Roman law, a child born to a free Roman woman and a slave, whose status is discussed later in Chapter 2, was considered a free (albeit extramarital) Roman (G.1.82). That was changed by the AD 52 *senatus consultum Claudianum*. The senate decree ruled that a woman who had intimate relations with a slave against the will of his owner (and despite the owner's warnings) could become a slave herself, and consequently bear slave children.

> G. 1.160: Maxima est capitis diminutio, cum aliquis simul et civitatem et libertatem amittit (...) item feminae, quae ex senatus consulto Claudiano ancillae fiunt eorum dominorum, quibus invitis et denuntiantibus cum servis eorum coierint.[102]
>
> *Capitis diminutio* is the greatest, when someone losses the citizenship and freedom at the same time. (...) Likewise, women who under the Claudian senate decree become slaves of those masters with whose slaves they had an intercourse against the will of these masters and despite of their warnings.

Sources referring to the *senatus consultum Claudianum* are less clear with regard to the status of children born of a union to which the slave's master consented, which may have been the scenario illustrated in *CIL* VI.3 20040. The crucial source is Gaius, although the passage has been the cause of some scholarly debate.

> G. 1.84: Ecce enim ex senatus consulto Claudiano poterat civis Romana, quae alieno servo volente domino eius coiit, ipsa ex pactione libera permanere, sed servum procreare; nam quod inter eam et dominum istius servi convenerit ex senatus consulto ratum esse iubetur. Sed postea divus Hadrianus iniquitate rei et inelegantia iuris motus restituit iuris gentium regulam, ut cum ipsa mulier libera permaneat, liberum pariat.
>
> And so then under the Claudian senate decree a Roman citizen, who had sexual intercourses with another person's slave with the master's consent, could in the virtue of *pactio* herself remain free, but bear slaves, for this what was agreed between her and the master of such slave was ordered to be valid under the *senatus consultum*. But thereafter the deified Hadrian moved by the unfairness of this matter and asymmetry of the law restored the rule of *ius gentium*, so that if a woman herself remains free, she bears the free.

[102] See also: P.S. 2.21a.1 & 17.

A literal reading of this passage would suggest that the *senatus consultum Claudianum* introduced a rule that children born of a free mother and a slave belonging to someone else should be slaves of their father's master, even in cases where the father's master did not disapprove of the union. (*Pactio* would have been an agreement between the woman and her partner's master confirming the master's consent and safeguarding her freedom). This was the general rule regulating free-slave unions until Hadrian restored the rule of *ius gentium*.[103] Solin must have used this interpretation when he wrote that the child, C. Iulius Sp. f. Hedynon, was a slave born to a freeborn mother as a result of the *senatus consultum Claudianum*.[104]

Paul Weaver proposed a different interpretation: between the time of the Claudian senate decree and the reign of Hadrian, a woman who lived with a slave with the consent of his master would have become his freedwoman, but her children would have been freeborn; if she kept her freeborn status by special agreement with her partner's owner (*pactio*), her children would be born slaves. After Hadrian restored the rule of *ius gentium*, she would no longer have been able to make such a *pactio*, as a woman could no longer sacrifice the freedom of her own offspring.[105] This interpretation provides us with three possible outcomes for the period between the *senatus consultum Claudianum* and Hadrian:

[103] A. Kacprzak, '*Servus ex libera natus*. Überlegungen zum senatusconsultum Claudianum', [in:] D. Feichtinger & I. Fischer (eds.), *Sexualität und Sklaverei* [= *Alter Orient und Altes Testament* CDLVI], pp. 63–82. See C. Castello, 'La condizione del concepito da libero e schiava e da libera e schiavo in diritto romano', *Studi in onore di Siro Solazzi*, Naples 1948, pp. 233–250; A. Storchi Marino, 'Restaurazione dei mores e controllo della mobilità sociale a Roma nel I secolo d.C.: il senatusconsultum claudiano *de poena feminarum quae servis coniungerentur*', [in:] F. Reduzzi Merola & A. Storchi Marino (eds.), *Femmes-esclaves : modèles d' interprétation anthropologique, économique, juridique : atti del 21. Colloquio internazionale GIREA, Lacco Ameno – Ischia, 27–29 ottobre 1994*, Naples 1999, pp. 391–426; B. Sirks, 'Der Zweck des Senatus Consultum Claudianum von 52 n. Chr.', *Zeitschrift der Savigny-Stiftung für Rechtsgeschichte RA* 122 (2005), pp. 138–149.

[104] Solin, *Beiträge zur Kenntnis* (cit. n. 95), p. 125.

[105] This interpretation is based on Tacitus, *Ann.* XII 53, who said that a woman having relationship with someone else's slave became his *liberta*, but did not comment on either *pactio* or status of children: P.R.C. Weaver, 'Gaius I. 84 and the S.C. Claudianum', *The Classical Review* 14.2 (1964), pp. 137–139.

1. without the consent of her partner's master, the woman would become a slave and bear slave children;

2. with the master's consent, but without *pactio*, she would become a *liberta* of the master, her children would be free;

3. with consent and *pactio* she would remain freeborn, but give birth to slave children.

If this hypothesis is correct, we could assume that C. Iulius Sp. f. Hedynon was freeborn to a mother who had become C. Iulius Primus' freedwomen.

Regardless of which interpretation of the *senatus consultum* we choose, certain problems remain: the *tria nomina* and filiation, even false, do not fit a slave boy, which status is suggested by the term *verna*. To accept either of them, we need to assume a wider meaning of *verna* including persons born free.[106] Another possibility is that the boy was freed which does not explain the filiation, however. Perhaps C. Iulius Sp. f. Hedynon was the natural son of a master and his slavewoman, who was then freed by his father.[107] As the natural son of his master he would not have suffered from the age limits imposed on manumission by the *lex Aelia Sentia* (G. 1.17). Or, the boy was manumitted against the *lex Aelia Sentia* and became a Iunian Latin. It is also possible that he died before obtaining his freedom, and that his description as freeborn was a matter of sentiment. Neither of these explanations are perfect, and the information is too limited for us to make definitive claims regarding C. Iulius Sp. f. Hedynon. However even the information we do have illustrates the difficulties in identifying a firm and universal rule for the application of the label *Spurii filius*. It is clear that the term served as a description of individuals born out of wedlock, but could also be used as a real filiation. The people described with this term were Romans who, for various reasons, had no legal father; this could be due either to social fatherlessness or to having a father who had been unable to hold *patria potestas* at the moment when the child was born. In

[106] Other *vernae* with filiations, see Herrmann-Otto, *Ex ancilla natus* (cit. n. 101), p. 44, who claimed that *verna* could be also 'im Hause des patronus als *ingenuus* geboren, als Kind von *liberti* im Haus des *patronus* geboren'.

[107] Herrmann-Otto, *Ex ancilla natus* (cit. n. 101), p. 43.

principle *Spurii filii* should refer only to those born free, but the sources illustrate that even this pattern could have exceptions.

5.2. *Roman law*

In Roman legal sources, the term *spurius* was used rather than the filiation *Spurii filius*. It is commonly held that, in the doctrinal sources of Roman law, it refers to a 'child born out of wedlock', and that the term was comparable or identical[108] to *vulgo quaesitus / conceptus*.[109] Roberto Fiori has suggested that *spurius* was used in two different senses:

1. It was simply the antithesis of *filius legitimus*. In such cases it would have referred to all children born out of wedlock who followed maternal status;
2. It was applied also in a more limited sense to children whose father was uncertain in social terms. In this sense, *spurius* would have constituted an antithesis to *naturalis*.[110]

The term was certainly applied as a generic description of 'extramarital' or 'bastard' children, both those who were fatherless and those begotten in non-marital unions. This usage is confirmed in numerous sources,[111] of which the most explicit is the definition given by Modestinus:

> D. 1.5.23 (Mod., *pand.* 1): Volgo concepti dicuntur qui patrem demonstrare non possunt, vel qui possunt quidem, sed eum habent, quem habere non licet. Qui et spurii appellantur παρὰ τὴν σποράν.

[108] R. Fiori, 'La struttura del matrimonio romano', *Bullettino dell'Istituto di diritto romano "Vittorio Scialoja"* 105 (2011), pp. 197–233, p. 224.

[109] Luchetti, *La legittimazione* (cit. n. 22), p. 12, n. 17.

[110] Fiori, 'La struttura' (cit. n. 108), p. 224.

[111] Luchetti, *La legittimazione* (cit. n. 22), p. 12, sources collected in n. 17.
Generic meaning: *Tit. Ulp.* 4.1 lists those who have status *sui iuris* – *spurii* are always *sui iuris*; D. 5.2.29.1: Ulpian (*opin.* 5) says that *spurii* have the right to the *querella inofficiosi testamenti* against their mother's will; D. 38.8.4: Ulpian (*reg.* 6) confirms that only the mother and maternal siblings

These who cannot indicate their father, or even those who can, but have one, whom they are not allowed to have, are described as 'commonly conceived'. And such (persons) are named *spurii* at the birth.

According to Fiori, *spurius* was used to denote the antithesis to *naturalis* in Gaius' passage on incest:

G. 1.64: Ergo si quis nefarias atque[112] incestas nuptias contraxerit, neque uxorem habere videtur neque liberos: itaque hi, qui ex eo coitu nascuntur, matrem quidem habere videntur, patrem vero non utique, nec ob id in potestate eius ⟨sunt, sed tales⟩[113] sunt, quales sunt ii, quos mater vulgo concepit: nam et hi patrem habere non intelleguntur, cum is etiam incertus sit; unde solent Spurii filii[114] appellari vel a Graeca voce quasi σποράδην concepti vel quasi sine patre filii.[115]

Thus, if anyone contracted a nefarious and incestuous marriage, it seems that he has neither a wife nor children. Therefore these who are born of this intercourse seem indeed to have a mother, whereas not of course a father. Because of this (they) are not under his power, but they are as those whom (their) mother casually conceived for those are not under-

are entitled to the succession after a *spurius* who died without a will; D. 50.2.3.2: Ulpian (*de off. proc.* 3) says that if *spurii* live honest lives, they could become *decuriones*, but legitimate children still have priority; D. 50.2.6 pr.: Papinian (*resp.* 1) says that *spurii* become decurions and therefore a person born of incest could become decurion too. In *CIL* XI 1147 (Veleia), an inscription of Trajan granting *alimenta* to children: the money was given to 263 *legitimi*, 34 *legitimae*, 1 *spurius* and 1 *spuria*. No categories between are visible. D. 49.15.25 (Marc. 14 *inst.*) refers to a situation of a child who was born in the captivity of parents married before they became captives. Such a child was considered *spurius*, if only the child and mother returned from the slavery (if the father returned too, such a child was under his power according to the *ius postlimini*).

[112] According to S. Solazzi, 'Glosse a Gaio I', [in:] *Scritti di diritto romano*, vol. VI, Naples 1972, pp. 153–267, pp. 205–207 (originally published in: *Studi in onore di Salvatore Riccobono*, vol. I, Palermo 1936, pp. 73–191): *nefarias atque* is a glossa.

[113] *suppl. ex* I. 1.10.12.

[114] I have changed the standard reading *spurii filii* into *Spurii filii*, on the understanding that if *spurii* is followed by *filius* or *filia* or *filii*, it was used in its basic form, as an element of false filiation and should thus be written with the capital letter, as all *nomina* are traditionally written in modern editions. Although it denotes 'extramarital child' or 'bastard', the term consists of the *nomen*.

[115] And *Ep. Gai* 4.8, I.1.10.12, Theoph., *Par.* 1.10.12: the *Epitome* and *Paraphrasis* use much harsher words to explain who *incerto patre* are – *si de adulterio concepti fuerint*, συμβαίνει τοὺς ἀπὸ πορνείας συλληφθέντας – which is an expression of the late antique attitude towards illegitimate children. See *infra*, pp. 254–257.

stood to have a father as he is uncertain. From which (people) customarily speak of 'sons of Spurius' or – in Greek tongue – as if conceived here and there – or as if sons without a father.

Fiori says that Romans recognised children born *ex incesto* as belonging to the category of *incerto patre* and equated them with the socially fatherless, thus the narrow category: *spurii (i.e. Spurii filii), quasi vulgo concepti*, antithesis to *naturales*. The use of *quasi* is revealing, as it refers to children not 'properly' *vulgo concepti*: the identity of the father is in fact known, but due to the atrocious nature of *incestum* he is counted as a father in neither the legal nor social sense, and his children are regarded in the same way as the fatherless. Fiori also notes that children of *incestum* must have had a lower position than other *spurii*,[116] yet the text on which his argument is based can be read in a number of ways. It is also possible that G. 1.64 has used *spurii* in its wider meaning, that is all children born out of wedlock.

In the first part of the passage, Gaius explains the standing of children born of incestuous unions. Children born of incest appear only to have a mother and not a father, because the marriage between their parents was void, even though the identity of the father is known. For this reason the children are not under the paternal power (*matrem quidem habere videntur, patrem vero non utique, nec ob id in potestate eius sunt*), the legal bond exists only between them and their mother, and had no father in legal terms. The description is valid for all children born out of *iustae nuptiae*, whose common characteristic is that they are not under the power of their fathers and they have no legal bond with the fathers (type 1).

In order to explain this 'fatherlessness' Gaius uses a comparison. He specifies that children who are not under the power of their fathers are similar to those conceived casually, *quos mater vulgo concepit*, and who are understood to have no father as his identity is uncertain, *nam et hi patrem habere non intelleguntur, cum is etiam incertus sit* (type 2) – the situation of any bastard is identical to those who do not even know who their fathers were, as in law they are not related to their fathers. Therefore, children of type 1 are not equated with those conceived casually, but merely compared to

[116] Fiori, 'La struttura' (cit. n. 108), pp. 224–225.

them, *quales sunt ii.*[117] Children of type 2 have two qualities: randomness of conception (a) and uncertainty of father (b).

Gaius then explains that those who are not under the power of their father (type 1), to which group children of incest belong, are referred to as *Spurii filii* (type 3). Children of type 3 are treated as if they had been conceived casually, *quasi σποράδην concepti* (a´) and as if the identity of their father was uncertain, *quasi sine patre filii* (b´), because they are not related to their fathers. Type 3 is therefore not equal to type 2, in the same way that type 2 is not equal to type 1. Children born of incest belong to types 1 and 3, but not to type 2, types 1 and 3 are equal. They may therefore be understood to belong to a wider category of children born out of wedlock, *quasi sine patre filii*, *Spurii filii*.[118]

This reasoning is supported by a passage from *Tituli ex corpore Ulpiani* devoted to the same problem. The passage is essentially the same as that in Gaius: a man who married a close relative contracted an incestuous marriage and could not therefore have *potestas* over his children as they were *quasi vulgo concepti spurii* (*Tit. Ulp.* 5.7).[119] It was not essential to include the comparison with children conceived casually: *spurii* were those born out of wedlock whom the father did not have *in potestate*, not merely children born to single mothers.

It is worth mentioning that the passage from Gaius has been preserved only in the fifth-century[120] *codex Veronensis.* The manuscript is not free from later *glossae* which were copied with the original *Institutes* as a single

[117] Or *tales sunt, quales sunt ii*, if we accept the reconstruction from the *Institutes* of Justinian.

[118] Rawson interpreted this passage in the same way, Rawson, 'Spurii' (cit. n. 21), p. 15: 'Gaius (1.64) defined *spurius* as a child deemed by the law to have no father. A man who formed a union against the rules of close relationship (*nefarias atque incestas nuptias*) was deemed to have neither wife nor children; children born of such a union were in the same position as those born of promiscuous intercourse (*ii quos mater vulgo concepit*). Such children had a mother, in the eyes of the law, but no father, and they were called *spurii* (but Gaius is uncertain about the etymology of the word)'.

[119] *Si quis eam, quam non licet, uxorem duxerit, incestum matrimonium contrahit ideoque liberi in potestate eius non fiunt, sed quasi vulgo concepti spurii sunt.* Repeated in *Col. Leg.* 6.2.1.4.

[120] Dating by M. Varvaro, 'Per la datazione del palinsesto veronese delle *Institutiones* di Gaio (Verona, B. Cap., Cod. XV)', *Scriptorium* 69.1 (2015), pp. 79–103.

text. Both Fiori's interpretation and my own therefore depend on a text which is not entirely reliable as a source.

Spurii in the narrower meaning can be perhaps seen in a constitution issued by Caracalla in August of AD 215 as a response to a certain Hostilia, who married a slave she thought had been freed. The *constitutio* states that her children, despite having a father, are to be recognised as *spurii,* as if they were born of a free mother and uncertain father. In this text *spurii* are indeed presented as children of single mothers. Yet, it could be also a reference to commonly known and general definition of *spurii*; as they had no father in the legal sense, they were *incerto patre*, even if the father raised them, as in the case of stable incestuous or free-slaves relationships.

> C.5.18.3: Imp. Antoninus A. Hostiliae: Si ignorans statum Erotis ut liberum duxisti et dotem dedisti isque postea servus est iudicatus, dotem ex peculio recipies et si quid praeterea tibi debuisse eum apparuerit. Filii autem tui, ut ex libera nati incerto tamen patre, spurii ingenui intelleguntur. PP VI k. Sept. Laeto II et Cereale conss.
>
> Emperor Antoninus Augustus to Hostilia: If you, not being aware of his status, married Eros and gave him a dowry as if he were a free man, and he was thereafter adjudged to be a slave, you will receive back the dowry and whatever else he owes you out of his *peculium*. But your sons are understood free-born *spurii,* as they were born of a free-born woman and an unknown father. Posted on 27th of August at the consulate of Laetus, for the 2nd time, and Cerealis.

It seems justified therefore that in the jurisprudential sources the term *spurius* was to describe any child who was not under the *potestas* of their fathers. Furthermore, the jurisprudential sources do not provide clear hint what the discussed term meant in non-legal language.

5.3. *Papyri*

While instances of the term *spurius* / *σπούριος* or the false filiation *Spurii filius* / *Σπουρίου υἱός* are not abundant in the papyri, they are nonetheless more numerous than any of the other descriptions discussed thus far.

The majority of documents containing the terms are census returns[121] – *SB* XXII 15704, *P. Flor.* I 5, *P. Oxy.* XLVII 3347 – and documents relating to civic status, such as *epikrisis* documents (*SB* I 5217 = *FIRA* III 6, *BGU* IV 1032 and *P. Oxy.* XII 1451), and registration of children (*P. Mich.* III 169 = *FIRA* III 4 = *CPL* 162), or application to *ephebeia* (*PSI* XVII 1691 discussed in Chapter 4). *Spurii* are attested once in a liturgy list (*SB* XX 14584 = *P. Lond.* III 1263 *descr.*, p. LXIX) and once in a will (*P. Select.* 14).

Among the census returns, only *SB* XXII 15704 = 131-Ar-20[122] (Karanis, after AD 138), ll. 61–88 is dated before the *constitutio Antoniniana*. It belongs to a longer document consisting of one land cession and three extracts from census returns. The four documents refer to the property matters of two families, one Roman and another Egyptian, but belonging to a privileged tax-group, presumably the *metropolitai*.

The passage where σπούριος appears is a copy of a census return submitted by Caius Sempronius Diogenes son of Sempronia Akousarion (no. 301), ll. 64–65: Γάιος Σεμπρώνιος Διογ̣[ένης] | σπούριος μητρὸς Σεμπρωνίας Ἀκου[σαρίου]. It is certain that Caius was a Roman citizen, as he was scrutinised by the prefect of Egypt in the very same year he submitted the return, l. 66: ἐπικε(κριμένος) τῷ̣ ις ⟨(ἔτει)⟩ ὑπὸ Φλαυίου Τιτιανοῦ ἡ̣γεμόν̣[ος]. He has the *nomen gentilicium* of his mother, and there is no mention of any man who might be identified as his father.

Two other census returns listing *spurii* are dated after AD 212. The earlier text (*P. Oxy.* XLVII 3347 = 215-Ox-1), dated to AD 216/7, comes from Oxyrhynchos and belongs to the census of AD 215, thus shortly after the edict of Caracalla. However *tria nomina* of the declarant – Titus Flavius Herminos – suggests that he was a citizen before AD 212. As in the case of Caius Sempronius Diogenes, above, he is described with the substantive

[121] On census and census returns, see: A. Jördens, *Statthalterliche Verwaltung in der römischen Kaiserzeit. Studien zum praefectus Aegypti* [= *Historia – Einzelschriften* CLXXV], Stuttgart 2009, pp. 63–94.

[122] The census returns quoted in this book have not only the *siglum* indicating their editions, but also the one given in the 'Catalogue of census declarations' in: R.S. Bagnall & B. Frier, *The Demography of Roman Egypt* [= *Cambridge Studies in Population, Economy and Society in Past Time*], Cambridge 2006².

σπούριος and a metronym, ll. 1–2: παρὰ Τίτου Φλαυίου Ἑρμε̣[ίνο]υ̣[123] σπουρίου μητρὸς Φλαυΐας Ταμερύλλης, and had his mother's *nomen gentilicium*. No further information relating to his civic or familial status was preserved.

The final text from this group comes from Arsinoe and is a return for the census of AD 243 (*P. Flor.* I 5 = 243-Ar-1). Here, both the declarant, Aurelia Thermoutharion, and her children, Aurelii Kopreion (no. 304) and N.N. (no. 305), described as σπουρίοι (l. 16), belonged to a family who acquired Roman citizenship under the *constitutio Antoniniana.* As in both of the previous cases, *spurius* is used as a substantive. The *nomen* of all three family members is the same, but in this case it cannot be interpreted as the acquisition of the maternal *nomen*; the text, in any event, is so fragmentary that it is impossible to determine whether or not a father was mentioned. The three belonged to the group of *katoikoi.* Thus, they were fiscally privileged new-Romans whose ancestors had been fiscally privileged Egyptians. The mother is described as κατοι|[κοῦσα ἀναγρα(φομένης) ἐπ' ἀμφ]ό̣δ̣ο̣υ̣ Τ̣αμείων (ll. 3–4). Both Calderini[124] and Bagnall[125] have suggested that the μὴ ἀνα[following second son's name should be reconstructed as μὴ ἀνα[γεγραμμένον], which could be an indicator of privileged status among Egyptians (new Romans still belonged to their former class so long as those classes continued to exist).[126]

[123] In the edition, the name is transcribed as Ἑρμ.[. . .]υ, reconstruction proposed in the commentary.

[124] CALDERINI, 'Ἀπάτορες' (cit. n. 1), p. 369.

[125] R.S. BAGNALL, 'Notes on Egyptian census declarations. I', *The Bulletin of the American Society of Papyrologists* 27 (1990), pp. 1–14, p. 4.

[126] According to www.papyri.info the expression (μὴ) ἀναγεγραμμένον ἐν ἐπιγεγενημένοις is attested mostly in documents relating to the census, it designated children of Egyptians of certainly or likely privileged fiscal status. Certain cases: *BGU* I 55 (Ptolemais Euergetis, AD 175); 109 (Ptolemais Euergetis, AD 121); 115 = *W. Chr.* 203 (Ptolemais Euergetis, AD 189); XIII 2226 (Ptolemais Euergetis, AD 202/3); *P. Brux.* 19 = *SB* V 8263 (Ptolemais Euergetis AD 117/8); *P. Oxf.* 8 (Ptolemais Euergetis, AD 104/5); *PSI* IX 1062 (Ptolemais Euergetis, AD 104/5); *SB* XX 14303, coll. II–III, ll. 39–58 (Ptolemais Euergetis, AD 147: see T. KRUSE, *Der Königliche Schreiber und die Gauverwaltung: Untersuchungen zur Verwaltungsgeschichte Ägyptens in der Zeit von Augustus bis Philippus Arabs (30 v. Chr. – 245 n. Chr.)*, vol. I, Munich 2002, p. 81, n. 46).

Probable: *BGU* IV 1069 R (Arsinoites, AD 245: an eldest son of a female declarant was described as, ll. 10–11: ἐπικεκριμέ|[νον], two younger, ll. 12–13: δύο μὴ ἀναγεγρα|[μμένους] ἐν ἐπιγεγενημένοις); *SB* XVIII 13369 (Ptolemais Euergetis, AD 147: a quarter of registration of a declarant given, ll. 3–4); *P. Münch.* III.1 70 (Ptolemais Euergetis, AD 119: a quarter of registration of a declarant given).

In the examples listed above, the term *σπούριος* seems to have had a meaning and function similar to *ἀπάτωρ* – a false filiation, or rather a substitute for a filiation, added to the description of individuals who had no father in neither the legal nor social sense (*infra*, pp. 80–91) – and was applied to Roman citizens. The term *σπούριος* was added after the name and followed by a metronym in the genitive and it seems to serve as the indication that the one who mattered for the status of a described person was the mother. It differes, therefore, from the use of the false filiation *Sp0 f0*, which was not accompanied by the metronym. Contrary to the texts discussed below, the census declarations provide no evidence that might allow us to speculate on the identity of the children's father or their mother's partner.

As all Romans were not liable for *laographia* before the *constitutio Antoniniana* we cannot expect to find *spurii* in tax lists; however *σπούριος* serves a similar function in a liturgy list from Ptolemais Euergetis (*SB* XX 14584 [before AD 253]), where we find, l. 35: *Ἀφροδίσιος σπούριος μητρὸς Θεον[ίλλης]* (no. 697) among those appointed for a liturgy. (This case similar to *P. Flor.* I 5, where new citizens added the description *σπούριος* instead of *ἀπάτωρ* perhaph as a sign of their Romanity.)

In documents relating to Roman citizenship acquisition, the term seems to have had a more technical, but similar meaning. *SB* I 5217 = *FIRA* III 6 (Theadelphia, AD 148) is a copy of an *epikrisis* issued for Caius Iulius Diogenes (no. 477) and Iulia Isarous (no. 478), two children of a Roman freedwoman, Iulia Primilla. Both children are described with a false filiation – which, unlike inscriptions, is written out in full – and as children born *ἐ[κ] μὴ νομίμων γάμ[ω]ν*:

Uncertain, too fragmentary: *BGU* I 128, col. I (Ptolemais Euergetis, AD 188/9); II 497 (Arsinoites, 2nd c.); *P. Ryl.* II 111 (Ptolemais Euergetis, AD 111).

The majority of non-Roman 'birth registrations' or 'birth returns' were filed by parents belonging to fiscally privileged orders, but this was not always the case (*P. Petaus* 1 *&* 2), as such declarations could serve not only in future *epikrisis*, but also as proof for an inheritance claim, see commentary A. Jördens, *P. Bingen* 105. Carlos Sánchez-Moreno Ellart has even suggested that the registration of children was obligatory for all Egyptians, but payers of full *laographia* simply did not keep copies for themselves, which, in his opinion, would explain why most surviving copies of birth returns belong to individuals of fiscally privileged groups: C. Sánchez -Moreno Ellart, '*ὑπομνήματα ἐπιγεννήσεως*: The Greco-Egyptian birth returns in Roman Egypt and the case of *P. Petaus* 1–2', *Archiv für Papyrusforschung* 56 (2010), pp. 91–129, p. 94.

ll. 19–23: *δι' ἧ[ς ἡ] Πρειμίλλα χρ̣[η]|ματ̣[ί]σασα Ἰουλία Πρειμίλλα ἐμαρτυροποιεῖτο εἶν[α]ι αὐ|τῆς τέκνα δί[δ]υμα τόν τε Γάϊον Ἰούλιον Σπουρίου υἱὸν | Διογένην καὶ Ἰουλία[ν] Σπουρίου θ̣υ̣γατέρα Ἰσαιοῦν | ἐ[κ] μὴ νομίμων γά̣μ[ω]ν.*

By which, Primilla, styled Iulia Primilla, attempted to prove that the twins – Caius Iulius son of Spurius Diogenes and Iulia daughter of Spurius Isarous (?) – not born of lawful marriage are hers.

The text also mentions Iulia Primilla's manumission certificate of AD 127/8 (ll. 16–17) and the *epikrisis* of her patron, Caius Iulius Diogenes, of AD 103/4 (ll. 13–16). These documents were of great importance in establishing her status: the *epikrisis* of her patron is noted in the document to prove that he was a Roman, while the other document proved that Iulia Primilla had been manumitted formally.[127] As a freedwoman formally freed by a Roman citizen, she became a Roman herself (ll. 8–10) and would have been able to transfer this status to her children if there was no father of lesser *status civitatis*.

The document does not mention whether or not the children were fathered by Caius Iulius Diogenes, as there would have been no need to include such information. His paternity has been assumed by Nelson and others on the basis of his will, *P. Select.* 14 (Arsinoite nome, after AD 127),[128] in which he left bequests to both Caius Iulius Diogenes the younger and his sister. In fact there is no clear indication that these siblings were his children: *σπούρια θυγάτηρ* in l. 15 is a reconstruction. While they do have the same ***nomen gentilicium*** as their mother's patron, it is also the ***nomen*** of their mother. The ***nomen*** is not decisive evidence of paternity, as the mother would have given them her own gentilicium regardless of the father.

A more convincing argument, as Nelson has pointed out, is the fact that Primilla was freed in the same year the children were born;[129] this suggests that her owner wanted the children to be born free. If Caius Iulius

[127] J.-P. Lévy, 'Les actes d'état civil romains', *Revue historique de droit français et étranger* 29 (1952), pp. 449–486, p. 481.

[128] C.A. Nelson, *Status Declarations in Roman Egypt* [= *American Studies in Papyrology* XIX], Amsterdam 1979, p. 45; J.A. Straus, 'Remarques sur quelques contrats de vente d'esclaves conservés sur papyrus', *Zeitschrift für Papyrologie und Epigraphik* 104 (1994), pp. 227–229, p. 227; S.E. Phang, *The Marriage of Roman Soldiers (13 BC – AD 235): Law and Family in the Imperial Army* [= *Columbia Studies in the Classical Tradition* XXIV], Leiden – Cologne 2001, p. 43.

[129] Nelson, *Status Declarations* (cit. n. 128), p. 45.

Diogenes was indeed the siblings' father, concealing his identity in the *epikrisis* document would have been unnecessary: as a Roman he would not have endangered the *status civitatis* of the children; nor would it have been necessary to reveal his paternity, as the *epikrisis* focused on civic, not familial status. On the basis of these circumstances, it seems probable that the children described as *Spurii filii* were born of a union between a slave and her master.

Another *epikrisis* document, dated almost 30 years later, comes from the Arsinoite nome (*BGU* IV 1032 [AD 173 or after]). It is based on a similar pattern to that found in *SB* I 5217, although the beginning of the text has been lost. In ll. 1–3, the *professio* of the child's N.N. Iulius Sp. f. N.N., mother in AD 147–148 is listed as one of the documents submitted at the *epikrisis*: [- *ca.* ? - ἑ]αυτῆς δέλτ[ον π]ρο|φ[ε]σσίωνος [ἐπ]ὶ σφραγείδων (l. σφραγίδων) ἐ[π]ὶ τοῦ ια (ἔτους) | θ[ε]οῦ Αἰλίο[υ] Ἀ[ν]τωνείνου. From this we can be certain that she was a freeborn Roman woman and that the citizenship of her children depended on this (*infra*, p. 60). As in *SB* I 5217 the child to be scrutinised is declared by his mother as a child ἐκ μὴ νομ[ί]μων γάμων (l. 10), and the description contains a false filiation written in full (l. 17); there is no evidence for or against the existence of a father.

P. Oxy. XII 1451 (Alexandria [?], AD 175) is the latest and longest document belonging to the *epikrisis* group discussed in this section; it contains an extract from the prefect's office confirming the *epikrisis* of slaves and children, Trunnia Marcella (no. 844) and Trunnius Lucilianus (no. 845), born of Trunnia, a Roman woman. The document postdates the *epikrisis* itself; it may have been written in regard to the citizenship of the daughter, Trunnia Marcella, but the reason why it was issued is not entirely clear.

As in the previous case (*BGU* IV 1032), the documents used to confirm that the children could be scrutinised as Romans were the *tabulae professionis* of their mother, their own *testationes*, and record of warrantors (*gnosteres*) who confirmed the children's status. As in both previous cases, the children are described as *Spurii filii* (ll. 17, 32); while the assertion that the children were born ἐκ μὴ νομίμων γάμων has not been preserved, its restitution in ll. 25–26 seems probable.

As *BGU* IV 1032, the document provides no information regarding the possible father. Sara Elise Phang suggested that in both *BGU* IV 1032 and

P. Oxy. XII 1451 the scrutinised children were born to soldiers;[130] yet scrutiny was important not only for the children of Roman soldiers, but for Romans in general, as all Romans were exempted from the poll-tax.[131] But even women exempted from the poll-tax had to pay taxes on their slaves, so certification of their own status could be important for the future scrutiny of their slaves. This, however, was not the only reason why a Roman mother would want to secure Roman citizenship for their children: only Roman children would have been able to inherit her estate, either as legally named heirs or in the event the mother died intestate (*infra*, pp. 277–282). For a young woman, an additional benefit of being Roman would have been the ability to marry a Roman citizen and produce legitimate Roman offspring for him.

Further information concerning the status of children can be found in the declarations made by mothers, *BGU* IV 1032, ll. 9–10: *ἐμαρτυρ[ο]ποιεῖτο εἶναι αὐτῇ υἱὸν τὸν ἐπικρεινόμενον* (l. *ἐπικρινόμενον*) *ἐκ μὴ νομ[ί]μων γάμων*: 'she has produced a testimony that the one to be scrutinised (born) not of a lawful marriage is her son' (the same phrase: *SB* I 5217, ll. 19–23, in *P. Oxy*. XII 1451, ll. 25–26 partly reconstructed). This, in my opinion, is a better understanding than 'were her children by unlawful marriage' as it was translated in *P. Oxy.* XII. If the texts wished to point out unlawfulness, *ἄνομος* would have been the more appropriate adjective. The meaning in this instance is that a child belonged to the mother who submitted them to scrutiny and was the one whose status was to be acquired. A *matrimonium iniustum* would only complicate the mother's claim, as it would require proof that the father was also Roman, otherwise a child could not acquire citizenship; under the *lex Minicia* – which was also followed in Egypt – children of Romans and non-Romans were supposed to follow not the maternal status but the worse one (*infra*, pp. 186–190). None of the three papyri discussed above mentions a father. Therefore, the *epikrisis* would have been the same regardless of whether the children were raised by a single mother or by parents who did not form any kind of marriage; for this reason we can safely assume that, in *epikrisis* documents, *Spurii filius/-a* was used as a general description of a 'bastard son or daughter'.

130 Phang, *Marriage of Roman Soldiers* (cit. n. 128), p. 44.

131 Phang, *Marriage of Roman Soldiers* (cit. n. 128), p. 45.

The last document that needs to be examined in this section is *P. Mich.* III 169 = *FIRA* III 4 = *CPL* 162 (AD 145), a birth declaration found in Karanis, but composed in Alexandria.[132] It was submitted by Sempronia Gemella, mother of twins, Marcii Sempronii Sokration (no. 852) and Sarapion (no. 851), and preserved on an actual diptych.[133] In the document, she testifies that she gave birth to twins, Sarapion and Sokrates, *incerto patre*, and explains that the *testatio* was made because the *lex Aelia et Sentia* forbade the registration of illegitimate children (*spurios spuriasve*) *in albo*.

The text became the subject of a vivid discussion in the scholarly literature, mainly because of the procedure it attests. According to Claudia Terreni, the *testatio* was made after *professio in actis* which, contrary to *professio in albo*, was accessible to illegitimate children but not obligatory until the time of Marcus Aurelius, after which it became mandatory to register all children within thirty days after their birth.[134] The *professio* was closely related to *epikrisis* because it could serve as a proof of citizenship and, as we have seen in the *epikrisis* documents above, was provided at the time of scrutiny. Perhaps the *testatio* also served other purposes, such as the acquisition of *ius trium liberorum* by the mother;[135] it therefore makes sense that it would have been subject to public control.[136]

It is commonly accepted by the scholarship that the twins registered by Sempronia Gemella were begotten of an informal union. The information provided by Sempronia Gemella about the boys' father was that he was unknown: *s[e] en[i]x̣ạm [esse] ẹx inc̣[ert]o p̣ạṭṛẹ* / γεγεννῆσθαι ἐξ ἀδήλου πατρός. This has provoked numerous hypotheses regarding his identity.

[132] A text similar but too fragmentary to discuss is *P. Wisc.* II 50 = *Ch. L. A.* XLVII 1439 (provenance unknown, AD 165).

[133] On the use of tablets in Roman Egypt, see E. MEYER, *Legitimacy and Law in the Roman World: Tabulae in Roman Belief and Practice*, Cambridge 2004.

[134] C. TERRENI, 'P. Mich 3.169: Il misterio di Sempronia Gemella', *Studia et documenta historiae et iuris* 62 (1996), pp. 573–582, p. 576; SÁNCHEZ-MORENO ELLART, '*Ipsis liberis*' (cit. n. 47), pp. 367–368. The opinions in this respect varied: *e.g.* according to Sanders it was a deed of purely private nature: *P. Mich.* III, pp. 162–163, while Cuq considered it to be an extract of the official document: É. CUQ, 'Les lois d'Auguste sur les declarations de naissance', [in:] *Mélanges Fournier*, Paris 1929, pp. 119–133, p. 129.

[135] SÁNCHEZ-MORENO ELLART, '*Ipsis liberis*' (cit. n. 47), p. 368; G. RIZZELLI, *Lex Iulia de adulteriis. Studi sulla disciplina di adulterium, lenocinium, stuprum*, Lecce 1997, p. 231.

[136] TERRENI, 'P. Mich 3.169' (cit. n. 134), p. 576.

It has been suggested that he was either Gemella's patron or her tutor, C. Iulius Saturninus, an accidental lover whose identity Gemella did not remember, or perhaps even a customer.[137] It has also been suspected that Gemella was abandoned by an unfaithful soldier or even had twins with a soldier closely related to her.[138] Peter van Minnen, in turn, suggested that Gemella had her children with Sokrates, a wealthy Egyptian inhabitant of Karanis.[139] A similar suggestion was offered by Claudia Terreni, who did not know the results of the archeological inquiry of the location of papyri in Karanis. According to her, the father would have been an Egyptian whose identity Gemella tried to hide in order to avoid the consequences of the *lex Minicia* and secure the Roman citizenship for her sons.[140] Almost all these explanations are based on the assumption that either the father was not proud enough of his relationship with Gemella to be indicated as the boy's father, that the nature of their relationship would have had a negative effect on the twins' legal standing, or that the mother was promiscuous and simply did not know the identity of the father. The father, however, did not appear because he did not matter; indicating him could even have complicated the children's claim for citizenship. The information provided by Gemella that children were *ex incerto patre* was not to hide the father, but to inform the authorities that there was no father to transfer his status to the twins.

We find a practical example of this in a passage of Scaevola preserved in the Digest.

> D. 22.3.29.1 (Scaev. dig. 9): Mulier gravida repudiata, filium enixa, absente marito ut spurium in actis professa est. Quaesitum est an is in potestate patris sit et matre intestata mortua iussu eius hereditatem matris adire possit nec obsit professio a matre irata facta. Respondit veritati locum superfore.

[137] Summarised with further literature by Terreni, 'P. Mich 3.169' (cit. n. 134), p. 577.

[138] J.F. Gilliam, 'Some Roman elements in Roman Egypt', *Illinois Classical Studies* 3 (1978), pp. 115–131, p. 120.

[139] P. van Minnen, 'House-to-house enquiries: An interdisciplinary approach to Roman Karanis', *Zeitschrift für Papyrologie und Epigraphik* 100 (1994), pp. 227–251, p. 242.

[140] Terreni, 'P. Mich 3.169' (cit. n. 134), pp. 579–580.

> A woman, who had been repudiated being pregnant, having given a birth to a son in the absence of her husband registered the son as *spurius* in the acts. The inquiry arose whether he was under the power of his father, and whether, because his mother had died intestate, he could acquire the maternal inheritance according to his (father's) order, and whether the *professio* made by the angry mother was not a hindrance. He responded that the space for truth was left.

The passage refers to a case in which a pregnant woman had been left by her husband and, because of her anger, she registered the child as *spurius* (*spurium in actis professa est*). When she died, the husband claimed to be *pater familias* of the boy in order to acquire his ex-wife's inheritance through the boy, who was his mother's heir according to the *senatus consultum Orfitianum*.[141] Scaevola says that, in this case, the declaration of the mother cannot be used as decisive proof of the boy's status. The text refers to a declaration similar to the one filled by Sempronia Gemella in which a child is registered as *spurius, natus ex incerto patre*. What matters in such a registration is not the identity of the father, but the status of the mother. Even if there was a father, he had little to do with either the registration or the *epikrisis*, except in cases where he was of a lower civic status and actually lived with the mother. *Spurius* and *Spurii filius* thus refer only to the status of a child with regard to their mother: it is a general term denoting a 'bastard' but also underlining the lack of a legal father or any relation to him with respect to the civic status.[142] Moreover, in the bureaucratic practice of Roman Egypt (or even wider), the term *spurius* developed into a technical term applied in two distinct ways: the first usage appears in deeds related to status, such as *epikrisis* and registrations of children, and was used when the civic rights of children were derived solely from the mother, while the second meaning was similar to ἀπάτωρ and was applied primarily in lists, census returns, *etc.*, but developed from the first usage.

[141] F. Schulz, 'Roman registers of births and birth certificates', *The Journal of Roman Studies* 32 (1942), pp. 78–91, pp. 81–82.

[142] In this contexts, the term *spurius* cannot be understood as 'child of an unknown father' which meaning Rawson suggested for D 22.3.29, because it is too narrow. See Rawson, 'Spurii' (cit. n. 21), p. 15.

It should be noted that, in private deeds in Egypt, Romans are never described as *Spurii filii*, regardless of whether they were fatherless or born in non-marital unions. In the will of Sabina Apollinarion from AD 172–173, the description is simply: [*Σα*]*βινία Ἀπολλωνάριον θυγάτηρ Σαβινίας Ἡρα̣ .* [. . .] (*PSI* XIII 1325, l. 9 [Phebihis, AD 172–175]), but in the majority of *testamenta* Romans are simply identified with their *nomina* without filiation. Because Romans in Egypt did not use filiations outside of the military context, *Sp. f.* never took the function of the false filiation, but was used only in certain types of documents to indicate the lack of a father who could transfer his status to the child. This observation supports the conclusion (discussed earlier) that *spf* was not an obligatory description, but a matter of choice, and that in Egypt the expression *Spurii filius* had a primarily technical meaning indicating not only the familial status, but also the Roman one of an individual described.

5.4. *Conclusion*

We should, in closing this section, attempt to explain the difference between *spurii* and *naturales*. An analysis of jurisprudential sources, papyri and inscriptions proves that a semantic difference undoubtedly existed between these two terms. Yet it seems that the difference is not in the *status libertatis* of either the children or their mothers, but in the relationships or lack thereof. *Naturalis* is used in contexts where familial relations matter, while *spurius* refers to the lack of the father from whom the status could be derived. *Naturalis* would have been applied when a father intended to manumit his son before he reached a certain age (G. 1.19), when a father was not allowed to pledge his slave children (P.S. 5.6.16), or when he gave up his son for adoption (G. 1.134); it indicated a blood relationship with another family member (not necessarily the father) which determined rights or obligations. *Spurius*, however, was applied only in situations where the lack of bonds between children and their father needs to be underlined, such as those inscriptions where individuals were described as *Spurii filii* despite their fathers being known, or the documents in which a mother registers the birth of a child who is technically *sine patre* (D. 22.3.29.1).

6. APATORES

The word ἀπάτωρ was known in Greek literature before it appeared in papyri in Roman Egypt,[143] where it was used to describe deities, such as Hephaestus, for whom no father was attributed. It could also be used to mean a man disowned by the father, ἄοικος, or to describe someone whose father had died.[144] The word was connected to illegitimate birth in some cases, but it did not denote the actual bastard, *e.g.* Ion described as ἀμήτωρ and ἀπάτωρ (Eur. *Ion* 108, 836–837).[145] In Roman Egypt, however, it became an element in the identification cluster in the position of missing patronym. Before discussing the meaning, however, it is worth saying a few words about its geographical distribution and the context in which it was applied.

6.1. *Geography*

Calderini[146] and Youtie[147] observed that the use of ἀπάτωρ was limited mostly to the Arsinoite nome during the second and third centuries. Indeed, the word is attested *ca.* 600 times in papyri from the Arsinoite nome. Malouta[148] and Calderini[149] also suggested that the term might have been used more widely; yet attestations from other nomes are few, and

[143] It is attested in earlier Greek literary sources (theological texts, tragedies, historical and philosophical works): Calderini, 'Ἀπάτορες' (cit. n. 1), p. 359; M. Malouta, 'The terminology of fatherlessness in Roman Egypt: ἀπάτωρ and χρηματίζων μητρός', [in:] J. Frösén, T. Purola & E. Salmenkivi (eds.), *Proceedings of the 24th International Congress of Papyrology, Helsinki, 1–7 August, 2004* [= *Commentationes Humanarum Litterarum* CXXII], Helsinki 2007, vol. II, pp. 615–623, p. 619.

[144] *TLG*, *s.v.* 'ἀπάτωρ'; *LSJ*, *s.v.* 'ἀπάτωρ'.

[145] Ogden, *Greek Bastardy* (cit. n. 4), pp. 170–171.

[146] Calderini, 'Ἀπάτορες' (cit. n. 1), p. 362, n. 5.

[147] H. Youtie, 'Ἀπάτορες. Law vs. custom in Roman Egypt', [in:] J. Bingen, G. Cambier & G. Nachtergael (eds.), *Le monde grec: pensée, littérature, histoire, documents. Hommages à Claire Préaux*, Brussels 1975, pp. 723–740 (reprinted in: H. Youtie, *Scriptiunculae posteriores*, vol. I, Bonn 1981, pp. 17–35), p. 726.

[148] Malouta, 'Terminology of fatherlessness' (cit. n. 143), p. 617.

[149] Calderini, 'Ἀπάτορες' (cit. n. 1), p. 362, n. 5.

would require further examination before being used as evidence for widespread application of the term outside of the Arsinoite nome.

6.1.1. Oxyrhynchites

The Oxyrhynchite papyri containing ἀπάτωρ were re-examined by Malouta, who proved that they were either wrongly attributed to the Oxyrhynchite nome or misread.[150] The only firm attestation of ἀπάτωρ in the Oxyrhynchite nome is *PSI* XV 1532 (Oxyrhynchos, AD 100–117), where it had the function different from usual (*infra*, pp. 99–100).

6.1.2. Elephantinites

The term occurs three times in the Elephantine ostraca. *O. Eleph. DAIK* 47 (Elephantine, AD 185) is a receipt of τέλος δερμάτων, a tax known through documents from Upper Egypt and the Arsinoite nome.[151] There are two payers of the tax, ll. 2-3: Pasenis (ἀπάτωρ) (no. 1747) and N.N. son of Pasenis. The former is not described explicitly as ἀπάτωρ, but labelled with the symbol // (as indicated in the *apparatus*) which the editor, Guy Wagner, resolved to (ἀπάτωρ) in the text transcription. The editor observed that the payers might have been relatives.[152] If he had not resolved // into ἀπάτωρ, Pasenis and N.N. would have have had the common patronym, Πασῆνις // καὶ .[. . . . . .] Πασήνεως. Moreover, they had the same profession which they practiced together (l. 3). As the name of the second payer is lost, we cannot be certain that the same symbol did not also follow his name. It is worth noting that while the // symbol is well-known in the context of taxation - usually, but not exclusively, it was used in tax lists to denote than an individual had paid the tax – there is only one other instance, in *O. Bodl.* II 832, where it might have been used to mean ἀπάτωρ.

[150] Malouta, 'Terminology of fatherlessness' (cit. n. 143), pp. 617–618.

[151] See the commentary in: *P. et O. Eleph. DAIK*, p. 41.

[152] *Ibidem*.

O. Bodl. II 832 (Elephantine, AD 179) is a receipt for ***potamophylakia***; the ostracon chronologically close to *O. Eleph. DAIK* 47.[153] There can be no doubt that the text comes from Elephantine, as it is made explicit in l. 2. Aditionally, the tax was collected by ***praktores*** known from other documents, Ailios Didymos and Hermodoros (ll. 1–2).[154] In *O. Bodl.* II 832 there is one tax-payer (no. 562), l. 3: *Βιῆγχις* // (ἀπάτωρ) μ̣ητ(ρὸς) *Θινβιηγχις* (l. *Θινβιήγχιος*), but the identification cluster differs from the one in *O. Eleph. DAIK* 47; here we find the metronym used as a substitute for the filiation (*infra*, pp. 78–79). The symbol // is placed in the position of the filiation and, as in the previous text, *O. Eleph. DAIK* 47, it was resolved by the editors to (ἀπάτωρ). Yet the position of the symbol does not prove that it was used to mean ἀπάτωρ: it could have also been the sign for 'no father', or 'without father', similar to the Latin *sine patre*, *e.g.* ἄνευ πατρός.

O. Eleph. DAIK 72 (Elephantine, AD 81–96), a tax receipt possibly for a poll-tax, is the only example among the Elephantine ostraca for which the reading of ἀπάτωρ seems fairly secure (no. 417): unlike the two previous ostraca, the word is written in full. Unfortunately, the fragment does not mention where the tax was paid. However, as the editor does not raise the possibility that it was paid somewhere else – the Arsinoite nome, for example – there are no reasons to reject it as an attestation of the term ἀπάτωρ in the late-first-century Elephantine. If we accept *O. Eleph. DAIK* 72 as evidence for the presence of the term in Elephantine, it makes the resolution of the symbol // to (ἀπάτωρ) in *O. Eleph. DAIK* 47 and *O. Bodl.* II 832 all more plausible, yet, certainly not secure.

6.1.3. Mendesian nome

There are three relevant documents, all concerning taxation, from the official archive of Thmouis, located in the Mendesios nome.[155] The first docu-

[153] The text was corrected and re-dated in R. Duttenhöfer, 'Korrekturen zu Ostraka aus Elephantine/Syene II', ***Zeitschrift für Papyrologie und Epigraphik*** 157 (2006), pp. 147–158, pp. 150 & 153.

[154] Duttenhöfer, 'Korrekturen zu Ostraka' (cit. n. 153), pp. 150–151.

[155] See *P. Ryl.* II, pp. 290–292, and *P. Thmouis*, pp. 1–4.

ment is related to *epikrisis* (*P. Ryl.* II 220 [Thmouis, AD 134–138]). It consists of seven fragments (A–G), containing lists of names grouped according to the location. Each list is organised in the following way: a location, followed by a list of boys belonging to this location, each one described by their name, patronym, papponym and metronym, information on the last census in which they were declared, the volume and page of the census register where they were recorded, information on the *epikrisis*, ἐπ(εκρίθη) (ἐτῶν), and physical characteristics; the lists concluded with the number of scrutinised boys, γ(ίνονται). Ἀπάτορες appear twice in the lists (nos. 481 and 482), E, l. 64: [Ποκροῦ(?)]ρις ἀπάτωρ ἐκ μη(τρὸς) Τια[- *ca.* ? -] and F, l. 81: [ἀπά]ṭωρ μητ(ρὸς) Ταποκρού[ριος]. Another ἀπάτωρ (no. 485) occurs in *P. Ryl.* II 221, fr. C, l. 32 (Thmouis, AD 200–225), a register of public land leasees. It consists of entries of people who were given land for cultivation, followed by guarantors, the date of the lease, its duration, type and the amount of land.

The final document from this location is *P. Thmouis* 1 = *PSI* I 104 + 105 + 107 (Thmouis, AD 180–192), a long and complicated roll believed to be a copy of an original series of tax reports and accounts by the royal scribe of the Mendesian nome. It concerns different types of unpaid taxes both on land and personal burdens. In one section regarding *laographia*, the texts refer to slaves who had been sold to people exempt from taxes, including citizens of Alexandria and Antinoopolis; it does not, however, make clear if or why this was a problem.[156] Only one short section of the text refers to *laographia* paid by free people, col. 158, l. 1 – 160, l. 22. A village scribe denounced 54 inhabitants of different villages who were either not on the lists of *laographia* payers or who had been inscribed there with incorrect names. A *kommogramateus* who took office after the denouncement informs us that some of those 54 could not be found in their supposed villages, some could not be identified, some were registered in Thmouis and Mendes, and some had already been added to *laographia* list. For this reason the payment of the tax was suspended. The cases were brought to the prefect, T. Furius Victorinus, who decided that they should be examined, but there is no further information regarding whether or not the investigation took place. The cases then went to the *conventus* of the prefect

[156] Detailed analysis of the text in: *P. Thmouis*, pp. 14–53.

M. Annius Syriacus who released those people from the tax, except for five persons registered in the metropolis, who were given a three-month moratorium, so that an examination of their rights could be made. Interestingly, all five were registered with an incorrect patronym, and one was even listed under the wrong name. Among those five, we find (no. 565): *Ἀπολλώνιος ἀπάτωρ ἐγ* (l. *ἐκ*) *μητρὸς* | *Σοήριος̣, δηλ(ωθεὶς) ἀναγρά(φεσθαι) ἐπὶ Θμούεως* | *δ ἀμφόδ(ου) ὡς Ἀπολλώνιο(ς) Στρά̣*|*[των(?)]ος μητρὸς [Σο]ήρ̣ιος* (159, ll. 21–23 – 160, l. 1).[157] As the archive consists of 16 published texts[158] (around one-third of all texts from the Mendesios nome)[159] and three contain *ἀπάτωρ*, it seems probable that the term was used in this nome, at least in administrative documents.

6.1.4. Other places

The only attestation of the term in the Western Desert is found in *P. Iand.* VII 142 (AD 164–165), from Kysis located in el-Kharga Oasis (Oasis Magna): l. 17 [- *ca.* 27 -] *ὑπὸ Πε̣τ[χ]ῶ(ντος [?]) τοῦ κ(αὶ) [Μα]ξίμου [ἀ]πάτ(ορος) μητ(ρὸς) Α̣ι̣[. . . ο]υ̣ ἀπὸ* [] (no. 520). Although *ἀπάτωρ* is a reconstruction, the editor, Joseph Sprey, does not explain his restitution in the commentary; for this reason, we must treat this attestation with some caution.

A list of payments in kind from the Memphite nome is preserved in *SB* XII 11011 (AD 130–175),[160] but it was written in the Arsinoite nome, perhaps in Karanis,[161] and cannot be counted as evidence of the term *ἀπάτωρ* outside the Arsinoite nome (no. 822).

There can, however, be no doubt that *BGU* XI 2019 = 187-Me-1 (Moithymis, AD 188) a census return submitted by a freedwoman Herakleia,

[157] See commentary in: *P. Thmouis*, pp. 169–173.

[158] TM Arch id: 43 on https://www.trismegistos.org/arch/index.php.

[159] According to www.papyri.info – the number is not necessarily exact, but gives an idea of the proportion.

[160] Malouta, 'Terminology of fatherlessness' (cit. n. 143), p. 618.

[161] An editor of the document provided rather firm prosopographical arguments which should allow us to accept the Arsinoite provenance: O.M. Pearl, 'Part of a daybook of payments in kind', *Zeitschrift für Papyrologie und Epigraphik* 10 (1973), pp. 55–62, p. 56.

comes from the Memphite nome and that it constitutes a *testimonium* for the term ἀπάτωρ (nos. 302–303). Yet Moithymis was close to the border with the Arsinoite nome[162] and it is possible that the appearance of the term is an example of terminological influence from the neighbouring nome.

Another attestation is *P. Bagnall* 32 (Ibion Panektyreos, AD 116/7), a document written in the Apollonopolite nome, and preserved perhaps in Hermopolis;[163] it is far enough from the Arsinoites, to be outside its sphere of terminological influence. In the document an individual described as ἀπάτωρ is one of the *epimeletai* addressing strategos Apollonios (l. 2: no. 824) with an oath. The reading of the term seems secure.

In a list of weavers (γέρδ(ιοι)), perhaps from Koptos, *O. Petr.* 320 = *O. Petr. Mus.* 505 (3rd c. AD), the entries include name and patronym; the description ἀπάτωρ μητ(ρὸς) Σεṿ() following the name Besis in line 7 seems to be a substitute for the patronym (no. 350).

Perhaps the most surprising attestation comes from the former temple of Hatshepsut (ŁAJTAR, *Deir el-Bahari*, no. 253 [Thebes West, 2nd c. AD]) and is found among inscriptions left by people who visited the temple of Amenhotep son of Hapu and Imhotep during the Roman period. It is the only instance of the term ἀπάτωρ among the plenitude of graffiti and inscriptions left on the walls of the temple, and it does not follow the usual scheme, ll. 1–3: τὸ προσκύνημα Ἀβασκάντọụ / υἱοῦ Θερμούθιος ἀπạ́ṭωρος (l. ἀπάτορος) καὶ τῇ | κυρία (l. τῆς κυρίας) μου μητρọ́ς (no. 87), as in *P. Soterichos* 7 (*infra*, p. 71). This could be interpreted in two ways. Ἀπάτωρ could constitute a part of the description of either the son, '*proskynema* of Abaskantos son of Thermouthis, the fatherless'; or the mother, '*proskynema* of Abaskantos son of fatherless Thermouthis'. The latter interpretation would mean that two methods of describing the fatherless had been applied in one identification cluster, or that the worshipper had chosen the mother as his geneological reference, skipping his patronym deliberately. It seems more likely, however, that ἀπάτωρ applies to Abaskanos, as the editor, Adam Łajtar, suggested.[164]

[162] As visible in both the map provided on www.trismegistos.org and in the Digital Atlas of the Roman Empire http://dare.ht.lu.se/places/36678.html via www.trismegistos.org.

[163] See commentary to *P. Bagnall* 32.

[164] A. ŁAJTAR, *Deir el-Bahari in the Hellenistic and Roman Periods. A Study of an Egyptian Temple Based on Greek Sources* [= *The Journal of Juristic Papyrology Supplement* IV], Warsaw 2006, p. 333.

The only evidence of ἀπάτωρ from outside Egypt comes from Syria, *P. Dura* 51 (Dura Europos, AD 225–275). It belongs to an extremely fragmentary text of undetermined nature which has been dated to the mid-third century. Interestingly, ἀπάτωρ, if read correctly, is the only word preserved in full in this text, but due to the state of preservation, there is no way to determine how the word was used. If we accept the editor's suggestion, based on the width of the columns, that the text was a list, ἀπάτωρ would probably have been used as filiation (no. 664).

6.1.5. Conclusion

While it is true that the majority of attestations of ἀπάτωρ come from the Arsinoite nome, we can nonetheless identify isolated *testimonia* from other places. The presence of the term in the archive of Bibliotheke of Thmouis is especially striking, as it suggests a wider application either in the Mendesian nome or in Thmouis herself. The *testimonia* from other nomes are far more problematic. It seems certain that ἀπάτωρ occurred outside of the Arsinoite nome at least occasionally, but we can neither prove nor disprove that it was widely applied in other nomes. Even if it was widely used, we do not know if it was throughout Egypt, or only in some regions. Attestations from the Arsinoite nome are obviously more numerous than those coming from other regions if only because the number of papyri from Arsinoite is incomparably higher than from any other place. The exact number of text is of course not possible to establish, but the platform Trismegistos provides the number of 3146 references to Arsinoites in documentary sources and 11285 attestations as provenance.[165] Documents from the Mendesian nome number only around one hundred, which can not even be taken into statistical account.

6.2. *Origin and purpose of apatores in documentary papyri*

In the vast majority of documentary papyri, ἀπάτωρ appears as a substitute for the paternal name. The identification cluster for ἀπάτορες was

[165] TM Geo 332 on www.trismegistos.org.

'person – ἀπάτωρ (– mother)': thus, *Διονύσιος ἀπάτωρ* (*μητρὸς Διονυσίας*). In the identification cluster for an individual with patronym, the order was 'person – father (– grandfather – mother)', thus *Διονύσιος Διονυσίου* (*τοῦ Διονυσίου μητρὸς Διονυσίας*).[166] The question we must ask is why this substitution occurred in Roman Egypt and when it first appeared.

According to Uri Yiftach, the term emerged as a response to the modified identification cluster in κατ' ἄνδρα reports – lists of individuals – in the Roman period: the Hellenistic formula, based on patronym and the 'population unit' to which an individual belonged, would have been replaced with a purely genealogical cluster. The appearance of ἀπάτωρ would have been connected with the increase of metronyms (and maternal papponyms) as an element within the identification cluster.[167]

In order to verify Yiftach's hypothesis, we must first examine whether the appearance of the term does indeed coincide with the beginning of Roman rule. The first attestation is dated to first years of the first century and comes from the Arsinoite nome (*P. Lond.* II 256 r. d, pp. 97–98, l. 18 [Kynopolis, AD 11]); it is a letter addressed by the chief of the association of public farmers, its secretary, and ***kommogrammateus***, to Akousilaos, *sitologos* of Lysimachis, listing *demosioi georgoi* and their duties in kind. The list of *georgoi* is arranged alphabetically, with each person described by his name and patronym. The term ἀπάτωρ, which follows the name Aphrodisios (no. 244) in l. 18 appears to have been used as a substitute for the patronym. This attestation, however, can not be interpreted as proof for widespread use of ἀπάτωρ in the early bureaucratic practices of Roman Egypt, as we do not find any further evidence until the end of the first century.

These early documents are only three in number: *P. Soterichos* 7, l. 7 (Theadelphia, AD 91), *O. Eleph. DAIK* 72 (AD 81–96), and *P. L. Bat.* XXV 28, ll. 9, 15, 16 and 18 (Arsinoites, AD 75–100). *P. L. Bat.* XXV 28 is possibly a register of seed given to public farmers in Soknopaiou Nesos (?);

[166] It is not clear why a false filiation separate from the Latin *Sp0 f0* developed. It could be that if *Sp0 f0* and *spurius* were associated with Romans, and it was therefore necessary to create a new false filiation so that locals were not confused with Romans. It may also be because *Spurii filius* had a technical meaning connected to civic status claims (*supra*).

[167] U. Yiftach, '*Apator metros*: The rise of a formula in bureaucratic perspective. Response to Maria Nowak', [in:] D. Lao & G. Thür (eds.), *Symposion 2015. Vorträge zur griechischen und hellenistischen Rechtsgeschichte (Coimbra, 1.–4. September 2015)*, Vienna 2016, pp. 115–120.

it lists people, lands and amounts of seed (nos. 813–816).[168] The ostracon from Elephantine, discussed above, is a receipt of payment. *P. Soterichos* 7 preserves the confirmation of a payment made by Soterichos, to a certain Sambas son of Mysthos and his wife. The wife is identified (l. 7) as *Τασουχᾶς Ἡραίδος ἀπάτωρ*, 'Tasouchas daughter of Herais, the fatherless' (no. 234). The identification is problematic, as it does not follow the usual pattern of 'person – *ἀπάτωρ* – mother'; instead the metronym precedes *ἀπάτωρ*. Either the case is incorrect (which could happen easily) and the description was intended to say that both the mother and daughter were fatherless, or the description was placed in the 'wrong' position (as in Łajtar, *Deir el-Bahari*, no. 253: *supra*, p. 69) which could, in turn, suggest that the term was new and the scribe was unfamiliar with its application. It may also be that the term was used for a function other than false filiation; placing *ἀπάτωρ* at the end of the identification cluster would offer clarification for why the metronym was given instead of the patronym. It would suggest the early usage, as later the term took the firm position of filiation within the identification cluster.

Additional evidence that the term emerged only in the late first century is the lack of attestations in early administrative archives containing lists of people, *e.g.* the record office archive of Kronion son of Apion of Tebtynis[169] or the Nemesion archive from Philadelphia.[170] Both archives were official, consisting of 192 and 62 preserved texts respectively, including documents listing people;[171] among them we find not even one *ἀπάτωρ*.

Our evidence for the first century thus consists of a mere four papyri, one early and three dated to the last quarter of the century, each of which is a different type of deed. The number is low compared to *ca.* 500 single

[168] See commentary to *P. L. Bat.* XXV 28.

[169] B. van Beek, 'Kronion son of Apion, head of the grapheion of Tebtynis', [in:] K. Vandorpe, W. Clarysse & H. Verreth (eds.), *Graeco-Roman Archives from the Fayum* [= *Collectanea Hellenistica – KVAB* VI], Leuven – Paris – Bristol, CT 2015, pp. 215–221.

[170] W. Clarysse, 'Nemesion son of Zoilos', [in:] Vandorpe *et al.* (eds.), *Graeco-Roman Archives* (cit. n. 169), pp. 256–258.

[171] On describing people in those archives, see M. Langellotti, 'Occupations and naming trends in first-century Tebtunis and Philadelphia', [in:] *Tell Me Who You Are* (cit. n. 34), pp. 147–182.

attestations of *ἀπάτωρ* in the second century.[172] Although the total number of papyri dated to the first century both in the Arsinoite nome and in Egypt more broadly is significantly lower than the second-century papyri, the difference is not great enough to account for the sudden increase in appearances of *ἀπάτωρ*.[173] The data suggests that *ἀπάτωρ* only became widespread one hundred years after the beginning of Roman rule.

That the term developed as a regular description only at the end of the first century does not exclude its connection to *κατ' ἄνδρα* reports. Among almost 500 individual *ἀπάτορες* collected in the online database *Roman Bastards*, nearly 400 are entries in various lists.[174] The proportion is even higher, if singular attestations are counted:[175] it is over 520 to 620, the total number of all appearances of the word in papyri.[176] Yet, the number of lists themselves is much lower than the number of attestations and individual *ἀπάτορες* – around 150 – as the term *ἀπάτωρ* usually occurs multiple times within a single list, *e.g.* the famous *Charta Borgiana* (*SB* I 5124 + Litinas, *Pap. Congr.* XXIII, pp. 399–405 [Tebtynis, AD 193]) which mentions 68 individual *ἀπάτορες* (nos. 581–648).

[172] Chronological distribution, see pp. 258–263.

[173] See W. Habermann, 'Zur chronologischen Verteilung der papyrologischen Zeugnisse', *Zeitschrift für Papyrologie und Epigraphik* 122 (1998), pp. 144–160.

[174] 1/05/2019: 499 individual *ἀπάτορες* vs. 396 individual *ἀπάτορες* on lists on romanbastards.wpia.uw.edu.pl. The numbers cannot be absolutely precise, as the database is being complemented and the identifications are not fully credible.

[175] *E.g.* Longinos also called Gemellos fatherless son of Taphois (no. 538), *Λογγεῖνος ὁ καὶ Γέμελλος ἀπάτωρ μη(τρὸς) Ταφῶιτος*, occurs 10 times in the Karanis tax roll (*P. Mich.* IV 223, ll. 21, 595, 1431 [AD 171/2]; *P. Mich.* IV 224, ll. 444, 1117, 2990, 4505 [AD 173]; *P. Mich.* IV 225, ll. 535, 1716, 1897 [AD 174]); Valerios fatherless son of Valeria (no. 539), *Οὐαλέριος ἀπάτωρ μη(τρὸς) Οὐαλερίας*, 19 times (*P. Mich.* IV 223, ll. 24, 354, 531, 865, 1050, 2565, 3561; *P. Mich.* IV 224, ll. 32, 471, 980, 1969, 2897, 3126, 5748; *P. Mich.* IV 225, ll. 243, 433, 1592, 2451, 2542); or Spartas son of Heraklous (no. 526) attested 8 times as either *ἀπάτωρ (μητρὸς) Ἡρακλοῦτος* or brother of Psenobastis (no. 527), *ἀδελφὸς μητ(ρὸς) τῆς αὐτῆς*, in the administrative archive of Theadelphia (*SB* XXIV 16329, l. 37 [AD 165]; *P. Berl. Leigh.* I 4, col. 3, l. 18 [AD 165]: leg. *Σπαρτᾶς ἀπ(άτωρ) Ἡρακ()* instead of *Σπαρτασᾶς Ἡρακ()*: J. France, 'Three papyri from Theadelpheia in Gent', *Zeitschrift für Papyrologie und Epigraphik* 123 [1998], pp. 135–144, p. 141; *P. Strasb.* I 55 = *C. Pap. Hengstl* 33, l. 12 [AD 173]; *BGU* IX 1891, ll. 84, 506 [AD 133]; *P. Col.* II.1 r 1a, col. 7, l. 10 [AD 134]; *p. Col.* II.1 r 2, col. 4, l. 17 [AD 129]; *P. Col.* V 1 v 3, col. 5, l. 113 [AD 155]).

[176] 1/05/2019: 524 and 622 on romanbastards.wpia.uw.edu.pl.

The two other significant groups of papyri in which ἀπάτωρ occurs frequently are census returns and receipts of payments of public burdens or confirming performance of a liturgy. In 12 census returns we find 27 individuals labelled as ἀπάτορες[177] – discussed in greater depth below – and an additional 26 individuals are attested as having performed their duty to the state or community (in money, kind or labour) in individual receipts.[178] These sources confirm Yiftach's hypothesis too, as they were used to count people in Roman Egypt and were issued on massive scale.[179]

Yet it is also interesting to note that ἀπάτωρ served as a description of individuals in private documents, such as contracts, wills or petitions concerning private law and individual matters; in these texts, the term would have been used by choice rather than official requirement. The number of ἀπάτορες in these sources amount to less than one tenth the number of fatherless individuals recorded on lists; but compared with either the census returns or receipts, persons described as ἀπάτορες in private deeds are more numerous, totalling over 30.[180] The term was therefore used in both administrative and private contexts,[181] although the use in lists and registers was more prevalent. Furthermore, the use of this label in private deeds might have developed only after it was introduced in administrative lists.

Before we can confirm Yiftach's hypothesis about κατ' ἄνδρα reports, some further reservations should be made. The majority of attestations of people come from second-century archives, and the nature of these archives determines the types of documents in which ἀπάτορες are attested. Almost one-third of the ἀπάτορες come from the administrative

[177] Nos. 199, 257, 258, 297–300, 302, 303, 307–314, 316–318, 320, 355, 356, 364, 365, 367, 837.

[178] Nos. 197, 232, 237, 238, 353, 354, 417, 492, 493, 495, 500, 505, 506, 508–510, 560–563, 568, 569, 579, 659, 693, 823, 826.

[179] Census declarations were based on patterns and written by professionals, so that they could be used by the administration. They were glutted together and kept as *tomoi synkollesimoi*: Bagnall & Frier, *Demography* (cit. n. 122), pp. 18–20.

[180] Nos. 201, 202, 228, 231–236, 323, 327, 348, 351, 352, 424, 433, 437, 452, 458, 476, 485, 486, 494, 496, 497, 499, 503, 504, 507, 511, 667, 674, 677, 689.

[181] This is not exclusively the case of the term ἀπάτωρ, as labels relating to different aspects to personal status were used both in private and administrative context, *e.g.* see '*xenos, epixenos*' in: T. Kruse, 'The labeling of strangers and aliens in Roman Egypt', [in:] *Tell Me Who You Are* (cit. n. 34), pp. 129–146.

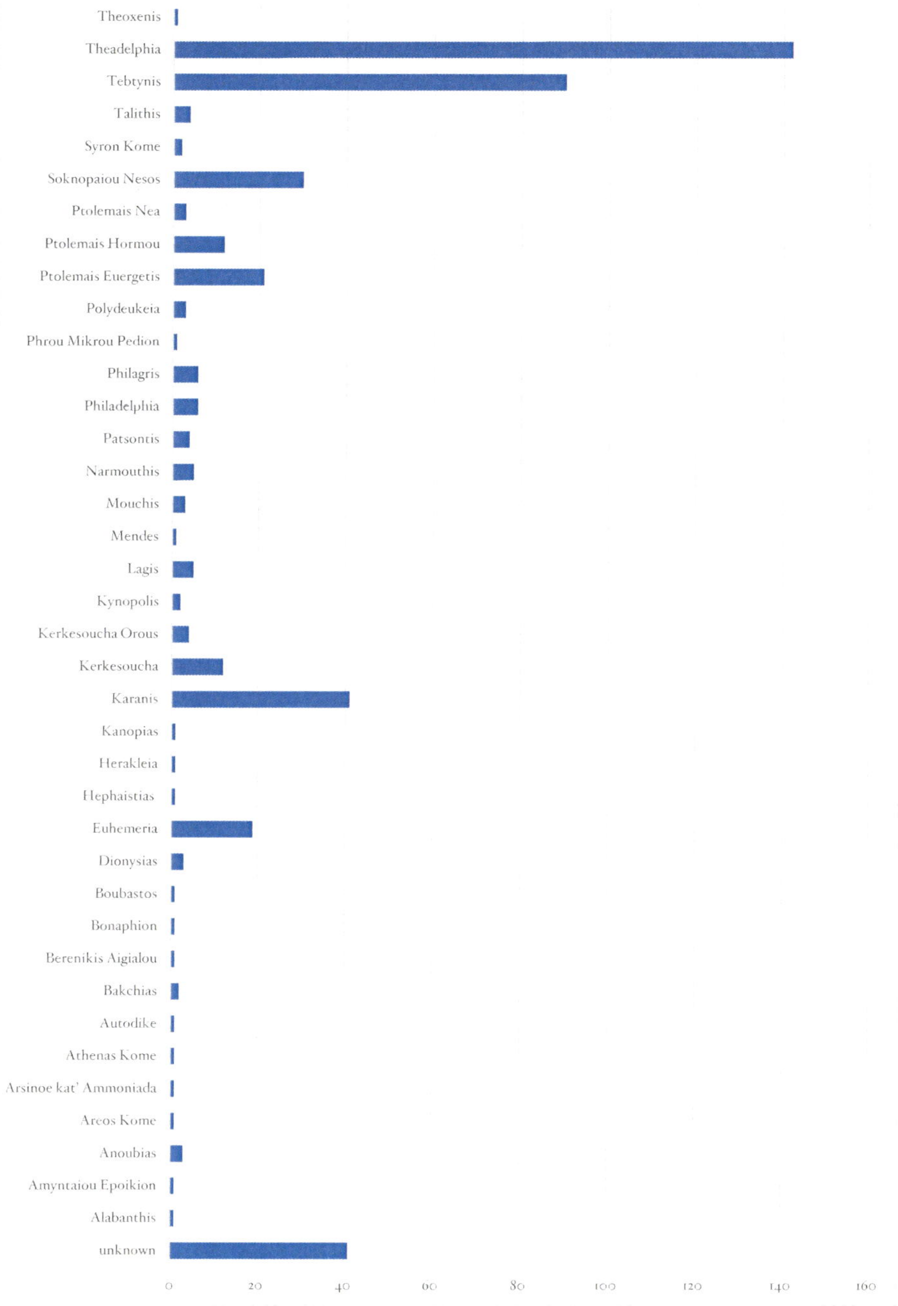

Fig. 1. Distribution of ἀπάτορες in the Arsinoite nome

archive of Theadelphia which consists of only official documents, mostly of κατ' ἄνδρα reports.[182] The Karanis tax rolls, although not as large as the Theadelphia archive – they consists only of four rolls and some fragments related to taxes – contains thousands of entries.[183] It seems logical to assume that lists, especially those containing numerous entries, provide the vast majority of individuals attested in papyri from the Arsinoite nome not only those described as 'fatherless'.

The label ἀπάτωρ should not be analysed in isolation. Another term used to underline and substitute filiation in Roman Egypt was χρηματίζων (χρηματίζουσα) μητρός, the geographical scope of which was limited to the Oxyrhynchite nome.[184] The literal meaning of the label is 'styled son/daughter of mother so-and-so', and unlike ἀπάτωρ it appears only with μητρός and mother's name in the genitive. Although it is a type of developed metronym, it draws attention to the lack of patronym in the same way as ἀπάτωρ.

Furthermore, the chronology of χρηματίζων μητρός is similar to chronology of ἀπάτωρ. The earliest attestations – two wills and one notification concerning payment of taxes on leased land[185] – come from the last two decades of the first century. One of the very earliest census returns (*P. Oxy.* II 254 = 19?-Ox-1) describes one individual solely with metronym, l. 11: ̣[- *ca.* 9 -] ων μη(τρὸς) Σινθεῶ(τος) ἄτεχ(νος) απε̣ ̣ ̣(). The lacuna is too small to allow for the reconstruction of both a name and χρηματίζων, thus ων must have been the ending of a personal name that proceeded μη(τρὸς), as Bagnall and Frier suggested.[186] The term χρηματίζων μητρός started to disappear from papyri around the same time as ἀπάτωρ (*infra*, pp. 258–263).

The distribution of the term among different types of document confirms, and even strengthens, our observations concerning the development of the label ἀπάτωρ in documentary papyri. There are 78 individuals identified as

[182] Full list of documents belonging to the archive in: K. Geens, 'Administrative archive of Theadelpheia', [in:] Vandorpe *et al.* (eds.), *Graeco-Roman Archives* (cit. n. 169), pp. 34–39.

[183] Full list of texts and bibliography in: K. Vandorpe & S. Van Beselaere, 'Tax rolls of Karanis', [in:] Vandorpe *et al.* (eds.), *Graeco-Roman Archives* (cit. n. 169), pp. 388–390.

[184] Malouta, 'Terminology of fatherlessness' (cit. n. 143), p. 616.

[185] *P. Oxy.* II 345 *descr.* = Benaissa, *ZPE* 170 (2009), pp. 160–161, no. 1, ll. 14–16 (AD 88) = no. 161; *P. Oxy.* I 104, ll. 10–11 (AD 96) = no. 162; *P. Oxy.* II 379 *descr.* = *Scritti Zabłocka*, pp. 135–143, l. 7 (AD 87–95) = no. 168.

[186] Bagnall & Frier, *Demography* (cit. n. 122), p. 181.

χρηματίζων μητρός.[187] Unlike ἀπάτωρ, χρηματίζων μητρός is found mostly in private documents, in which content and personal descriptions were decided by individuals rather than officials. Among these documents we find contracts, unilateral legal deeds, declarations concerning property held by private individuals, and petitions sent by individuals to officials. A total of 42 people are described as χρηματίζων μητρός in private documents.[188] Only seven are recorded in census returns,[189] with an additional 17 in various lists,[190] and the rest in official texts, including oaths taken by officials, oath certificates (*libelli*), and official correspondence. The distribution of texts by genre illustrates that in the Oxyrhynchite nome χρηματίζων μητρός was used as means of self-description (contracting parties, witnesses, officials) and description (references in legal deeds, heirs) in the context of private law.

Was the context of application for χρηματίζων μητρός very different from that of ἀπάτωρ? It seems unlikely. The difference in typological distribution can be explained by the state of the surviving evidence. There are only seven χρηματίζοντες μητρός in three census returns, while 27 individuals labelled as ἀπάτορες occur in 12 census returns. This disproportion, however, simply reflects the distribution of census returns: the majority come from the Arsinoite nome, and Arsinoite census returns are over four times as numerous as Oxyrhynchite ones.[191] We may also note that five χρηματίζοντες μητρός are attested in three Oxyrhynchite wills (four heirs and a ***kyrios***),[192] while ἀπάτωρ is attested only once as a witness to a will from the Arsinoite nome;[193] however there are three times as many Oxyrhynchite wills as Arsinoite ones.[194] Therefore, the use of ἀπάτωρ and χρηματίζων μητρός seems to correspond to the general typological distribution of papyri.

[187] See www.romanbastards.wpia.uw.edu.pl, *s.v.* 'χρηματίζων μητρός'.

[188] Nos. 161–172, 174, 175, 178, 181, 182, 184, 187, 189–193, 195, 359, 369–372, 377, 379–381, 387, 391, 392, 395–398, 402.

[189] Nos. 315, 357, 358, 360–363.

[190] Nos. 173, 176, 179, 180, 194, 373–376, 382, 384, 388–390, 393, 394.

[191] Bagnall & Frier, *Demography* (cit. n. 122), pp. 6–7.

[192] Nos. 162, 165–167 (heirs), 168 (kyrios).

[193] No. 231.

[194] See Nowak, *Wills* (cit. n. 44), pp. 271–342.

The question which remains to be answered is whether the appearance of these terms was connected to the role of the metronym in Roman-era identification clusters. It has been noted that metronyms took on increased importance during the Roman period. Mark Depauw[195] and Yanne Broux[196] explained the phenomenon in terms of Roman provincial tax policies.[197] Furthermore, the rise of metronyms – including those serving as substitutes for patronyms – cannot be observed at the very beginning of Roman rule, but only from the late first century, which corresponds with our chronologies for *ἀπάτωρ* and *χρηματίζων μητρός*.[198]

Yet, the simple lack of a patronym within the identification cluster was also as a label of fatherlessness in Roman Egypt.[199] In such cases, the metronym was used in its place.[200] The description is attested concurrently to *ἀπάτωρ* and *χρηματίζων μητρός*. Yet, it is difficult to estimate the scale of application. Broux and Depauw estimated that, of the 14,409 identification clusters extracted from Trismegistos that contain a metonym, 9.2% consist of a sole metronym (1.2% of those are followed by the maternal papponym).[201] Yet, a significant number (*ca.* 1300) of those cases classified by Broux and Depauw as the 'person – mother (– grandfather)' cluster are *ἀπάτορες* and individuals described as 'person – *ἀδελφός/υἱός* – mother', where the element *ἀδελφός/υἱός* refers to the individual listed immediately before. In these cases, the patronym (or *ἀπάτωρ*) constitutes a part of the description, but it can be supplemented from the description of the relative to whom the term *ἀδελφός* or *υἱός* refers, *e.g.*:

[195] M. Depauw, 'Do mothers matter? The emergence of metronymics in early Roman Egypt', [in:] T.V. Evans & D.D. Obbink (eds.), *The Language of the Papyri*, Oxford 2010, pp. 120–139.

[196] Y. Broux & M. Depauw, 'The maternal line in Greek identification: Signalling social status in Roman Egypt (30 bc – ad 400)', *Historia* 64.4 (2015), pp. 467–478.

[197] The infrequent use of metronym in the Ptolemaic period was due to the influence of Egyptian onomastic/descriptive practices: M. Depauw, 'The use of mother's names in Ptolemaic documents. A case of Greek-Egyptian influence', *The Journal of Juristic Papyrology* 37 (2007), pp. 21–29; Broux & Depauw, 'Maternal line' (cit. n. 196), pp. 468 & 476–477.

[198] Broux & Depauw, 'Maternal line' (cit. n. 196), p. 471, fig. 2.

[199] He identified only two Hellenistic texts where a metronym was used for people without father's name: Depauw, 'Use of mother's names' (cit. n. 197), p. 24.

[200] Calderini, '*Ἀπάτορες*' (cit. n. 1), p. 362, n. 3.

[201] Broux & Depauw, 'Maternal line' (cit. n. 196), p. 472, tab. 1.

P. Mich. IV 224, ll. 2129–2131 (Karanis, AD 173): / Ὀννῶφ(ρις) Πεθέως τοῦ Πεθέως μη(τρὸς) Ταοννώφρεως | φυλάκ(ων) (δραχμαὶ) δ
/ Πτολεμαῖος υἱὸς μη(τρὸς) Ταπεθ(έως) φυλάκ(ων) (δραχμαὶ) δ

/ Onnophris son Petheus son of Petheus of the mother Taonnophris (paid) 4 drachmae for the guard tax.
/ Ptolemaios (his) son of the mother Tapetheus (paid) 4 drachmae for the guard tax.

ll. 175–176: / Χαιρήμων Ἥρωνος τοῦ Ὀρσενούφ(εως) μη(τρὸς) Διδύμης (δραχμαὶ) δ̣
/ Ἀχειλλᾶς ἀδελφ(ὸς) μη(τρὸς) τῆς αὐτῆς (δραχμαὶ) δ

/ Chairemon son of Heron son of Orsenouophis of the mother Didyme (paid) 4 drachmae.
/ Achillas (his) brother of the same mother (paid) 4 drachmae.

As Broux and Depauw have observed, there were cases – *e.g.* in mummy labels – in which the use of sole metronym was justified by reasons other than the lack of patronym.[202] Some descriptions by metronyms could be scribal omissions. Therefore, it is not really possible to assume how many people described with sole metronyms were indeed fatherless.

It seems possible that, at some point after a century of Roman rule in Egypt, the simple metronym (along with other methods of identification for those who had no patronym) was no longer sufficient to indicate that someone had no patronym. A need for greater precision in identification may have led to the appearance of ἀπάτωρ and χρηματίζων μητρός, but these terms did not replace the metronym completely. It is tempting to suggest that they were developed by the Roman administration for documents containing multiple entries and then spread all over the evidence as a handy descriptive method. Although neither terms appears to have been an obligatory part of the identification of the fatherless, ἀπάτωρ became the predominant method of identifying people without a patronym in the second-century Arsinoite nome. The term is present in all second-century archives containing a large enough sample of documents: the tax rolls from Karanis, the administrative archive of Theadelphia, the Petaus archive, or the archive of *sitologoi* from Soknopaiou Nesos. Furthermore, the time when the term started being used in a regular

[202] Broux & Depauw, 'Maternal line' (cit. n. 196), p. 474.

way, that is last decades of the first century, coincides with the full 'Romanisation' of the administration in the Arsinoite nome, which would have taken place in the 60s of the first century, as suggested by Tomasz Derda.[203] If this is indeed the right observation, it would confirm that the term developed in the administrative milieu, but immediately was adopted for private use.

Finally, it is difficult – perhaps impossible – to exclude the possibility that additional methods were applied concurrently with ἀπάτωρ and matronyms. A good example is the tax register recently re-edited by Alain Martin and Rosario Pintaudi.[204] The register contains 111 entries listing 113 tax-payers of whom 77 names have been preserved.[205] Among those 77, not even one is described as ἀπάτωρ or with a metronym. This fact has not escaped the attention of the editors, who suggested that people described with υἱός plus a feminine name in the genitive, or those without patronym but labelled by their profession, might have been fatherless.[206] This, of course, is one possible scenario, but it is equally possible that the list is too short and that the names of the fatherless have simply not been preserved in the fragment we possess.

6.3. *Meaning*

In scholarly literature, the term ἀπάτωρ is recognised as a description referring to extramarital birth. Carl Wessely was the first to observe and comment on this phenomenon.[207] Calderini identified the term as being related to illegitimacy and proposed that not only the term, but the very phenomenon of illegitimacy, only appeared in Egypt during Roman times.[208] He further suggested that the majority of people described as ἀπάτορες would have

[203] T. Derda, *Arsinoites Nomos. Administration of the Fayum under Roman Rule* [= *The Journal of Juristic Papyrology Supplement* VII], Warsaw 2006, pp. 282–283.

[204] A. Martin & R. Pintaudi, 'Le journal fiscal *SB* XXVI 16560: une réédition', *Aegyptus* 95 (2015), pp. 25–42.

[205] Martin & Pintaudi, 'Le journal fiscal *SB* XXVI 16560' (cit. n. 204), p. 39.

[206] Martin & Pintaudi, 'Le journal fiscal *SB* XXVI 16560' (cit. n. 204), pp. 36 (comm. to l. 33) & 37 (comm. to l. 37).

[207] C. Wessely, *Karanis und Soknopaiu Nesos. Studien zur Geschichte antiker Cultur- und Personenverhältnisse*, Milan 1975 (reprint), p. 30.

[208] Calderini, 'Ἀπάτορες' (cit. n. 1), p. 359.

been the offspring of Roman soldiers who were banned from legally marrying before their release from military service; when Calderini was writing, the ban was understood to have been binding until the end of the second century.[209] The opinion of Calderini was further endorsed by Youtie,[210] who did not, however, claim that the ἀπάτορες consisted entirely of soldiers' children, and was aware that the description continued to appear in the papyri even after soldiers were allowed to marry;[211] some of the fatherless were children born of mixed unions (listed in the *Gnomon of idios logos*) not recognised as marriages by the Roman rulers.[212] Bagnall, in turn, disagreed with the idea that ἀπάτορες were primarily children of soldiers, but maintained that they were children born of stable unions between people who were not legally married due to the unequal social standing of the partners, especially freeborn-freedwoman.[213] Although Bagnall used ἀπάτορες as his starting point, his case study based on the archive of *nekrotaphoi* from Kysis was devoted primarily to those described with a sole metronym. However, all of the studies devoted to ἀπάτορες in Roman Egypt have come to the same basic conclusion: that they were mostly children begotten of unions which the Roman administration did not recognise as marriages. This has become the widely accepted view repeated in papyrological editions. In my opinion, the term ἀπάτωρ had a different meaning in Roman Egypt and as principle did not apply to persons born in 'informal' unions.

6.3.1. Plutarch

In the most literal sense ἀπάτωρ would refer to a person who has no father at all. Yet, 'fatherless' is an ambiguous terms, as it could denote a person

[209] The discussion on whether AD 197 was indeed the date when the ban abolished, see pp. 206–209.

[210] Youtie, 'Ἀπάτορες' (cit. n. 147), p. 737.

[211] *Ibidem*, p. 732.

[212] *Ibidem*, pp. 738–739.

[213] R.S. Bagnall, 'Illegitimacy in Roman and late antique Egypt', [in:] T. Derda, A. Łajtar & J. Urbanik (eds.), in collaboration with A. Mirończuk & G. Ochała, *Proceedings of the 27th International Congress of Papyrology, Warsaw 29.07–3.08 2013* [= *The Journal of Juristic Papyrology Supplement* XXVII], Warsaw, vol. I, pp. 5–17.

with no legitimate father, or an individual whose father died, or who had no father in both legal and social sense. Our understanding of who was considered to be fatherless is not helped by the fact that none of the texts from Roman Egypt bother to comment on the matter.[214] However, a text from outside Egypt – Plutarch's *Roman Questions* – provides some insight into how the term ἀπάτωρ was perceived in the early days of the Empire (*Moralia* 288 E-F):

Διὰ τί τοὺς ἀπάτορας 'σπορίους' υἱοὺς καλοῦσιν; Οὐ γάρ, ὡς Ἕλληνες νομίζουσι καὶ λέγουσιν οἱ ῥήτορες ἐν ταῖς δίκαις, συμφορητοῦ τινος καὶ κοινοῦ σπέρματος γεγόνασιν, ἀλλ' ἔστιν ὁ Σπόριος τῶν πρώτων ὀνομάτων, ὡς ὁ Σέξτος καὶ ὁ Δέκιμος καὶ ὁ Γάιος. τὰ δὲ πρῶτα τῶν ὀνομάτων οὐχ ὁλογραφοῦσιν ἀλλ' ἢ δι' ἑνὸς γράμματος, ὡς τὸν Τίτον καὶ τὸν Λούκιον καὶ τὸν Μᾶρκον, ἢ διὰ δυοῖν, ὡς τὸν Τιβέριον καὶ τὸν Γναῖον, ἢ διὰ τριῶν, ὡς τὸν Σέξτον καὶ τὸν Σερούιον. ἔστιν οὖν καὶ ὁ Σπόριος τῶν διὰ δυοῖν γραφομένων, τοῦ σ καὶ τοῦ π. γράφουσι δὲ διὰ τούτων καὶ τοὺς ἀπάτορας "σίνε πάτρε" οἷον ἄνευ πατρός, τῷ μὲν σ τὸ "σίνε" τῷ δὲ π τὸ "πάτρε" σημαίνοντες. τοῦτ' οὖν τὴν πλάνην ἐποίησε, τὸ διὰ τῶν αὐτῶν γραμμάτων τὸ "σίνε πάτρε" καὶ τὸν Σπόριον γράφεσθαι. Λεκτέον δὲ καὶ τὸν ἕτερον λόγον, ἔστι δ' ἀτοπώτερος· τοὺς γὰρ Σαβίνους φασὶ τὸ τῆς γυναικὸς αἰδοῖον ὀνομάζειν σπόριον, εἶθ' οἷον ἐφυβρίζοντας οὕτω προσαγορεύειν τὸν ἐκ γυναικὸς ἀγάμου καὶ ἀνεγγύου γεγενημένον.

For what reason are ἀπάτορες called *spurii filii* (or spurious sons)? Not, as the Greeks believe and rhetors in court say, because they were begotten of something contributed by many (?) and common seed; but Spurius is a *praenomen* like Sextus and Decimus and Caius. They do not write first names in full, but by one letter, as Titus (T.) and Lucius (L.) and Marcus (M.); or by two, as Tiberius (Ti.) and Cnaeus (Cn.); or by three, as Sextus (Sex.) and Servius (Ser.). Spurius, then, is one of those written by two letters: Sp. by those they write also ἀπάτορες *sine patre*, that is to say without father, indicating *sine* by s and *patre* by p. This, then, caused the error, the writing of the same abbreviation for *sine patre* and for Spurius. I must state the other explanation also, but it is somewhat absurd: They assert that the Sabines use the word *spurius* for the *pudenda muliebria*, and it later came about that they called the child born of an of an unmarried and unbetrothed woman by this name, as if in mockery.[215]

[214] Yiftach, '*Apator metros*' (cit. n. 167), p. 115.

[215] Plutarch, *Moralia*, vol. IV: *Roman Questions. Greek Questions. Greek and Roman Parallel Stories. On the Fortune of the Romans. On the Fortune or the Virtue of Alexander. Were the Athenians*

In this passage Plutarch notes that, in his own time, *spurii filii* had the same meaning as ἀπάτορες; yet this was incorrect in his opinion, as the word *spurius* has no etymological connection with the term ἀπάτωρ, fatherless. *Spurius*, originally a *praenomen*, emerged as a noun meaning 'fatherless' only from the confusion between the expression *sine patre filius* and the filiation *Spurii filius*, which were abbreviated in the same way, *spf*. Thus, in Plutarch's time ἀπάτωρ was incorrectly used as a counterpart of *spurii filius* or simply *spurius*.

It is important to note that Plutarch elsewhere uses the term νόθος to denote a bastard;[216] his use of ἀπάτωρ – a counterpart of *spurius* in the early Empire – must therefore have served a more specific purpose. The chronology supports such a reasoning: *Roman Questions* were written around the same time as the emergence of the onomastic phenomenon discussed in this section.[217] It may be that Plutarch attempted to clarify the Latin term by using a Greek term with a similar (or even identical) meaning and context of application.

As demonstrated in the section above, *spurius* was used in Roman legal practices of the second century as a general term denoting a person born out of wedlock, or simply as an antonym of a legitimate child. Interestingly, some works of classical jurisprudence apply the Greek etymology in regard to *spurii*, *e.g. vel a Graeca voce quasi* σποράδην *concepti* (G. 1.64) or παρὰ τὴν σποράν (D. 1.5.23: Mod., *pand*. 1). This could be the etymology to which Plutarch refers: ὡς Ἕλληνες νομίζουσι καὶ λέγουσιν οἱ ῥήτορες ἐν ταῖς δίκαις, συμφορητοῦ τινος καὶ κοινοῦ σπέρματος γεγόνασιν. It seems, therefore, that Plutarch must have known the legal or technical definitions of *spurius*, if he was able to refer to current etymologies. As the term *spurius* was a new Latin term in Plutarch's time (*supra*, pp. 36–37), it is possible that it had the same meaning in both legal and everyday language.

More Famous in War or in Wisdom? [= *Loeb Classical Library* CCCV], tr. F.C. Babbitt, London 1936, with modifications.

[216] *E.g. Solon* 7.3.6; *Lysander* 22.6.6; *Alexander* 9.8.2; *Pericles* 24.10.1; 37.4.4.

[217] One of Plutarch's late works written certainly after AD 96, Domitian's death: *The Roman Questions of Plutarch: A New Translation, with Introductory Essays & a Running Commentary*, ed. H.J. Rose, New York 1974, pp. 46–48.

Finally, Plutarch was not an Egyptian author, and we cannot be certain whether his understanding of ἀπάτωρ applied to Chaeronea, to Rome, to the Roman East in general, or to the whole of the empire. Hence, it is not possible to decide whether the term ἀπάτωρ was used by Plutarch as an exact counterpart of *spurius* or the word of the closest meaning, a child *sine patre*, thus a category to which Gaius referred as 'concieved casually'. It is, however, certain that it was not to denote a child born of a union of partners who were not legally married, which was Youtie's interpretation of the discussed passage.[218]

6.3.2. Papyri

There is at least one instance in the papyri where the word ἀπάτωρ might have been used in the same sense as *spurius*. It appears in a text which belongs undoubtedly to the sphere of Roman law, *P. Diog.* 18, but the exact meaning of the term is uncertain; we will return to this passage in detail in the final chapter. Apart from this example, the term ἀπάτωρ seems to have been used in the papyri to describe a person who was actually, not only legally, fatherless, thus with a narrower meaning than *spurius*. (Although the number of ἀπάτορες may seem to be high, it represents only tiny percentage of the Egyptian population between the first and third centu-

[218] YOUTIE, 'Ἀπάτορες' (cit. n. 147), p. 730. Youtie claimed that *spurius*/ἀπάτωρ should be interpreted as 'without legal father'; his argument was based on the final part of Plutarch's text – τὸν ἐκ γυναικὸς ἀγάμου καὶ ἀνεγγύου γεγενημένον – providing the translation 'the child born of a woman who has not entered into a formal marriage'. This interpretation, however, seems unjustified: the passage is a part of yet another etymology of the word *spurius* which Plutarch himself rejects as being even more far-fetched (ἀτοπώτερος) than the first one. According to this second etymology (repeated by Isidor of Sevilla, *Etym.* 9.5.24), *spurius* came from the Sabines, who named female genitalia *spurius*, and later used the same word to describe a child born ἐκ γυναικὸς ἀγάμου καὶ ἀνεγγύου. Furthermore, Youtie's translation 'of a woman who has not entered into a formal marriage' is not ideal. It is also worth noting that Plutarch used this etymology to explain why *spurius* could be used as an insult, while Youtie observed that, in Plutarch's time, there was nothing shameful in having children from long-term life partners instead of legal spouses.

ries.[219] Thus the interpretation is not unrealistic from the statistical point of view.)

A source which seems to confirm this narrow meaning of the word ἀπάτωρ is a group of census returns from Egypt which include household members described as either ἀπάτωρ or χρηματίζων μητρός (*supra*):[220]

1. *P. Mil. Vogl.* III 193a = *SB* VI 9495.1a = 145-Ar-1 (Tebtynis, AD 147): Hero ἀπάτωρ declared by her mother, Kroniaina daughter of Herakleios, 13 years old (no. 307);

2. *P. Mil. Vogl.* III 194a = *SB* VI 9495.2a = 145-Ar-3 (Tebtynis, AD 146/7): Sarapias ἀπάτωρ of Thermion, declared by her mother-in-law Herais, 18 years old (no. 308);

3. *P. Berl. Leihg.* III 52B (ined.) = 145-Ar-19 (Philagris, AD 147): six siblings ἀπάτορες of Thermouthis, Harphesis, 30 years old (no. 309), Hatres, 22 years old (no. 310), Orseus, 20 years old (no. 311), Hermes, 16 years old (no. 312), Heras, 14 years old (no. 313), Ponneis, 16 years old (no. 314) declared by the eldest brother Harphesis;

4. *BGU* I 90, and *BGU* I 224; 225; II 410; 537; and *P. Grenf.* II 55 (copies addressed to different officials) = 159-Ar-13 (Soknopaiou Nesos, AD 161): Isarion ἀπάτωρ of Tanephremmis declared by her husband, 13 years old (no. 257);

5. *SB* XVIII 13289, and *P. Berl. Leihg.* I 16c (copy) = 159-Ar-16 (Theadelphia, AD 161): Horion *vel* Horios ἀπάτωρ of Tapheus declared himself as the only household member, 33 years old (no. 258);

6. *BGU* II 447 = *BGU* I 26 = 173-Ar-9 (Karanis, AD 175): Thakiaris[221] ἀπάτωρ of Taos declared by her male relative, 12 years old (no. 297);

[219] In a personal communication, Yanne Broux informed me that she could distinguish 66,831 different people in texts from the Fayum dated between AD 80 and 284. They are mentioned 104,252 times.

[220] The majority of census returns including fatherless household members were identified by Bagnall and Frier.

[221] Corrected from Xanaris to Tha[k]iaris: J. Cowey & D. Kah, 'Bemerkungen zu Texten aus BGU I–IV. Teil I: Zensusdeklarationen', *Zeitschrift für Papyrologie und Epigraphik* 163 (2007), pp. 147–182, p. 170.

7. *BGU* I 117 = Ar-187-8 (Ptolemais Euergetis, AD 189): N.N., 29 years old (no. 316), and Sarapous, 8 years old (no. 317), *ἀπάτορες* declared by their male relative;

8. *BGU* XI 2019 = 187-Me-1 (Moithymis, AD 188): Senamounis,[222] 20 years old (no. 302), and Tastoous, 12 years old (no. 303), *ἀπάτορες* declared by their mother, Herakleia, freedwoman;

9. *BGU* XI 2018 = 187-Ar-26 (Karanis, AD 188/9): Ptolemais, 25 years old (no. 298), Thol..., 15 years old (no. 299), and Taesis, 4 years old (no. 300), *ἀπάτορες* sisters (?) declared by their male relative,[223] Petosorapis;

10. *SB* XXIV 15987 = *SB* XIV 11355 = 187-Ar-32 (Ptolemais Euergetis, AD 208–209): Hermione *ἀπάτωρ* of Herois, former wife of a declarant, Didymos, and his son's mother (no. 367);

11. *P. Strasb.* IV 257 = 201-Ar-1 (Tebtynis, AD 203): Tolis *alias* Helledore *ἀπάτωρ* household member, 54 years old (no. 318);

12. *P. Tebt.* II 446 = *SB* XX 14168 = 215-Ar-8 (Ptolemais Euergetis, AD 217): Aurelia Protous *ἀπάτωρ*, declarant (?) (no. 321);

13. *BGU* III 971 = 229-Ar-2 (Ptolemais Euergetis, AD 245): Thermoutarion *ἀπάτωρ* of Thermoutharion, declarant (no. 199);

14. *P. Oxy.* LXXIII 4956 (Peenno, AD 146/7): Tnepheros *χρηματίζουσα μητρός* Senpapos, declarant (no. 357);

15. *P. Oxy.* LXXIII 4957 (Sesphtha, AD 147): Leontas *χρηματίζων μητρός* Tanouphis, declarant, 40 or over 40 years old (no. 358);

[222] *Σεναμοῦνι(ν) Αβι*, but Bagnall claimed the second name with no other indication is suspicious and suggested the reading *ἀργ(ήν)*: R.S. BAGNALL, 'Notes on Egyptian census declarations. IV', *The Bulletin of the American Society of Papyrologists* 29 (1992), pp. 101–115, p. 114.

[223] The first editor, Herwig MAEHLER, *BGU* XI, proposed the reading *τὰς σ̣ . [θ]υγ(ατέρας)* before *Πτολεμαΐδα ἀπάτορα (ἐτῶν) κε καὶ Τκολλ ̣ ()ν ἀδελ(φὴν) ἀπάτορα (ἐτῶν) ιε καὶ Θαῆσιν ἄλλ[η]ν ἀπάτορα (ἐτῶν) δ* and claimed that the women were daughters of Petsorapis' wife, who was the mother of the legitimate daughter, Soeris, declared in the same census. The eldest and middle sisters would thus have been born long before the marriage of their mother and Petsorapis and the subsequent birth of Soeris, while the youngest may have been born after both the birth of Soeris and the divorce of her parents; these events, moreover, would not have prevented the couple from living in a common household and raising all four girls together. This interpretation is possible, but rather unlikely. Youtie chose instead to read the missing word in line 10 as *συγγενεῖς* and identified the three sisters as the daughters of Petsorapis' sister or brother, and suggested that their parents would have maintained an informal relationship lasting at least 22 years and ending with the death of one of the partners: H. YOUTIE, 'BGU XI 2018', *Zeitschrift für Papyrologie und Epigraphik* 9 (1972), pp. 133–137.

16. *P. Bagnall* 38 (Oxyrhynchos, AD 174 [?]): Tachonsis χρηματίζουσα μητρός N.N., household member (no. 315);

17. *P. Oxy.* LXXIV 4989 (Oxyrhynchos, AD 175): Ploution, 36 years old (no. 360), Andromachos, 34 years old (no. 361), Harmiusis (no. 362), and N.N. (no. 363), χρηματίζοντες μητρός Didyme daughter of Plutarchos, declared by their mother.

All of these census returns which include mention of fatherless individuals were submitted either by mothers who were neither divorced nor married, or by other relatives. Furthermore, there is not even one case in which we can detect a possible figure who might have been the father of the fatherless. This is not necessarily the case for children born of unions that were certainly not marriages; not only they were not labelled with ἀπάτωρ (or a similar term), but they often have a patronym. We will return to this problem in Chapter 2, but it is worth providing a few cases which will help to determine the precise meaning of ἀπάτωρ.

The most obvious example can be found in papyri which include a patronym in descriptions of children born of slaves. In Roman law a slave could not be a father in the legal sense, as he could neither hold *patria potestas* nor leave an inheritance. For these reasons children born to a slave and a free woman were free, as they acquired their status from their mother (G. 1.80), but extramarital. This rule was recognised as belonging to *ius gentium* (G. 1.84) thus, broadly speaking, to the rules of Roman law recognised by Romans as common to all people. It is, therefore, reasonable to assume that the rule applied to people who had no Roman citizenship, but were Roman subjects, *i.e. peregrini*. This conclusion is based not only on analogy and common sense, but on the papyrological sources themselves.[224]

There are not many papyri which mention free-born sons of slaves, but they do exist; such cases include *P. Ryl.* II 103 = *Sel. Pap.* II 314 (Ptolemais Euergetis, AD 134), *SB* I 5124 (Tebtynis, AD 193), *P. Brux.* I 19 = *SB* V 8263 (Ptolemais Euergetis, AD 117/8), and *P. Harr.* II 180–189 (Ptolemais Euergetis, AD 134–146). *P. Ryl.* II 103 was composed in AD 134 in Ptolemais Euergetis as an *epikrisis* application for a certain Herakleides, and was sub-

[224] The problem of the status of children born to slaves is discussed in details in Chapter 2, pp. 103–120.

mitted by his already-scrutinised (l. 21) elder brother Horion. Both brothers were not only free-born, but were even entitled to metropolite status. The important detail is that their mother Lykarous (no. 832), a free-born woman, is described as a daughter of Herakleides slave of Ischyrion:[225]

> *P. Ryl.* II 103, ll. 3–4: [παρὰ] Ὡρίω[ν]ος τοῦ [Ἡρ]ακλείδου τοῦ Ἡρακλείδου μητρὸς Λυκαροῦτος τῆς Ἡρακλείδου | [δο]ύλου Ἰσχ[υρί]ων[ο]ς τοῦ Πάπου τῶν ἀπὸ τῆς μητροπ(όλεως) ἀναγραφομένω(ν) ἐπ' ἀμφόδο(υ) Βιθ(υνῶν) Ἄλλω(ν) Τόπ(ων).
>
> From Horion son of Herakleides son of Herakleides, his mother being Lykarous daughter of Herakleides slave of Ischyrion son of Papos, from among those with metropolitan status, registered in the quarter of Bithynians and Other Areas.

> ll. 16–19: ἡ δὲ | [Λυκαροῦς Ἡ]ρακλείδο(υ) δούλου Ἰσχυρίω[ν]ος τοῦ Πάπου μητρὸς Διδύμης τῆς Ἑρμᾶ ἀπεγρά(φη) | [τῶι η (ἔτει) θεοῦ[226] Οὐεσπ]ασιανοῦ ἅμα τῆι μη[τ]ρὶ κ[α]ὶ ἀδελφοῖς ἐπ' ἀμφόδο(υ) Σεκν[ε]βτ(υνείου), ἥτις | [καὶ αὐτὴ ἐτελεύτησε] μετὰ τ[ὴ]ν τοῦ ι[ϛ] (ἔτους) Ἁδριανο[ῦ] Κ[αίσ]αρος τοῦ κυ[ρί]ου κατ' οἰκί(αν) ἀπογραφήν.
>
> And Lykarous daughter of Herakleides slave of Ischyrion son of Papos, her mother being Didyme daughter of Hermas, was registered together with (her) mother and siblings in the 8th year of the deified Vespasian, in the quarter of the temple of Seknebtunis; and she died after the household census of the 16th year of Hadrian Caesar the lord.

P. Brux. I 19 = *SB* V 8263 = 117-Ar-3 is a census return for the year AD 117. Theon, the declarant,[227] lists among the members of his household:

1. Dioskoros, a slave owned equally by Laberia, Theon's wife, and her sister Horaiane, a weaver, ll. 4–8;

[225] *P. Ryl.* II 103 discussed in detail in: M. Nowak, 'Fatherless among οἱ ἀπὸ τῆς μητροπόλεως – a revision', *Zeitschrift für Papyrologie und Epigraphik* 208 (2018), pp. 213–225.

[226] θεοῦ supplemented by W. Liesker & P.J. Sijpesteijn, 'More remarks on some imperial titles in the papyri. III', *Zeitschrift für Papyrologie und Epigraphik* 63 (1986), pp. 281–290, p. 282 = *BL* VIII 292.

[227] R.S. Bagnall, 'Notes on Egyptian census declarations. V', *The Bulletin of the American Society of Papyrologists* 30 (1993), pp. 35–56, p. 38.

2. Alexous daughter of Hermas and Tasoucharion, apparently a free woman, but described as *γυνὴ Διοσκόρου δούλ(ου)*, ll. 23–24: *Ἀλεξοῦς Ἑρμᾶ τ[οῦ] Ἑρμᾶ μη(τρὸς) Τασουχ(αρίου) τῆ(ς) Σύρο(υ) | γυνὴ Διοσκόρου δούλ(ου)*;

3. Pasion, the one year old son of Dioskoros and Alexous, ll. 14–16: *Πασίων υἱὸ(ς) Δι[οσκό]ρο(υ) δούλ(ου) Λαβερίας | μητ(ρὸς) Ἀλεξοῦτ(ος) τ[ῆς] Ἑρμᾶ* (no. 833);

4. Alexous, their daughter, l. 25: *Ἀλεξοῦς θυγ(άτηρ) α(ὐτῶν)* (no. 834);

5. Taharyotis, their daughter, l. 26: *Ταρεῶτις ἄλλη θυγ(άτηρ) τῶν α(ὐτῶν)* (no. 835).

As a confirmation that we are not dealing with a scribal error in *P. Brux.* I 19, Pasion also appears in a series of receipts for poll tax (*P. Harr.* II 180–189) for years 134, 136, 137, 139, 140, 141, 143, 144, 145, and 146, in which he is described as: *Πασίων Διοσκόρου δούλου Λαβερίας μητρὸς Ἀλεξάνδρας*.[228]

Finally, in the famous *Charta Borgiana* we find a man described as Protas son of Heron slave of Protas (no. 615) listed among those who performed the five-days liturgy of canal work, *SB* I 5124, ll. 200–201: *Πρωτᾶς Ἥρωνος δού(λου) Πρωτᾶ μη(τρὸς) Ταόρσεω(ς)*.[229] All these people were children of slave fathers. While they were certainly extramarital, this was not an obstacle to being labelled as the sons of their fathers. It is important to note that the census returns, tax receipts and liturgy lists, especially those of the *Charta Borgiana*, are documents where the term *ἀπάτωρ* occurs often; thus if the terms *ἀπάτωρ* and *χρηματίζων μητρός* were applied to people born and raised in stable relationships which were not considered marriages, children of slave-free unions would be first to have it.

The similar case is soldiers who were banned to have children before their *missio honesta*, thus their children were legally fatherless (*infra*, pp. 120–127). Three of the seven cases found in the famous *Papyrus Cattaoui*

[228] The name of the mother differs, but the editor explained that Alexous could be a hypocoristic form of Alexandra or the difference between matronyms in *P. Harr.* II 180–189 and *P. Brux.* I 19 could be interpreted as a scribal mistake – a scribe would have written mistakenly the name of Laberia's mother instead of the name of the mother of Pasion. See commentary in: *P. Harr.* II, p. 52. The case of Pasion is discussed in: Nowak, 'Fatherless among *οἱ ἀπὸ τῆς μητροπόλεως*' (cit. n. 225), p. 220.

[229] The identification as a son of a free woman and slave: A. Martin, 'En marge de la Charta Borgiana', *Chronique d'Égypte* 75 (2000), pp. 118–125, pp. 124–125.

(Alexandria [?], after AD 142) concerned the legitimacy of children born to Roman soldiers. One case (col. III, ll. 11–22) concerned the *epikrisis* of two boys born to a Roman soldier and his Roman concubine during his time of service (ll. 14–15); in the document it becomes clear that the father had no right to present his sons for scrutiny. The official in charge of Roman citizenship, in this case the prefect Q. Rutilius Lupus (AD 114–117),[230] concludes his remarks with the sentence, ll. 21–22: *νόμιμον | δὲ π̣α̣τ̣έρα αὐτῶν ποιεῖν οὐ δ̣ύνομα[ι]* (l. *δύναμαι*) – 'I cannot make you their legitimate father'. Although the boys are recognised as extramarital in the legal sense, they are described neither as *ἀπάτορες* nor *spurii* (*Spurii filii*).

A similar conclusion can be drawn from the case of Chrotis, an Alexandrian citizen, who wanted her son born of an Alexandrian serving in the army to be recognised as legitimate son in regard to the testamentary succession so she turned to the same prefect (col. IV, ll. 1–15). The prefect's decision was similar, ll. 13–14: *Οὐκ ἐδύνατο Μαρτιά[λιος] | στρατευόμενος νόμιμον υἱὸν ἔχειν*, 'Martialis as a soldier could not have a legitimate son'. Again the boy is described as neither *Spurii filius* nor *ἀπάτωρ*. The case of Octavius Valens (col. IV, l. 16 – col. V, l. 26) offers further confirmation. The prefect ruling in a case concerning *epikrisis* decided that the sons of Octavius Valens could not be scrutinised as citizens as they were not his legitimate sons; neither of the sons are described as *ἀπάτορες*.

SB XXII 15704 (Karanis, after AD 138), discussed in the section devoted to *spurii*, provides an excellent example of the use of patronyms which were only social, but not legal. Besides Caius Sempronius Diogenes *spurius* of Sempronia Akousarion (no. 301), this document also mentions another individual born out of wedlock, Apronius son of Marcus son of Apronius *eques*. Apronius was an Egyptian of privileged fiscal status: in the extract from the census return for AD 117 he is described in l. 47 as *λαογρ(αφούμενος)*, thus partially exempt from *laographia*.[231] By the time of the census return for AD 131, he is said to be *ὑπερετὴς ἀπολύσιμ(ος) τῆς | λαο̣γρ(αφίας) ιε (ἔτει) (ἐτῶν) ξα*[232] (ll. 28–29), fully exempt from paying *laographia* in the 15th year

[230] PHANG, *Marriage of Roman Soldiers* (cit. n. 128), p. 24.

[231] SANCHEZ-MORENO ELLART, '*ὑπομνήματα ἐπιγεννήσεως*' (cit. n. 126), p. 103.

[232] Yet, perhaps he was 62 then. See R.S. BAGNALL, 'The people of P. Mich. Inv. 5806', *Zeitschrift für Papyrologie und Epigraphik* 105 (1995), pp. 253–255, p. 254.

of Hadrian (AD 130/1) as he had reached an age when he was no longer liable for taxes. This proves that he was not a Roman. It is possible he did not obtain Roman citizenship because his father had died before being released from the army; he is described not as a veteran but as ἱππεύς (ll. 27 and 46). Yet, Apronius is not described as ἀπάτωρ; indeed, he had a patronym.

In the *Gnomon of idios logos*[233] – which will be discussed at greater length in Chapter 4 – none of the paragraphs describing the legal situation of children born to parents of unequal civic status use the term ἀπάτωρ (or νόθος or *spurius*). Children are referred to simply as τέκνα (*BGU* V 1210, l. 47: ιγ τὰ ἐξ ἀστῆς καὶ ξένọυ γενόμενα τέκνα ξένα γẹίνεται) or οἱ ἐξ (...) γενόμενοι (*e.g. BGU* V 1210, l. 109: λη οἱ ἐξ ἀστῆς καὶ Αἰγυπτίου γενόμενοι μένουσι μὲν Αἰγύπτιοι). In my article published in 2015, I argued that these texts provide evidence that ἀπάτωρ was not a formal descriptions;[234] since then I have become convinced that the term ἀπάτωρ does not appear because the texts describe people who were not 'fatherless children', but rather the offspring of unions classified as marital or quasi marital; we shall return to this point soon.

The problem concerning the most numerous group of sources attesting discussed here terms, the tax lists, is that we do not possess enough information to determine which entries refer to children of unions. The patronyms following the names of payers or liturgists is a simple name in the genitive; neither the civic status of the father, nor the type of bond that connected him with the woman who bore his child is indicated. Yet, even in the lists we can find traces of the hypothesis introduced above. One example is Isas son of Tiberius Claudius Antoninus, a payer of *laographia* (*P. Mich.* IV 223, ll. 1803, 2316 [Karanis, AD 171/2]). Both his name and the fact he was liable for poll-tax are proof that Isas was not a Roman; however his father's name – and, indeed, all three parts of the *tria nomina* – are Roman. If Isas was the marital son of his father, he would be Roman himself and certainly not a payer of

[233] On the *Gnomon*, see Th. KRUSE, 'Der Gnomon des Idios Logos im Lichte der Terminologie für Verwaltungsrichtlinien im Imperium Romanum', [in:] K. HARTER-UIBOPUU & T. KRUSE (eds.), *Studien zum „Gnomon des Idios Logos": Beiträge zum Dritten Wiener Kolloquium zur antiken Rechtsgeschichte*, forthcoming.

[234] NOWAK, 'Ways of describing illegitimate children' (cit. n. 11), pp. 211–212.

laographia. The fact that he was born out of *matrimonium iustum* did not stop the scribes responsible for the list from using the patronym.

Therefore, people described as ἀπάτωρ or χρηματίζων μητρός do not have patronym as a rule, and the terms never occur in a context that might otherwise allow us to determine who their father was; while people who were undeniably begotten of non-marital unions were often identified with their fathers. These two observations would suggest that the term was used to identify an individual who was without a father in both the legal and social senses, in other words an individual associated only with their mother. The only individual identified with both patronym and the term ἀπάτωρ is the famous Tamystha *alias* Thamistis, a case which requires careful examination.

6.3.3. Tamystha's case

P. Lond. II 324, p. 63 = *W. Chr.* 208 (Prosopites, AD 161) is a letter addressed by Anikos to his sister Tamystha. It contains extracts from two census returns for the year AD 131 (131-Pr-1) and 145 (145-Pr-1) performed in the Prosopite nome. The addressee of the letter is described with the term ἀπάτωρ:

> ll. 29–34: Ἄνικος Χενθνούφιος τῇ ὁμομ|ητρίῳ μου ἀδελφῇ Ταμύσθᾳ ἀπάτορι χαίρειν. ἀνα|δέδωκά σοι τὰ προκίμενα ἀντίγραφα τῶν ἀ|πογραφῶν, ὧν ἐπιδείξω τὰ ἴσα ἐν καταχωρι|σμῷ, ὁπ[ό]ταν χρεία ἦν εἰς ἀπόδειξιν τοῦ εἶναί με [ὁ]μομ[ήτ]ριόν σου ἀδελφ[ό]ν.
>
> I, Anikos son of Chenthnouphis, to my maternal fatherless sister Tamystha, greetings. I have delivered to you the above copies of the census records, whose originals I shall display in the registry, whenever it is necessary to prove that I am your maternal brother.

Tamystha is not, however, described as ἀπάτωρ in the extracts from the census returns copied in the letter. Indeed the extracts might lead us to the opposite conclusion: she is recorded as the sister of her brother and the daughter of their parents.

ll. 10–14 (census return for AD 131): *Θενθνοῦπις Ἀνίκου τοῦ Παθερμουθίου | μη(τρὸς) Θάσειτος Ἑρπαῆσις (ἐτῶν) με. | Δημητροῦς Σωτηρίχου ἡ γυνὴ μη(τρὸς) Θαμίστις. | Θαμίστις ἡ θυγάτηρ (ἐτῶν) vac. ? | Ἄνικος ὁ ἀδελφὸς τῶν αὐτῶν γονέω(ν) ἀφῆλ(ιξ) (ἐτῶν) ς.*

Thenthnoupis son of Anikos son of Pathermouthios, his mother being Thaseis daughter of Herpaesis, 45 years old; his wife Demetrous daughter of Soterichos, her mother being Thamistis; daughter Thamistis [blank] years old; Anikos, her brother from the same parents, a minor, 6 years old

ll. 26–29 (census return for AD 145): *Χεντμοῦφις Ἀνίκου τοῦ Παθερμούθιος | μη(τρὸς) Θάσ[ει]τος Ἑρπαήσιος μεταλικὸς (ἐτῶν) νβ. Ἄνικος ὁ υἱὸς | μη(τρὸς) Δημητροῦτος Σωτηρίχου (ἐτῶν) κ. Θαμίστις ἡ ἀδελφὴ | τῶν αὐτῶν γονέων (ἐτῶν) κδ.*

Chentmouphis son of Anikos son of Pathermouthis, his mother being Thaseis daughter of Herpaesis, miner, 52 years old; his son Anikos, his mother being Demetrous daughter of Soterichos, 20 years old, Thamistis his sister of the same parents, 24 years old.

The document seems to confirm that a person twice described as the daughter of her father Kenthnoupis (written also as Thenthnoupis and Chentmouphis) could also be described as ἀπάτωρ, which would offer evidence that the category of ἀπάτορες was legal rather than social. Youtie claimed that Thamistis *alias* Tamystha could have been a daughter born to Demetrous and another man before she married Kenthnoupis but raised by Kenthnoupis and 'something drastic must have taken place to effect so far-reaching a revision in the legal status of Thamistis *alias* Tamystha'; the woman, once declared as having been born of the same parents as her brother, at some point became 'fatherless'. Youtie claims that such a 'diminution' of familial status was not uncommon in Roman Egypt: *P.Bour.* 42 (Hiera Nesos, AD 166/7) lists Kastor son of Tapasmutis formerly known (as his real status was discovered during some kind of investigation) as son of Ision (l. 564).[235] After the death of Kenthnoupis there might have been a problem with the succession. If Kenthnoupis was not her father, Thamistis *alias* Tamystha would not have been entitled to inherit anything from his estate and her brother would have been the sole

[235] YOUTIE, 'Ἀπάτορες' (cit. n. 147), p. 725.

heir.[236] The procedure of depriving the woman of the familial status would therefore have been initiated by the brother (or the father before his death). Then the document with the census records would have been issued for the benefit of Thamistis *alias* Tamystha, perhaps in regard to issues concerning her and her brother's common mother, or to legal problems concerning the relationship between the siblings: εἰς ἀπόδειξιν τοῦ εἶναί με [ὁ]μομ[ήτ]ριόν σου ἀδελφ[ό]ν (ll. 33–34).

This explanation seems unlikely, as the text does not mention any procedure or investigation which would have resulted either in a change or correction to the status of Thamistis *alias* Tamystha, or the act of *apokeryxis* undertaken by Kenthnoupis.[237] If such a procedure indeed took place, the information on it would have been essential. Otherwise the document would not be comprehensible, as the same person is once fatherless and once described with the patronym. In fact, the extracts from the census returns provided by Anikos would have been proof of her legitimacy and would thus have worked to Thamistis *alias* Tamystha's benefit not only in maternal succession. As a sister τῶν αὐτῶν γονέων she would have been entitled to inherit from her father along with her brother; using the returns as evidence in an inheritance case would have weakened Anikos' legal position, not strengthened it.

Sabine Huebner has proposed that the girl may have been adopted by Kenthnoupis after he had married her mother.[238] In this case, however, there would be no reason for describing her as ἀπάτωρ, as she would have had a father. Such an interpretation would only make sense if the adoption had been revoked; it seems unlikely, however, this crucial fact would have been omitted in the document.

Bagnall and Frier observed that the returns were not copied very carefully: there are mistakes in the spelling of names (*e.g.* three variants of Kenth-

[236] Youtie, 'Ἀπάτορες' (cit. n. 147), pp. 724–725.

[237] In classical Athenian law, *apokeryxis* served as a means of excluding a child from the *oikos* and resulted in the dissolving of familial bonds between the father, who undertook the act, and his child. The function of *apokeryxis* in Egypt is not obvious, but it might have served as a simple disinheritance, see J. Urbanik, 'Dioscoros and the law (on succession): *lex Falcidia* revisited', [in:] J.L. Fournet (ed.), *Les archives de Dioscore d'Aphrodité cent ans après leur découverte. Histoire et culture dans l'Égypte byzantine*, Paris 2008, pp. 117–142, pp. 124–127.

[238] S. Huebner, *The Family in Roman Egypt. A Comparative Approach to Intergenerational Solidarity and Conflict*, Cambridge 2013, p. 178.

noupis), in grammatical cases, and in people's ages. Even the name of the Anikos' sister is recorded in two variants: Thamistis, a name attested only in this document, and Tamystha, a reasonably popular Graeco-Egyptian name. This variation has been used as grounds to suggest that the information concerning the woman's status may be inaccurate.[239] I myself, quite wrongly, tried to prove that Thamistis and Tamystha were two different persons.[240]

Another scenario is that Thamistis *alias* Tamystha was a daughter of Kenthnoupis and Demetrous from before they had married. Her status would not have mattered during the lifetime of her parents, which would explain why she was described as a legitimate daughter (or simply as daughter) in the census, but it may have become more important at some point, perhaps when it came to succession. This explanation would support Youtie's theory that ἀπάτορες were usually begotten of parents who had formed stable relationships but could not marry due to restrictions introduced by the Romans.[241] (Although there is nothing to suggest that Thamistis *alias* Tamystha's parents were of unequal status, or to explain what would have canceled this inequality so they could eventually marry.) If this is the case, one has to accept that the legitimation of natural children was forbidden among Egyptians: Tamystha *alias* Thamistis would have remained ἀπάτωρ despite the subsequent marriage of her parents and despite being socially and administratively recognised as her father's daughter. Romans could not provide legitimacy for their children by marriage until late antiquity,[242] but our sources do not provide evidence that the same prohibition was applied to Egyptians. Reasoning *per analogiam* would not be justified in this case, as the institutions of Roman family law did not usually apply to non-Romans in Egypt.

The onomastic habit cultivated within this family seems to support the hypothesis that Tamystha was an outsider within the family: Kenthnoupis, father of Anikos and Tamystha, had three brothers and each one, includ-

[239] BAGNALL & FRIER, *Demography* (cit. n. 122), p. 42.

[240] M. NOWAK, 'The fatherless and family structure in Roman Egypt', [in:] *Symposion 2015* (cit. n. 167), pp. 100–114.

[241] YOUTIE, 'Ἀπάτορες' (cit. n. 147), pp. 238–239.

[242] *Legitimatio per subsequens matrimonium*, by which an illegitimate child became legitimate through subsequent marriage of their parents, was introduced by Constantine. While his constitution was not preserved, the text may be restored thanks to Zeno's constitution (C. 5.27.5 pr.): see *infra*, p. 302.

ing Kenthnoupis, named his first-born son Anikos (ll. 9, 18, and 24) which was the name of their father. Moreover, two of the four brothers named their first-born daughters Thaseis (ll. 8 and 19), which was their mother's name. The youngest brother did not have a daughter, and Kenthnoupis recorded Thamistis *alias* Tamystha as his only daughter. If she was indeed his first-born daughter she should have been named Thaseis, but was instead named after her maternal grandmother (l. 12) (Fig. 2). If Thamistis *alias* Tamystha was not related to Kenthnoupis, she would as ἀπάτωρ have received her name from her mother's closest relative.

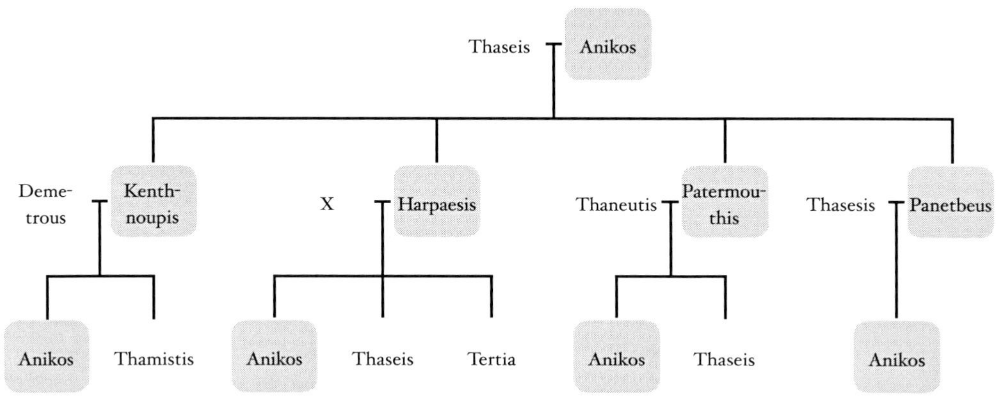

Fig. 2. Family tree of Thamistis *alias* Tamystha

Yet, the onomastics can also be explained in such a way that supports Tamystha's legitimate status:

a) There could have been an elder sister named Thaseis who died after the first recorded census return was completed. As a second daughter, Thamistis *alias* Tamystha would have been named after the maternal grandmother,[243] exactly as Tertia, the second daughter of Tamystha's uncle Herphaesis and his wife, daughter of Horos and Tertia (see Fig. 2).

b) Thamistis *alias* Tamystha could have been named after her maternal mother for reasons unknown to us – the family's onomastic pattern did not have to be absolute.

[243] Hobson, 'Naming practices' (cit. n. 88), p. 161.

The above explanations justifying the familial status of Thamistis *alias* Tamystha are not as unlikely as they may seem. We have already noted that ἀπάτωρ had more than one meaning, one of which was a child orphaned by their father. Perhaps, in addressing his sister, Anikos wanted to underline both the fact that their father had died and that they shared a common mother: τῇ ὁμομητρίῳ μου ἀδελφῇ.

BGU II 648 = *W. Chr.* 360 = *Sel. Pap.* II 284 (Prosopites, AD 164 or 196) provides a further argument. The document is a petition addressed to an official, perhaps the *epistrategos*, by Tamystha daughter of Kenthnouphis. The applicant claims that her father had left her a plot of land as a share in his inheritance, but her uncle, Panetbes, and her cousin, Thaesis daughter of Patermouthis, took it from her by force. In the petition she asks the official to order the *strategos* of the Prosopite nome to force the relatives to give the land back. It seems probable that we are dealing with the same family (Fig. 2), as Jean Yoyotte[244] and Jan Quaegebeur[245] noticed, but as far as we can tell from the document, the reason the uncle and cousin took the land from Tamystha had nothing to do with doubts about her marital birth and inheritance rights, but rather the fact that she did not cultivate the land.

ll. 8–16: ὁ τούτου ἀδελφὸς Πανετβῆς καὶ | Θαῆσις Πατερμούθεως ἀνεψιά μου βι|αίως ἀντι[λ]αμβάνονται τ[ο]ῦ πατρικοῦ | μου μέρους προφάσει γεωργίας βασιλικῆς | γῆς, εἰς ἣν γυνὴ οὖσα οὐκ ὀφείλω καθέλ|κεσθαι κατὰ τὰ ὑπὸ τῶν ἡγεμόνων καὶ | ἐπιτρόπων περὶ τούτου διατεταγμένα, | ἐπεὶ καὶ ἄτεκν[ός] εἰμι καὶ οὐδὲ ἐμαυτῆι | ἀπαρκεῖν δύναμαι.

His brother, Panetbes, and my cousin, Thaesis daughter of Patermouthis, lay hold on my paternal share by force on the pretext of the cultivation of royal land, which I, as a woman, ought not to be compelled to undertake, according to ordinances of the prefects and procurators in this regard, since I am both childless and am not able to provide for myself.

[244] J. YOYOTTE, 'Une étude sur l'anthroponymie gréco-égyptienne du nome prosôpite', *Bulletin de l'Institut français d'archéologie orientale* 55 (1955), pp. 125–140, pp. 126–127.

[245] J. QUAEGEBEUR, 'Considérations sur le nom propre égyptien Teëphthaphônukhos', *Orientalia Lovaniensia Periodica* 4 (1973), pp. 85–100, p. 98.

It is not entirely clear if there was any connection between this document and the letter from Anikos. The census reports could have been sent by Anikos to support Tamystha's claim against her relatives – the conflict would have started at least three years before the petition to the *epistrategos* from AD 164 – or even to support her claim to the land before the conflict had even started. It is also possible that *P. Lond.* II 324, p. 63 = *W. Chr.* 208 is wholly unrelated to the land left by Kenthnouphis; it could just as easily concern the succession after Demetrous or the relationship between Anikos and Tamystha. Nevertheless, *BGU* II 648 offers proof that Tamystha, described as ἀπάτωρ in *P. Lond.* II 324, p. 63 = *W. Chr.* 208, was in fact her father's daughter, which is the same conclusion suggested by the extracts from the census returns. *P. Lond.* II 324, p. 63 = *W. Chr.* 208 therefore provides us with evidence that ἀπάτωρ could be used to describe an individual whose father had died. Does this, however, mean that we need to re-assess our understanding of ἀπάτορες?

Before examining further sources, we must add one reservation: *P. Lond.* II 324, p. 63 = *W. Chr.* 208 is the only document attesting the term ἀπάτωρ in the Prosopite nome. As mentioned above, the geographical dispersion of documents containing the term ἀπάτωρ is unequal and, as such, we cannot be certain whether it was used with consistent meaning and function throughout Egypt or, more broadly, the Roman world. In other words, we cannot apply the proposed meaning from this document onto other uses of ἀπάτωρ in Roman Egypt. Yet, two further observations cast some doubt as to whether the term ἀπάτωρ was used solely to denote people born out of wedlock in Roman Egypt.

In some documents we find both ἀπάτωρ and μητρός applied concurrently. This is the case in the archive of *sitologoi* from Soknopaiou Nesos.[246] In the archive, the nomenclature follows a definite pattern. In *SPP* XXII 169 (Soknopaiou Nesos, AD 216), a grain list, Melas (no. 673) in lines 10 and 52 is described as Μέλας ἀπάτ(ωρ) μητ(ρὸς) Σοηροῦτος, and Horion (no. 475) in line 26 appears as Ὡρίων μητ(ρὸς) Θαεισᾶτος. In *SB* XIV 11715 = *SPP* XXII 167 = *SPP* XII 67 (Soknopaiou Nesos, AD 209), a copy of a κατ' ἄνδρα list, Paeis

[246] On the archive, see K. Geens & W. Clarysse, 'Tax collectors from Socnopaiou Nesos in the early third century', [in:] Vandorpe *et al.* (eds.), *Graeco-Roman Archives* (cit. n. 169), pp. 383–386.

son of Talbauis (no. 466) is styled as *Πάεις ἀπάτωρ μητ(ρὸς) Ταλβαύεως*,[247] while Panephremmis son of Teknas (no. 658)[248] and Horion son of Thaisas (no. 475) are described by their metronyms without the addition *ἀπάτωρ*.[249] Should it mean that *ἀπάτ(ωρ) μητ(ρός)* describes something different than *μητ(ρός)* in this archive or even, more broadly, in the Arsinoite nome? Perhaps *ἀπάτωρ* occurred when the father was died.

It seems rather unlikely. First, in other multi-entry lists concurrences of the two categories are rare, *e.g.* in the Karanis tax rolls[250] or in the administrative archive of Theadelphia.[251] Second, already Calderini observed that in some lists the number of *ἀπάτορες* is relatively high, while in others it is low. In two *laographia* lists belonging to the administrative archive of Theadelphia, *BGU* IX 1891 (AD 133) and 1892 (AD 133), *ἀπάτορες* constituted over 10% of all entries, while only 1% of those recorded in the Karanis tax rolls – which were still unpublished when Calderini was writing – were labelled as fatherless.[252] Even if we take into consideration only those lists where the number of *ἀπάτορες* is the highest, the numbers are still too low to allow for a definitive re-interpretation; this is especially true for poll-tax lists, which represent the entire male adult population of a given place.

[247] *SB* XIV 11715, col. 2, l. 2; col. 3, l. 2; col. 4, l. 2; col. 5, l. 2; col. 6, l. 2; col. 7, l. 2; col. 8, l. 2; col. 9, l. 2; col. 10, l. 2; col. 11, l. 2: D.H. SAMUEL, 'Taxation at Socnopaiou Nesos in the early third century', *The Bulletin of the American Society of Papyrologists* 14 (1977), pp. 161–207, pp. 196–197, no. 63.

[248] *SB* XIV 11715, col. I, l. 43; col. II, l. 43; col. III, l. 40; col. IV, l. 43; col. V, l. 42; col. VII, l. 40; col. VIII, l. 40; col. IX, l. 39, col. X, l. 42: SAMUEL, 'Taxation at Soknopaiou Nesos' (cit. n. 247), pp. 198–199, no. 79.

[249] With a metronym without *μητρός*, *Ὡρίων Θαεισᾶτος* (*BGU* II 392, l. 19 [AD 208]), and with a metronym preceded by *μητρός*, *Ὡρίων μητ(ρὸς) Θασιᾶτος* (*SB* XIV 11715, col. 1, l. 40; col. 2, l. 39; col. 3, l. 36; col. 4, l. 39; col. 5, l. 38; col. 7, l. 36; col. 8, l. 36; col. 9, l. 35; col. 10, l. 3; *SPP* XXII 84, l. 12 [AD 200–225]; *SPP* XXII 2, l. 13 [AD 207/8]; *SPP* XXII 169, l. 26 [AD 216]): SAMUEL, 'Taxation at Socnopaiou Nesos' (cit. n. 247), pp. 204–205, no. 119.

[250] The list of documents belonging to the archive, see K. VANDORPE & S. VAN BESELAERE, 'Tax rolls of Karanis', [in:] VANDORPE *et al.* (eds.), *Graeco-Roman Archives* (cit. n. 169), pp. 388–390.

[251] The list of documents belonging to the archive, see K. GEENS, 'Administrative archive of Theadelphia', [in:] VANDORPE *et al.* (eds.), *Graeco-Roman Archives* (cit. n. 169), pp. 34–39.

[252] CALDERINI, 'Ἀπάτορες' (cit. n. 1), p. 363.

According to Bagnall and Frier, the average age of death for those who survived until the age of five was 43,7.[253] Even if this number is not fully reliable – as the authors themselves cautioned – it cannot be too far from the truth; even if the average life expectancy was slightly higher than Bagnall and Frier propose it would have been considerably lower than it is today.[254] They also observed that the median male age at the time of first marriage was around 25.[255] It should also be noted that men started paying *laographia* when they were 14 and continued to pay it until they reached the age of 62. Taking all this into consideration, we can assume that the average father of a 14-year-old boy would have been in his late thirties or early forties. Furthermore, teenagers were only one of the age categories within such lists; the majority of tax payers were older. Even if we discount the Karanis tax rolls and look only at the two *laographia* lists from Theadelphia, it is difficult to believe that the number of individuals whose fathers were dead at the moment they were entered onto the list amounts to only 10% of the total. The number is far too low to allow interpreting ἀπάτορες as men whose fathers died.

A striking case is *PSI* XV 1532 (Oxyrhynchos, AD 100–117),[256] a general property return submitted to the *bibliotheke enkteseon*.[257] The land declared

[253] Bagnall & Frier, *Demography* (cit. n. 122), p. 105.

[254] Bagnall & Frier, *Demography* (cit. n. 122), pp. 106–109.

[255] Bagnall & Frier, *Demography* (cit. n. 122), p. 116.

[256] Yet, the dating is not secure and the papyrus could be later. *Terminus ante quem* is AD 150. See commentary to *PSI* XV 1532.

[257] *E.g.* F. Burkhalter, 'Archives locales et archives centrales en Égypte romaine', *Chiron* 20 (1990), pp. 191–216; K. Maresch, 'Die Bibliotheke Enkteseon im römischen Ägypten. Überlegungen zur Funktion zentraler Besitzarchive', *Archiv für Papyrusforschung* 48.1 (2002), pp. 233–246; F. Lerouxel, 'Les femmes sur le marché du crédit en Égypte romaine (30 av. J.-C. – 284 apr. J.-C.). Une approche néo-institutionnaliste', *Les cahiers du Centre de recherches historiques* 37 (2006), pp. 121–136; idem, 'The private credit market, the bibliotheke enkteseon, and public services in Roman Egypt', *Annales. Histoire, Sciences Sociales* 67.4 (2012), pp. 629–659; A. Jördens, 'Öffentliche archive und römische Rechtspolitik', [in:] K. Lembke, M. Minas-Nerpel & S. Pfeiffer (eds.), *Tradition and Transformation: Egypt under Roman Rule. Proceedings of the International Conference, Hildesheim, Roemer- and Pelizaeus-Museum, 3–6 July 2008* [= *Culture and History of the Ancient Near East* XLI], Leiden 2010, pp. 159–179; eadem, 'Nochmals zur bibliotheke enkteseon', [in:] G. Thür (ed.), *Symposion 2009: Vorträge zur griechischen und hellenistischen Rechtsgeschichte (Seggau, 25.–30. August 2009)* [= *Akten der Gesellschaft für griechische und hellenistische Rechtsgeschichte* XXI], Vienna 2010, pp. 277–290;

in the *apographe* is described as having been inherited from Thonis, a deceased brother (no. 163):

> *PSI* XV 1532, ll. 11–20: [κ]ạτήντησεν εἴς μ[ε] | ἐξ ὀνόματος τοῦ ἀδ[ελ]|φοῦ μου Θώνιος χ[ρη]|ματίζοντος μητρ̣[ὸς] | τῆς αὐτῆς [τ]ẹτẹλ̣[ευτηκότος | τ]ῷ γ (ἔτει) [Τρ]ạịạ[νοῦ Καίσαρος | τ]ọῦ κυρίου ἀτ̣ẹ́κ̣ṿọụ κ[αὶ ἀ]|διαθέτου καὶ ἀπάτ̣ọρο[ς ἐ]|π' ἐμοὶ μόνῳ ἀδελφῷ [καὶ] | κ̣ληρονόμῳ.
>
> (it) fell to my share in the name of my brother Thonis, styled the son of the same mother, who died in the 3rd year of Trajan Caesar, the lord, childless, without a will, and fatherless, having me as his only brother and heir.

Although *de cuius* was described by the metronym, χρηματίζων μητρός, the term ἀπάτωρ was applied as a *terminus technicus* with a broader meaning than we have seen thus far. The term, together with ἄτεκνος and ἀδιάθετος, was used to demonstrate that the declaring brother was preceded by neither children, father, nor testamentary heirs.[258] The term ἀπάτωρ, therefore, does not indicate whether *de cuius* was born out of wedlock, (although it was true), but that there was no father who would be entitled to the inheritance before Thonis, as the term ἀδιάθετος is used to point out that no binding will existed at the time of *de cuius*' death. Whether the will was revoked or never made did not matter; what mattered was that there existed no heirs who could claim the inheritance according to the will. The same applies to ἀπάτωρ, there was no father who could claim the inheritance.

The conclusion, therefore, seems obvious. The term ἀπάτωρ in Roman Egypt, if used as an element of a personal identification cluster described those born out of wedlock, and applied only to cases in which the father was absent both legally and socially. The term, therefore, is not the counterpart of Latin *spurius* which had broader meaning. Although the case of Tamystha, the property return from Oxyrhynchos, and tutor application discussed in Chapter 5, prove that the above meaning was not the only possible – the term could also have been used to describe an individual

J.L. Alonso, 'The *bibliotheke enkteseon* and the alienation of real securities in Roman Egypt', *The Journal of Juristic Papyrology* 40 (2010), pp. 11–54.

[258] The term was often used in substitution clause in wills made for non-Romans before the *constitutio Antoniniana*. See Nowak, *Wills* (cit. n. 44), pp. 271–342.

whose father had died or *spurius* or a person who had no father for whatever reason.

CONCLUSION

The examination of terms applied to persons born out of wedlock has allowed us to confirm certain theories proposed by other scholars, and to formulate new ones. The section devoted to *naturalis* and *spurius* / *Spurii filius/-a* demonstrates that the two terms were used for two very different purposes. The adjective *naturalis* was applied to indicate blood bonds between relatives, legitimate or otherwise, while *spurius* served to denote personal status. This appears to have been the case not only in Roman Egypt, but throughout the Empire. With regard to the term ἀπάτωρ, the sources demonstrate that it took on a special meaning and function in Roman Egypt: when used as a substitute for filiation in a personal identification cluster, it may be interpreted as a sign that the individual in question was both legally and socially fatherless. If applied outside the identification cluster, however, it had other meanings.

CHAPTER TWO

FATHERLESS CHILDREN WHO HAD FATHERS

INTRODUCTION

THE TERMINOLOGICAL STUDIES presented in the previous chapter allowed us to identify a group who could legitimately be classified as fatherless; their lack of a father in the social sense was indicated by their identification clusters, which either skipped the patronym or replaced it with the metronym or with another special term ἀπάτωρ. However an additional group existed within the social landscape of Roman Egypt – and the Roman Empire in general – whose identification cluster did not lack the patronym, but who did not legally have fathers, and were thus recognised under the law as *sine patre*. These individuals will be examined in the present chapter.

1. CHILDREN OF SLAVE FATHERS

Children who were born free of a slave parent, were the first group to be classified as legally fatherless as they were considered to be non-marital. Yet not all children with a slave parent were born free. It is therefore necessary to reconstruct the rules by which *status libertatis* was acquired before we can discuss the familial standing of free persons born of free-unfree unions.

1.1. *Status libertatis*

Under Roman law, the children born of unions between slaves and free individuals could have either free or slave status. If the mother was a slave, her offspring were also slaves, regardless of the status of the father;[1] unless the mother had been free at any time during her pregnancy (*favor libertatis*: G. 1.89; P.S. 2.24.3). According to the *Institutes* of Gaius (G. 1.82) and *Tituli ex corpore Ulpiani* (*Tit. Ulp.* 5.9), the *status libertatis* of children born from unions between slaves and free persons depended on the mother, in as much as they were non-marital children. However exceptions to this rule were introduced for children born of free mothers and slave fathers.

The already discussed *senatus consultum Claudianum* of AD 52 noted that the children of a free woman and a slave belonging to someone other than the woman could be born slaves; yet the *status libertatis* depended on whether the slave's master had agreed to the slave's union with a free woman. However if children were fathered by a slave belonging to their mother, there were no legal issues until the time of Constantine, which problem is discussed in the last chapter.[2]

The Claudian senate decree was not the only law to contradict the general rule of *status libertatis* acquisition. Gaius, shortly after his discussion on the *senatus consultum Claudianum* (G. 1.86), refers to another *lex*. The *lex* states that boys born to a free man who had conceived them with a slave whom he had believed to be free should be free, while children born to a woman who knew that her partner was someone else's slave, were to be considered slaves.

> G. 1.86: Sed illa pars eiusdem legis **salva est**, ut ex libera et servo alieno, quem sciebat servum esse, servi nascantur. Itaque apud quos talis lex non est, qui nascitur iure gentium matris condicionem sequitur, et ob id liber est.

[1] The regular study of different configurations of *status libertatis* of fathers and slave children in inscriptions outside of the *familia Caesaris*, see E. Herrmann-Otto, *Ex ancilla natus: Untersuchungen zu den „hausgeborenen" Sklaven und Sklavinnen im Westen des Römischen Kaiserreiches* [= *Forschungen zur antiken Sklaverei* XXIV], Mainz 1993, pp. 83–98.

[2] See D. Liebs, 'Sie liebte ihren Sklaven', [in:] J. Hallebeek *et al.* (eds.), *Inter cives necnon peregrinos: Essays in Honour of Boudewijn Sirks*, Göttingen 2014, pp. 409–428.

> But this part of the same *lex*, which says that (children) of a free woman and someone else's slave of whom she knew to be a slave are born slaves, is still biding. So among those, for whom this *lex* is not (biding), whoever is born, they follow the maternal condition, and because of this they are free.

The former ruling concerning freedom of sons by unfree mother was abolished by Vespasian who considered it inconsistent, but the latter was in force still in Gaius' time. This passage constitutes the only mention of this *lex*, which must have predated Vespasian. It was perhaps issued during the reign of Augustus, and might be one of his *leges* on manumissions.[3] Its relationship to the *senatus consultum Claudianum* has become the subject of intense scholarly debate.

This *lex* could not have applied to the same range of cases as the Claudian senate decree. Gaius refers to the *lex* as *salva est*, suggesting it was still in force in his time, and had not been changed by the ruling of Hadrian which altered the *senatus consultum Claudianum* in regard to situations in which a free woman stayed with someone else's slave with the consent of the slave's master (G. 1.84: *supra*, pp. 45–48). Carlo Castello argued that the *senatus consultum Claudianum* would have applied only to women in a relationship with someone else's slave, as the status of children born to such unions was already regulated by the *lex* referred to in G. 1.86.[4] Yet, this interpretation contradicts Gaius' own description of the *senatus consultum Claudianum*, G. 1.84: *senatus consulto Claudiano poterat civis Romana ... ipsa ex pactione libera permanere, sed servum procreare*.

An alternative interpretation proposed by Agnieszka Kacprzak suggests that the *lex* would have applied to all children born of a free mother and slave father, while the *senatus consultum* would have regulated only the status of those born in a *contuberium*.[5] The *lex* would thus have been limited to children born of free women and slaves who did not form any type of relationship. Such a ruling would obviously have been ineffective, which

[3] A. Kacprzak, '*Servus ex libera natus* – Überlegungen zum *senatusconsultum Claudianum*', [in:] D. Feichtinger & I. Fischer (eds.), *Sexualität und Sklaverei*, Münster 2018, pp. 63–82, p. 69.

[4] C. Castello, 'La condizione del concepito da libero e schiava e da libera e schiavo in diritto romano', [in:] *Studi in onore di Siro Solazzi*, Naples 1948, pp. 233–250, p. 239.

[5] Kacprzak, '*Servus ex libera natus*' (cit. n. 3), p. 71.

might explain why it is referred to only by Gaius, and why Hadrian did not intervene against it.[6]

The explanation is convincing, but the passage *apud quos talis lex non est* remains problematic. The question is, therefore, to whom the *lex* did not apply. It says that children to whom the law does not apply follow the free condition of mothers. Certainly individuals whose mother did not know that her partner was a slave and, for this reason, were not subject to the *lex*. A woman unaware of her partner's slave status would have been free from the *capitis diminutio maxima*, as she would have been ignorant of the facts and not the law.[7] She would thus have kept her freedom and with it the right to bear free children. This would have been an exception to the *lex*, but one based on the general rule, while *apud quos talis lex non est* in G. 1.86 seems to refer to other cases.

It could refer to a group to whom the law did not apply at all. Philipp Eduard Huschke and William Buckland were both of this opinion, interpreting the *lex* as a *lex Latina*, valid only for Latins,[8] while John Crook suggested that it would have applied to *Latinae Iunianae*. If these interpretations are close to the truth, Romans would have been considered *apud quos talis lex non est*, free from the rule of this particular *lex*.[9] Yet the opposite reasoning, as proposed by Kacprzak, seems more justified: the *lex* would have regulated the status of Roman children in *ius civile*, while *ius gentium* would have applied to others, *i.e.* peregrines, who would follow the status of their mothers.

The rule of maternal status acquisition to which Gaius refers is traceable in the province of Egypt, where it applied to the status of children

[6] Kacprzak, '*Servus ex libera natus*' (cit. n. 3), p. 72.

[7] D. 22.6.9 pr. (Paul. *de iuris et facti ignorantia*): *(…) Regula est iuris quidem ignorantiam cuique nocere, facti vero ignorantiam non nocere*.

Women even mistaken of law could impose a protection against its effects, see L. Winkel, 'Forms of imposed protection in legal history, especially in Roman law', *Fundamina* 16.1 (2010), pp. 578–587, pp. 583–585.

[8] *Gaii Institutionum iuris civilis commentarii quattuor*, P.E. Huschke (ed.), Leipzig 1886, p. 194; W.W. Buckland, *The Roman Law of Slavery. The Condition of the Slave in Private Law from Augustus to Justinian*, Cambridge 1908, pp. 398–399.

[9] J. Crook, 'Gaius, *Institutes* I 84–86', *The Classical Review* 17.1 (1967), pp. 7–8.

born to peregrine women and slaves.[10] In the papyri, there are at least three cases of freeborn children of slave fathers and free mothers, thus children whose free status might have depended on the *iuris gentium regula* mentioned by Gaius G. 1.84 and 86 (*supra*, pp. 87–89):

1. Lykarous daughter of Herakleides, slave of Ischyrion, of mother Didyme daughter of Hermas (no. 832 in *P. Ryl.* II 103 = *Sel. Pap.* II 314 [Ptolemais Euergetis, AD 134]);

2. Pasion, Alexous, and Taharyotis children of Dioskoros, slave of Laberia and Horaiane, of mother Alexous daughter of Hermas (nos. 833–835 in *P. Brux.* 19 = *SB* V 8263 = 117-Ar-3 [Ptolemais Euergetis, AD 117/8]; Pasion, no. 833, is attested also in *P. Harr.* II 180–189 [Ptolemais Euergetis, AD 134–146]);

3. Protas son of Heron, slave of Protas (no. 615 in *SB* I 5124 [Tebtynis, AD 183]).

All listed individuals were born after the discussed *lex* and *senatus consultum Claudianum* had been issued (AD 52). In *P. Ryl.* II 103, Lykarous is mentioned as having been registered for the first time with her mother and siblings in the quarter of the temple of Seknebtynis in the eighth year of Vespasian (ll. 16–18).[11] She would thus have already been born by the census of the year AD 75. The same can be said of the children of Dioskoros in *P. Brux.* I 19: the youngest of the siblings, Pasion, was born one year before Hadrian became emperor.

The analysis of G. 1.86 and these cases illustrate that the basic rule of the maternal status acquisition discussed by Gaius also applied to peregrines in Roman Egypt. If we could prove that the rule that children fol-

[10] Observed already by Rafał TAUBENSCHLAG, *The Law of Greco-Roman Egypt in the Light of the Papyri. 332 BC – 640 AD*, Warsaw 1955², p. 73.

[11] Taubenschlag was of the opinion that Lykarous' parents did not live together, because he claimed that the rule known from Gortyn and the *Syro-Roman Law Book* according to which a free woman who cohabited with a slave bore slaves was applied: TAUBENSCHLAG, *Law of Greco-Roman Egypt* (cit. n. 10), p. 73, n. 28. Yet, it does not seem to be a justified view. On *P. Ryl.* II 103, see M. NOWAK, 'Fatherless among οἱ ἀπὸ τῆς μητροπόλεως – a revision', *Zeitschrift für Papyrologie und Epigraphik* 208 (2018), pp. 213–225. On the Gortynian regulation concerning children born of free mother and unfree father, see p. 112.

lowed the *status libertatis* of their mothers had been brought to Egypt only by Romans, this might suggest that Romans created a rule binding for Romans and non-Romans of the Empire, and then excluded Romans by introducing a *lex* belonging to *ius civile*.

1.1.1. Children of slave fathers before Romans

In her monograph on slavery in Graeco-Roman Egypt, Iza Bieżuńska-Małowist noted that the evidence for free women living with slaves during the Ptolemaic period was limited to the Zenon's archive:[12] *P. Cair. Zen.* III 59369 = *C. Ptol. Sklav.* I 15 (Krokodilopolis, 241 BC); IV 59620 = *C. Ptol. Sklav.* I 79 (Arsinoites, 248–239 BC); and 59621 = *C. Ptol. Sklav.* I 80 (Arsinoites, 248–239 BC).[13] The first of these texts does not attest very much:[14] it is a letter addressed to Zenon, written by a man named Philemon. Philemon says that he had brought a suit against his father-in-law, Herakleides, regarding some land, but that Herakleides, perhaps to avoid legal proceedings, countered with the accusation that his son-in-law had been a slave. As a result of this accusation, Philemon was taken into custody. It appears that Zenon played some part in this episode, as Philemon asks Zenon to inform the *strategos* that Philemon is not a slave so that he may be freed from his imprisonment.[15]

It is not known whether Philemon was indeed a slave or if he was falsely denounced by his father-in-law.[16] Even if he had once been a slave, it seems unlikely that he would have entered into marriage with Herakleides' daughter as a slave.[17] It is more probable that either he did not know of his status,

[12] K. VANDORPE, 'Zenon son of Agreophon', [in:] K. VANDORPE, W. CLARYSSE & H. VERRETH (eds.), *Graeco-Roman Archives from the Fayum* [= *Collectanea Hellenistica – KVAB* VI], Leuven – Paris – Bristol, CT 2015, pp. 447–455.

[13] I. BIEŻUŃSKA-MAŁOWIST, *L'esclavage dans l'Égypte gréco-romaine. Première partie : période ptolémaïque*, Wrocław – Warsaw – Cracow – Gdańsk 1974, p. 120.

[14] *C. Ptol. Sklav.*, p. 83.

[15] Reconstruction proposed by SCHOLL in *C. Ptol. Sklav.*, p. 82.

[16] *C. Ptol. Sklav.*, p. 83.

[17] Bieżuńska Małowist and Seidl believed that the text is a proof for marriages between slaves and free women in Ptolemaic Egypt: BIEŻUŃSKA-MAŁOWIST, *Esclavage dans l'Égypte gré-*

or he purported to be free. The latter would be a case of status usurpation, and would explain both the radical steps taken by Herakleides and the harsh reaction of the *strategos*. If this interpretation is correct, the document does not offer proof that Herakleides allowed his daughter to enter voluntarily into marriage with a slave, but is rather an illustration of the measures taken against slaves falsely claiming to be free in order to marry free women.

A more convincing piece of evidence for the union of free women and slaves is found in two drafts of a petition belonging to the same archive of Zenon (*C. Ptol. Sklav.* I 79 = *P. Cair. Zen.* IV 59620 and 80 = *P. Cair. Zen.* IV 59620). The petition was written by Zenon to the king about a house which was occupied by a woman named Arsinoe who claimed she had built it. Zenon, in turn, claims the house had been built for him by his own slave, Eutychos; Zenon also mentions that Eutychos lived with Arsinoe and had had children with her, *P. Ptol. Sklav.* I 79, ll. 8–9: καὶ ἔμπροσθεν αὐτῆι συνεῖναι | καὶ τέκνα αὐτῶι ὑπάρχειν ἐξ αὐτῆς. The status of these children cannot be determined from the passage, as we cannot be certain whether Eutychos had indeed formed a 'marriage' with Arsinoe or if he simply lived with her and fathered her children. According to Pavlovskaja, it is notable that Zenon made no claims concerning Eutychos' children, suggesting they might have been free.[18] The petition was, however, concerned with the house; the children were mentioned only because Zenon wanted to explain that Arsinoe was emotionally close enough to Eutychos (as his life partner and mother of his children) to persuade him to help her to win the case, in this case seeking *asylum* in the Sarapeum in order to avoid providing testimony about the house.

Among Ptolemaic Demotic documents we find one case potentially related to the status of children born to a free woman and a slave belonging to another person. It is two ostraca from the Theban region dated to the mid-second century BC, *DO BM* 26669 = *O. Tempeleide* 38 and *DO BM* 26206 = *O. Tempeleide* 39.[19] The later text, *DO BM* 26206 = *O. Tempeleide* 39, consists of

co-romaine I (cit. n. 13), p. 120; E. SEIDL, *Ptolemäische Rechtsgeschichte* [= *Ägyptologische Forschungen* XXII], Glückstadt 1962², p. 106, but Scholl raised doubts about it, *C. Ptol. Sklav.*, p. 83.

[18] E.S. GOLUBCOVA, A.I. PAVLOVSKAJA & T.V. BLAVATSKAJA, *Die Sklaverei in hellenistischen Staaten im 3.–1. Jh. v. Chr.*, Wiesbaden 1972, pp. 254–255.

[19] On the dating, see U. KAPLONY-HECKEL, *Die demotischen Tempeleide*, vol. I: *Text*, Wiesbaden 1963, p. 95.

an oath taken as the result of an ownership claim over a slave, Pamontu son of Pshendjehuti. *DO BM* 26669 = *O. Tempeleide* 38 suggests that Pshendjehuti, Pamontu's father, would have been a slave, while *O. Tempeleide* 39 mentions that he was married to Pamontu's mother and that he even provided a kind of 'Eheurkunde'.[20] Since Pamontu was an object of the property claim, he might have been a slave, which would mean that a child born to a free mother and slave father would have followed the paternal status. Yet it is not explicit that Pamontu's mother is free, rather her free status is only implied by the mention of the 'Ehefrauenschrift' in *O. Tempeleide* 39: it is not difficult to imagine a similar agreement if the woman had belonged to another master.[21] It might have been a deed regarding the ownership of future offspring and other claims between masters of 'spouses'. Finally, even if the mother was free, this document cannot be used as proof for children of Eutychos and Arsinoe were also slaves because rules applied by Egyptian and Greek speaking individuals could vary. (We could easily imagine that the children of Eutychos and Arsinoe were free, while Pamontu son of Pshendjehuti was a slave.)

The Egyptian sources from before Alexander the Great provide us with no direct analogies. Yet there is one further case, from Aramaic papyri, which illustrates that much depended on interested parties themselves and there might have been no obvious rule. The papyri in question are part of the Ananiah archive from Elephantine, dated to the Persian period.[22] It is a series of documents attesting the marriage of the archive's owner to a slave-girl, Tamet,[23] and its legal consequences. The earliest document concerning the marriage is the marriage deed itself, which does not list Tamet as one of the parties, but rather her master Meshullam. The con-

[20] S. Lippert, *Einführung in die altägyptische Rechtsgeschichte* [= *Einführungen und Quellentexte zur Ägyptologie* V], Berlin 2008, p. 113.

[21] For analogous cases, see D. Lewis, 'Slave marriages in the laws of Gortyn: A matter of rights?', *Historia* 62.4 (2013), pp. 390–416.

[22] The best preserved Aramaic texts from Elephantine come from either this archive or Mibtahiah archive: B. Porten, 'Egypt. Elephantine', [in:] R. Westbrook (ed.), *A History of Ancient Near Eastern Law* [= *Handbook of Oriental Studies. Section 1. The Near and Middle East* LXXII], vol. II, Leiden – Boston 2003, pp. 863–881, p. 863.

[23] On the status of Tamet and its evolution from slave to free, see B. Porten & H.Z. Szubin, 'The status of the handmaiden Tamet: A new interpretation of Kraeling 2 (TAD B3.3)', *Israel Law Review* 29.1–2 (1995), pp. 43–64.

tract, in addition to protecting Tamet in the case of divorce and ensuring her property claims in the case of widowhood,[24] regulated the situation of the couple's son Pilti. If Ananiah should ever divorce Tamet, Meshullam was entitled to claim Pilti. Otherwise, he was not entitled to the boy at all and would indeed be forced to pay a penalty if he tried to claim Pilti (*Pap. Eleph. Eng.* B36 [449 BC]). What does this mean for the boy's status? Was he free conditionally or was he a slave[25] who could act as free because his master, Meshullam, provided him with such 'freedom' in the contract?

Another child born to Ananiah and Tamet was Jehoishma. Twenty two years after the marriage contract, Meshullam set free both Tamet and Jehoishma on his death. Both women were to serve Meshullam as a son or daughter would support their father and, after his death, they were to support Meshullam's son Zaccur.[26] If the two women failed in this obligation, a high monetary penalty would be imposed on them (*Pap. Eleph. Eng.* B39). Jehoishma thus became Zaccur's sister, and it was Zaccur who later gave her into a marriage and provided her with a dowry.

It is worth stressing that the Aramaic papyri from Elephantine do not represent pure Jewish law.[27] They contain elements common throughout Ancient Near Eastern law, and a strong Egyptian influence is visible.[28] The family to whom the archive belonged lived in Elephantine under Persian rule, and its members were subjects of the Persian king, his officials and courts.[29]

The material from Egypt is not enough, but also comparative studies are not especially helpful in establishing a pre-Roman pattern of status acquisition by children born to free and unfree partners in the 'classical Greek world'. Herodotus, talking about the Lycians, found it extraordinary that Lycian children took their names from their mothers, *καλέουσι ἀπὸ τῶν μητέρων ἑωυτοὺς*

[24] For the detailed analysis of the contract, see PORTEN & SZUBIN, 'Status of the handmaiden Tamet' (cit. n. 23).

[25] PORTEN & SZUBIN, 'Status of the handmaiden Tamet' (cit. n. 23), p. 59.

[26] As Yaron has, however, pointed out this contractual clause should not be necessarily connected with the Hellenistic *παραμονή*, but interpreted as an independent legal phenomenon: R. YARON, *Introduction to the Law of the Aramaic Papyri*, Oxford 1961, p. 100.

[27] Cowley even claimed that Pentateuch was unknown to Jews of the fifth-century Elephantine: A. COWLEY, *Aramaic Papyri of the Fifth Century BC*, Oxford 1923, p. XXVIII.

[28] YARON, *Introduction* (cit. n. 26), pp. 114–128.

[29] See PORTEN, 'Egypt. Elephantine' (cit. n. 22), pp. 863–870.

καὶ οὐκὶ ἀπὸ τῶν πατέρων (1.173.4); he goes on to note that if a female citizen lives with a slave, their children are considered *γενναῖα*, well born, *καὶ ἢν μέν γε γυνὴ ἀστὴ δούλῳ συνοικήσῃ, γενναῖα τὰ τέκνα νενόμισται* (1.173.5). That the adjective refers to citizenship is made clear later in the same sentence, where it is specified that children of a male citizen and a foreign woman are born *ἄτιμα*, deprived of civic rights, *ἢν δὲ ἀνὴρ ἀστὸς καὶ ὁ πρῶτος αὐτῶν γυναῖκα ξείνην ἢ παλλακὴν ἔχῃ, ἄτιμα τὰ τέκνα γίνεται* (1.173.5). This passage should be seen less as proof of status acquisition among Lycians than as an illustration of what was considered standard among Athenians or even Greeks: Herodotus writes that these rules were specific to Lycians and not shared by any other peoples, *ἓν δὲ τόδε ἴδιον νενομίκασι καὶ οὐδαμοῖσι ἄλλοισι συμφέρονται ἀνθρώπων* (1.173.4), suggesting that the custom would have been viewed as highly irregular. Indeed, the idea of granting citizenship to children of slaves was appalling to Herodotus, which is why he bothers to mention it at all; we cannot, however, be certain how he perceived the question of freedom.

From around the same time as Herodotus, we find an interesting passage from the Great Code at Gortyn.[30] Columns VI and VII confirm that the union of a free women and a slave belonging to someone other than the woman were not only known, but even had some social recognition;[31] the status of the offspring was a matter for the lawgiver.

> *IC* VI 56 – VII 10: [------- *αἴ κ᾽ ὁ δõλος*] | *ἐπὶ τὰν ἐλευθέραν ἐλθὸν ὀπυίει*, | *ἐλεύθερ᾽ ἔμεν τὰ τέκνα. αἰ δέ κ᾽* | *ἀ ἐλευθέρα ἐπὶ τὸν δõλον, δõλ᾽ ἔμ|εν τὰ τέκνα. αἰ δέ κ᾽ ἐς τᾶς αὐτ|ᾶς ματρὸς ἐλεύθερα καὶ δõλα* | *τέκνα γένεται, ἒ κ᾽ ἀποθάνει ἀ* | *μάτερ, αἰ κ᾽ ἒι κρέματα, τὸνς ἐλε|υθέρονς ἔκεν. αἰ δ᾽ ἐλευθέροι* | *μὲ ἐκσεῖεν, τὸνς ἐπιβάλλον|τανς ἀναιλε̃θαι.*
>
> (If the *dolos*) goes to a free woman and marries her, their children shall be free; but if the free woman goes to the *dolos*, their children shall be *doloi.* And if free and *dolos* children should be born of the same mother, in a case where the mother dies, if there is property, the free children are to have it, but if there should be no free children born of her, the heirs are to take it over.[32]

[30] *The Law Code of Gortyn*, ed., tr. & comm. R.F. Willetts, Berlin 1967, p. 8.

[31] As David Lewis excellently proved, this and other passages of the Great Code concerning relationships between slaves or free and slaves cannot be interpreted as a proof that such unions had any legal recognition similar to marriage: Lewis, 'Slave marriages' (cit. n. 21).

[32] Tr. Lewis, 'Slave marriages' (cit. n. 21), p. 404.

The rule governing status acquisition is interesting for any student of Roman law: something as trivial as the domicile chosen by the couple was decisive in determining whether or not the child would be free. There is, however, a logic behind the rule: a woman capable of providing a house for her and her offspring would have had the right to keep and raise her children, while one who had to move into the household of her partner's owner would already have had an extremely low social standing and almost no economic resources, which would not have allowed her to provide for her children. The logic behind the rule, in any event, seems to have been quite distant from the later legal traditions shaped by Roman law.

All of the above cases illustrate that the sources from Ptolemaic Egypt, and the comparative material, offer insufficient evidence from which to reconstruct a pattern for the acquisition of *status libertatis* by free-unfree unions before the Roman era. We cannot exclude that the problem of status would have been regulated differently depending on place and time, or even that it would have been left to the discretion of the parties involved. We can observe only that status acquisition was not coherent, which could have given the Romans good cause to introduce a uniform rule of *ius gentium*.

1.2. *Family status*

1.2.1 Roman law

While unions between free and slaves were not uncommon in the Roman Empire,[33] unions between free women and slaves belonging to the Imperial House are especially well-attested.[34] In everyday life, slaves recognised themselves as the fathers of their free children, and the epigraphic sources

[33] See an overview of such unions in J. Kolendo, 'L'esclavage et la vie sexuelle des hommes libres à Rome', *Index* 10 (1981), pp. 288–297.

[34] Paul Weaver proposed that, in the early imperial period, stable unions between free women and imperial slaves were not isolated cases, and there are examples in which a mother and child(ren) have the same non-Imperial *nomen*, *e.g. CIL* VI 8444 and 33781: P.R.C. Weaver, *Familia Caesaris. A Social Study of the Emperor's Freedmen and Slaves*, Cambridge 1972, pp. 141–142. The marriage of free women by slaves must have been rather rare outside of the *familia Caesaris*. Weaver estimated that the number of such unions among all slaves involving

suggest that this recognition would not have been denied to them within the communities in which they lived.[35] There is, however, no unique descriptive pattern applied to children born of slave fathers: they could be represented as *Spurii filii*,[36] with the adjective *naturalis*, but they appear also without any special description, simply as sons and daughters.[37]

There were cases in which the law had to recognise familial bonds between slaves, or between slaves and their free close relatives. Familial bonds with or between slaves were notably recognised and binding in regard to incest and the prevention thereof (D. 23.2.14.2–3: Paul. *ad ed.* 35; D. 23.2.8: Pomp. *ad Sab.* 5; D. 23.2.56: Ulp. *disp.* 3). The same applied to *in ius vocatio* (D. 2.4.4.3: Ulp. *ad ed.* 5).[38] Although a free father could sell, pledge, or bequeath his slave children as any other slaves, bonds between him and them had legal recognition in some situations: a natural father could, for example, free his children (and also other groups of slaves) before reach-

unions accounted for a maximum of 10%, and suggested that a more probable number would be below 5%: Weaver, *Familia Caesaris* (cit. *supra*), pp. 186–188.

[35] J.B. Mispoulet, 'Du nom et de la condition de l'enfant naturel romain', *Nouvelle revue historique de droit français et étranger* 9 (1885), pp. 15–63, p. 17: 'C'est ainsi que nous voyons, dans certaines inscriptions, les esclaves qui, légalement, n'ont ni père ni mère, décrire leur filiation. C'est ce même sentiment qui a créé la parenté naturelle, bien avant qu'elle ait été sanctionnée par le législateur'.

[36] *CIL* VI 29513 (Rome, AD 50–300: no. 1195): *D(is) M(anibus) / L(ucio) Voluseno Sp(uri) f(ilio) / Victori / Volusena Restit(uta) / et Agrypnus Caes(aris) / fil(io) piissimo vix(it) / ann(os) V m(enses) VI*. 'To the spirits departed. Volusena Restituta and Agrypnus of Caesar (established) for L. Volusenus Sp. f. Victor, the most pious son, who live 5 years and 6 months'.

Interestingly, there are few inscriptions attesting the expression *filius naturalis* applied to a child whose father was a slave, *e.g.* *CIL* X 7822 (Sardinia, 2nd–3rd c. AD).

[37] *E.g.* *CIL* VI 18424 (2nd c. AD): *D(is) M(anibus) Fl(aviae) Saturninae / sanctissimae fil(iae) vix{s}it / an(nos) XIII d(ies) III comparavit / Fl(avia) Successa mater et sibi suis/que contubernali suo Satur/nino Caes(aris) n(ostri) posterisq(ue) / eorum*. 'To the spirits departed. Flavia Successa provided for (her) most just daughter Flavia Saturnina, who lived 13 years and 3 days, for herself and her family, her partner Saturninus, slave of our Caesar, and their descendants'.

Discussed among other similar cases by M. Krawczyk in: 'Paternal onomastical legacy vs. illegitimacy in Roman epitaphs', [in:] M. Nowak, A. Łajtar & J. Urbanik (eds.), *Tell Me Who You Are. Labelling Status in the Graeco-Roman World*, Warsaw 2017, pp. 101–122, pp. 104–106.

[38] Buckland, *Roman Law of Slavery* (cit. n. 8), p. 78; Herrmann-Otto, *Ex ancilla natus* (cit. n. 1), p. 39, n. 13.

ing adulthood (G.1.18–19) and appoint them as his heirs (D. 28.8.11: Javol. *ex post. Lab.* 4; D. 42.8(9).17.1: Jul. *dig.* 49).[39]

These bonds were sometimes described within the framework of the familial terminology, and even in jurisprudential sources we find terms such as *pater*, *filius*, and *frater*,[40] but not frequently, and with good reason: slaves had no familial status at all. Under Roman law, slaves could not be subject to family law, and could not therefore enter into *matrimonium* (or: did not have *conubium*) with anyone whatsoever.[41] Categories such as *sui* or *alieni iuris* simply did not and could not apply to them. They had no agnatic relatives, nor even *cognati* (D. 38.8.1.2: Ulp. *ad ed.* 46).[42] In principle they could not acquire property for themselves,[43] and consequently could neither inherit nor become *de cuius*.

Although slaves could have a wife and children after manumission (D. 28.1.14: Paul. *reg.* 2),[44] they had no legal ancestors (*adgnati* and *gentiles*).[45] The familial name of the *libertus* was bound to the family of his patron – this is visible in the onomastics, as freedmen took the *nomina gentilicia* of their patrons and, after the late Republican period, even their *praenomina*[46] – but their family itself was technically new.[47] When a slave acquired free-

[39] Herrmann-Otto, *Ex ancilla natus* (cit. n. 1), pp. 85–86.

[40] Herrmann-Otto, *Ex ancilla natus* (cit. n. 1), p. 39.

[41] E. Volterra, 'La nozione giuridica del *conubium*', [in:] E. Volterra, *Scritti giuridici*, II, Naples 1992, pp. 277–320 (reprinted from *Studi Albertario*, II, Milan 1950, pp. 348–384), p. 296.

[42] Buckland, *Roman Law of Slavery* (cit. n. 8), p. 77; Herrmann-Otto, *Ex ancilla natus* (cit. n. 1), pp. 38–39.

[43] Yet, on slaves' *peculium* and their ability to undertake legal deeds, see I. Buti, *Studi sulla capacità patrimoniale dei servi* [= *Pubblicazioni della Facoltà di Giurisprudenza dell'Università di Camerino* XIII], Naples 1976.

[44] C. Cosentini, *Studi sui liberti. Contributo allo studio della condizione giuridica dei liberti cittadini*, vol. I, Catania 1948, p. 39.

[45] Cosentini, *Studi sui liberti* (cit. n. 44), p. 40.

[46] H. Solin, 'Name', [in:] G. Schöllgen, H. Brakmann, S. de Blaauw, T. Fuhrer *et al.* (eds.), *Reallexikon für Antike und Christentum. Sachwörterbuch zur Auseinandersetzung des Christentums mit der antiken Welt*, vol. XXV, Stuttgart 2013, coll. 723–795, coll. 765–766.

[47] Cosentini, *Studi sui liberti* (cit. n. 44), p. 40.

dom, their civic status depended on the person who freed them, not on their parents (D. 38.2.1 pr.).[48]

In other words, under Roman law a freedman could be a father but not a son, and for this reason freedmen did not use filiation,[49] *libertinus ... nec patrem habuisse videtur, cum servilis cognatio nulla sit* (*Tit. Ulp.* 12.3),[50] did not inherit from their parents by *intestate*, not even from their mothers (P.S. 4.10.2), and were succeeded by their patron or patron's descendants. Slaves and freedmen cannot, therefore, be considered as either extramarital or marital children; slaves existed outside the Roman family in the legal sense, and freedmen existed only partially within that system, as they were the first of their family and had no officially recognised ancestry.

Under these circumstances, free children begotten by slave fathers must have had the same status as those who had no father in social terms. This is confirmed in Roman sources:

> I. 1.4 pr.: sed et si quis ex matre libera nascatur, patre servo, ingenuus nihilo minus nascitur: quemadmodum qui ex matre libera et incerto patre natus est, quoniam vulgo conceptus est.
>
> But was anyone born of a free mother, (their) father (being) a slave, they are born free none the less: just as one who was born of a free mother and unknown father, because they were conceived casually.

The rule certainly predates Justinian, as it can also be found in the *Tituli ex corpore Ulpiani*, 5.10, and in a constitution of Caracalla from August AD 215 (C. 5.18.3: *supra*, pp. 52–53) as the response to a question posed by a certain Hostilia, who married a slave whom she thought had been free. The emperor's answer was that the dowry and other obligations should be paid back to her from her (*ex*-[?]) partner's *peculium*; with regard to the children, the emperor decided that they were free, but *spurii*. Caracalla's

[48] In principle slaves freed in a formal way, thus in a will, by inscription into census list (as long as the census was performed) or throughout the fictional process, by Romans became Romans. Yet, if the manumission was not formal, or with the abuse of the *lex Aelia et Sentia*, a freed person became a Junian Latin, which status was introduced by the *lex Iunia* issued at the reign of Augustus (G. 3.56): A. Watson, *Roman Slave Law*, Baltimore 1987, p. 28.

[49] Freedmen with filiations in: Solin, 'Name' (cit. n. 46), col. 766.

[50] Herrmann-Otto, *Ex ancilla natus* (cit. n. 1), p. 39.

reply refers to the same rule found in Justinian's *Institutes*: children born of a free woman and a slave were *incerto patre nati*, *spurii* (*filii autem tui, ut ex libera nati incerto tamen patre, spurii ingenui intelleguntur*).

1.2.2. Local law – Egypt

Sources from Roman Egypt tell us little in regard to the legal standing of slaves and freedmen and their position within the family, especially when compared to the information preserved in Roman legal sources. This may be due to the relatively low number of slaves in Egypt:[51] it is estimated that slaves made up around 10% of the population.[52] As freedmen were freed slaves, their number would have constituted only a certain percentage of this 10%, which would make their total number very low indeed. If the estimates are correct,[53] the small number of slaves and freedmen could explain why information on their legal position is limited. However, the sources referring to slave and freed inhabitants of Egypt belong to legal practice and do not provide the same kind of systematic information as, for example, the *Institutes* of Gaius. Rather, they attest the rights and obligations of individuals, not the lack thereof, and if slaves were considered

[51] M. GIBBS, 'Manufacture, trade, and the economy', [in:] Ch. RIGGS (ed.), *The Oxford Handbook of Roman Egypt*, Oxford 2012, pp. 38–55, p. 43.

[52] Bagnall and Frier estimated that slaves constituted around 8.5% of village population and *ca.* 13.4% of metropolitan inhabitants. This would make the overall number around 11% for the total Egyptian population in the early imperial period. Much earlier, Iza Bieżuńska-Małowist, having considered previous estimates, suggested that the number of slaves in Roman Egypt would have not exceeded 10%. She noticed, however, that the situation in Alexandria might have been different, and the number of slaves located there higher: R.S. BAGNALL & B. FRIER, *The Demography of Roman Egypt* [= *Cambridge Studies in Population, Economy and Society in Past Time*], Cambridge 2006², p. 70, n. 69; I. BIEŻUŃSKA-MAŁOWIST, *L'esclavage dans l'Égypte gréco-romaine. 2. Période romaine*, Wrocław – Warsaw – Cracow – Gdańsk 1977, pp. 156–158.

[53] Yet, the estimations for the number of slaves in the Roman Empire varied significantly, especially that the views of the total population of the early Empire (before the Antonine plague) are different. The summary of the discussion in: W. SCHEIDEL, 'Quantifying the sources of slaves in the early Roman Empire', *The Journal of Roman Studies* 87 (1997), pp. 156–169; IDEM, 'Human mobility in Roman Italy, II: The slave population', *The Journal of Roman Studies* 95 (2005), pp. 64–79. Some authors claimed that any estimation of the number of slaves would be a guess-work, *e.g.* HERRMANN-OTTO, *Ex ancilla natus* (cit. n. 1), p. 3.

incapable of doing anything, we should not be surprised that this incapability is left unattested.

There are, nonetheless, some papyri from which we can draw several conclusions about the status of slaves in Egypt and note certain similarities with Roman institutions. First, it seems that, in Roman times, slaves who belonged to non-Romans could neither inherit nor leave property to heirs, even by means of a local will.[54] As Hans Kreller rightly observed, the occasional obligation for heirs to give something to slaves – for example, in celebration of the testator's birthday (*P. Oxy.* III 494, ll. 23–25) – should not be understood to mean that slaves had the ability to acquire *mortis causa*.[55] Such cases are rather obligations imposed on free heirs.

Second, freedmen and slaves were not related to their parents on a descriptive level. In papyri dated to the Roman period, the identity of slaves and freedmen was determined by their patronage, not their natural descent,[56] and in identification clusters it is the patron who appears in place of the father:[57]

> N.N. + ἀπελεύθερος + patron's name in genitive (+ patron's patronym (+ papponym and matronym)): Διονύσιος ἀπελεύθερος Διονυσίου (τοῦ Διονυσίου (τοῦ Διονυσίου μητρὸς Διονυσίας))
> N.N. + δοῦλος + owner's name in genitive (+ patron's patronym):[58] Διονύσιος δοῦλος Διονυσίου (τοῦ Διονυσίου)

[54] H. Kreller, *Erbrechtliche Untersuchungen auf Grund der graeco-aegyptischen Papyrusurkunden*, Leipzig – Berlin 1919, pp. 304 & 311–312.

[55] Kreller, *Erbrechtliche Untersuchungen* (cit. n. 54), pp. 311–312.

[56] R.S. Bagnall, 'Freedmen and freedwomen with fathers?', *The Journal of Juristic Papyrology* 21 (1991), pp. 7–8, p. 7; J.A. Straus, *L'achat et la vente des esclaves dans l'Égypte romaine. Contribution papyrologique à l'étude de l'esclavage dans une province orientale de l'Empire romain* [= *Archiv für Papyrusforschung. Beiheft* XIV], Munich 2004, p. 271.

[57] See N. Istasse, 'Trois notes sur les affranchis dans les papyrus de l'Égypte romaine', *Chronique d'Égypte* 76 (2001), pp. 202–208, who corrected reading of patronyms of freedmen in a few documents.

[58] In legal documents the mother's name was sometimes added, ἐκ (μητρὸς) δούλης N.N., if she was the property of the same owner. The reason for adding the mother's name was to assure the other party of a contract (or heirs or authorities) that the slave named in the deed was indeed a slave and belonged to the person disposing it: Straus, *L'achat et la vente des esclaves* (cit. n. 56), p. 271. Sometimes a similar piece of information appears in census returns:

instead of:

name + patronym (+ papponym and matronym): *Διονύσιος Διονυσίου (τοῦ Διονυσίου μητρὸς Διονυσίας)*

The identification cluster suggests further that in the case of slaves the patronage substituted familial bonds, which suggests that slaves were not recognised as relatives. The rules governing the acquisition of *status civitatis* of freedmen may also offer hints regarding the familial status of slaves and freedmen in Roman Egypt. Slaves, as we know, had neither civic nor fiscal status of their own; this applied not only to slaves belonging to Romans, but to those owned by all civic groups in Egypt. As owners were liable to pay taxes for their slaves, they registered their slaves in the fiscal groups to which they themselves belonged. The rule that slaves should follow the fiscal category of their masters, is expressed in *PSI* X 1146 (Tebtynis, after AD 138), ll. 11–12: *οἱ δοῦ|λοι λ̣α̣ο̣γ̣ρ̣αφοῦνται ὡς οἱ δεσπόται*, 'slaves are subjects to *laographia* as their masters', and further supported by *epikrisis* applications submitted on behalf of slaves belonging to fiscally privileged groups.[59] The scrutiny of a slave into a privileged group depended on whether their master also belonged to this group.[60] The parents of the slaves would not have been relevant in such applications and are thus never mentioned.

Slaves acquired their own civic status at the time of their manumission, and their new status seems to have depended entirely on the status of their former master: slaves freed by Roman masters became Romans themselves, those affranchised by *peregrini* became *peregrini*, which is discussed in detail in the next chapter. Natural parents did not figure into the process at all, even if they had won their freedom before their child: even if a slave had been born to free father, they would not have acquired

BAGNALL & FRIER, *Demography* (cit. n. 52), pp. 157–158. The reason for including a name of slave's mother in a census declaration was perhaps the same as in the case of legal deeds.

[59] J.A. STRAUS, 'Le statut fiscal des esclaves dans l'Égypte romaine', *Chronique d'Égypte* 48 (1973), pp. 364–369.

[60] STRAUS, 'Le statut fiscal des esclaves' (cit. n. 59); C.A. NELSON, *Status Declarations in Roman Egypt* [= *American Studies in Papyrology* XIX], Amsterdam 1979, p. 5; E. MEYER, 'Freed and Astoi in the Gnomon of the Idios Logos and in Roman Egypt', [in:] K. HARTER-UIBOPUU & T. KRUSE (eds.), *Studien zum „Gnomon des Idios Logos": Beiträge zum Dritten Wiener Kolloquium zur antiken Rechtsgeschichte*, forthcoming.

the status of their father on being freed, but rather the status of their patron. (*E.g.* if a Roman citizen had a son with a slave woman belonging to an Egyptian, the child would be born the slave of their mother's Egyptian owner and, if freed by this Egyptian, would acquire Egyptian status.)

A letter from Pliny to Hadrian requesting Roman citizenship for a physician, Harpokras, suggests that the acquisition of the former master's civic status was either standard practice in the Roman Empire, or at very least a phenomenon not limited to Egypt, 10.5.2: *Est enim peregrinae condicionis manumissus a peregrina*. Under this model, there would have been no connection between the status of a freed person and the status of their parent(s), which would have been the case for free children; slave status depended solely on the patron.[61]

As slaves were not allowed to own property, they possessed nothing that could be transferred to their children by inheritance. They were not described by their blood bonds, but by patronage. Finally, they had no status of their own which they could transfer to their children. It would therefore seem that children born to free peregrine mothers and a slave father belonging either to a Roman or peregrine owner would have been treated as fatherless, exactly as they would have been under Roman law.

2. FATHERLESS CHILDREN OF FREE FATHERS

2.1. *Soldiers and veterans*

Slave status was not the only obstacle to becoming a father in Roman law. Children born to soldiers during their military service were also considered to be legally fatherless. As this matter has already received attention from numerous scholars, we need only provide here a summary. From early imperial times,[62] soldiers were deprived of *uxoris iure ducendi facultas* to ensure *disciplina militaris*. Their situation during their time of service

[61] E. Volterra, 'Manomissioni di schiavi compiute da peregrini', [in:] *Studi in onore di Pietro de Francisci*, vol. IV, Milan 1956, pp. 73–106, pp. 101–102.

[62] On the chronology, see B.P. Campbell, 'The marriage of soldiers under the Empire', *The Journal of Roman Studies* 68 (1978), pp. 153–166.

was in this respect similar to that of slaves, but the ban on marriage was temporary, lasting only from recruitment to discharge.

The ban is attested in literary,[63] juridical[64] and papyrological sources,[65] and it applied to soldiers of all units, legions, *auxilia* and fleet,[66] both to Romans and those who only became Romans at their *missio honesta*. This is illustrated by the case of Octavius Valens and his sons, preserved in *P. Cattaoui*, in which a Roman magistrate declared an Alexandrian marriage to be void because the husband was serving in the army (*infra*, p. 145). A child born to a regular soldier between the reign of Augustus and end of the second or beginning of the third century – a matter discussed in the final chapter of this book – was always considered extramarital, and never *legitimus*. This in turn determined their position within the family and succession: they neither belonged to the family of their fathers, nor could they inherit from them without a will.

The legal standing of children conceived in the army was ameliorated by the *testamentum militis* or the constitution of Hadrian, which allowed such children to request *bonorum possessio* after their fathers in the class *unde cognati*. As both Hadrian's edict and the *testamentum militis*[67] are mentioned in the *Gnomon of idios logos*, there can be no doubt that they were applied in legal practice, which is further confirmed by the papyri discussed below.

> *BGU* V 1210, ll. 96–98: λδ. τοῖς ἐν στρατείᾳ καὶ ἀπὸ στρατείας[68] οὖσι σ̣υνκεχώρηται διατίθεσθα[ι] | καὶ κατὰ Ῥωμαικὰς καὶ Ἑλληνικὰς διαθήκας καὶ χρῆσθαι οἷς βούλ|ωνται ὀνόμασι, ἕκαστον δὲ τῷ ὁμοφύλῳ καταλείπειν καὶ οἷς ἔξ[εσ]τ̣ι̣ν̣.

[63] Presented in S.E. PHANG, *The Marriage of Roman Soldiers (13 BC – AD 235): Law and Family in the Imperial Army* [= *Columbia Studies in the Classical Tradition* XXIV], Leiden – Cologne 2001, pp. 16–21.

[64] PHANG, *Marriage of Roman Soldiers* (cit. n. 63), pp. 86–114.

[65] Papyri and *diplomata* in: PHANG, *Marriage of Roman Soldiers* (cit. n. 63), pp. 22–85.

[66] CAMPBELL, 'Marriage of soldiers' (cit. n. 62), p. 154.

[67] On *testamentum militis*, see J.F. STAGL, 'Das *testamentum militare* in seiner Eigenschaft als *ius singulare*', *Revista de estudios histórico-jurídicos: Sección derecho romano* 36 (2014), pp. 129–157, with further literature.

[68] § 34 of the *Gnomon* (*BGU* V 1210, ll. 96–98) provides the information that τοῖς ἐν στρατείᾳ καὶ ἀπὸ στρατείας οὖσι were entitled to make a military will, which provoked various interpretations in regard to the scope of persons entitled to the privilege, *i.a.* veterans. Yet, Ulrike Babusiaux re-interpreted this paragraph successfully proving that ἀπὸ στρατείας οὖσι

34. It was agreed that those who are in the army and those outside the army can make a Roman will or a Greek will and to apply words as they wish, it is allowed for them to bequeath (their property) to anyone of their rank.

BGU V 1210, ll. 99–100: *λε. τοὺς στρατευομένους καὶ ἀδιαθέτους τελευτῶντας ἐξὸν τέκνοι[ς] καὶ συγγενέσι κληρονομεῖν, ὅταν τοῦ αὐτοῦ γένους ὦσι οἱ μετερχ[όμε]ν̣ο̣ι̣.*[69]

35. Children and relatives are allowed to inherit after soldiers who died without a will whenever they follow the kin of deceased.

Paragraph 34 could be perhaps identified with Hadrian's edict also survived in a copy (*BGU* I 140 = *Sel. Pap.* II 213 [Alexandria (?), AD 119]). It allowed children born to soldiers during their military service to request *bonorum possessio* from their fathers in the same class as testators' collaterals, that is *unde cognati*, the third group of persons who could request *bonorum possessio*. It seems that both passages of the *Gnomon* deal with situations in which the children were of different civic status than their fathers, which would prevent succession under normal circumstances.[70] Thus, as long as the fathers died while serving in the army, their children had some rights regarding succession. If not the privileges, the situation might be complicated for soldiers' families.

This is illustrated by *VBP* IV 72 (Ankyron, after AD 117/8), a record of a dispute regarding some property inherited by Sarapas and his sister from their father who served in the legion. Those parts of the text which mention the reason for the dispute have been lost, but it must have concerned the title according to which the property was acquired. Sarapas declared both of his father's names: Psenamounis, his original name, and Marcus Longinus Valens, which he took after enrolling in the army (ll. 12–15). Sarapas also mentions that, in AD 117/8, he and his sister declared the inheritance they had acquired from Longinus (ll. 16–20) and underlined

encompassed civilians exposed to danger in the enemy's land. See U. Babusiaux, 'Römisches Erbrecht im Gnomon des Idios Logos', *Zeitschrift der Savigny-Stiftung für Rechtsgeschichte RA* 135 (2018), pp. 108–177, pp. 162–167, with further literature.

[69] Preserved also in *P. Oxy.* XLII 3014, ll. 1–4. Yet, the paragraph was obviously longer, after the words with which the paragraph in *BGU* V 1210 ended *P. Oxy.* XLII 3014 continued, *ἐὰν δὲ μὴ* | [- *ca.* 10 -] .[. . . .] . . . *η π̣α̣ρ̣ε̣μβολη vac. ? vac. ?*

[70] Babusiaux, 'Römisches Erbrecht' (cit. n. 68), p. 172.

once again that their father had originally been known as Psenamounis (ll. 20–21). The text then informs us that the children of legionary soldiers were allowed to inherit after their fathers.

> Fr. B ctr., ll. 21–24: ἔξεστι δὲ καὶ τοὺς | ἐν λεγεῶ]νι στρατευομένους κληρονομεῖσθαι ὑπὸ τέ|[κνων. οὐ] τότε γὰρ γείνονται Ῥωμαίων πολεῖται (l. πολῖται), ὅταν | [ἀπολυθ]ῶσι πληρώσαντες τὰ τῆς στρατείας.
>
> It is allowed that children inherit after those who serve in legions. They do not, however, become Roman citizens until they are dismissed from the army having completed their service.

Another land declaration is then mentioned along with the information that the father had died before it was submitted. One final piece of important information is given in the text: the father died before he was released from the army, ll. 30–32: τετελεύτη|[κε δ' ὁ] πατήρ μου μετὰ τὸ ι [(ἔτος)] Δομιτιανοῦ Καί|[σαρος τοῦ κ]υρίου [. .]υν . [. . .] . . ἐπεὶ οἱ τῶν στρατι|[ωτῶν - *ca.* ? -] . ατοι . ν ἀ[πογρά]φονται ι . [.] . α . . .

This would mean that someone had approached Sarapas and his sister claiming that they were not allowed to inherit the estate of Psenamounis *alias* Longinus, possibly arguing that Psenamounis *alias* Longinus had died after his *missio honesta*. As a veteran he would certainly have been a Roman, and as a legionary soldier he would not have transferred Roman citizenship to his children. For this reason, Sarapas wished to demonstrate that his father had died before being released from his service. The phrase ἔξεστι δὲ καὶ τοὺς | [ἐν λεγεῶ]νι στρατευομένους κληρονομεῖσθαι ὑπὸ τέ|[κνων] is not a reference to the *epistula Hadriani*,[71] which was not issued until later, the father died still at the reign of Domitian, neither to *testamentum militis*, because the heirs do not mention any will. It simply illustrates the situation when the privileges did not apply.[71*]

[71] As suggested in the edition, *VBP* IV, p. 66.

[71*] Although in theory only Romans should be recruited to legions, non-Roman recruitment happened often, as illustrated by the discussed text. Such recruits should be given the citizenship at the recruitment, but at the 29th International Congress of Papyrology in Lecce, Dominic Rathbone provided some examples illustrating that it was not always the case (Pompeius Niger: Roman soldiers and citizenship reconsidered). I have heard this paper only after I had finished writing this book, but it changed my interpretation of *VBP* IV 72, which I originally considered to be a reference to *testamentum militis*.

When Roman soldiers were released from their service they regained the privilege of *conubium*. But what happened to children begotten before their fathers were discharged? Were they submitted to the *potestas* of their father and became *legitimi*, or did they remain outside of their father's agnatic family? And what happened to children born of peregrine mothers? There is no simple answer to these questions, because soldiers belonging to different units had a different *status civitatis*. Legionary soldiers were recruited among freeborn Romans, yet it was also possible for peregrines, especially holding local citizenship (*e.g.* of Alexandria), to be enrolled in the legions, chiefly in those periods when the recruitment of Romans was difficult.[72] Praetorians and urban units also recruited Roman citizens.[73] From the time of Claudius, non-Roman auxiliary soldiers and individuals serving in the fleet were granted Roman citizenship at their *missio honesta*.[74] In such cases citizenship was given not only to the soldiers, but also to their children (and perhaps grandchildren), if they were born of peregrine mothers; the soldiers also obtained *ius conubii* for current or future peregrine[75] life partners.[76]

In AD 140, the privilege was limited for auxiliary soldiers: any children born to them during their military service were no longer granted citizenship.[77] Fleet veterans, however, acquired all three privileges – citizen-

[72] See M. Sołek, '*Origo castris* and the local recruitment policy of the Roman army', *Novensia* 26 (2015), pp. 103–115, with further literature.

[73] Only legionary soldiers, however, did not obtain *diplomata* at the end of their service: Phang, *Marriage of Roman Soldiers* (cit. n. 63), pp. 54 & 61.

[74] G. Wesch-Klein, 'Recruits and veterans', [in:] P. Erdkamp (ed.), *A Companion to the Roman Army*, Malden – Oxford – Victoria 2007, pp. 435–450, p. 439.

[75] The *communis opinio* is that wives were not granted with the citizenship: B. Pferdehirt, *Die Rolle des Militärs für den sozialen Aufstieg in der römischen Kaiserzeit*, Bonn 2002, p. 223.

[76] M. Kaser, *Das römische Privatrecht. Erster Abschnitt. Das altrömische, das vorklassische und klassische Recht*, Munich 1971², p. 316.

[77] Yet, centurions and decurions were still granted the citizenship for their children after AD 140: P. Weiss, 'Die vorbildliche Kaiserehe. Zwei Senatsbeschlüsse beim Tod der älteren und der jüngeren Faustina, neue Paradigmen und die Herausbildung des ‹antoninischen› Prinzipats', *Chiron* 38 (2008), pp. 1–466, pp. 34–35. Yet, they had to prove that children were born to them of stabile unions during their service at the army: W. Eck, 'Die Veränderungen in Konstitutionen und Diplomen unter Antoninus Pius', [in:] M.A. Speidel & H. Lieb (eds.), *Militärdiplome. Die Forschungsbeiträge der Berner Gespräche von 2004*, Stuttgart 2007, pp. 87–104, pp. 92–93.

ship, *civitas liberorum* and *conubium* – also after AD 140. Legionaries appear not to have been granted *ius conubii* towards *peregrinae* both before and after AD 140, nor did they obtain the privilege of Roman citizenship for children born to non-Roman mothers.[78] Yet, this rule did not apply to all legionary soldiers: it was possible for those recruited as peregrines to receive both privileges at their discharge.[79]

It remains unclear whether children born during the military service of their fathers – and granted *civitas* at their fathers' discharge – were also made subjects to *patria potestas*. As principal, the decisive moment in determining whether children were legitimate was the time of conception (G. 1.89). Thus, only those conceived in marriage were *legitimi* subjected to *patria potestas*. Yet, soldiers' children might have been a special case. Unfortunately, no texts address this issue directly.

The idea that *missio honesta* did not result automatically in legitimation and had no effect on the familial status of children is suggested in G. 1.57. Gaius claims that some veterans obtain *conubium* with *Latinae* and *peregrinae* whom they marry *post missionem*. In reference to the children, the texts says: *et qui ex eo matrimonio nascuntur, et cives Romani et in potestatem parentum fiunt*. There is no mention of children born during the term of service.

As Sara Elise Phang has observed, another passage from Gaius discussing peregrines acquiring Roman citizenship does not list *missio honesta* among the ways in which a father could acquire *patria potestas* over his children.[80] New Roman citizens could only acquire parental power over previously-born sons through *rescriptum principis*.[81]

[78] S. Waebens, 'Reflecting the "change in AD 140". The veteran categories of the *epikrisis* documents revisited', *Zeitschrift für Papyrologie und Epigraphik* 180 (2012), pp. 267–277, p. 270.

[79] Campbell claimed that at least from the reign of Domitian legionaries had to receive *conubium* and *civitas liberorum*, but Phang argued for the contrary: J.B. Campbell, *The Emperor and the Roman Army: 31 BC – AD 235*, Oxford 1984, p. 440; Phang, *Marriage of Roman Soldiers* (cit. n. 63), pp. 68–75.

[80] G. 1.65–75: Phang, *Marriage of Roman Soldiers* (cit. n. 63), pp. 309–310.

[81] Phang, *Marriage of Roman Soldiers* (cit. n. 63), pp. 310–311. The further part of the Gaian text says that obtaining *potestas* over children was not automatic, but required careful consideration of the Emperor, especially if children were young: *quod ita demum is facit, si causa cognita aestimaverit hoc filiis expedire; diligentius autem exactiusque causam cognoscit de impuberibus absentibusque: et haec ita edicto divi Hadriani significantur*.

G. 1.93: Si peregrinus sibi liberisque suis civitatem Romanam petierit, non aliter filii in potestate eius fiunt, quam si imperator eos in potestatem redegerit (...).

If a peregrine applies for (a grant of) Roman citizenship for him and his children, his children will be under his power no differently than only if the emperor brings them under his power.

Yet, auxiliary soldiers (*peregrini*) acquiring citizenship through *honesta missio* might have been subjects to *leges speciales*. Such *leges speciales* are not mentioned in the sources. Furthermore, the process of claiming *patria potestas* for a child born outside of a recognised union would have required a special privilege, which does not appear in the *diplomata* issued for auxiliary soldiers:

ipsis liberis posterisque eorum civitatem dedit et conubium cum uxoribus quas tunc habuissent cum est civitas iis data aut si qui caelibes essent cum iis quas postea duxissent dumtaxat singuli singulas.

[The emperor] has granted to them, their children and their offspring citizenship and the right of marriage (*conubium*) with the wives they had when citizenship was granted to them, or, if they were unmarried, with those whom they married afterwards, limited to one spouse for each man.[82]

The most probable scenario is, therefore, that these children who received citizenship at the *missio honesta* of their fathers were not submitted to *patria potestas*.[83] The acquisition of paternal status would thus have been a special privilege rather than an automatic condition of legitimacy.

Although the children of soldiers were not recognised as their marital offspring, it is not visible on the descriptive level. Roman children of soldiers often had the *gentilicia* of their fathers, belonged to their *tribus*, and were described with their real filiations.[84] Such descriptive practice was popular in inscriptions throughout the empire:[85] In an epitaph from Inter-

[82] Formula reconstructed and translated by Waebens, 'Reflecting the "change in AD 140"' (cit. n. 78), p. 271.

[83] Pferdehirt, *Die Rolle des Militärs* (cit. n. 75), p. 225.

[84] Phang, *Marriage of Roman Soldiers* (cit. n. 63), p. 312.

[85] See K. Friedl, *Der Konkubinat im kaiserzeitlichen Rom. Von Augustus bis Septimius Severus* [= *Historia – Einzelschriften* XCVIII], Stuttgart 1996, p. 257.

cisca in Panonia, Manilia Crescentia, woman described as *filia naturalis*, bore the gentile name of her father (no. 1726):

> *Alba Regia* II (1970), p. 123, no. 448 = *RIU* V 1242 (Intercisa in Pannonia, AD 150–300): D(is) [M(anibus)] / G(aio) Manil[io ---] / leg(ionis) II Ad(iutricis) na[t(ione) --- domo] / Galatia Anc[yra q(ui) v(ixit) a(nnos) ---] / Manilia Cres[centia (?) filia] / naturalis her[es prima et] / Manilia Nicia [liberta (?) et] / [co]niux sec[unda heres] / [b]ene m[erenti f(aciendum) c(uraverunt)].
>
> To the spirits departed. For well-deserving Caius Manilius ... of the *legio II Adiutrix* of the nation ... from Ancyra in Galatia who lived ... years, Manilia Crescentia, natural daughter and first heir, and Manilia Nicia, freedwoman, wife and second heir, took charge for erecting (this epitaph).

Paternal identification was applied also to children born of peregrine mothers who did therefore not share the *status civitatis* of their father. Such a case is the already mentioned Apronius son of Marcus labelled as *Ἀπρώνιος υἱὸς Μάρκου* | *ἱππέως μητρὸς Κρονοῦτος τῆς* | *Μάρ⟨ων⟩ος* (*SB* XXII 15704, ll. 26–28 [Karanis, after AD 138]), thus described with the regular identification cluster containing the patronym; another is Caius Apolinarius Niger son of Caius Iulius Niger who is discussed later in this chapter (*infra*, p. 220). In other words, children of soldiers were described in the same terms as fully legitimate children, even if they were not. As Sara Elise Phang noted, this phenomenon is easily explained: the children of soldiers were not bastards, but were acknowledged as their father's progeny at the social level. Their fatherlessness was strictly legal.[86] In this respect this group is similar to free children born of slaves.

2.2. *Incest*

Undoubtedly, children born of partners who could not have *conubium* due to close family bonds[87] belonged to the group whose fathers although known were never recognised by law. Prohibited relationships included those between parents and children and between siblings; intimate rela-

[86] PHANG, *Marriage of Roman Soldiers* (cit. n. 63), p. 312.

[87] VOLTERRA, 'Conubium' (cit. n. 41), pp. 296–297.

tionships between first-cousins or between nieces and uncles were regulated differently in various periods of Roman history. Incest applied not only to agnatic relatives, but to anyone related by blood, including slaves if the blood bonds were close enough; in the classical period the prohibition was extended to close relatives by marriage.[88]

In a passage quoted above in Chapter 1, Gaius explained that children born to incestuous couples had the status of *spurii*, they did not belong to the family of their fathers (G. 1.64). Gaius' description is repeated in various sources (*Tit. Ulp.* 5.7; *Col. Leg.* 6.2.1.4; *Ep. Gai* 4.8; I. 1.10.12). As Philippe Moreau noted, until late Antiquity none of them suggest that children born of incestuous union would have had a different (or worse) position than other Romans born out of wedlock.[89] This is confirmed directly in a fragment ascribed to Papinian, who explained that individuals born in the result of incest could become *decuriones*, because the fact that they had come from incest was not their fault.[90] This illustrates that the perception of incest did not translate into the offspring born in such circumstances.

> D. 50.2.6 pr. (Pap. *resp.* 1): Spurii decuriones fiunt: et ideo fieri poterit ex incesto quoque natus: non enim impedienda est dignitas eius qui nihil admisit.
>
> *Spurii* become decurions, and therefore someone born of incest is able to become (a decurion), the dignity is not hindered from a person who has committed nothing.

Although incest among Romans was punished,[91] it was neither penalised nor prohibited for non-Romans in the Empire. The 'endogamous

[88] On the detailed scope of prohibition within time, see P. Moreau, *Incestus et prohibitae nuptiae : conception romaine de l'inceste et histoire des prohibitions matrimoniales pour cause de parenté dans la Rome antique*, Paris 2002, pp. 167–331. The author focused not solely on stable unions, but also referred to affairs of shorter duration.

[89] Moreau, *Incestus et prohibitae nuptiae* (cit. n. 88), p. 363. See, however, B. Rawson, '*Spurii* and the Roman view of illegitimacy', *Antichthon* 23 (1989), pp. 10–41, p. 15; R. Fiori, 'La struttura del matrimonio romano', *Bullettino dell'Istituto di diritto romano "Vittorio Scialoja"* 105 (2011), pp. 197–233, pp. 224–225.

[90] S. Corcoran, 'The sins of the fathers. A neglected constitution of Diocletian on incest', *Journal of Legal History* 21.2 (2000), pp. 1–34, p. 6; Rawson, '*Spurii*' (cit. n. 89), p. 15.

[91] How persons guilty of incest were punished depended on many factors, *i.a.* the period when the incest happened, or whether it was a stable union or an extramarital affair: Moreau, *Incestus et prohibitae nuptiae* (cit. n. 88), pp. 352–353.

marriages' of brother and sister in Roman Egypt – including the union of full siblings – has raised many controversies among scholars, both in regard to their origin[92] and their exact nature.[93] It is certain, however, that such marriages were especially popular among fiscally privileged groups of Egyptians, such as metropolite class,[94] and were recognised by Romans as legitimate unions. This acceptance is well attested in official documents, such as census returns and *epikrisis* documents, in which non-Roman individuals openly declare that their spouse was their sibling. The legal recognition of 'endogamous unions' extended beyond Egypt, into the Near East, and parts of Greece, but obviously applied only to non-Romans.[95] While these customs were tolerated by law, they were despised in Latin literature and associated with barbaric practices.[96]

The provinces would thus have been governed by two different policies: incest among non-Romans was not only tolerated as sexual behaviour, but also produced legitimate offspring, while for Romans it was a punishable offence, yet without negative effects for the offspring. As the *Gnomon of idios logos* attests, Roman incest resulted in the illegitimacy of both the union and its offspring: in paragraph 23 of the version of the *Gnomon* published as *BGU* V 1210, we find not only the general rule prohibiting Romans from marrying their sisters and aunts (while still allowing them to marry the daughters of their brothers), but also a reference to a specific

[92] See J. Mélèze Modrzejewski, *Droit et justice dans le monde grec et hellénistique* [*The Journal of Juristic Papyrology Supplement* X], Warsaw 2010, pp. 368–371, with further literature.

[93] A scholarly discussion arose from an article by Sabine Huebner, who suggested that brother-sister marriages were in fact adoptions of sons-in-law into brides' families. Although intelligent and interesting the hypothesis attracted criticism due to the lack of sources confirming Huebner's interpretation. See, *i.a.*, S. Huebner, 'Brother-sister marriage in Roman Egypt: A curiosity of humankind or a widespread family strategy?' *The Journal of Roman Studies* 97 (2007), pp. 21–49; S. Remijsen & W. Clarysse, 'Incest or adoption? Brother-sister marriage in Roman Egypt revisited', *The Journal of Roman Studies* 98 (2008), pp. 53–61; J. Rowlandson & R. Takahashi, 'Brother-sister marriage and inheritance strategies in Greco-Roman Egypt', *The Journal of Roman Studies* 99 (2009), pp. 104–139.

[94] Bagnall & Frier, *Demography* (cit. n. 52), p. 129: 'Among the metropolitan marriages, some forty percent (17 of 43) are between close kin – more than one marriage in every three'.

[95] Moreau, *Incestus et prohibitae nuptiae* (cit. n. 88), pp. 90–91; Corcoran, 'The sins of the fathers' (cit. n. 90), p. 10.

[96] Moreau, *Incestus et prohibitae nuptiae* (cit. n. 88), pp. 88–89.

case in which Pardalas, a curator of the *idios logos*, confiscated the property of siblings who lived in an incestuous union (*BGU* V 1210, ll. 70–72).[97] The paragraph is certainly proof that incest between Romans was not treated with full severity in Egypt.[98] Such acts of magnanimity could happen also outside Egypt, an example of which is a passage ascribed to Marcellus, D. 23.2.57a: Marc. *ad Pap de adult.* The emperors Marcus Aurelius and Lucius Verus allowed children born to a niece and her maternal uncle who had been ignorant of their blood bonds to 'keep' their legitimate status.[99] It is difficult to determine why some cases received lighter treatment,[100] but it is certain that there was no lenience in regard to unions between children and parents.

Matters were further complicated after the *constitutio Antoniniana*, which granted Roman citizenship to everyone within the empire.[101] Although the papyrological evidence for incest after AD 212 is meagre,[102] it must still have been practiced, as attestations of brother-sister marriages occur occasionally after Caracalla's grant. One of such marriages postdating the *constitutio Antoniniana* comes from the Theognostos *alias* Moros archive from Hermopolis.[103] The marriage was between the archive's last owner, Aurelius Theognostos *alias* Moros, and his sister, Dioskorous. One

[97] Another example of 'sister-brother' union could be *P. Mich.* VIII 465: O. MONTEVECCHI, 'Endogamia e cittadinanza romana in Egitto', *Aegyptus* 59 (1979), pp. 137–144, pp. 142–144.

[98] It is, however, uncertain whether Pardalas restored punishing brother-sister marriages, if contracted by Romans, or to the opposite he reduced the sanction. The interpretation depend on what meaning *μέντοι* had in the second part of the paragraph: S. RICCOBONO, *Gnomon dell'idios logos*, Palermo 1950, pp. 147–149.

[99] MOREAU, *Incestus et prohibitae nuptiae* (cit. n. 88), p. 356.

[100] A. GUARINO, 'Studi sull' "incestum"', *Zeitschrift der Savigny-Stiftung für Rechtsgeschichte RA* 63 (1943), pp. 175–267, p. 245.

[101] In the older literature, there were doubts whether the edict of Caracalla granted the Roman citizenship to Egyptians, but nowadays *communis opinio* is that Egyptians were included to the universal grant. See V. MAROTTA, 'Egyptians and citizenship from the first century AD to the *constitutio Antoniniana*', [in:] L. CECCHET & A. BUSETTO (eds.), *Citizens in the Graeco-Roman World*, Leiden 2017, pp. 172–198.

[102] BAGNALL & FRIER, *Demography* (cit. n. 52), p. 127.

[103] On the archive, see P.J. SIJPESTEIJN, 'Theognostos alias Moros and his family', *Zeitschrift für Papyrologie und Epigraphik* 76 (1989), pp. 213–218; P. VAN MINNEN, *P. Bagnall* 56, pp. 317–319; and the list of texts belonging to the archive TM Arch id: 241 at https://www.trismegistos.org/arch/.

of the documents belonging to the archive is *P. Pintaudi* 42 (Hermopolis, AD 234/5), a receipt of money accepted by a wet-nurse from Theognostos and his sister-wife for nourishing their son, Hermaios (ll. 5–6: ῠἱοῦ [σο]υ Ἑρμ[αίου μητρὸς Δ]ιοσ[κο]ρ̣οῦτο̣[ς ἀδελ]|φῆ[ς σου]). The document was written over twenty years after Caracalla's edict, but the boy is described as the son of his parents, and the mother in turn appears as her husband's sister, even though Dioskorous could not have had *conubium* with her brother under Roman law, nor would their son have been considered legitimate. As we know, however, the filiation should not be interpreted as proof that an individual was born legitimate. The only thing the document attests is that, two decades after Caracalla's edict, a brother and sister considered themselves married and had a son. Whether or not they considered him legitimate is difficult to say, but as they issued a birth registration for him, it seems likely that they did.[104]

Another less certain example comes from AD 223/4, only twelve years after Caracalla's grant. *P. Oxy.* XLIII 3096 is a petition to the *amphodogrammateus* for the correction of an entry in the γραφὴ ἀφηλίκων. The boy whom the petition concerned was entered incorrectly, as the *alias* of the father and papponym had been left apart.

> *P. Oxy.* XLIII 3096, ll. 5–16: ἐπειδὴ ἔμαθον τὸν υἱόν μου | Ἡρᾶν μητρὸς Ταύριος ὁμογνησίας | ἀδελφῆς ἐν τῇ καταχωρισθείσῃ τῷ | διελθόντι β (ἔτει) γραφῇ ἀφηλίκων | ἐν τάξει τρισ⟦ .⟧καιδεκαετῶν (l. τρεισκαιδεκαετῶν) καὶ|τὰ γραφικὴν πλάνην τετάχθαι | Ἡρᾶν Διογένους μητρὸς Ταυσείριος | ὁμογνησίας ἀδελφῆς τοῦ πατρὸς | (δωδεκάδραχμον) ἀπὸ γυμνασίου δέον Ἡρᾶν Διογέ|νους τοῦ κ̣α̣ὶ̣ Π̣α̣υ̣σ̣ε̣ι̣ρ̣ί̣ω̣ν̣ο̣ς̣ Δ̣ι̣ο̣γ̣έ̣|νους μητρὸς Ταύριος ὁμογνησίας | ἀδελφῆς τοῦ πατρό̣ς̣.
>
> Since I have learned that my son Heras, whose mother is Tauris, my full sister, had been entered to the registered list of minors for the last 2nd year in the category of thirteen-year-olds by a scribal error as 'Heras son of Diogenes of the mother Tauseiris, full sister of the father, payer of twelve drachmae from the gymnasion', the needed (description is) 'Heras son of Diogenes *alias* Pauseirion son of Diogenes of the mother Tauris, full sister of the father.

[104] The boy seems to be mentioned in an unpublished child register of AD 234 (P. Lond. 947 [1] k + m): VAN MINNEN, *P. Bagnall* 56, pp. 318–319.

The boy, clearly born of an incestuous union, was recognised as legitimate not only by the parents, but also by the authorities who entered him on the *γραφή ἀφηλίκων*. He was, therefore, entitled to enter the group of *οἱ ἀπὸ τοῦ γυμνασίου*, which suggests that he might have been considered a legitimate child of his father, as perhaps only such children had the access to this group which is discussed in detail in next chapters. The fact that Heras was recognised as legitimate, however, does not help us to prove or disprove that 'brother-sister' relationships were tolerated after AD 212. The boy was accepted to *οἱ ἀπὸ τοῦ γυμνασίου* in the second year of Alexander Severus (AD 222/3),[105] which means he would have been born shortly before Caracalla's edict when, as Orsolina Montevecchi noted, such unions were still perfectly legal.[106] The text proves only that children born to endogamous unions did not lose their legitimate status.

One text which suggests the continuity of incestuous marriages many years after the *constitutio Antoniniana* is *PSI* V 457 (Oxyrhynchos, AD 269), another application for the registration of a boy in the group *οἱ ἀπὸ τοῦ γυμνασίου*. The application, dated over half a century after the universal grant, was submitted by Marcus Aurelius Flavius, for the scrutiny of a nephew born to his sister (ll. 5–6: *ὁ τῆς ὁμογνησίας μου ἀδελφῆς Κοπροῦ[τος] | υἱὸς Μᾶρκος Αὐρήλ(ιος) Φλαύιος Βησαρίωνος*). The boy's father was Besarion, whom Peter Sijpesteijn recognised as the brother of the applicant, which would also make him the brother of his wife.[107] This interpretation is based on the fact that Marcus Aurelius Hermophilos provided for the scrutiny of his nephew, Marcus Aurelius Flavius, the same credentials he had presented at his own scrutiny (ll. 16–17: *ἐμὲ δὲ προσβ(εβηκότα) ἐπ(ικεκρίσθαι) τ[ῷ] α (ἔτει) Δεκ[ίων] | ἐπὶ τ(αῖς) προκ(ειμέναις) ἀποδ(είξεσιν)*).[108] Sijpesteijn explained the difference of papponyms in Besarion and Hermophilos' descriptions (ll. 3 and 13) as the result of a name change or the fact that the grandfather may have had two names.[109] The explanation is not

[105] Commentary to l. 8 in *P. Oxy*. XLIII 3096.

[106] MONTEVECCHI, 'Endogamia e cittadinanza' (cit. n. 97), p. 141.

[107] P.J. SIJPESTEIJN, 'Some remarks on the epicrisis of *οἱ ἀπὸ γυμνασίου* in Oxyrhynchus', *The Bulletin of the American Society of Papyrologists* 13 (1976), pp. 181–190, p. 187.

[108] SIJPESTEIJN, 'Remarks on the epicrisis' (cit. n. 107), p. 185.

[109] SIJPESTEIJN, 'Remarks on the epicrisis' (cit. n. 107), p. 186.

convincing, especially as studies on double names have developed significantly since it was first proposed.[110]

The common credentials nonetheless suggest that Besarion and Hermophilos would have been brothers. Therefore, either the declaration by Hermophilos that credentials were the same or the papponym of either of Besarion or Hermophilos is incorrect. The former solution was postulated by Orsolina Montevecchi. The document might have been a copy for the family archive and could have contained credentials for the maternal side, or been based on an incorrect pattern.[111] It is perhaps easier to assume a mistake in the papponym as Sijpesteijn did.

If the young man presented for *epikrisis* was indeed born of siblings, it is not stated openly in the document. We should not, in any event, be surprised that incestuous unions continued to exist in Egypt and other Eastern provinces after AD 212, as Diocletian took strong measures against them (discussed in the final chapter). It is, however, impossible to measure or even estimate how often such unions occurred or, how they were viewed by local authorities.[112] Nevertheless, the document should not be interpreted as proof that the Romans were accepting of such practices, but rather the opposite.

CONCLUSION

Children born of couples consisting of one partner who could not marry – either temporarily (soldiers) or at all (slaves) – or of parents too closely related are well attested in papyri. Legally they were of the same standing as those who had no father whatsoever, but their social position was different as they did have fathers in reality. This is visible even at a descriptive level. Perhaps the best label for this category of children is 'extramarital',

[110] Y. Broux, *Double Names and Elite Strategy in Roman Egypt* [= *Studia Hellenistica* LIV], Leuven 2015, esp. pp. 107–151.

[111] O. Montevecchi, 'PSI V 457. Un caso di endogamia o una semplificazione del formulario?', *Aegyptus* 73 (1993), pp. 49–55.

[112] W. Uxkull-Gyllenband, *Der Gnomon des Idios Logos. II. Der Kommentar*, Berlin 1934 (= *BGU* V.1), p. 38.

as they were born of parents who could not marry. Being extramarital also resulted in illegitimate status. Obviously, the cases discussed here were not the only kinds which could produce extramarital children. Roman law recognised other situations in which there could be no marriage, such as the prohibition imposed on tutors and their closest agnates from marrying their female wards, or the limitations of the *leges Iuliae*.[113] Such unions are, alas, not visible in the surviving material from Roman Egypt.

[113] See, *e.g.*, C. Castello, *In tema di matrimonio e concubinato nel mondo romano*, Milan 1940; E. Nardi, 'Sui divieti matrimoniali delle leggi augustee', *Studia et documenta historiae et iuris* 7 (1941), pp. 112–146; B. Rawson, 'Family life among the lower classes at Rome in the first two centuries of the Empire', *Classical Philology* 61.2 (1966), pp. 71–83; R. Astolfi, *La lex Iulia et Papia*, Milan 1996⁴, pp. 103–109; L. Desanti, 'Costantino e il matrimonio fra tutore e pupilla', *Bullettino dell'Istituto di diritto romano "Vittorio Scialoja"* 89 (1986), pp. 443–463; Th. McGinn, *Prostitution, Sexuality, and the Law in Ancient Rome*, Oxford 1998; S. Treggiari, *Roman Marriage. Iusti Coniuges from the Time of Cicero to the Time of Ulpian*, Oxford 1991; Fiori, 'La struttura' (cit. n. 89).

CHAPTER THREE

THE FATHERLESS AND THEIR STATUS

IN THE PRESENT CHAPTER we will examine the acquisition of status by the fatherless; the term, in this case will refer both to those who were fatherless in the legal and social sense, as well as those individuals discussed in the previous chapter who were fatherless in the legal sense despite having fathers who were acknowledged at the social level. The rules of status acquisition for children born of couples of different *status civitatis* will be discussed separately in Chapter 4.

Before AD 212, the inhabitants of the Roman Empire were not a homogenous group governed by a single set of laws, but were divided into Romans and peregrines. In Roman Egypt, the latter group was further divided into *astoi* and *Aigyptioi*. Such a division was not exclusive to Egypt, as local citizenship was recognised by Romans throughout the Roman world. Each group was allowed to follow different sets of rules in matters concerning family, personal status or succession, but even within those groups certain issues (*e.g.* marriage) could be handled in different ways. Rules were often based on past traditions and were applied on a case by case basis.[1] It is important to note that 'peregrine' rules were applied by Roman officials in Egypt – even, as in the case of the incest ban, if they opposed the basic

[1] On the status of 'peregrine law' in Egypt and reasons why it was applied at all in Roman times and summary of the scholarly discussions thereof, see J.L. ALONSO, 'The status of peregrine law in Egypt: "customary law" and legal pluralism in the Roman Empire', *The Journal of Juristic Papyrology* 43 = *Special Issue. Papyrology AD 2013* (2013), pp. 351–404.

principles of Roman law – yet they were not applied equally in every case.[2] If we are to establish the rules applying to status acquisition, each group of fatherless individuals must be examined separately; only then can we determine whether there were separate sets of rules governing *status civitatis*, or whether there existed a uniform pattern.

1. ROMANS

Under Roman law, children born of marriage were entitled to the status of their father, albeit with exceptions (discussed in the next chapter). This rule is expressed briefly in the *Tituli ex corpore Ulpiani* and explains that the status of children depended on marriage:[3]

> *Tit. Ulp.* 5.8: Conubio interveniente liberi semper patrem sequuntur; non interveniente conubio matris conditioni accedunt (...).
>
> If there is *conubium*, children always follow (their) father; if there is no *conubium*, they take the mother's status.

The rule that children could only follow paternal status when *conubium* existed between the parents is also attested outside of the legal sources (Cic., *Top.* 3.62, or Isid., *Et.* 9.21),[4] suggesting that fatherless individuals born to Roman women followed the maternal status, and that such children were defined as the *spurii* of their mothers (G. 1.64 and *Tit. Ulp.* 5.7, *Col. Leg.* 6.2.1.4, *Ep. Gai* 4.8). This is also well attested in the *epikrisis* deeds discussed in Chapter 1.

The rule appears also in Gaius. After a discussion of the *lex* regulating the status of children born to a free father who was unaware his partner

[2] Alonso, 'The status of peregrine law in Egypt' (cit. n. 1), pp. 352–353.

[3] E. Volterra, 'L'acquisto della cittadinanza romana e il matrimonio del peregrino', [in:] E. Volterra, *Scritti giuridici*, vol. II, Naples 1992, pp. 257–276 (reprinted from *Studi in onore di Enrico Redenti*, vol. II, Milan 1951, pp. 403–442), p. 262.

[4] E. Volterra, 'La nozione giuridica del *conubium*', [in:] *Scritti giuridici*, vol. II, Naples 1992, pp. 277–320 (reprinted from *Studi in memoria di Emilio Albertario*, vol. II, Milan 1950, pp. 348–384), pp. 298–299.

was a slave (G. 1.85), and of children born to a free woman and a slave belonging to someone else (G. 1.86: *supra*), he notes:

> G. 1.87: Quibus autem casibus matris et non patris condicionem sequitur qui nascitur, iisdem casibus in potestate eum patris, etiamsi is civis Romanus sit, non esse plus quam manifestum est.
>
> It is abundantly clear that in those cases in which a child takes its mother's status and not its father's, the child is not under its father's *potestas* even if the father is a Roman citizen.[5]

The text is problematic. If it is a commentary on the *lex* regarding the children of free individuals and slaves (G. 1.85–86, discussed in Chapter 2),[6] we must assume that G. 1.87 refers to the second part of G. 1.86: *Itaque apud quos talis lex non est, qui nascitur, iure gentium matris condicionem sequitur et ob id liber est*, and is therefore an elaboration of the rule of *ius gentium* stating that children of free mothers follow the status of their mothers. Siro Solazzi, however, argued that G. 1.87 would have applied to Roman women who married a peregrine thinking he was Roman (G. 1.68),[7] which is what the next sentence in the passage says:

> Et ideo superius rettulimus quibusdam casibus per errorem non iusto contracto matrimonio senatum intervenire et emendare vitium matrimonii eoque modo plerumque efficere, ut in potestatem patris filius redigatur.[8]
>
> This is why we explained above that in certain cases where, owing to some mistake, a civil marriage fails to be contracted, the senate intervenes to cure the defect in the marriage and in most cases by so doing causes the son to be brought into his father's *potestas*.[9]

[5] Tr. F. de Zulueta in: *The Institutes of Gaius. Part I. Text with Critical Notes and Translation*, Oxford 1946 with minor modifications.

[6] L. Arends Olsen, *La femme et l'enfant dans les unions illégitimes à Rome. L'évolution du droit jusqu'au début de l'Empire*, Bern 1999 , p. 230.

[7] S. Solazzi, 'Glosse a Gaio I', [in:] *Studi in onore di Salvatore Riccobono*, vol. I, Palermo 1936, pp. 73–191 (reprinted in *Scritti di diritto romano*, vol. VI, Naples 1972, pp. 153–267).

[8] Solazzi himself considered this part of the text be a post-Gaian emendation: Solazzi, 'Glosse a Gaio. I' (cit. n. 7), pp. 211–212.

[9] Tr. F. de Zulueta (cit. n. 5).

The passage refers again to the rule that only children begotten in marriage could follow the status of their father. In the case of a marriage contracted in ignorance between a Roman woman and a peregrine, the Roman citizenship of children could be saved by granting it also to the father (G. 1.68). So long as we do not attempt to maintain a distinction between the acquisition of freedom and citizenship, G. 1.87 may be interpreted as a commentary on both the *lex* concerning the children of slaves and free men, and on people of different *status civitatis*; for Romans *status civitatis* and *status libertatis* were inseparable.[10]

The passages from G. 1.85–86 constitute a commentary to the *lex* which introduced exceptions whereby some children born of free and slave unions could follow the paternal status despite the general rule that children should always follow their mother in cases where there was no marriage. G. 1.85 begins with the error by a free spouse about the *status libertatis* of a slave 'wife', which would not affect the status of children, as they would simply have been slaves belonging to their mother's owner; the *lex*, however, introduces an exception to the general rule, in which male offspring are considered free if the father was mistakenly convinced that his 'spouse' was free. The same *lex* introduces another exception: children did not follow the status of their mother, if she had them with a slave belonging to someone else. An exception to this exception could be made if the mother had taken a slave as her 'spouse' in ignorance; in this case her children remained free, thus following the general pattern of status acquisition. In the following passage (G. 1.86), the general rule is asserted with reference to those to whom the exceptions of the *lex* did not apply: these individuals followed the maternal status, *iure gentium matris condicionem sequitur*. In G. 1.87 the general rule is explained once again, this time in the context of *patria potestas*, which applied to both freedom and citizenship (unfree fathers could not hold *patria potestas*, and their children could not therefore follow their status). The three sections (G. 1.85–87) may thus be understood as referring to a single general rule according to which children would acquire the status of their mothers in cases where there was no *conubium* between their parents, and explains several possible exceptions to this rule which could result in changes to either the *status libertatis* or *status civitatis*.

[10] E. Volterra, 'Manomissione e cittadinanza', [in:] *Studi in onore di U.E. Paoli*, Florence 1956, pp. 695–716, pp. 697–699.

As we saw in the previous chapter, the general rule by which *status libertatis* was acquired from mothers applied to both Romans and non-Romans and belonged to *ius gentium*. If the rule of G. 1.87 is the same rule expressed in G. 1.86, illustrated in more general terms, we must understand it as referring to a concept wider than the framework of the Roman family. If this is true, the passage may in fact refer to the rule of *ius gentium*, which is referred to directly in G. 1.86.

The notion that this rule applied to single mothers of peregrine status is confirmed in G. 1.90, in which the status of children born to a woman who had lost her citizenship is explained: children born of a marriage from before *capitis deminutio* were Romans, *si vero volgo conceperit, peregrinum ex ea nasci*.

1.1. *Status vs. Roman onomastics*

In the case of fatherless individuals, maternal status acquisition was not limited to citizenship. It is visible also at the level of Latin onomastics. In earlier literature, it was rather accepted that Roman children born out of wedlock were always given the maternal *nomen gentilicium*.[11] Indeed, a number of sources would appear to confirm his statement,[12] but it is obviously not the only possible scenario. On the one hand, not every legally fatherless individual was given the *nomen* of their mother; on the other hand, not every person bearing their mother's *nomen* was born out of wedlock.

Studies on individuals bearing the maternal *nomina gentilicia* have been recently conducted by Małgorzata Krawczyk[13] and Tuomo Nuorluoto.[14] The two authors, having investigated two different sets of sources, arrived

[11] *E.g.* J.B. Mispoulet, 'Du nom et de la condition de l'enfant naturel romain', *Nouvelle revue historique de droit français et étranger* 9 (1885), pp. 15–63, p. 60; H. Thylander, *Étude sur l'épigraphie latine : date des inscriptions – noms et dénomination latine – noms et origine des personnes*, Lund 1952, pp. 90–91.

[12] See www.romanbastards.wpia.uw.edu.pl, *s.v.* 'maternal *nomen*'.

[13] M. Krawczyk, 'Paternal onomastical legacy vs. illegitimacy in Roman epitaphs', [in:] M. Nowak, A. Łajtar & J. Urbanik (eds.), *Tell Me Who You Are. Labelling Status in the Graeco-Roman World*, Warsaw 2017, pp. 107–128.

[14] T. Nuorluoto, 'Emphasising matrilineal ancestry in a patrilineal system: Maternal name preference in the Roman world', [in:] *Tell Me Who You Are* (cit. n. 13), pp. 257–281.

at two different (although not mutually exclusive) conclusions. Nuorluoto demonstrated that, in certain cases, the maternal *nomen* was given to the children of perfectly legitimate marriages.[15] The main factor responsible for choosing the maternal *nomen*, especially for a daughter, would have been the considerably higher prominence of the mother and her family, than that of the father.[16] It is not therefore surprising that the practice is attested mostly in the highest strata of Roman society, *i.e. ordo senatorius*, for whom familial standing was of undoubted importance.

Krawczyk, whose focus was on children bearing the paternal *cognomina*, analysed over a hundred epitaphs from the city of Rome and distinguished a number of sources in which the maternal *nomen* was indeed a sign of illegitimacy. She further observed that a significant portion of those cases refer to children born to a freedwoman or, less frequently, a freeborn woman and a slave.[17] Indeed, in cases of children born to slave fathers or those raised by single mothers, there is no one apart from the mother whose *nomen* a child could acquire, especially if there was no known false *nomen gentilicium* for bastard children. Such children would therefore have borne the maternal *nomina*, specifically the *nomina gentilicia* of either the mother's father or patron.[18] Yet it does not necessarily illuminate the model of illegitimacy in the Roman Empire, nor the connection between law and onomastic practice.[19]

Clear instances of people born out of wedlock bearing the paternal *gentilicia* are fewer. This is because inscriptions provide only limited information on prosopography, while in order to be certain that a person

[15] Observed already by H. Solin, 'Name', G. Schöllgen, H. Brakmann, S. de Blaauw, T. Fuhrer *et al.* (eds.), *Reallexikon für Antike und Christentum. Sachwörterbuch zur Auseinandersetzung des Christentums mit der antiken Welt*, vol. XXV, Stuttgart 2013, coll. 723–795, col. 761.

[16] The most illustrious example studied by Nuorluoto is Poppaea Sabina, wife of emperor Nero. Her father was T. Ollius, but she assumed the *nomen* of her maternal grandfather, Poppaeus Sabinus, holder of highest offices and honours: Nuorluoto, 'Emphasising matrilineal ancestry' (cit. n. 14), pp. 265–266.

[17] Krawczyk, 'Paternal onomastical legacy' (cit. n. 13), pp. 110–112.

[18] Yet, sometimes it could be difficult to determine whether a child indeed had a maternal *nomen* or they were freedmen themselves, see Krawczyk, 'Paternal onomastical legacy' (cit. n. 13), *passim*.

[19] Krawczyk, 'Paternal onomastical legacy' (cit. n. 13), pp. 115–116.

with a paternal *nomen* was legally fatherless, we would need an additional description, as *sp() f()*,[20] or information that the parents were not married. This is obvious when the father was a slave or a soldier, but becomes more problematic if the father was free or a freed civilian. Only occasionally do the inscriptions allow us to understand that parents were not married.

This appears to have been the case in a first century inscription from Lombardia (Scarpizzolo) discussed by Mispoulet:

> *CIL* I 4153 = *Inscr. Ital.* X 960: P(ublius) Mucius Biraci f(ilius) / sibi et / Nevia⟨e⟩ Sp(uri) f(iliae) / Tertullae concubin(ae) / et Muciae Verae f(iliae) / t(estamento) f(ieri) i(ussit).
>
> Publius Mucius son of Biracus ordered in his will (this epitaph) to be made for him, and Nevia Tertulla daughter of Spurius, his concubine, and Mucia Vera, his daughter.

Jean Baptiste Mispoulet[21] and Susan Treggiari[22] interpreted Mucia Vera to be the legitimate daughter of Publius Mucius' previous marriage, on the understanding that only legitimate children bore the *nomina* of their fathers. Yet, Publius Mucius might have been a soldier, as Andreas Kakoschke noted that the filiation, *Biraci filius*, derives from the *cognomen*, and that the form 'Pränomen + Gentiliz + cognominale Filiation' was characteristic for legionary soldiers from Northern Italy in the first century AD.[23] If Publius Mucius indeed served in the army and had his daughter born after his enrolment, Mucia Vera was legally fatherless and the paternal *nomen* would be the sign of actual paternity, not the legal one. Such a practice is attested also outside of Italy, which we discussed in Chapter 2. Some texts discussed in Chapter 1 attest individuals described as *sp() f()* with different *nomina* than their mothers, which suggests that they might have had the parental *nomina* too. All the above illustrates the relationship between

[20] As in *CIL* VI.2 8148 *&* 15007 discussed in Chapter 1.

[21] Mispoulet, 'Du nom et de la condicion' (cit. n. 11), p. 37.

[22] S. Treggiari, 'Concubinae', *Papers of the British School at Rome* 49 (1981), pp. 59–81, p. 69.

[23] A. Kakoschke, 'Annotationes Epigraphicae VII. Zu einigen Inschriften aus den römischen Provinzen Germania inferior und Germania superior', *Frankfurter elektronische Rundschau zur Altertumskunde* 34 (2017), pp. 1–29, p. 18, esp. n. 67 (https://doi.org/10.21248/fera.32.191).

status acquisition and onomastics existed, but the onomastics should not be treated as a certain marker of illegitimacy or legitimacy.

2. STATUS ACQUISITION: NON-ROMANS

The question we must now ask is whether the rule concerning status acquisition by fatherless individuals – in which the child follows their mother's status – applied to non-Romans too. We shall also ask whether the rule applied to all groups of *peregrini* indiscriminately – which would suggests that the rules of status acquisition for non-Romans were provided by Romans as *ius gentium* and existed independently from local laws and concepts – or if it depended on the group of people to which it was applied. The latter seems more probable especially in regard to local citizenships in the East predating the Roman period, or to groups framed on institutions which had existed before the Romans arrived, such as the gymnasial group.

We do not need to prove that a child born out of wedlock to a single Egyptian mother became a simple peregrine; however the status of children born to fiscally privileged groups of Egyptians, and to citizens of *poleis*, could be more problematic. The Egyptians who constituted the most numerous group among inhabitants of Roman Egypt, were not fully homogenous in the legal sense. Among them, some paid a lower rate of *laographia* and were entitled to privileges such as the corn dole. Their position reminds to some extent *status civitatis* in regard to rules concerning its acquisition.[24] Thus, all these groups should be discussed in separate sections.

2.1. *Astoi*

Citizens of Alexandria, Ptolemais Hermiou, Naukratis, and Antinoopolis enjoyed a different *status civitatis* in Egypt than the *peregrini Aegyptii*;

[24] Exact standards and privileged rates of *laographia* in particular nomes, see A. Monson, 'Late Ptolemaic capitation taxes and the poll tax in Roman Egypt', *The Bulletin of the American Society of Papyrologists* 51 (2014), pp. 127–160, tab. 6 at p. 156.

Roman citizenship was granted to the latter on the condition that they first obtain local citizenship of either Alexandria or one of the other *poleis*.[25] Citizens were fully exempt from *laographia*, and enjoyed other privileges such as exemption from liturgies in the *chora*.[26] *Astoi* were also subject to different sets of laws; yet, these laws were not the result of an on-going legislative process.[27] Nor were they produced in the same way and at the same time. Thus they differed considerably in content. Except for Antinoopolis, the laws of the *poleis* dated back to Hellenistic times or even earlier,[28] were based on laws of different Greek poleis and further developed to some extent independently by each of the three *poleis* in the Ptolemaic period.[29] Thus, the best would be to study each city separately.

Our sources for citizenship of Alexandria, Ptolemais Hermiou and Naukratis are insufficient to provide a full picture of status acquisition for any of them, and the majority of information regarding the status of citizens in Roman Egypt comes from the *Gnomon of idios logos* which refers to *astoi*[30] and only rarely to Alexandrians, which suggests that Roman admin-

[25] A dominant opinion is that Egyptians could not become Romans, if they had not acquired a citizenship of one of the *poleis* before. See D. Delia, *Alexandrian Citizenship during the Roman Principate* [= *American Classical Studies* XXIII], Atlanta 1991, pp. 39–45; more recently V. Marotta, 'Egyptians and citizenship from the first century AD to the *constitutio Antoniniana*', [in:] L. Cecchet & A. Busetto (eds.), *Citizens in the Graeco-Roman World. Aspects of Citizenship from the Archaic Period to AD 212*, Leiden – Boston 2017, pp. 172–198, who has suggested that the status of Egyptians would have been comparable to *peregrini dediticii Aeliani* before late second century (pp. 187–190).

[26] Yet the tax privileges are attested directly only for Alexandria and Antinoopolis, see A. Jördens, *Statthalterliche Verwaltung in der römischen Kaiserzeit. Studien zum praefectus Aegypti* [= *Historia – Einzelschriften* CLXXV], Stuttgart 2009, pp. 331–338.

[27] J. Mélèze Modrzejewski, *Droit et justice dans le monde grec et hellénistique* [= *The Journal of Juristic Papyrology Supplement* X], Warsaw 2010, pp. 114–115.

[28] Naukratis was funded much earlier, in the 7th c. BC, but the status of *polis* it could have only since the Ptolemaic period: J. Mélèze Modrzejewski, 'Bibliographie de papyrologie juridique: 1972–1982 (III.3)', *Archiv für Papyrusforschung* 32 (1986), pp. 97–147, p. 121.

[29] J. Mélèze-Modrzejewski, *Loi et coutume dans l'Égypte grecque et romaine* [= *The Journal of Juristic Papyrology Supplement* XXI], Warsaw 2014, pp. 88–89.

[30] In previous scholarship, the *astoi* from the *Gnomon* were understood to mean Alexandrians, but since Diana Delia's monograph on Alexandrian citizenship, it has become accepted that the term applied in the *Gnomon* refers more generally to citizens of the *poleis*. See Delia, *Alexandrian Citizenship* (cit. n. 25), pp. 13–20.

istration perceived the matter of status uniform for all *cives peregrini* with some special regulations for Alexandrians. While much of the information in this section refers specifically to Alexandrians, the conclusions may be understood to apply to citizens of all three *poleis*.

It was assumed that the laws of Alexandria were based on Athenian ones, thus the citizenship was granted only to the children of married Alexandrians.[31] This is supported by the admission procedure which was focused on ancestry and membership. The ordinary procedure consisted of the following steps.

Since early Ptolemaic times, the acquisition of citizenship had been closely related to the institution of *ephebeia*.[32] Access to the *ephebeia* involved *eiskrisis*,[33] a personal examination of candidates which took place in the Great Serapeum and for which written proof of status was required.[34] Young men who submitted to *eiskrisis* and went through one year of *ephebeia*[35] were then further scrutinised to become Alexandrians[36] which procedure was carried out by the prefect of Egypt[37] and ended with

[31] P.M. Meyer, 'Papyrus Cattaoui. II. Kommentar', *Archiv für Papyrusforschung* 3 (1906), pp. 67–105, p. 85.

[32] Ephebate and citizenship of Alexandria were connected from the Ptolemaic times, as it is explicit from the letter of Claudius to the Alexandrians, *P. Lond.* VI 1912 = *C. Pap. Jud.* II 153 = *Sel. Pap.* II 212 (Alexandria, AD 41). The chronology is discussed in detail in: A.S. Chankowski, *L'éphébie hellénistique. Étude d'une institution civique dans les cités grecques des îles de la Mer Égée et de l'Asie Mineure*, Paris 2010, pp. 174–179, with further literature. Perhaps ephebate existed also in Ptolemais and Naukratis already in the Hellenistic times: *ibidem*, p. 180.

[33] C.A. Nelson, *Status Declarations in Roman Egypt* [= *American Studies in Papyrology* XIX], Amsterdam 1979, pp. 47–59.

[34] The procedure is reconstructed in: J.E.G. Whitehorne, 'Becoming an Alexandrian citizen', *Comunicazioni* 4 (2001), pp. 25–34.

[35] Wolff claimed that men born of *engraphos gamos* became citizens when they turned 14 years old; although they needed to undergo *eiskrisis* they did not need to complete the *ephebeia* (*P. Flor.* III 382 = *P. Flor.* I 57; ll. 67–91 = *W. Chr.* 143 [Hermopolites, AD 233]): H.J. Wolff, *Written and Unwritten Marriages in Hellenistic and Postclassical Roman Law* [= *American Philological Association Philological Monographs* IX], Haverford, PA 1939, pp. 42–43.

[36] A. Bowman & D. Rathbone, 'Cities and administration in Roman Egypt', *The Journal of Roman Studies* 82 (1992), pp. 107–127, pp. 114–115.

[37] A. Jördens, 'Status and citizenship', [in:] C. Riggs (ed.), *The Oxford Handbook of Roman Egypt*, Oxford 2012, pp. 247–259, p. 252.

enrolling to demes and tribes.[38] Only exceptionally the citizenship was granted to adults.[39]

The documentation referring to *ephebeia* and the acquisition of Alexandrian citizenship concerns indeed young men born of Alexandrian marriages (or marriages between an Alexandrian and *aste* of another polis).[40] Furthermore, there are no surviving examples of Alexandrians described directly as fatherless. While there are arguments against the idea that individuals born out of wedlock were excluded from Alexandrian citizenship, they are not especially strong, based on two uncertain cases and some observations regarding the system by which Alexandrian status was acquired in the Roman period.

The most important case comes from the famous *Cattaoui Papyrus* (col. IV, l. 16 – col. V, l. 26). It concerns Octavius Valens, a soldier and Alexandrian, who had at least three sons during his military service, all born to a certain Cassia Secunda. In AD 142, he submitted an application for the scrutiny of his eldest, but the request was rejected by the prefect, C. Valerius Eudaimon, who argued that:

1. the boy was born during his father's military service, and thus could not be legitimate, col. V, ll. 4–6: *ἐξερχομέ|νου εἴτε ἐν τάξει εἴτε ἐν σπείρᾳ εἴτε [ἐ]ν εἴλῃ ὁ γεννη|θεὶς οὐ δύναται εἶναι νόμιμος υἱός*;

2. because the boy was not the legitimate son of an Alexandrian, he could not become an Alexandrian himself, col. V, ll. 6–8: *μὴ ὢν δὲ | νόμιμος υἱὸς τοῦ πατρὸς ὄντος Ἀλεξανδρέως Ἀλε|ξανδρεὺς οὐ δύναται εἶναι.*

[38] Yet, Bowman and Rathbone proposed that *ephebeia* was the way through which Alexandrians were admitted to the gymnasial group, which consisted only of some Alexandrians: BOWMAN & RATHBONE, 'Cities and administration' (cit. n. 36), pp. 113 & 115.

[39] The most frequently discussed case is that of Harpokras, an Egyptian freedman, for whom Pliny the Younger petitioned for Roman citizenship (Plin., *Ep.* 10.5, 6, 7, 10). As Harpokras had to become a citizen of Alexandria before he could become Roman, he was granted Alexandrian citizenship by Trajan. Yet the letters between Pliny and Trajan suggest that this was far from standard procedure (Plin., *Ep.* 10.7: *Civitatem Alexandrinam secundum institutionem principum non temere dare proposui*). It is also clear that certain individuals, including the champions in *agones*, could be rewarded citizenship by the city itself, but the procedure is unattested: DELIA, *Alexandrian Citizenship* (cit. n. 25), p. 29.

[40] DELIA, *Alexandrian Citizenship* (cit. n. 25), p. 54.

The latter sentence suggests that having an Alexandrian father would have been crucial for becoming a citizen. This is, however, not so obvious. Scholarly literature regarding this case tends to focus on the status of the boy's parents, Octavius Valens and Cassia Secunda. Octavius Valens was clearly an Alexandrian, he might have been a Roman.[41] The *Cattaoui Papyrus* offers no information about Octavius Valens' unit; it says only that he served in a cohort, ἐν σπείρᾳ, which could refer to either the *cohors* of legion or *auxilia*.[42] His *duo nomina* suggest that the more possible interpretation is *auxilia*,[43] which suggest that Octavius Valens was only an Alexandrian. We need to remember, however, that *P. Catt.* is not an official list of soldiers, so the *praenomen* might be simply omitted in the text.

Octavius Valens' life partner, Cassia Secunda, is also described with Latin *duo nomina*, which is enough, as women did not have *praenomina*. She had a proper Roman name[44] – her *cognomen* was not Greek – and it does not seem unreasonable to propose that she was indeed a Roman.[45] Yet she is often identified as an Alexandrian in the scholarly literature.[46] According to Sara Phang, if she had been a Roman, the prefect would have referred not only to

[41] A 'double citizenship' was well-known in the Empire before AD 212. It meant that a person held both Roman and local citizenship at the same time: J.A. CROOK, *Law and Life of Rome, 90 BC – AD 212*, Ithaca 1984, pp. 38–40. On the conflict of laws in regard to double citizenship, see V. MAROTTA, 'Doppia cittadinanza e pluralità degli ordinamenti. La Tabula Banasitana e le linee 7–9 del Papiro di Giessen 40, col I', *Archivio giuridico Filippo Serafini* 236 (2016), pp. 461–491, pp. 470–486, with further literature.

[42] Even if he was not a Roman before his recruitment, as one of *epikrimenoi* he could have been a legionary soldier. See P. SCHUBERT, *P. Diog.*, pp. 19–20.

[43] Mann claimed that Octavius Valens would have been an auxiliary soldier because registers of Roman citizens from the early Principate contain *praenomina*, while the lists who name people with *duo nomina* are lists of auxiliary or fleet soldiers: J.C. MANN, 'Name forms of recipients of diplomas', *Zeitschrift für Papyrologie und Epigraphik* 139 (2002), pp. 227–234.

[44] Indeed soldiers of auxiliary units and fleet took or were rather given Roman *nomina* despite of not having the citizenship yet. It is, however, different from taking a Roman name and pretending to be a Roman acting before Roman officials. See MAROTTA, 'Egyptians and citizenship' (cit. n. 25), pp. 183–186 & 189, n. 75.

[45] J. LESQUIER, *L'armée romaine d'Égypte d'Auguste à Dioclétien* [= *Mémoires publiés par les membres de l'Institut français d'archéologie orientale du Caire* XLI], Cairo 1918, p. 188, n. 1.

[46] *E.g.* MANN, 'Name forms' (cit. n. 43), p. 227; S.E. PHANG, *The Marriage of Roman Soldiers (13 BC – AD 235): Law and Family in the Imperial Army* [= *Columbia Studies in the Classical Tradition* XXIV], Leiden – Cologne 2001, p. 28.

the ban on soldiers' marriages, but also to the *lex Minicia* in his justification for why the boy could not be recognised as an Alexandrian citizen.[47]

This argument does not stand up to scrutiny. According to the *lex Minicia* discussed in the next chapter, if a Roman female married a peregrine the children were always peregrines, regardless of whether or not there was *conubium* (G. 1.77); the *lex Minicia* ruled that children of these unions should follow the lower status (G. 1.78). This means that the children of Octavius Valens and Cassia Secunda would have been Alexandrians, thus the opposite of what Phang suggested.[48] In fact, the *lex Minicia* would not have been relevant to the case of Octavius Valens' sons, because there was no marriage between Octavius Valens and Cassia Secunda under either civil law or *ius gentium*. Octavius Valens was a soldier and soldiers were not allowed to marry; not only would they have been prevented from contracting a marriage under *ius civile*, but there could not have been any marriage whatsoever. The *lex Minicia* did not apply to the children of soldiers. Nor did the status of the mother matter to the prefect: Octavius Valens requested status for his son, but the son could not follow the paternal status as he was not legitimate.[49] This is exactly what the prefect said to justify his decision.

When examining the cases preserved in the *Cattaoui Papyrus*, we must remember that they were collected and copied specifically to serve as precedents against Tertia Drusilla whose opponent wish to prove that she could neither marry a soldier nor produce legitimate offspring for him. The seven cases were thus assembled to illustrate that, in Roman law, marrying a soldier resulted in neither a 'mixed union' nor a 'quasi-marriage', but in no marriage at all, and that soldiers had no legal rights towards their children: they could transfer neither their status – including Alexandrian citizenship – nor their property to their child, except in a will.

A similar scenario is preserved in *BGU* VII 1662 (AD 182), a *homologia* confirmation:[50] Longinia Nemesilla paid some money on behalf of her

[47] Phang, *Marriage of Roman Soldiers* (cit. n. 46), p. 28.

[48] Which Meyer already noted: Meyer, 'Cattaoui. Kommentar' (cit. n. 31), p. 86.

[49] Meyer, 'Cattaoui. Kommentar' (cit. n. 31), p. 85.

[50] H.-A. Rupprecht, *Studien zur Quittung im Recht der gräco-ägyptischen Papyri* [= *Münchener Beiträge zur Papyrusforschung und antiken Rechtsgeschichte* LVII], Munich 1972, p. 52.

underage sons, heirs to their father, Marcus Valerius Turbo. The sum was paid by virtue of the bequest made by him in favour of his another daughter, Kyrilla. Kyrilla was an *aste* (ll. 2 and 12: *Κυρίλλα θυγάτηρ Μάρκου Οὐαλερίου Τούρβωνος ἀστή*) married to an Alexandrian (l. 12); other family members – Longinia Nemesilla, her husband and Kyrilla's father, Marcus Valerius Turbo, and his sons, Marci Valerii Montanus and Longinus *alias* Numisianus – were all Romans.[51]

The editors of *BGU* VII recognised Marcus Valerius Turbo as a veteran on the basis of other three texts: *BGU* VII 1565, 1574, and 1692 = *FIRA* III 3 = *CPL* 152.[52] Marcus Valerius Turbo first appears in AD 144 as a father registering his legitimate son Marcus Valerius Maximus, born to Antonia Casullute (*BGU* VII 1692). In *BGU* VII 1565, dated to AD 169, Marcus Valerius Turbo is labelled *στρατιώτης* (l. 6). Finally, in *BGU* VII 1574 dated to AD 176/7, Marcus Valerius Turbo appears again but is labelled neither as a soldier nor a veteran.

We cannot be certain whether or not Marcus Valerius Turbo who appears in these four texts was in fact the same person,[53] but it seems likely. All four texts come from the same excavation season in Philadelphia and are dated within the time-span of a single lifetime: in AD 144 M. Valerius Turbo became a father, and by AD 182 he was already dead. If Marcus Valerius Turbo was indeed enrolled in the army, this would have happened after AD 144, the year when he submitted the *professio* for his legitimate child. Furthermore, if he was able to produce a *legitimus* he must have been Roman before his recruitment. If he had been recruited shortly after the *professio*, he would have reached the end of his military career by the end of 60s or the beginning of the 70s, which would explain why he is labelled as *στρατιώτης* in *BGU* VII 1565, as well as the lack of this description in *BGU* VII 1574 and 1662. If this reconstruction is correct, it would mean

[51] That they were Romans is proved not only by the onomastics, but also by the mention that Marcus Valerius Turbo made a Roman will (ll. 7 & 14), and Longinia Nemesilla acted without a guardian because of *ius trium liberorum* (ll. 3–4 & 19–20).

[52] *BGU* VII 1565, comm. to l. 6.

[53] J.F. GILLIAM, 'Notes on Latin texts from Egypt', [in:] J. BINGEN, G. CAMBIER & G. NACHTERGAEL (eds.), *Le monde grec: pensée, littérature, histoire, documents. Hommages à Claire Préaux*, Brussels 1975, pp. 766–774, reprinted in: J.F. GILLIAM, *Roman Army Papers*, Amsterdam 1986, pp. 363–371, p. 366.

that Marcus Valerius Turbo had children with three different women: Marcus Valerius Maximus with Octavia before his recruitment, Kyrilla with an *aste*, with whom he lived during his time of his service, and, finally Marci Valerii Montanus and Longinus *alias* Numisianus with Longinia Nemesilla after his discharge. [54] If Kyrilla was indeed born while her father was still a soldier – in *BGU* VII 1662 she is listed as being about 30 – then she would have been a fatherless *aste*; this in turn would prove that status acquisition in such cases did indeed follow the mother. We cannot be, however, certain to which *polis* Kyrilla belonged.

It would be possible to reconstruct conventional treatment of the fatherless based on what we know of the system. The Romans, as we have mentioned, allowed provincials to apply local laws from before the conquest, although in some cases they did introduce and enforce their own rules.[55] Status acquisition may have been one of the legal points which the Romans wished to make uniform under *iuris gentium regula*. (This seems probable even from reading the *Gnomon* whose paragraphs refer simply to *astoi* not to citizens of Naukratis or Ptolemais.) There are a handful of arguments in favour of this interpretation. In regard to *astoi* (and Alexandrians) the rule of status acquisition from the lesser parent certainly applied to unions of a Roman and an *astos* or *aste*: their children became *peregrini cives* not *peregrini Aegyptii*. This is attested in both the *Gnomon* (*BGU* V 1210, ll. 111–112) and in deeds of legal practice (*e.g. P. Tebt.* II 316, col. III, ll. 30–71; *BGU* XIII 2223; *PSI* XVII 1691). The *Gnomon* also illustrates that *astoi* who married Egyptians in ignorance were treated in the same way as Romans who, through their ignorance, married peregrines, and would thus have been allowed to prove their mistake and transmit the higher status to their offspring (*BGU* V 1210, ll. 128–129). These elements of status acquisition, which we shall discuss in the next chapter, strongly suggests that the acquisition of citizenship of the *poleis* in Roman Egypt was shaped according to Roman rules.

[54] According to Phang, Kyrilla would have been his daughter born when still served in the army, Nemesilla and the two boys would have been been his legitimate family settled after the discharge, but Phang did not include Marcus Valerius Maximus: PHANG, *The Marriage of Roman Soldiers* (cit. n. 46), p. 220.

[55] On this topic, see A. JÖRDENS, 'Keine Konkurrenz und dennoch Recht: Zum Umgang Roms mit den lokalen Rechten', [in:] D. LEÃO & G. THÜR, *Symposion 2015. Vorträge zur griechischen und hellenistischen Rechtsgeschichte (Coimbra, 1.–4. September 2015)*, Vienna 2016, pp. 237–250.

Elizabeth Meyer made similar discoveries in her study on freedmen of *astoi*. In analysing the *Gnomon of idios logos*, she noticed that standing of both citizens and the freedmen of *astoi* in private law was similar or even the same in regard to marriages and wills;[56] this suggests that they would have shared the same status: in other words, freedmen of *astoi* became *astoi*.[57] Unfortunately, evidence is meagre outside the *Gnomon* – the two major documents are *P. Hamb.* IV 270 (Alexandria, 2nd–3rd c. AD)[58] and *P. Oxy.* XXII 2349 (Oxyrhynchos, AD 70)[59] – and the conclusions we can draw from them are not necessarily coherent with those from the *Gnomon*.

In *P. Hamb.* IV 270, a woman petitioning an *epistrategos* to appoint a *tutor* for her is described as a freedwoman of a man having *demotikon* Althaieus and a citizen herself.

> *P. Hamb.* IV 270, ll. 3–6: *παρὰ Ἀλεξάνδρας Ἀνμωṿ[ίου τοῦ Διοσ]|κ̣όρου ἀστῆς ἀπελευθέρα[ς Ἰσιδώρου] | Ἰ̣σιδώρου τοῦ Ἰσιδώρου . . [- ca. 7 - τοῦ] | καὶ Ἀλθαιέως*
>
> from Alexandra daughter of Anmonios son of Dioskoros, *aste*, freedwoman of Isidoros son of Isidoros son of Isidoros ... also called Althaieus

The woman is both an *aste* and the freedwoman of a citizen, which supports the evidence of the *Gnomon*. Yet the description is curious: although Alexandra is a freedwoman, she has a patronym.[60] Nathaël Istasse suggested that the patronym might have been a false filiation connected either with Alexandra's profession (?) or her membership in the Alexandrian civic

[56] E. MEYER, 'Freed and *astoi* in the *Gnomon of the Idios Logos* and in Roman Egypt', [in:] K. HARTER-UIBOPUU & T. KRUSE (eds.), *Studien zum „Gnomon des Idios Logos": Beiträge zum Dritten Wiener Kolloquium zur antiken Rechtsgeschichte*, forthcoming.

[57] This is also the observation made by I. BIEŻUŃSKA-MAŁOWIST, 'Les affranchis dans les papyrus de l'époque ptolémaique et romaine', [in:] *Atti dell'XI Congresso Internazionale di Papirologia, Milano, 2–8 settembre 1965*, Milan 1966, pp. 433–443, p. 433, or J.A. STRAUS, 'Le statut fiscal des esclaves dans l'Égypte romaine', *Chronique l'Égypte* 48 (1973), pp. 364–369.

[58] MEYER, 'Freed and *astoi*' (cit. n. 56).

[59] MEYER, 'Freed and *astoi*' (cit. n. 56).

[60] It is a reconstruction with no parallels, but any other supplement does not seems likely. See D. HAGEDORN, commentary to *P. Hamb.* IV 270, p. 168.

body.[61] If the latter is correct, it would explain why freed persons are not attested among Alexandrians (and would also explain the absence of the fatherless among citizens of Alexandria). The other attestation of a freedwoman belonging to the Alexandrian citizen body comes from *SB* XIV 11388 (Arsinoites, AD 161–169), an application for registration among the ephebes.[62] The mother of the candidate appears to be a freedwoman,[63] yet ἀπε̣[λευθέρα] in line 2 is reconstructed and the reading of the epsilon is not fully certain.[64]

The second document, *P. Oxy.* XXII 2349 (Oxyrhynchos, AD 70) concerns a contract between a soldier, Caius Julius Saturninus, and Herakleides son of Apion. Before enrolling in the legion and assuming a new Roman name, Saturninus had been an Alexandrian, a fact which is pointed out in the document. Also mentioned in the deed is Saturninus' freedman, Dionysios *alias* Theopompos, who was to act as the *curator* of his master's property. Dionysios had been freed before Saturninus had enrolled in the army. As Meyer rightly observed, although the freedman would have been an Alexandrian, both *demotikon* and tribe are absent from his description, which is especially visible in comparison to his patron's description, whose pre-recruitment identity contains them (ll. 5–6).

Meyer interpreted the status of freedmen as follows: freedmen of Alexandrians would have been Alexandrians of lower status, second-class citizens who were not registered in the Alexandrian demes.[65] This is the category applied by Fraser to children born of Alexandrians and women of the *chora*.[66] Meyer argued that freedwomen able to bear citizens would have

[61] N. Istasse, 'Trois notes sur les affranchis dans les papyrus de l'Égypte romaine', *Chronique d'Égypte* 76 (2001), pp. 202–208, p. 204.

[62] Whitehorne, 'Becoming an Alexandrian' (cit. n. 34), p. 28.

[63] Delia, *Alexandrian Citizenship* (cit. n. 25), p. 144.

[64] R. Coles, 'New documentary papyri from the Fayum', *The Journal of Juristic Papyrology* 18 (1974), pp. 177–187, p. 180.

[65] Meyer, 'Freed and *astoi*' (cit. n. 56).

[66] P.M. Fraser, *Ptolemaic Alexandria*, Oxford 1972, pp. 41–42; K. Vandorpe & S. Waebens, 'Women and gender in Roman Egypt: the impact of Roman rule', [in:] K. Lembke, M. Minas-Nerpel & S. Pfeiffer (eds.), *Tradition and Transformation: Egypt Under Roman Rule. Proceedings of the International Conference, Hildesheim, Römer- und Pelizaeus-Museum, 3–6 July 2008*, Leiden 2010, pp. 415–435, p. 420.

had an equivalent status to female citizens, while freedmen would become citizens deprived of political rights, comparable to Junian Latins.[67] The similarity is supported by comparison with the limitations on succession rights imposed on freedmen of Romans and *astoi*.[68] Meyer concludes that the acquisition of civic and fiscal status by freedmen, including the freedmen of Alexandrians, was a Roman innovation introduced by Augustus;[69] yet despite being citizens, the freedmen of Alexandrians would have not been granted all Alexandrian political rights, responsibilities, or privileges.[70]

This reasoning is convincing, although it seems implausible that the freedmen were second-class citizens. Fraser conceived of this category as Ptolemaic, while Mayer claims that the status of freedmen of *astoi* was developed in the time of Augustus 'as part of Augustus' "cargo of *eunomia* and abundance"'.[71] (These are not mutually exclusive things, because Romans might have used Hellenistic solution, if it served their purposes.) Furthermore, the comparison between Alexandrian freedmen (or persons freed by *astoi* in general) and Junian Latins does not hold. The latter were neither lesser Romans nor Romans at all, but were assimilated to the colonial Latins by a legal fiction of the *lex Iunia* and *lex Aelia Sentia* dated to the reign of Augustus.[72] Although they could become Roman citizens relatively easily, they were not initially Romans.[73]

The comparison with formal freedmen is more accurate, as freedmen could not perform many public functions, and could not even enroll as legionary soldiers.[74] Yet two important reservations should be made. First,

[67] Meyer, 'Freed and *astoi*' (cit. n. 56).

[68] Meyer, 'Freed and *astoi*' (cit. n. 56).

[69] Meyer, 'Freed and *astoi*' (cit. n. 56).

[70] Meyer, 'Freed and *astoi*' (cit. n. 56).

[71] Meyer, 'Freed and *astoi*' (cit. n. 56).

[72] A considerable number of publications was devoted to Junian Latins. See M. Hirt, 'In search of Junian Latins', *Historia* 67 (2018), pp. 288–312.

[73] See, however, G. Camodeca, 'Per una riedizione dell'archivio ercolanese di L. Venidius Ennychus. II', *Cronache Ercolanesi* 36 (2006), pp. 187–209, illustrating that a Junian Latin might have needed the approval of local decuriones in order to achieve the *civitas*.

[74] Y. Le Bohec, *The Imperial Roman Army*, tr. R. Bate, London – New York 2000, p. 87. See *Ch. L. A.* XLVI 1364 = *CPL* 102 = *FIRA* III^2 7 in which a part of an oath taken by a legionary soldier was that he was born free Roman; P. Schubert, *P. Diog.*, p. 19.

freedmen deprived of some public rights (*e.g.* exclusion from the juries, public priesthoods or senatorial order) shared some of their limitations concerning the participation in public life with other disadvantaged citizens, among them the urban poor.[75] Second, in addition to gaining freedom and citizenship, Roman freedmen were registered in a *tribus*,[76] yet the lack of *deme* and *phile* is used as the primary argument for why the Alexandrian freedmen in *P. Oxy.* XXII 2349 would have been citizens of the second category. To this we add that neither the *Gnomon* nor other sources provide any evidence that freedmen of the *poleis* were deprived of public rights.

Yet Meyer further observed that, not only was the status of citizens and their freedmen comparable, but that the restrictions concerning inheritance rights imposed on freedmen by *astoi* were similar to those imposed on Roman freedmen. We might therefore suspect that the status of Alexandrian freedmen (or those freed by *astoi* in general) depended on the status of their former masters, and that this rule was introduced by the Romans, who provided similar safeguards for the rights of former masters as were found in Roman law. Yet, before assuming so, it should be helpful to examine what status had freedmen before Romans.

2.1.1. Excursus: Freedmen before Romans

In his famous letter to the inhabitants of the Thessalian city of Larissa (*ILS* 8763: 214 BC), Philip V referred to the Roman practice of accepting former slaves as citizens as both irregular and exceptional, but also as a strength of Rome.[77] The text suggests that, for Philip, the exclusion of freedmen from citizenship was normal, perhaps a rule within the Hellen-

[75] H. Mouritsen, *The Freedman in the Roman World*, Cambridge – New York 2011, p. 73, with further literature.

[76] On distribution of freedmen among tribes, see Mouritsen, *Freedman* (cit. n. 75), pp. 75–78, with further literature.

[77] G. Purpura, 'Diritti di patronato e *astikoi nomoi* in P. Oxy. IV, 706', [in:] *Iuris vincula. Studi in onore di Mario Talamanca*, vol. VI, Naples 2001, pp. 465–483, p. 472; Ch. Bruun, 'Slaves and freed slaves', [in:] Ch. Bruun & J. Edmondson (eds.), *The Oxford Handbook of Roman Epigraphy*, Oxford 2014, pp. 605–626, p. 605.

istic legal *koine*.[78] In classical Greece, freedmen did not become citizens of the *polis* to which their former owner belonged.[79]

Sources regarding the status of freedmen in Hellenistic Egypt are far from satisfying. The identification cluster 'N.N. + ἀπελεύθερος + patron's name', which places the former owner into the position of slave's 'father', occurs only in papyri from the Roman era as counterpart of the Latin identification cluster 'N.N. + *l(ibertus)* + patron's name'.[80] The Hellenistic identification cluster, however, is not necessarily significant in the matter of status acquisition: ἀπελεύθερος had not been part of personal descriptions in Greek epigraphy before the Romans introduced it. In regard to slaves the name of an owner could be even indicated the same way as filiation, i.e. 'N.N. + name in genitive'. Without additional context, it is impossible to determine whether Διονύσιος Διονυσίου means 'Dionysios son of Dionysios' or 'Dionysios slave of Dionysios'.[81] If this identification cluster was applied to both slaves and freedmen, it would put the former master in exactly the same position as in Latin inscriptions, where the patron is substituted for the father. This substitution

[78] *Koiné juridique*, see Mélèze Modrzejewski, *Loi et coutume* (cit. n. 29), pp. 148–149.

[79] D. Lewis & S. Zanovello, 'freedmen/freedwomen, Greek', [in:] *Oxford Classical Dictionary*, 2017 online edition (retrieved 8 Oct. 2018, from http://classics.oxfordre.com/view/10.1093/acrefore/9780199381135.001.0001/acrefore-9780199381135-e-8019).

Even ignoring the controversial matter of the civic group to which Athenian *apeleutheroi* belonged – metics or foreigners or *apeleutheroi* – it seems certain that they belonged to one and same status, no matter who freed them: status did not depend on their former master. This problem was widely discussed in the scholarly literature, see *e.g.* A. Calderini, *La manomissione e la condizione dei liberti in Grecia*, Milan 1908, pp. 360–364; C. Bearzot, 'Né cittadini né stranieri: *apeleutheroi* e *nothoi* in Atene', [in:] M.G. Angeli Bertinelli & A. Donati (eds.), *Il cittadino, lo straniero, il barbaro, fra integrazione ed emarginazione nell'antichità. Atti del I Incontro Internazionale di Storia Antica (Genova 22-24 maggio 2003)* [= *Serta antiqua et mediaevalia* VII], Rome 2005, pp. 77–92; A. Dimopoulou-Piliouni, 'Apeleutheroi: metics or foreigners?', *Dike* 11 (2008), pp. 27–50; D. Kamen, *Status in Classical Athens*, Princeton – Oxford 2013, p. 43; J.D. Sosin, 'A metic was a metic', *Historia* 65.1 (2016), pp. 2–13, with further literature.

[80] A. Calderini, *Manomissione* (cit. n. 79), pp. 311–312; R. Scholl, 'Ἀπελεύθεροι im ptolemäischen Ägypten', *Archiv für Papyrusforschung* 36 (1990), pp. 39–42; Meyer, 'Freed and *astoi*' (cit. n. 56).

[81] B.H. McLean, *An Introduction to Greek Epigraphy of the Hellenistic and Roman Periods from Alexander the Great down to the Reign of Constantine (323 BC – AD 337)*, Ann Arbor 2002, pp. 93–94, 103.

would be, however, different than in the cluster 'N.N. + ἀπελεύθερος + patron's name', as the indication of the patron's position is absent.

Our investigation is made no easier by the fact that sources concerning freedmen and manumissions in Hellenistic Egypt are scarce, and half of the surviving examples refer to testamentary manumission, in which the slave has not yet been freed and is thus described without filiation or patron.[82] Fortunately there are at least two cases which shed some light on the 'civic' status of freedmen in Ptolemaic Egypt. First of them is *P. Eleph.* 3 & 4 = *C. Ptol. Sklav.* 36 a & b dated to the early third century BC. They are two agreements between Elaphion, described as 'Syrian', and two Arcadian men, Antipatros (*P. Eleph.* 3) and Pantarkes (*P. Eleph.* 4); the agreements are assisted by two different *kyrioi* (Pantarkes [*P. Eleph.* 3] and Dion [*P. Eleph.* 4]). According to these deeds, Elaphion paid 300 drachmae of *tropheia* (equivalent for upbringing?) to Antipatros (*P. Eleph.* 3) and 400 to Pantarkes (*P. Eleph.* 4); the men, in turn, were not allowed to bring a lawsuit against Elaphion to exact the *tropheia*, nor were they allowed to enslave her. Otto Rubensohn, the editor of *P. Eleph.*, suggested the woman was a courtesan. The scenario might have been as follows: Elaphion stayed with Antipatros, then changed her 'sponsor' to Pantarkes, who acted as her *kyrios* in the first agreement; the repayment of *tropheia* would thus have been made to Antipatros, allowing Elaphion to move in with Pantarkes. After a few months the scenario repeats: Elaphion finds a new 'sponsor', Dion, who repays Pantarkes, the previous 'sponsor'. This interpretation, although interesting, cannot be accepted for a number reasons, primarily because both agreements were made not between the two men, but between the men and the woman herself.

Some decades later, Erhard Grzybek proposed dating of the documents[83] in which *P. Eleph.* 3 (Jan.–Feb. 282 BC) postdates *P. Eleph.* 4 (Jun.–Jul.

[82] I. Bieżuńska-Małowist, *L'esclavage dans l'Égypte gréco-romaine. Première partie: période ptolémaïque*, Wrocław – Warsaw – Cracow – Gdańsk 1974, p. 128; *C. Pap. Sklav.*, p. 145. The low number of manumissions could be perhaps explained by the low number of slaves in Hellenistic Egypt even in comparison to Roman period: W. Clarysse & D. Thompson, *Counting the People in Hellenistic Egypt*, vol. II: *Historical Studies*, Cambridge 2006, p. 267: the authors estimated that tax-liable slaves accounted for 3.8% of the adult population.

[83] E. Grzybek, 'Die griechische Konkubine und ihre „Mitgift" (*P. Eleph.* 3 und 4)', *Zeitschrift für Papyrologie und Epigraphik* 76 (1989), pp. 206–212, p. 207.

283 BC) by half a year.[84] On the basis of the new dating, he suggested that Elaphion was a free concubine who brought her quasi-dowry as *tropheia*. Her first partner was Pantarkes who received 400 drachmae for Elaphion's maintenance; after seven months, however, she exchanged him for Antipatros to whom she gave 300: the amount of the previous *tropheia*, less 100 drachmae which were kept by Pantarkes as compensation for the fact that his time with Elaphion was so brief.[85]

Joseph Partsch proposed yet another interpretation: Elaphion may have been a slave co-owned by Antipatros and Pantarkes and freed by them for the price of 700 drachmae. The *tropheia* would thus be the price for Elaphion's freedom paid separately to her former masters in two instalments. The instalments may have been different because Antipatros and Pantarkes owned Elaphion in unequal parts. This seems the best interpretation, as it explains the details of the agreements, specifically the penal clause forbidding enslavement and the exclusion of further money claims by Antipatros and Pantarkes, more convincingly. This explanation also does not rely too much on conjecture and takes into account the woman's name, a matter to which we will return shortly.[86]

If this interpretation of the texts is accurate, these documents could be relevant to the status of freedmen in Hellenistic Egypt: both parties in both agreements bore different 'ethnic' descriptions: Although Elaphion is described as a Syrian,[87] her name is the diminutive of the Greek noun ἔλαφος, 'deer', which suggests that she might have been either a house-born slave or acquired as a child; she would have been given her name

[84] A.E. SAMUEL, *Ptolemaic Chronology* [= *Münchener Beiträge zur Papyrusforschung und antiken Rechtsgeschichte* XLV], Munich 1962, pp. 20–24.

[85] See GRZYBEK, 'Die griechische Konkubine', (cit. n. 83). The interpretation was accepted by the editors of B. PORTEN *et al.*, *The Elephantine Papyri in English. Three Millennia of Cross-Cultural Continuity and Change*, Leiden – New York – Cologne 1996, pp. 414–415.

[86] J. PARTSCH, *Griechisches Bürgschaftsrecht. I. Teil. Das Recht des altgriechischen Gemeindestaats*, Leipzig 1909, p. 351, n. 5; U. WILCKEN, 'Papyrus-Urkunden', *Archiv für Papyrusforschung* 5 (1913), pp. 198–300, p. 209; R. SCHOLL in *C. Ptol. Sklav.*, p. 141; BIEŻUŃSKA-MAŁOWIST, *Esclavage dans l'Égypte gréco-romaine* I (cit. n. 82), pp. 128–129.

[87] *C. Ptol. Sklav.*, p. 142.

by an owner, and may not have had a Syrian identity of her own.[88] Her ex-masters appear as Arcadians, which means that Elaphion did not adopt the *patris* of her masters after her manumission but the one referring to even distant but real origin.[89]

The Ptolemaic *patris* is, however, not an equivalent of Roman *status civitatis*. In fact, numerous labels referring to *patris* circulated in Ptolemaic Egypt; these terms could refer to cities (Athenian), places which no longer existed (Myosian), or even regions (Cretan).[90] While these 'ethnic' labels did not refer only to the Greek speaking world, indigenous population never used them; Egyptians instead used the formula 'ὁ ἀπό + place' to specify their domicile.[91] It should be noted that an individual who included 'Athenian' as a part of their description was not necessarily a citizen of Athens or subject to Athenian law.[92] Rather, the label referred to the former homeland of an individual or their ancestors in the early period,[93] and may no longer have had any legal value.[94]

They certainly had the descriptive one, however. In the early third century a royal *prostagma* was issued which established the rules for how people should

[88] See: D. Lewis, 'Notes on slave names, ethnicity, and identity in Classical and Hellenistic Greece', [in:] *Tell Me Who You Are* (cit. n. 13), pp. 183–213, p. 201.

[89] According to Scholl, the substantive 'Syrian' became a synonym for slaves who, if not born at home, often came from Syria: *C. Ptol. Sklav.*, p. 142. In Ptolemaic Egypt, however, slaves also bore other ethnic descriptions: Lewis, 'Notes on slave names' (cit. n. 88), pp. 200–203.

[90] Mélèze Modrzejewski, *Loi et coutume* (cit. n. 29), pp. 107–108.

[91] Observed by E. Bickermann, 'Beiträge zur antiken Urkundengeschichte. I: Der Heimatsvermerk und die staatsrechtliche Stellung der Hellenen im ptolemäischen Ägypten', *Archiv für Papyrusforschung* 8 (1927), pp. 216–239; Mélèze Modrzejewski, *Loi et coutume* (cit. n. 29), p. 108, n. 80; M. Depauw, 'Elements of identification in Egypt, 800 BC – AD 300', [in:] M. Depauw & S. Coussement (eds.), *Identifiers and Identification Methods in the Ancient World* [= *Orientalia Lovaniensia Analecta* CCXXIX], Leuven – Paris – Walpole, MA 2014, pp. 82–83.

[92] Bickermann, 'Beiträge. I' (cit. n. 91), p. 223; Mélèze Modrzejewski, *Loi et coutume* (cit. n. 29), p. 107.

[93] C. Fischer-Bovet, 'Official identity and ethnicity: comparing Ptolemaic and Early Roman Egypt', *Journal of Egyptian History* 11 (2018), pp. 208–242, p. 220. Yet, in the second and first centuries B.C. *patrides* could denote occupational groups or status groups: U. Yiftach, 'Did *BGU* XIV 2367 work?', [in:] Depauw & Coussement (eds.), *Identifiers* (cit. n. 91), pp. 103–118, pp. 110–111.

[94] The summary of the discussion on these descriptions, see K. Goudriaan, *Ethnicity in Ptolemaic Egypt* [= *Dutch Monographs on Ancient History and Archaeology* V], Amsterdam 1988, pp. 1–7.

be described in legal deeds. While the ordinance itself has not been preserved, its content is known thanks to *BGU* XIV 2367 (Alexandria [?], late 3rd c. BC) and *P. Hamb.* III 168 (provenance unknown, mid-3rd c. BC or before).[95] Of the four groups mentioned in the text – soldiers, citizens, citizen-soldiers, and others – only the last group had to include their *patris* within their identification cluster.[96] The appearance of the *patris* in the identification cluster placed people in the group of 'others' and offered proof that the person was neither a citizen of Alexandria, Naukratis or Ptolemais nor a member of the army. This was important in the legal sense, as *politai* were subjects to the laws of their *poleis* with their own administration of justice.[97]

It also suggests that ethnic descriptors must also have carried a specific meaning, as it would have otherwise been sufficient to write 'Egyptian' or 'Hellen'. As Uri Yiftach noted, the ordinance appeared around the same time as the re-organisation of the justice system by Ptolemy II Philadelphos.[98] His 'Justizdiagramma' established two types of courts in the Egyptian *chora*: the court of *laokritai* – composed of Egyptian priests – for the Egyptians, and the *dikasterion* for Greeks.[99] Subjects of *dikasteria* consisted not only of 'Greeks', but also those considered 'barbarians' by the Greeks – *e.g.* Thracs or Jews – while the courts of *laokritai* oversaw cases brought forth by Egyptians.[100] The laws applied in each type of court obviously varied.[101] The distinction between them, however, was neither total nor especially strong, and it was, in fact, the language of the deed that decided which court should be used. In other words, if any controversy should arise as the result of a Demotic contract between an 'Athenian' and

[95] YIFTACH, '*BGU* XIV 2367' (cit. n. 93).

[96] See Nomenklaturregel in: FISCHER-BOVET, 'Official identity and ethnicity' (cit. n. 93), tab. 1.

It is probable that this rule did not originate with the *prostagma* referred to in *BGU* XIV 2367, but were already in use, as in *P. Eleph.* 3 & 4 or discussed by Yiftach *P. Eleph.* 2: YIFTACH, '*BGU* XIV 2367' (cit. n. 93), p. 106.

[97] MÉLÈZE MODRZEJEWSKI, *Loi et coutume* (cit. n. 29), pp. 88–102.

[98] YIFTACH, '*BGU* XIV 2367' (cit. n. 93), p. 107.

[99] H.J. WOLFF, *Das Justizwesen der Ptolemäer*, Munich 1970², pp. 37–63.

[100] MÉLÈZE MODRZEJEWSKI, *Loi et coutume* (cit. n. 29), p. 204.

[101] MÉLÈZE MODRZEJEWSKI, *Loi et coutume* (cit. n. 29), pp. 98–109 and *passim*.

a man 'from Pathyris', it would be heard by a *laokritai* court:[102] *patris* did not determine the laws applied to its bearer.[103]

The function of the *patris* was therefore descriptive, as Uri Yiftach demonstrated,[104] but it might also have been cultural.[105] It was certainly not the equivalent of Roman *status civitatis*. In regard to Elaphion, designated as Syrian despite her ex-masters being Arcadian, we can only conclude that the identity of the freed person did not depend fully on their ex-masters.

This observation is supported by two papyri published in 2002, *SB* XXVIII 16852 & 16853 (Antaiopolis, 132 BC).[106] *SB* XXVIII 16852 is an notarial manumission of Thermouthis, a six-year-old girl, by two soldiers, Zenodoros and Sosibios, both described as Milesians, although the description at that time did not necessarily refer to their familial homeland.[107] Although the two were perhaps related, they were not brothers, and had owned the girl jointly.[108] In the manumission document (*SB* XXVIII 16852), the girl is described only by her name, age, and physical features, τὴν ἑαυτῶν δούλην, ἧι ὄνομα Θερμοῦθις, ἐτῶν ἓξ μελίχρουν στρογγυλο|πρόσωπον (ll. 12–13).[109] In the second document (*SB* XXVIII 16853), a proclamation of Thermouthis manumission found rolled in the manumission deed,[110] the description is different: Τερμοῦθις | ἡ ἐξ Εὐφροσύνης (ll. 1–2). Although

[102] Clarysse & Thompson, *Counting the People* II (cit. n. 82), p. 143.

[103] The *patris* element may have played another important role. Although it was not itself a tax category, those with a Greek *patris* were placed in the tax-category of Hellens and exempted from the symbolic one-obol tax. Yet, this group consisted not only of 'Greeks', but also indigenous Egyptians, including those who held important offices within the Hellenistic state. *P. Eleph.* 3 & 4 are too early to be connected to the salt-tax. On the tax-Hellens, see Clarysse & Thompson, *Counting the People* II (cit. n. 82), pp. 138–147.

[104] Yiftach, '*BGU* XIV 2367' (cit. n. 93).

[105] Mélèze Modrzejewski, *Loi et coutume* (cit. n. 29), p. 108.

[106] N. Quenouille, 'Eine Sklavenfreilassung aus der Ptolemäerzeit (P. UB Trier S 135-2 und 135-12)', *Archiv für Papyrusforschung* 48.1 (2002), pp. 67–97.

[107] Yiftach, '*BGU* XIV 2367' (cit. n. 93), pp. 110–111. Yet, the editor recognised it as a proper ethnic: Quenouille, 'Eine Sklavenfreilassung' (cit. n. 106), pp. 81–82.

[108] Quenouille, 'Eine Sklavenfreilassung' (cit. n. 106), pp. 68–69.

[109] The similar description was perhaps applied in another fragmentary agoranomic manumission dated to 110 BC – *SB* XIV 11998.

[110] On the procedure, see Quenouille, 'Eine Sklavenfreilassung' (cit. n. 106), pp. 88–96.

the newly freed girl had no label related to her *patris* – which is not surprising in the late second century BC – she is described by a familial bond, in this case her metronym, not by the relation of patronage. Her Egyptian name and the fact that her mother's identity was known both suggest that she was a house-born slave; if she was not described with reference to her former masters, the metronym would have been the only available label.

2.1.2. *Astoi*: a conclusion

The conclusions we can draw from these documents are unsatisfactory. The sources do not inform us of the status of former slaves freed by *astoi*, although they do suggest that, in Ptolemaic Egypt, former slaves referred to their own geographic and familial origin rather than that of their patron.

Obviously, Romans did not impose rules applied to themselves and their freedmen onto the *peregrini* in any strict sense. This means that the Romans did not subject peregrines to *ius civile* – which they could not have done directly anyhow – but rather imposed rules which they considered to be binding for everyone. This is illustrated by the example discussed above of children born to free mothers and slave fathers: the principle is simple for peregrines, but for Romans it had many exceptions. The same appears to have been the case for status acquisition by freed persons. Although freedmen of Romans acquired Roman citizenship at the time of manumission, this happened only if the manumission was performed properly and within the limitations imposed at the beginning of the Empire. The status of freedmen therefore depended on the method of manumission. Roman manumissions are not traceable among non-Romans; on the contrary, pre-Roman methods of manumission continued to survive in local laws during the Roman period.[111] Furthermore, there were no limitations introduced by Romans on peregrine freedmen similar to those found in the *lex Aelia Sentia* and *lex Fufia Caninia*. It seems more probable that the status

[111] See, *e.g.*, M. YOUNI, 'Transforming Greek practice into Roman law: manumissions in Roman Macedonia', *Tijdschrift voor Rechtsgeschiedenis* 78 (2010), pp. 313–342.

model for freedmen was enforced as *iuris gentium regula* as the Romans believed it to be a rule that should be shared by all people.

Since Eduardo Volterra, it has been accepted that peregrine freedmen acquired *status civitatis* after their manumittors according to *ius gentium*.[112] Yet, the jurisprudential sources suggesting this are not numerous. A fragment of Ulpian's *Opinions* says that freedmen have the same *origo* and domicile as their patrons (D. 50.1.6.3: *Libertini originem patronorum vel domicilium sequuntur*), yet this is not the same as citizenship.[113] In the fragmentary C. 10.40.7 pr., Diocletian and Maximian list *manumissio* as one of the ways by which people acquire citizenship.[114] Even if the acquisition of status from the manumittor was indeed the rule of *ius gentium*, there may have been exceptions: entire groups or territories could have been exempted and allowed to follow different rules, especially given that Roman law usually respected the obstacles concerning manumission in peregrine laws (Fr. *dosith*. 12).[115] It suggests that not only slaves by *astoi* acquired the status of their patrons, but it might become a general rule for non-Romans.

The question we must ask is whether Romans applied their rules for status acquisition only to freedmen or to everyone. The latter seems more probable. In an influential article, Alan Bowman and Dominic Rathbone observed that the rules in the *Gnomon* governing the marriage and succession of *astoi* resemble 'Augustus' marital and testamentary legislation at Rome'. The authors, however, avoided suggesting a direct influence, saying 'we should perhaps admit the possibility of cross-fertilization between Alexandria and Rome in the development of this legislation'.[116] If the above observation is indeed true, the cases of Kyrilla and of the sons of Octavius Valens could be interpreted as proof, albeit not especially strong, that the fatherless children of *astai* would have been accepted among the *peregrini cives* of Egypt.

[112] E. Volterra, 'Manomissioni di schiavi compiute da peregrini', [in:] *Studi in onore di Pietro de Francisci*, vol. V, Milan 1956, pp. 73–106.

[113] On the *origo* as mostly fiscal category, see D. Nörr, 'Origo Studien zur Orts-, Stadt- und Reichszugehörigkeit in der Antike', *Tijdschrift voor Rechtsgeschiedenis* 31 (1963), pp. 525–600.

[114] Volterra, 'Manomissioni' (cit. n. 112), pp. 102–103.

[115] Volterra, 'Manomissioni' (cit. n. 112), pp. 92–93.

[116] Bowman & Rathbone, 'Cities and administration' (cit. n. 36), p. 116.

2.1.3. Antinoopolis: special case

Antinoopolis is a case special among the Egyptian *poleis*, as it was only founded in AD 130,[117] and its founder, Hadrian, wished for the city to play a special role in Egypt.[118] While Antinoopolis was organised along the lines of other *poleis*, it also enjoyed certain privileges (it had, for instance, a *boule*). The laws of Antinoopolis were based on those of Naukratis (*W. Chr.* 27) which were, in turn, based to some extent on Milesian law, as Naukratis was originally a colony of Miletus. However this does not mean that Milesian laws were translated exactly into those of Naukratis, nor that Hadrian simply 'transplanted' the laws of Naukratis to Antinoopolis; citizens enjoyed not only the usual privileges of *astoi*, such as exemption from *laographia*, but also some additional benefits, such as a special alimentation fund granted by Hadrian.[119]

The new *polis* needed citizens, and this might suggest that obtaining citizenship of Antinoopolis was relatively easy. Attestations collected by Myrto Malouta illustrate that many *katoikoi* from the Arsinoite nome became citizens of Antinoopolis in the first decades of the city's existence.[120] It does not, however, exclude the possibility that other groups of *peregrini Aegyptii* entitled to the lower *laographia* rate were accepted as citizens of the new city. It is likely that citizens of Ptolemais (*P. Würz.* 9 = *W. Chr.* 26 [Arsinoite nome, AD 161–169]),[121] Alexandria and Naukratis could also acquire the citizenship of Antinoopolis. It remains unclear, however, whether they could hold 'double local citizenship' or had to give up their former one. In the later period, a relatively high number of

[117] Other propositions of dating, see summarised in: MÉLÈZE MODRZEJEWSKI, *Loi et coutume* (cit. n. 29), p. 90, n. 8.

[118] Summary of scholarly opinions why Hadrian founded Antinoopolis, see F. STRUM, 'Ha conferito Adriano uno statuto personale speciale agli Antinoiti?', *Iura* 43 (1992), pp. 83–97, p. 85.

[119] Listed and discussed in: STRUM, 'Uno statuto personale speciale' (cit. n. 118); P. SCHUBERT, 'Antinoopolis', [in:] R.S. BAGNALL *et al.* (eds.), *The Encyclopedia of Ancient History*, online edition 2012; IDEM, *P. Diog.*, pp. 26–30.

[120] SCHUBERT, *P. Diog.*, p. 25; M. MALOUTA, 'Antinoite citizenship under Hadrian and Antoninus Pius. A prosopographical study of the first thirty years of Antinoopolis', *The Bulletin of the American Society of Papyrologists* 46 (2009), pp. 81–96.

[121] SCHUBERT, *P. Diog.*, p. 25.

Romans (mostly veterans) are attested among the citizens of Antinoopolis.[122] It would thus seem that Romans, citizens of other *poleis*, and privileged Egyptians (although not perhaps payers of full *laographia*), could become citizens of the new city.

This special status of the city suggests that rules of the admission to its citizenship should not have been restrictive, including admission of fatherless children of female citizens. The best example comes from the archive of Gemellus Horion.[123] It is a census return filled for Tasoucharion (no. 355) and her two children, Caia Apolinaria and Gemellus Horion, the last owner of the archive (187-Ar-27). The census return concerns a landed property located in Karanis and was submitted to authorities from the Arsinoite nome, although the owners did not reside in the declared property.

> *P. Mich.* VI 370 (Karanis, AD 189), ll. 7–14: *ὑπάρχει τοῖς | φροντιζομένοις ὑ̣π' ἐμοῦ Τασου|χαρίῳ ἀπάτορι μη(τρὸς) Σαραπιάδος | Ἀντινοείδι* (l. *Ἀντινοίδι*) *μητρὶ τῶν ὑπογεγρα(μμένων) | ἐν τῇ κώμῃ οἰκί(α) καὶ αὐλ(ὴ) καὶ (τρίτον) μέρος | ἑτ(έρας) οἰκί(ας) καὶ Γαίᾳ Ἀπολ̣ι̣ναρίᾳ καὶ Γεμέλλῳ Ὡρίωνι υ̣ἱ̣ο̣ῖ̣ς Ἀντινοεῦσι | κοινῶς ἐξ ἴσου οἰκ̣ί̣(α) κτλ.*
>
> There belong to persons whom I represent, to Tasoucharion fatherless daughter of Sarapias, citizen of Antinoopolis, mother of the below described, a house, courtyard and third share of another house in the village, and to Caia Apolinaria and Gemellus Horion, her children, citizens of Antinoopolis, jointly and in equal shares a house, *etc.*

There can be little doubt that the woman whose filiation is substituted by *ἀπάτωρ* belonged to the citizens' body of Antinoopolis.

Furthermore, individuals described with their sole metronym occur in second-century ephebic lists from Antinoopolis (*I. Portes* 5, 6, 9 *&* 10 and *SB* I 4965). The descriptive pattern applied in these registers is simple:

[122] MALOUTA, 'Antinoite citizenship' (cit. n. 120), p. 86.

Yet despite possessing citizenship of the polis, the veterans often lived in the Arsinoites, as illustrated in the archives of Marcus Lucretius Diogenes and Gemellus Horion.

[123] See the family tree in: H. YOUTIE, *P. Mich.* VI, p. 118, and corrected in: TM Arch. id 90; R. SMOLDERS, 'Gemellus Horion', [in:] K. VANDORPE, W. CLARYSSE *&* H. VERRETH (eds.), *Graeco-Roman Archives from the Fayum* [= *Collectanea Hellenistica – KVAB* VI], Leuven – Paris – Bristol, CT 2015, pp. 143–149.

a) 'person – patronym', *e.g. I. Portes* 9 (Antinoopolis, AD 163), l. 12: *Ἑρμίας Διοσκόρου*; l. 13: *Σερῆνος ὁ καὶ Σαραπάμμων Ὡρίωνος*

b) 'person – metronym', *e.g. I. Portes* 9, l. 14: *Ἀμμώνιος Δημητριοῦτος*

The metronym lacks *μήτηρ* in the genitive and is identical to the patronym, which is not unusual in inscriptions, but provided researchers with difficulties. Youtie, as discussed later in the section devoted to the gymnasial group, suggested that individuals bearing only metronyms on the ephebic list of the Leontopolis inscription were *ἀπάτορες*, which translates to the lists from Antinoopolis.[124] Kent Rigsby, who published one of the ephebic inscriptions from Antinoopolis (*SEG* XXVIII 1458), noticed that the number of people identified with only metronyms was too high – *ca.* 15% on both lists from Antinoopolis and Leontopolis – to be interpreted as *ἀπάτορες*.[125] He suggested that 'one listed that parent who was a citizen of the city'.[126] In his study on *SEG* XL 1568, Jean Bingen identified individuals labelled with metronyms as children of the so-called mixed unions between *astai* and non-*astoi* possessing the right of *epigamia*, which meaning is investigated later in Chapter 4.[127] None of these three statements oppose one another. Youtie included people born to 'mixed unions' as *ἀπάτορες*, thus by suggesting that *SEG* XL 1568 contains *ἀπάτορες* he was referring specifically to people born to a citizen and a non-citizen.[128] Yet, Rigsby obviously interpreted *ἀπάτορες* the way they are interpreted in Chapter 1, thus he was also right claiming that the number of people with metronyms was too high to represent only fatherless boys.

In these lists, and in other texts which do not provide a patronym in the description of a citizen of Antinoopolis, we are indeed unable to distinguish between fatherless individuals and those born of mixed unions

[124] H. YOUTIE, '*Ἀπάτορες*. Law vs. custom in Roman Egypt', [in:] BINGEN, CAMBIER & NACHTERGAEL (eds.), *Le monde grec* (cit. n. 53), pp. 723–740 (reprinted in: H. YOUTIE, *Scriptiunculae posteriores*, vol. I, Bonn 1981, pp. 17–35), p. 730.

[125] K. RIGSBY, 'An ephebic inscription from Egypt', *Greek, Roman and Byzantine Studies* 19 (1978), pp. 239–249, p. 248, n. 28.

[126] RIGSBY, 'Ephebic inscription' (cit. n. 125), p. 248.

[127] J. BINGEN, 'L'inscription éphèbique de Léontopolis (220 *p.C.*)', *Chronique d'Égypte* 76 (2001), pp. 209–229, p. 221.

[128] YOUTIE, '*Ἀπάτορες*' (cit. n. 124), pp. 738–740.

consisting of one citizen of Antinoopolis, as the description ἀπάτωρ was not used in Antinoopolis (*P. Mich.* VI 370 was written in the Arsinoite nome). Yet, it is very likely that both categories of children could acquire citizenship of the *polis* because, as we will demonstrate in Chapter 4, both mothers and fathers could transfer it to their offspring.

2.2. *Privileged Egyptians*

The exact relationship between the metropolite, gymnasial and *katoikoi* orders still remains a subject of scholarly debate. It was once thought that οἱ ἀπὸ τοῦ γυμνασίου constituted a group within the metropolite order, making them a kind of 'super elite', a privileged group within a privileged group.[129] Although this idea is no longer as widely held, the precise distinction between the groups is not certain. It seems that *metropolitai* were a fiscal class introduced by the Romans near the beginning of their rule in Egypt, gymnasial group, which also entitles to the lower *laographia* rate was based on Greeks of the *chora* from Ptolemaic times.[130] While the rules governing the groups were similar, they were not identical due to the different origin and purpose of the both classes of Egyptians.[131] It was membership in the gymnasial group that decided admission to the corn dole[132] and to the highest local offices.[133] Our sources also confirm that priests

[129] J. Mélèze-Modrzejewski, 'Entre la cité et le fisc. Le statut grec dans l'Égypte romaine', [in:] F.J. Nieto (ed.), *Symposion 1982. Vorträge zur griechischen und hellenistischen Rechtsgeschichte (Santander, 1.–4. September 1982)*, Cologne – Vienna 1989, pp. 241–280 (reprinted in: *Droit impérial et traditions locales*, Aldershot 1990, n° I) and others referred there.

[130] P. van Minnen, 'Αἱ ἀπὸ γυμνασίου: Greek women and the Greek elite in the metropoleis of Roman Egypt', [in:] H. Melaerts & L Mooren (eds.), *Le rôle et le statut de la femme en Égypte hellénistique, romaine et byzantine : acts du colloque international, Bruxelles – Leuven, 27–29 novembre 1997* [= *Studia Hellenistica* XXXVII], Paris 2002, pp. 337–353, p. 338 and *passim*; J. Rowlandson, 'Dissing the Egyptians: legal, ethnic and cultural identities in Roman Egypt', [in:] A. Gardner, E. Herring & K. Lomas (eds.), *Creating Ethnicities & Identities in the Roman World*, London 2013, pp. 213–247, p. 222.

[131] Rowlandson, 'Dissing the Egyptians' (cit. n. 130), p. 223.

[132] See M. Nowak, 'Get your free corn: The fatherless in the corn-dole archive from Oxyrhynchos', [in:] *Tell Me Who You Are* (cit. n. 13), pp. 215–228.

[133] Rowlandson, 'Dissing the Egyptians' (cit. n. 130), pp. 223–224.

enjoyed a special fiscal status: they were fully exempted from taxes and liturgies perhaps as early as the late Ptolemaic period.[134]

The last group is the *katoikoi* or '*katoikoi*[135] from the total of 6,475 Greek men in the Arsinoite' (*κάτοικοι τῶν ἐν (τῷ) Ἀρσινοίτῃ (νομῷ) ἀνδρῶν Ἑλλήνων ͵ϛυοε*),[136] which is attested in the Arsinoite nome and consisted of members registered in Ptolemais Euergetis,[137] in the Roman era it included individuals who paid only 20 drachmae of *laographia* instead of 40.[138] *Katoikoi* have been recognised as an Arsinoite equivalent of the gymnasial group elsewhere.[139]

2.2.1. Metropolite group

Peter van Minnen observed that the rules of admission to the metropolite group mirrored the rules governing the acquisition of Roman citizenship.[140] If this was the case, we would expect to find fatherless individuals among the *metropolitai* and this is exactly what the sources illustrate. At

[134] MONSON, 'Late Ptolemaic capitation taxes' (cit. n. 24), pp. 150–152.

[135] Yet, the same term *κάτοικος* was used to denote a land-holder in general in Roman period: D. CANDUCCI, 'I 6475 cateci greci dell'Arsinoite', *Aegyptus* 70 (1990), pp. 211–255, p. 212.

[136] And other descriptions, see CANDUCCI, '6475 cateci' (cit. n. 135), pp. 222–223. The name referred originally to the first Greek settlers of the Fayum at the time of Ptolemy II Philadelphos: *ibidem*, p. 226.

[137] It is possible that the group existed also in the Herakleoplite nome: CANDUCCI, '6475 cateci' (cit. n. 135), p. 212.

[138] The existence of the group as a fiscal class is first attested in AD 52, but it seems most likely that the fiscally privileged categories of *katoikoi* and Hellens in the late Ptolemaic period prefigured the Roman-era *katoikoi* and gymnasial classes: MONSON, 'Late Ptolemaic capitation taxes' (cit. n. 24), p. 159. Yet, see O. MONTEVECCHI, 'Problemi di un'epoca di transizione. La grecità d'Egitto tra il I^{a} e il I^{p}', [in:] B. KRAMER, W. LUPPE, H. MAEHLER & G. POETHKE (eds.), *Akten des 21. Internationalen Papyrologenkongresses, Berlin, 13.–19. 8. 1995* [= *Archiv Beiheft* III], Stuttgart – Leipzig 1997, vol. II, pp. 719–726.

[139] E. BICKERMANN, 'Beiträge zur antiken Urkundengeschichte. II: *Ἀπογραφή, οἰκογένεια, ἐπίκρισις, Αἰγύπτοι*', *Archiv für Papyrusforschung* 9 (1930), pp. 24–46, p. 43; VAN MINNEN, '*Αἱ ἀπὸ γυμνασίου*' (cit. n. 130), p. 343; ROWLANDSON, 'Dissing the Egyptians' (cit. n. 130), p. 225.

[140] VAN MINNEN, '*Αἱ ἀπὸ γυμνασίου*' (cit. n. 130), pp. 340–341.

least five texts[141] from between the reign of Hadrian and mid-third century confirm that the fatherless were granted membership of the *metropolis*. As these cases have been discussed in a separate article,[142] they need only be summarised here:

1. Lykarous, fatherless metropolite daughter of a slave and metropolite mother (no. 832): *P. Ryl.* II 103 (Ptolemais Euergetis, AD 134), an *epikrisis* document for her son submitted by another son who was already scrutinised;
2. Hermione ἀπάτωρ daughter of Herois (no. 367), whose metropolite status is based on the interpretation of *SB* XXIV 15987 (*recto*: Ptolemais Euergetis, AD 208/9) and *SB* XIV 11714 (*verso*: Ptolemais Euergetis, AD 208/9);
3. Dideis explicitly described as ἀπάτωρ ἀπὸ τῆς μητροπόλεως (no. 327): *P. Petaus* 22 (Syron Kome, AD 185 or after);
4. Her brother Theon not described explicitly as ἀπάτωρ, but with no patronym (no. 831);
5. Aurelius Epimachos, described as χρηματίζων μητρός, holder of πρακτορεία σιτικῶν μητροπολιτικῶν λημμάτων (no. 186): *P. Oxy.* XLIII 3097 (Oxyrhynchos, AD 224/5).

The only text which might cast some doubt on the notion that the fatherless were admitted to the metropolite order is a fragment of *P. Thmouis* 1 (col. 158, l. 1 – col. 160, l. 22), which we have already mentioned in Chapter 1. The passage concerns the fiscal status of a group of people who had been wrongly omitted or erroneously registered on the list of *laographia* payers. The case went through several stages and, after the examination by the prefect, the status of only five people remained unclear. The prefect ruled that the five, who were registered in the metropolis but were perhaps unable to prove their status before him (col. 159, l. 10), had three months to prove by scrutiny that they retained the right (l. 12) to lower *laographia* or exemption. The list, containing three people from the village Psenacho and two from Mendes, is given.

[141] In M. Nowak, 'Fatherless among οἱ ἀπὸ τῆς μητροπόλεως – a revision', *Zeitschrift für Papyrologie und Epigraphik* 208 (2018), pp. 213–225, p. 224, I included *SB* XII 10953, but a fatherless individual mentioned there belongs to either *katoikoi* or *metropolitai*, so he was moved to section 2.4.

[142] Nowak, 'Fatherless among οἱ ἀπὸ τῆς μητροπόλεως' (cit. n. 141).

P. Thmouis 1, col. 159, l. 19 – col. 160, l. 15 [entries numbered by MN]:

Of those from the village of Psenacho and registered in Thmouis:
1. Apollonios fatherless son of the mother Soeris indicated as registered in the 4th quarter of Thmouis as Apollonios son of Straton, his mother being Soeris;
2. xx son of Nechthe[...], his mother being Thauris, indicated as registered in the 11th quarter of Thmouis as Ti[...]n son of Ailourion, his mother being Isidora;
3. Apollonios son of Protarchos, his mother being Tryphaina, indicated as registered in the 11th quarter of Thmouis as Apollonios son of Isidoros, his mother being Tryphaina; there are 3.

Of those from Mendes:
4. Psois son of Horos, his mother being Tanoupis, indicated as registered as Psois son of [...]epis, his mother being Tanoupis;
5. Horos, his brother, indicated as registered as with the same name; there are 2.[143]

The text shows that an individual described as ἀπάτωρ registered himself or was registered in the metropolis using a patronym. This might constitute proof that Apollonios required a patronym in order to register as fiscally privileged, or, even further, that one needed a patronym to be admitted into the metropolite order.[144] Yet among this group of people whose fiscal status needed to be clarified, we also find one registered with an incorrect name,

[143] *τῶν μὲν ἐπ̣ὶ̣ κ̣ώμης Ψεναχὼ | παραγεν(ομένων) καὶ ἐπὶ Θμούεως ἀναγρα(φομένων)· | Ἀπολλώνιος ἀπάτωρ ἐγ* (l. *ἐκ*) *μητρὸς | Σοήριο̣ς, δηλ(ωθεὶς) ἀναγρά(φεσθαι) ἐπὶ Θμούεως | δ ἀμφόδ(ου) ὡς Ἀπολλώνιο(ς) Στρά̣|[των(?)]ος μητρὸς [Σο]ήρ̣ιος, | [. . .]π̣ους Νεχθε[. . .] μη(τρὸς) Θαύριος, | [δηλ(ωθεὶς)] ἀναγεγρά(φθαι) ἐπ[ὶ Θμ]ούεως ια | [ἀ]μφόδου ὡς Τι[. .]ν Αἰλουρίωνος | [μη]τρὸς Ἰσιδώρα̣ς, | [Ἀπο]λ̣λώνιος Πρωτά̣[ρ]χου μητρὸς | [Τ]ρυφαίνης, δηλ(ωθεὶς) ἀναγρά(φεσθαι) ἐπὶ ⟨Θμούεως⟩ ια | ἀμφόδ(ου) ὡς Ἀπο[λ]λώνιος Ἰσιδώρου | μητρὸς Τρυφαίνης, γί(νονται) γ, | τῶν δὲ ἐπὶ Μένδητος· | Ψόι̣ς Ὥρου μητρὸ(ς) Τανούπιος, δηλ(ωθεὶς) | ἀναγρά(φεσθαι) ὡς Ψόις . . . .ήπιος μη(τρὸς) | Τανούπιος, | Ὧρος ὁ ἀδελφός, δηλ(ωθεὶς) ἀ̣ν̣α̣γ̣ρ̣άφεσθαι | ἐπὶ τοῦ αὐτοῦ ὀνό(ματος), (γίνονται) β̣.*

[144] This is how the editor, Sophie Kambitsis, interpreted the passage, as she provided a reference to *P. Bour.* 42 and quoted Youtie (‘*Ἀπάτορες*’ [cit. n. 124], p. 725) on investigation which was to reveal that the real status of Kastor from *P. Bour.* 42 was ἀπάτωρ.

patronym and metronym (2), and two with patronyms different from their real ones (3 and 4); furthermore it is difficult to determine if Horos, the last person on the list, provided the same incorrect patronym as his brother recorded in the previous entry or registered using full description of his brother (5).[145] There is nothing in the passage to provide us with any hint as to why those people were registered incorrectly: we do not know if they were admitted to the privileged group on the basis of fraudulent data – they may have given the patronym or full name of a privileged individual who had died – or if they had simply been entered incorrectly into the register and had run into difficulties providing relevant proof of their identity. Regardless of whether they were not entitled to the lower *laographia* rate, or merely unable to prove that right before the prefect, the prefect gave them another chance to confirm that they belonged to the metropolite class. We would therefore be justified in concluding that, if fatherless men could not be accepted in the metropolite group, Apollonios would not have been given the three-month grace period in which to prove his fiscally privileged status by undergoing scrutiny (again?).

There is another possible explanation: the list of five people might not have been compiled as a part of the prefect's decision, but rather included later as proof that they were not eligible for the lower *laographia* rate. Even if this were the case, it would not stand as proof that ἀπάτορες could not be admitted to the metropolite order, but only that certain Apollonios was registered as son of Straton despite of being fatherless.

2.2.2. *Katoikoi*

Jane Rowlandson noted that the rules of admission to the *katoikoi* were similar to the rules governing metropolite status, but differed significantly from those governing admission to the gymnasial group.[146] This means that we could expect fatherless individuals in this group. Indeed, Aristide Calderini noticed fatherless individuals in *P. Flor.* I 5, a census return

[145] ἀ̣ν̣α̣γ̣ρ̣άφεσθαι | ἐπὶ τοῦ αὐτοῦ ὀνό(ματος) could refer to his brother's description or state that he is how he was entered to the register.

[146] Rowlandson, 'Dissing the Egyptians' (cit. n. 130), p. 225.

dated to AD 244/5 submitted by Aurelia Thermoutharion of the *katoikoi*. She is described with her patronym, papponym (in lacuna), metronym, and *κατοι*|[...] *ἀναγρα(φομένης) ἐπ' ἀμφ]ό̣δ̣ο̣υ̣ Τ̣αμείων* (ll. 3–4), for which Roger Bagnall proposed the restitution *κατοι*|[*κοῦσα*].[147] Lines 14–16 contain a list of people belonging to Aurelia Thermoutharion's household, including two sons, Kopreios and N.N., described as *σπούριοι*. After the description, only *μὴ ανα̣*|[...] is preserved. Calderini's restitution *μὴ ἀνα̣*|[*γεγραμμένους*] was confirmed by Bagnall.[148] As the declarant was described as *κατοι*|[*κοῦσα*], she was registered in one of the *amphodoi* of Ptolemais Euergetis,[149] and her sons were labelled as *μὴ ἀνα̣*|[*γεγραμμένους*]; this would suggest that the family were *katoikoi* and children's status was acquired from the mother.

Another document that strengthens the conclusion drawn above, *BGU* III 971, is dated as late as AD 245, but contains extracts of three deeds – one *epikrisis* and two census returns – produced earlier. Lines 1–8 contain a copy or extract of the *epikrisis* of two boys, Apollinarios and Ammonios, to the *katoikoi* group;[150] the document was submitted by their parents, Doras and Tamystha, and is dated to AD 194/5.[151] Lines 8–15 are a copy or abstract of a census return for the year 229 (229-Ar-2). The declarant is Ammonios son of Doras (one of the brothers scrutinised in lines 1–8) who is described as being listed in the register of *katoikoi* in the quarter of Hermouthiake,

[147] R.S. Bagnall, 'Notes on Egyptian census declarations. I', *The Bulletin of the American Society of Papyrologists* 27 (1990), pp. 1–14, p. 4.

[148] A. Calderini, '*Ἀπάτορες*', *Aegyptus* 33 (1953), pp. 358–369, p. 369; Bagnall, 'Notes. I' (cit. n. 147), pp. 4–5. Calderini proposed to read Kopreios' father's name: *κακ Δείου*. Bagnall recognised this restitution as not very likely, but he did not exclude it. Indeed, in legal documents, both *spurius* and *Spurii filius* underline the lack of the father and the bond with the mother. The function of *spurius* in lists and census returns resembles *ἀπάτωρ*, and was therefore never followed by the patronym; however the sample size for this is limited. Although *spf* was sometimes included in Latin inscriptions with the indication of the father, *spurius* + patronym is not attested. See Chapter 1.

[149] Quarter of Tameia is attested as the quarter where *katoikoi* were registered: Canducci, '6475 cateci' (cit. n. 135), p. 225.

[150] O. Montevecchi, 'Nerone a una polis e ai 6475', *Aegyptus* 50 (1970), pp. 5–33, p. 22; Canducci, '6475 cateci' (cit. n. 135), p. 216; C. Sánchez -Moreno Ellart, '*ὑπομνήματα ἐπιγεννήσεως*: The Greco-Egyptian birth returns in Roman Egypt and the case of *P. Petaus* 1–2', *Archiv für Papyrusforschung* 56 (2010), pp. 91–129, p. 117.

[151] Date after R. Ziegler, 'Bemerkungen zur Datierung dokumentarischer Papyri und Ostraka', *Zeitschrift für Papyrologie und Epigraphik* 114 (1996), pp. 157–161, p. 160.

where his parents were also registered (ll. 2–3). A list of household members includes his wife, Thermoutharion ἀπάτωρ (l. 13), and their daughter (l. 14). Unfortunately the description of the wife has been lost (ll. 13–14), but the text preserves that she was registered in the same *amphodon* as her husband. Lines 16–21 preserve a fragment of a copy of the census return for the year 243 (243-Ar-4). The declarant (on behalf of her son) is the widowed Thermoutharion, described this time with a sole metronym instead of ἀπάτωρ. Only the beginning of her son's description has survived, l. 21:]Ἀμμωνίου τοῦ Δωρ[, which Bagnall reconstructed to [καὶ τὸν γενόμενόν μοι ἐκ τοῦ | γενομένου μου ἀνδρὸς] Ἀμμωνίου τοῦ Δωρ[ᾶ υἱὸν - *ca.* ? -].[152]

Bagnall pointed out that *BGU* III 971 must have been compiled in connection with some procedure related to status, perhaps *epikrisis*;[153] the three documents may have been gathered as proof that one of Doras and Thermoutharion's children, perhaps their son, was eligible to become a *katoikos*. If this is the case, we may suggest that Thermoutharion, despite being ἀπάτωρ, belonged to the *katoikoi* as well,[154] or that the status was acquired from the father with no regard to the identity of the mother. The former interpretation is more plausible.

However, Daniela Canducci suggested that these two texts might attest to the endogamous marriages popular and significant among *katoikoi* before AD 212, that were kept hidden by presenting the children as fatherless.[155] This interpretation, however, is more than unlikely, as Thermoutharion ἀπάτωρ must have been born before the *constitutio Antoniniana*. In the census of 229 she is listed as a wife and mother, and her husband Ammonios was *ca.* 50 years old at that time. It is likely that they were married before the *constitutio Antoniniana*, and if the children had been born before the *constitutio*, there would have been no reason to disguise them as fatherless, which is discussed in Chapter 2. Furthermore, neither of the documents contains even the slightest suggestion of brother-sister marriages. Obvi-

[152] Reading and reconstruction proposed in: R.S. Bagnall, 'Notes on Egyptian census declarations. IV', *The Bulletin of the American Society of Papyrologists* 29 (1992), pp. 101–115, p. 113.

[153] Bagnall, 'Notes. IV' (cit. n. 152), p. 112.

[154] Canducci included her on the list of *katoikoi*: D. Canducci, 'I 6475 cateci greci dell'Arsinoite. Prosopografia', *Aegyptus* 71 (1991), pp. 121–216, pp. 199 – 200.

[155] Canducci, '6475 cateci' (cit. n. 135), p. 244.

ously, the sources are too few and too late to allow for any firm conclusions; they nonetheless suggest the possibility that fatherless persons were admitted to the *katoikoi* order.[156]

The material is not abundant, but we can reason by analogy of freedmen as in regard to *astoi*. Basing on *BGU* I 55 and 138, we could suspect that freedmen were included to the group of *katoikoi*.[157] The most obvious example is *BGU* I 138 (Ptolemais Euergetis, AD 188/9), a census return for the year 187 (187-Ar-18), in which one of the declared individuals is *Δεῖος Ἥρωνος νεωτέρου Καπίτ[ωνος τοῦ καὶ . . . | μη(τρὸς)] Βησοῦτος ἀπελευθέρας Ἑρμιόνης τῆς Διδᾶ κάτοι[κος ἐπικεκριμέ]νο]ς (ἐτῶν) λα* (ll. 7–9). Deios is described having undergone an *epikrisis* to the group of *katoikoi*. It is important to note that his mother, Besous, was a freedwoman of a certain Hermione who was daughter of *katoikos*; as the mother of a person declared as *katoikos*, Besous would have been eligible to marry a *katoikos* and produce children who could be scrutinised to this order. The mother therefore belonged to the group, as the children of people of unequal *status civitatis* followed the lower status, which problem is discussed separately. The text thus suggests that a freedwoman could have acquired a privileged status from her patron.

A similar situation is attested in *BGU* I 55 (Ptolemais Euergetis, AD 175 or after), a document containing census returns from the years 159 (159-Ar-1) and 173 (173-Ar3), which lists the family of Mysthes *alias* Ninnos, *katoikos* (ll. 13–14). Mysthes was married to Zosime, a freedwoman of Ammonarion (ll. 3–4 and 18). Ammonarion's father, Marion, is listed as a member of the *katoikoi* in the census of AD 159. In both census returns the children of Mysthes and Zosime were declared, for AD 159, ll. 7–8: Ammonios, 5 years old, and Didymos, 4 years old;[158] for AD 173, ll. 19–21: N.N., 11 years old, Dioskoros, 10 years old, N.N., 9 years old, and Isidora, 8 years old. The children declared for the year 159 were each described as *μὴ ἀναγεγρ(αμμένα) ἐν*

[156] Montevecchi claimed that only children of *katoikoi* could become *katoikoi* themselves: MONTEVECCHI, 'Nerone' (cit. n. 150), p. 24.

[157] CANDUCCI, '6475 cateci' (cit. n. 135), p. 234.

[158] The third child possible, but not very likely: J. COWEY & D. KAH, 'Bemerkungen zu Texten aus *BGU* I–IV. Teil I: Zensusdeklarationen', *Zeitschrift für Papyrologie und Epigraphik* 163 (2007), pp. 147–182, p. 149.

ἐπιγεγενημένοις (l. 8), and the same description occurs in line 20 after the name of the first son, while the adverb ὁμοίως appears after Dioskoros and his 9-year old brother (ll. 20 and 21). This way of labelling children in census declarations could be proof that they were entitled to membership in one of the privileged groups.[159] Interestingly enough, the father of Mysthes was also married to a freedwoman (ll. 1–2: Aphrodite *alias* Aphroditous), but Mysthes' mother was another free woman, Herais, as suggested by his metronym in line 13.

Concluding, two examples of fatherless individuals in the group of *katoikoi* survived, but both postdate the *constitutio Antoniniana*. Nor can we rely on the indirect argument of freedmen, as the sources are not numerous and attest only freedwomen among *katoikoi*.

2.2.3. Gymnasial order

As Peter van Minnen wrote, the rules of admission to οἱ ἀπὸ τοῦ γυμνασίου at the beginning of the Roman period would have been rather loose and favoured the acquisition of status after fathers. In other words, to gain admission to the gymnasial group, it was sufficient to have a father who also belonged to the group.[160] This observation suggests that fatherless individuals may not have been able to gain admission. Yet a decision by the Roman government closed the order around one century after the beginning of the Roman rule, between 50s and 70s,[161] and the Roman provincial administration imposed restrictions on the admission of new members to the gymnasial group. According to Peter van Minnen, this would have excluded the offspring of mothers who did not belong to the group (discussed in Chapter 4), but not included the fatherless and freedmen.

Indeed, the importance of ancestry for membership of the gymnasial order suggests that children born of single mothers would have not been eligible to join after the order was closed. From the late first century, an applicant had to prove several generations of ancestry on both the father's

[159] See *supra*, p. 55, n. 126.

[160] van Minnen, '*Αἱ ἀπὸ γυμνασίου*' (cit. n. 130), p. 340.

[161] van Minnen, '*Αἱ ἀπὸ γυμνασίου*' (cit. n. 130), pp. 341–342.

and mother's side.[162] It also seems that the adopted children of gymnasial couples could be excluded from the order. In some Oxyrhynchite *epikrisis* applications fathers had to swear that their child was begotten and not adopted, as in *P. Oxy.* X 1266, ll. 32-37 (Oxyrhynchos, AD 98), which problem is discussed in detail in Chapter 4.

As van Minnen pointed out, the requirement of gymnasial ancestry could not be fulfilled by freedmen (nor by ἀπάτορες), who simply did not have ancestors.[163] Yet, the observation that freedmen (and the fatherless) could not satisfy the requirement applied to candidates born of lawful marriage does not necessarily prove that freedmen and ἀπάτορες were excluded from the group. For those outside the regular system, the requirements for status acquisition would have been based on different criteria, as it was for Roman citizenship or metropolite status: freedmen acquired both Roman citizenship and metropolite status of their patrons, while the fatherless followed their mothers; both of these scenarios differed from the 'basic' rule. The extensive proof of ancestry required from members born to couples should not therefore be taken as proof that those outside the traditional family system – *i.e.* freedmen and bastards – were not admitted at all.

Furthermore, Youtie observed that ten fatherless persons were recorded on the list of ephebes who took part in the ephebic game in Leontopolis,[164] *SEG* XL 1568 = *SB* VIII 9997 (Leontopolis, AD 220).[165] None of the boys recorded was labelled as ἀπάτωρ, perhaps because this indicator was not used in the region,[166] but they were described with the sole metronym, ll. 21–22: *Βησα|ρίων Θεανοῦτος*, or as ἐκ μητρός, *e.g.* l. 27: *Νεμεσίων ἐγ μητρὸς Ἀμμωναρίου Κοΐντου*. This observation is important, since, according to the traditional view, ephebes were the ones who were further scrutinised to become members of the gymnasial group, which system was an

[162] See especially VAN MINNEN, '*Αἱ ἀπὸ γυμνασίου*' (cit. n. 130) and Y. BROUX, 'Creating a new local elite. The establishment of the metropolitan orders of Roman Egypt', *Archiv für Papyrusforschung* 59.1 (2013), pp. 143–153 with references to previous literature.

[163] VAN MINNEN, '*Αἱ ἀπὸ γυμνασίου*' (cit. n. 130), p. 345.

[164] For *υἱός* / *θυγάτηρ* as an element of the identification cluster, see D. HAGEDORN, 'Zur Verwendung von *υἱός* und *θυγάτηρ* vor dem Vatersnamen in Urkunden römischer Zeit', *Zeitschrift für Papyrologie und Epigraphik* 80 (1990), pp. 277–282.

[165] YOUTIE, '*Ἀπάτορες*' (cit. n. 124), p. 730.

[166] For the discribution of the term, see pp. 64–70.

imitation of the model of the acquisition of citizenship of *poleis*.[167] It is, however, uncertain, whether all ephebes were scrutinised for the gymnasial group.[168] Although the text is dated to AD 220, after Septimius Severus had granted *boulai* to the metropoleis, it is possible that the *ephebeia* functioned according to earlier rules, in which case the text could be interpreted as referring to the gymnasial class in Leontopolis.

Jean Bingen confirmed that Youtie's observation on the presence of men described only with metronym among ephebes was significant,[169] but sought another explanation. According to him, individuals described with only their metronyms would not have been ἀπάτορες, but rather the children of so-called mixed unions. He based this assumption on comparison with Antinoopolis, as people with sole metronyms are present not only in *SEG* XL 1568, but also on the ephebic lists from Antinoopolis (*I. Portes* 5, 6, 9 *&* 10 and *SB* I 4965). Those on the lists from Antinoopolis described with only their metronyms would not have been ἀπάτορες, but rather the children of so-called mixed unions between citizens and non-citizens admitted to citizenship of Antinoopolis due to the right of *epigamia*. The children of such unions would have been described with sole metronyms because their right to become ephebes (and citizens of Antinoopolis) depended on their mother. If the father was not mentioned it was because he had no bearing on the child's future citizenship.[170]

[167] *E.g.* NELSON, *Status Declarations* (cit. n. 33), p. 59; FISCHER-BOVET, 'Official identity and ethnicity' (cit. n. 93), p. 231.

Montevecchi, however, claimed that *ephebeia* would have been reserved for the *astoi* only: O. MONTEVECCHI, 'Efebia e ginnasio. In margine a B. Legras, Néotês', *Aegyptus* 80 (2000), pp. 133–138, p. 135.

[168] According to Nelson, a boy admitted to the *ephebeia* could be left aside of the gymnasial group because of the insufficient maternal ancestry: NELSON, *Status Declarations* (cit. n. 33), pp. 58–59.

Taubenschlag suggested that becoming an ephebe would have been a first step of joining the gymnasial group and the examination for the gymnasium admitted the candidates to the *ephebeia* too. Consequently, almost every ephebe would have eventually belonged to the gymnasial order: R. TAUBENSCHLAG, *The Law of Greco-Roman Egypt in the Light of the Papyri, 332 BC – 640 AD*, Warsaw 1955², pp. 640–641.

John Whitehorn suggested that *ephebeia* was in fact a higher level of the gymnasial group: J.E.G. WHITEHORNE, 'The ephebate and the gymnasial class in Roman Egypt', *The Bulletin of the American Society of Papyrologists* 19 (1982), pp. 171–184.

[169] BINGEN, 'Inscription éphèbique' (cit. n. 127), p. 215.

[170] BINGEN, 'Inscription éphèbique' (cit. n. 127), p. 221.

Furthermore, Leontopolis had obtained the right to organise the Antinoopolite games and organised them according to Antinoopolite rules. This would suggest that Leontopolis admitted boys born of mixed unions to the *ephebeia* on the grounds such individuals were also allowed in Antinoopolis.

The Leontopolis list, however, is unusual. It is divided into three groups: the winners of the agon, other ephebes and the category under the heading, ll. 50–52:

> *Καὶ οἱ ἐν τάξει ὑπερμε|γεθῶν καὶ ἄλλων καταδεῶν τὴν ὄψιν παραδεχθέντες ὑπὸ τοῦ κρα|τίστου ἐπιστρατήγου.*

This group should include two categories of boys, ὑπερμεγέθεις and καταδεεῖς τὴν ὄψιν, who were not included in the list as regular ephebes, but who were admitted by the *epistrategos* only after they (or their parents) complained.[171] Marcus Tod suggested that they would have been excluded due to physical disability;[172] Jean Bingen thought the group consisted of boys too young to be included on the list of ephebes, καταδεεῖς τὴν ὄψιν, as well as those who had not been presented to the *ephebeia* at the proper age, but only later.[173] A high proportion of young men listed in this category were described with sole metronyms. They would have been admitted only as the result of an appeal brought by their parents before the *epistrategos*, ll. 53–57 and 60–61. Those seven would have been rejected initially, along with twelve other candidates, due to conservatism and a lack of enthusiasm from the local magistrates for the new rules of admission.[174] This, however, does not explain why some boys described by metronyms (ll. 21–22, 27 and 44) would have been admitted immediately without appealing to the *epistrategos*.

Obviously if Bingen's interpretation of *SEG* XL 1568 is correct, the inscription tells us nothing about the admission to οἱ ἀπὸ τοῦ γυμνασίου, but only into the civic body of Antinoopolis (*infra*, pp. 163–164). However, even if we reject this hypothesis as too speculative, the decision to reject

[171] M.N. Tod, 'An ephebic inscription from Memphis', *The Journal of Egyptian Archaeology* 37.1 (1951), pp. 86–99, p. 96.

[172] Tod, 'Ephebic inscription' (cit. n. 171), p. 95.

[173] Bingen, 'Inscription éphèbique' (cit. n. 127), pp. 223–224.

[174] Bingen, 'Inscription éphèbique' (cit. n. 127), p. 225.

does not allow us to conclude that the fatherless were indeed admitted to the gymnasial order of Leontopolis. The fact that the majority of individuals with sole metronyms were added to the categories of people who would have not been included in the *ephebeia* under normal circumstances, ὑπερμεγέθεις and καταδεεῖς τὴν ὄψιν, suggests that the situation is irregular. We cannot use an irregular (and thus-far unexplained) scenario to determine the regular rules for the admission to the *ephebeia* and to the gymnasial group. Therefore, the discussed inscription should not be interpreted as proof for the admission of fatherless to the *ephebeia* in Leontopolis.

The lack of proof for the admission of fatherless individuals to the gymnasial group suggests that the maternal status acquisition did not work in this group. This conclusion is further supported by information from the corn dole of Oxyrhynchos. The sources, which I discussed in detail in another publication, tell us that neither the fatherless nor freedmen were admitted to the *epikrithentes*, the group primarily eligible for the corn dole. This is because the group of *epikrithentes* was based on the membership in either the gymnasial order or the *ephebeia*. It seems that fatherless sons of mothers belonging to the group were admitted only later in the special group of *homologoi*.[175]

If freedmen were indeed excluded, the hypothesis that only those able to prove legitimate lineage were allowed into the order seems even more plausible. The evidence for the exclusion of freedmen, however, is far from certain. In *P. Oxy.* I 171 = *SB* XXII 15353 (Oxyrhynchos, AD 146/7), a census return for AD 145 (145-Ox-2,) we find a family consisting of Hierax son of Hakoris, who describes himself as ἀπὸ γυμνασίου (l. 13), and Hierax, a son born to the declarant of a freedwoman Alexandra, ll. 14-16: Ἱέραξ υἱός \μου/ μ̣η̣τ̣ρ̣ὸς Ἀλεξάνδρας | ἀπελευθ̣[έρας - *ca.* 18 -] | ἀπογρα(φόμενος) ἐπ[ὶ τοῦ αὐτοῦ ἀμφόδου]. Although the description of Hierax belonging to the gymnasial group has not been preserved, we can assume he was a member, as the members of the gymnasial order are totalled up directly after him in ll. 17–18: ὡς εἶνα[ι *ca.* 20 ἀπὸ τοῦ] | γυ̣μν[ασίου *ca.* 18].[176] The text suggests that, even after the closure of the order, a person born to a freed mother

[175] Nowak, 'Get your free corn' (cit. n. 132).

[176] D. Montserrat, G. Fantoni & P. Robinson, 'Varia descripta Oxyrhynchita', *The Bulletin of the American Society of Papyrologists* 31 (1994), pp. 11–80, p. 31.

could belong to the order. It is difficult to say if this example proves a rule or is simply an exceptional case. Yet if a freedwomen could be the mother of someone belonging to the group, freedmen would also have been admitted to the order; and if freedmen were admitted, it is likely that fatherless children would also be accepted. This hypothetical reconstruction is, however, based on only one source.

Finally, Youtie observed the presence of [*Ψεναvο(?)*]*ῦ̣πις ἀπάτωρ μη(τρὸς)* [*Πνεφ*]*ε̣ρῶτος* and *Μύσθης ἀπάτωρ μη(τρὸς) Ταορσε|νούφεως* among priests of Bacchias and payers of *laographia* at the lower rate (*P. Bacch.* 2 = *SB* VI 9320 {Bakchias, AD 171}, ll. 19 and 41–42).[177] Although there are no more surviving texts attesting fatherless priests, the explanation proposed by Youtie that Egyptian priests were given priesthoods following the maternal line would hold well.[178]

2.2.4. Fatherless individuals in privileged unidentified groups

There are a few fatherless individuals in the papyri who could be identified as payers of lower *laographia*, but the groups to which they belonged cannot be determined. Among those who paid *laographia* at the privileged rate, we have already mentioned Pasion son of the slave Dioskoros (no. 833), recorded in the census return for AD 117 (*P. Brux.* I 19 {Ptolemais Euergetis, AD 117/8}). Pasion is further recorded in receipts for poll tax (*P. Harr.* II 180–189 {Ptolemais Euergetis}) for the years 134, 136, 137, 139, 140, 141, 143, 144, 145 and 146, in which he is described as Pasion son of Dioskoros slave of Laberia. He paid only twenty drachmae of *laographia*, which was the privileged rate in the Arsinoite nome.[179] As far as his status is concerned, the only information provided in the receipts is that he paid his tax in the Phremei quarter, which is one of the quarters where *katoikoi* were registered.[180] Yet, this offers no certain indication of his status.

[177] YOUTIE, '*Ἀπάτορες*' (cit. n. 124), p. 733.

[178] YOUTIE, '*Ἀπάτορες*' (cit. n. 124), pp. 733–734.

[179] MONSON, 'Late Ptolemaic capitation taxes' (cit. n. 24), tab. 6 at p. 156.

[180] CANDUCCI, '6475 cateci' (cit. n. 135), p. 225.

Another individual belonging to the privileged group of Egyptians is Aretion ἀπάτωρ, son of Thermouth(), registered in an *amphodon* of Ptolemais Euergetis and payer of *laographia* at the privileged rate (no. 560): *SB* XII 10953 (Ptolemais Euergetis, AD 172).

It has been recognised in the scholarly literature that certain offices were only given to members of privileged groups; among these Christelle Fisher-Bovet included *sitologoi*.[181] There are several fatherless individuals who served in this position, including one of the *sitologoi* from Euhemeria reporting to the royal scribe in *P. Stras.* VI 526 (Euhemeria, AD 156/7) who, in line 6, seems to be described as ἀπάτωρ (no. 425). Two other examples come from the archive of Petaus. Asklas (no. 329) and Potamon are mentioned on a list of recently appointed *sitologoi* (*P. Petaus* 59, ll. 29 and 68 [Ptolemais Hormou, AD 185]). As all instances come from the Arsinoite nome, the individuals may have been either *katoikoi* or members of the metropolite order.

CONCLUSION

The examination of status acquisition from mothers throughout Roman Egypt offers few certain conclusions, largely due to the state of sources. As we demonstrated in Chapter 1, people described as fatherless constituted only a tiny percentage of the population; furthermore, direct descriptions are limited to two nomes. Futhermore, identifying members of groups partly or fully exempted from *laographia* is often problematic.

For these reasons, we must rely on analogies and comparison. It seems that the membership in the metropolite group was based on the Roman rules of status acquisition. Yet, those rules would not have been an imitation of *ius civile*, the law applied to Romans themselves, but would rather have belonged to *ius gentium*. Based on other evidence and indirect arguments, we can assume that the same was true for *katoikoi*, while the rules governing οἱ ἀπὸ τοῦ γυμνασίου remain puzzling, as it is difficult to state what the group was for: its function may not have been simply fiscal, but

[181] Fischer-Bovet, 'Official identity and ethnicity' (cit. n. 93), p. 232.

it was certainly not a *status civitatis*. For this group both the admission of fatherless individuals and the application of Roman rules is doubtful.

Additional proof that the Romans imposed rules of status acquisition from *ius gentium* onto all groups in Egypt is fact that the *Gnomon of idios logos* – which devotes much attention to the status of children whenever it was problematic – never discusses fatherless individuals. This may have been the case because their status, as acquired from their mothers, never raised controversies. This picture of status acquisition should be completed with the next chapter.

mother: Roman → child: Roman
mother: local citizen → child: local citizen
mother: citizen of Antinoopolis → child: citizen of Antinoopolis
mother: Egyptian → child: Egyptian
mother: metropolite Egyptian → child: metropolite Egyptian
mother: gymnasial Egyptian → child: Egyptian (full poll tax)
mother: catoecic Egyptian → child: catoecic Egyptian

Tab. 1. Fatherless individuals in Roman Egypt according to the civic/fiscal status

CHAPTER FOUR

MIXED UNIONS

IN THIS CHAPTER, we shall closer examine the social and legal standing of children resulting from 'mixed unions'. Youtie identified the children of 'mixed unions' in Roman Egypt as ἀπάτορες on the grounds of the *Gnomon of idios logos*, he also interpreted 'mixed unions' as having been forbidden or at least discouraged.[1] However this may not have been entirely the case, as we shall see in this chapter. The final question posed in this chapter is on the impact which a position of a child born to a mixed union had on a legal standing of such individuals.

1. PTOLEMAIC EGYPT

In classical Greek, there were a few terms used to describe a bastard: νόθος, παρθένιος, and σκότιος were all applied to children born of unmarried parents. While νόθος often referred to the child of a concubine, it could be used more generally for anyone born out of wedlock; παρθένιος and σκότιος both referred to the offspring of unwed women.[2] Before the introduction of Pericles' Citizenship Law in the mid-fifth century BC, it

[1] H. YOUTIE, 'Ἀπάτορες. Law vs. custom in Roman Egypt', [in:] J. BINGEN, G. CAMBIER & G. NACHTERGAEL (eds.), *Le monde grec: pensée, littérature, histoire, documents. Hommages à Claire Préaux*, Brussels 1975, pp. 723–740 (reprinted in: H. YOUTIE, *Scriptiunculae posteriores*, vol. I, Bonn 1981, pp. 17–35), p. 738.

[2] D. OGDEN, *Greek Bastardy in the Classical and Hellenistic Periods*, Oxford 1996, p. 18. The term σκότιος was, however, used also to denote concubine's bastards: *ibidem*.

did not matter whether a mother-concubine was a citizen of Athens or not, as children became Athenians after their fathers.[3] After Pericles' Law, which restricted Athenian citizenship to individuals born of two Athenian parents, however, the meaning of *νόθος* shifted to either 'offspring of foreign mother' or 'children of concubine', as we can see in later Greek literature.[4] In Hellenistic inscriptions, *νόθος* developed into a civic category: a child of a mother who did not belong to the community of the father.[5] It is worth noting that sometimes *nothoi* constituted a category between citizens and *xenoi*, thus a kind of separate *status civitatis.*[6] The meaning of *nothos* in Ptolemaic Egypt, as we mentioned in Chapter 1, is not entirely clear, although it does not seem to have been applied to children begotten of 'mixed unions' as it was in certain other parts of the Hellenistic world. Furthermore, we possess relatively little surviving information regarding such unions in Ptolemaic Egypt.

As Daniel Ogden wrote, it became necessary for Greek newcomers to Egypt to marry women of different cultures or political entities; this is a kind of universal truth for conquered lands and is often visible in founding myths of Greek colonies. Ogden further observed that, after the initial period of *commixtio sanguinis*, the new political entities would often restrict access to themselves, thus providing a precise line of demarcation between themselves and 'barbarians'.[7] While the former phenomenon is certainly visible in the papyri, it is difficult to confirm whether or not Hel-

[3] M. Silver, *Slave-Wives. Single Women and 'Bastards' in the Ancient Greek World: Law and Economics Perspectives*, Oxford 2018, p. 169. Whether *nothoi* were indeed full citizens or only with lesser political privileges, see *ibidem*, pp. 169–176, with further literature.

[4] J.J. Vélissaropoulos-Karakostas, 'Les nothoi hellénistiques', [in:] E. Harris & G. Thür (eds.), *Symposion 2007. Vorträge zur griechischen und hellenistischen Rechtsgeschichte (Durham, 2.–6. September 2007)* [= *Akten der Gesellschaft für griechische und hellenistische Rechtsgeschichte* XX], Vienna 2008, pp. 253–274, p. 253; Silver, *Slave-Wives* (cit. n. 3), p. 169.

[5] Vélissaropoulos-Karakostas, 'Les nothoi' (cit. n. 4); L.M. Günther, 'Nothoi und nothai – eine Randgruppe in der hellenistischen Polis? Zur Auswertung der einschlägigen Inschriften Milets', [in:] A. Matthaei & M. Zimmermann (eds.), *Stadtkultur im Hellenismus* [= *Die hellenistische Polis als Lebensform* IV], Heidelberg 2014, pp. 133–147.

[6] J. Mélèze-Modrzejewski, 'Dryton le crétois et sa famille ou les mariages mixtes dans l'Égypte hellénistique', [in:] *Aux origines de l'Hellénisme, la Crète et la Grèce. Hommage à Henri Van Effenterre présenté par le Centre G. Glotz*, Paris 1984, pp. 353–377, p. 355.

[7] Ogden, *Greek Bastardy* (cit. n. 2), pp. 323–327.

lenistic Egypt entered the second phase described by Ogden, as marital restrictions are nearly impossible to trace.

The most obvious case is the Hellenes of the *chora* who labelled themselves with a variety of descriptions referring to *patris*, some of which were not even Greek. The relatively high number of 'inter-marriages' between them attested in the papyri suggest that such individuals were not subject to any marital restrictions. Such marriages are also early: the very first preserved Greek marital contract from Egypt was between Herakleides the Temnitan and Demetria the Koan (*P. Eleph.* 1 [310 BC]). These observations should not be a surprise, as there was no legal distinction between 'Hellenes' of the *chora* in Ptolemaic Egypt.[8] Descriptions discussed in the previous chapter such as 'Macedonian' or 'Athenian' did not indicate that the individuals had a separate *status civitatis*, but were rather a sign of ancestry and/or cultural appurtenance and documentary identification. In later periods, the ethnic descriptions became less significant; while some developed into designations of a specific group or status, such as the famous Persian of the *epigone*.[9]

The 'inter-marriages' between Greek newcomers and the indigenous population constitute a separate problem. As we mentioned in the previous chapter, there was both a cultural and legal distinction between 'Hellenes' and 'Egyptians', which is most apparent in the double system of courts which decided cases according to language. Yet couples described in terms of both local descent and Greek origin are relatively well attested in the source material.[10] The earliest record of a 'Graeco-Egyptian' marriage is *W. Chr.* 51 = *I. Fayoum* I 2 = *SB* I 1567 (244–221 BC), an inscription from Krokodilopolis: daughters of this Graeco-Egyptian couple bore *patris* of their father, but were given both Greek and Egyptian names.[11]

[8] MÉLÈZE-MODRZEJEWSKI, 'Dryton le crétois' (cit. n. 6), pp. 360–361.

[9] U. YIFTACH, 'Did BGU XIV 2367 work?', [in:] M. DEPAUW & S. COUSSEMENT (eds.), *Identifiers and Identification Methods in the Ancient World. Legal Documents in Ancient Societies*, vol. III [= *Orientalia Lovaniensia Analecta* CCXXIX], Leuven – Paris – Walpole, MA 2014, pp. 103–118, pp. 110–111.

[10] R. TAUBENSCHLAG, *The Law of Greco-Roman Egypt in the Light of the Papyri. 332 BC – 640 AD*, Warsaw 1955², p. 104, n. 8: examples provided.

[11] MÉLÈZE-MODRZEJEWSKI, 'Dryton le crétois' (cit. n. 6), p. 363.

The existence of such unions and their resulting children has long been recognised in the scholarly literature,[12] and has been supported by a variety of not stringent but probable arguments, *e.g.* frequency of double Graeco-Egyptian names,[13] identification clusters consisting of a Greek name and Egyptian patronym or Egyptian name and Greek patronym, or bilingual family archives.[14] There is nothing to suggest that restrictions on marriages between 'Hellenes' and 'Egyptians' were imposed by law.

Regulations regarding mixed unions might have been more restrictive for citizens of Naukratis, Alexandria and Ptolemais, whose citizenship was to some extent comparable to the Roman concept of *status*. Although it is nearly impossible to reconstruct the rules that might have applied to mixed families in the Egyptian *poleis* of the Ptolemaic period, it has been suggested that the rule of double descent might have been applied in Naukratis. Only two pieces of evidence, however, support such an argument: Athenaeus (4.149 d) claims that there existed a 'law of marriage' in Naukratis, and *W. Chr.* 27, discussed later in thich chapter, mentions that citizens of Antinoopolis had *epigamia* towards Egyptians, while citizens of Naukratis did not.[15]

This evidence does not allow for anything more than conjecture. First, status acquisition in *poleis*, as discussed in Chapter 3, might have been redefined by Romans, thus it may be that *W. Chr.* 27 refers not to Hellenistic, but Roman prohibition.[16] Second, even if the prohibition discussed in *W. Chr.* 27 predated the Roman presence in Egypt, the meaning of the

[12] See V. Ehrenberg, *L'État grec*, Paris 1976, p. 254, or Taubenschlag, *Law of Greco-Roman Egypt* (cit. n. 10), pp. 104–108, who believed mixed unions to be regularly contracted in the Egyptian *chora*. This view has been, however, nuanced by Mélèze-Modrzejewski, 'Dryton le crétois' (cit. n. 6).

[13] Reservations in regard to the onomastics as a tool for studying mixed unions, see M. Grassi, 'Matrimoni misti e onomastica nella Siria d'età romana: il caso di Dura Europos', [in:] S. Marchesini (ed.), *Atti del Convegno Matrimoni misti: una via per l'integrazione tra i popoli. Mixed Marriages: A Way to Integration among Peoples. Convegno multidisciplinare internazionale (Verona – Trento, 1–2 dicembre 2011)*, Trento 2012, pp. 127–138, pp. 129–131.

[14] Critics of those arguments, see Mélèze-Modrzejewski, 'Dryton le crétois' (cit. n. 6), pp. 362–374.

[15] Mélèze-Modrzejewski, 'Dryton le crétois' (cit. n. 6), pp. 356–357.

[16] Ogden, *Greek Bastardy* (cit. n. 2), p. 356.

term 'Egyptian' changed considerably between the seventh century BC, when the city was founded, and the second century AD. It is impossible to reconstruct the marital laws of Naukratis solely on the basis of *W. Chr.* 27, nor can we say whether or not the city allowed *metroxenia* or *patroxenia*.[17]

We possess comparably little information regarding the marital laws of Hellenistic Alexandria and Ptolemais,[18] but it is accepted that they did not accept offspring of mixed unions among their citizens. A supposed Alexandrian-Egyptian family is attested in a third-century Demotic tax list, *P. Lille dém.* III 101 = *P. Count.* 4, ll. 61–65. Willy Clarysse identified the head of this family, Monimos son of Kleandros (l. 61), as the son of Kleandros, Alexandrian. Kleandros, in turn, appears in one of the wills *P. Petrie*² I 1, ll. 55–56, in which he acts as a *kyrios*.[19] In 1988, Clarysse suggested that Monimos might have been an Alexandrian who married a non-Alexandrian and had a non-Alexandrian daughter.[20] In *P. Count.*, Clarysse and Dorothy Thompson noted that it was uncertain whether Monimos had followed the Alexandrian status of his father, as he was liable for the salt tax as other Hellens.[21] It is thus difficult to say who was the last Alexandrian in this family and how they became non-Alexandrians. Yet, it happened at some point.

Dryton's archive provides us with some information regarding Ptolemais. Dryton had been a cavalry officer and described himself as both Cretan and a citizen of Ptolemais,[22] although his second family was highly Egyptianised.[23]

[17] Term *patroxenos* is actually not attested in the Greek sources, I use it after OGDEN, *Greek Bastardy* (cit. n. 2), p. 19.

[18] Theories on Alexandria, see summarised in OGDEN, *Greek Bastardy* (cit. n. 2), pp. 348–355.

[19] W. CLARYSSE, 'Une famille alexandrine dans la chora', *Chronique d'Égypte* 63 (1988), pp. 137–140. The same Monimos may be attested in *I. Fay.* III 207, commentary to *P. Count.* 4, ll. 61–64, in *P. Count.*, pp. 139–140.

[20] CLARYSSE, 'Une famille alexandrine' (cit. n. 19), p. 139.

[21] *P. Count.*, p. 140.

[22] See M. VALLET, 'Dryton et la citoyenneté ptolémaïte : statut juridique et stratégies sociales', *Chronique d'Égypte* 88 (2013), pp. 125–146.

[23] J.K. WINNICKI, 'Ein ptolemäischer Offizier in Thebais', *Eos* 60 (1972), pp. 343–353, p. 352; K. VANDORPE, 'Apollonia, a businesswoman in a multicultural society (Pathyris, 2nd–1st centuries BC)', [in:] H. MELAERTS & L. MOOREN (eds.), *Le rôle et le statut de la femme en Égypte hellénistique, romaine et byzantine : acts du colloque international, Bruxelles – Leuven, 27–29 novembre 1997* [= *Studia Hellenistica* XXXVII], Paris 2002, pp. 325–336.

He was married twice:[24] the first wife was described as *aste*,[25] while the second lacked any label. The son born of the first wife, Sarapias daughter of Esthladas, possessed citizenship,[26] but the five daughters with the second wife, Apollonia *alias* Senmouthis, are not described as citizens.[27] They married Egyptians, and gave only Egyptian names to their children: *e.g.* the eldest, Apollonia *alias* Senmouthis, was married to Kaies son of Pates.[28]

We cannot draw many conclusions from the two attested cases in which *astoi* married people of the *chora* and had children with them. It is logical to assume that rules concerning the status of children born to people belonging to different *poleis* would have developed, as this also happened in other parts of the Hellenistic world.[29] Although these rules have not been preserved, it is possible to make further conjectures based on the *Gnomon of idios logos*, which we will discuss below.

2. THE ROMAN ERA

2.1. *Unions with Romans*

For Romans, as 'mixed union' could be defined any marriage contracted between a Roman and a non-Roman. Whether such unions were recognised as legitimate depended entirely on the *conubium*[30] (G. 1.76; *Tit.*

[24] Documents belonging to the archive were being published gradually providing new data, thus at some point it was discussed whether Dryton had two or three wives: N. Lewis, 'Dryton's wives: two or three?', *Chronique d'Égypte* 57 (1982), pp. 317–321. Yet, now, there could be no doubt that he had only two, see *P. Dryton*, pp. 27–29.

[25] Arangio-Ruiz recognised her as an Alexandrian: V. Arangio Ruiz, 'Intorno agli *astoi* dell'Egitto Greco-Romano', *Revue internationale des droits de l'Antiquité* 4 (1950 = *Studi de Visscher*), pp. 7–20. This recognition does not seem credible any more: D. Delia, *Alexandrian Citizenship during the Roman Principate* [= *American Classical Studies* XXIII], Atlanta 1991, pp. 13–21.

[26] G. Plaumann, *Ptolemais in Oberägypten: ein Beitrag zur Geschichte des Hellenismus in Ägypten*, Leipzig 1910, p. 21.

[27] *Ibidem*, p. 22.

[28] Vandorpe, 'Apollonia, a businesswoman' (cit. n. 23), p. 336.

[29] Vélissaropoulos-Karakostas, 'Les nothoi' (cit. n. 4).

[30] *Ius conubii* could be granted individually, as in the case of veterans (G. 1.57) or to entire groups usually together with the *ius commercii* since early republican times: A. N. Sherwin-

Ulp. 5.3).[31] It has already been pointed out that Romans recognised marriages between peregrines, which was important in regard to citizenship.[32] Similarly, it does not appear that unions between Romans and non-Romans without *conubium* would have been entirely deprived of the status of marriage under Roman law.[33] Such unions were not *matrimonia iusta*, but still *matrimonia* (G. 1.87: *non iusto contracto matrimonio*).[34]

Three paragraphs in the *Gnomon* (39, 46 and 52) deal with marriages between peregrines and Romans. The concessions by which a Roman could marry an Egyptian is expressed in § 52 of the *Gnomon*.

BGU V 1210, l. 137: *νβ. Ῥωμαίοις ἐξὸν Αἰγυπτίαν γ[ῆμα]ι.*

52. Romans are permitted to have Egyptian wives.

The text states clearly that Romans could marry Egyptian women. Such a sentence, however, seemed completely unacceptable to the earliest modern editors of the *Gnomon*, who proposed that ⟨οὐκ⟩ should be restituted before ἐξόν.[35] This view has not been shared by subsequent commentators equivo-

WHITE, *The Roman Citizenship*, Oxford 1973², p. 32. Before 338 BC, there was no need for *ius conubii* because Latins could marry Romans and Latins from other communities without any restrictions. It was only the war of 341–338 BC when Rome acquired undoubtedly hegemonic position and could grant privileges to its allies: S.T. ROSELAAR, 'The concept of *conubium* in the Roman Republic', [in:] P.J. DU PLESSIS (ed.), *New Frontiers: Law and Society in the Roman World*, Edinburgh 2013, pp. 102–122, pp. 108–110.

31 On the meaning of the word, see ROSELAAR, 'The concept of *conubium*' (cit. n. 30), p. 103.

32 E. VOLTERRA, 'L'acquisto della cittadinanza romana e il matrimonio del peregrino', [in:] E. VOLTERRA, *Scritti giuridici*, vol. II, Naples 1992, pp. 257–276 (reprinted from *Studi in onore di Enrico Redenti*, vol. II, Milan 1951, pp. 403–442), p. 262.

33 B. RAWSON, '*Spurii* and the Roman view of illegitimacy', *Antichthon* 23 (1989), pp. 10–41, p. 12.

34 V. SANNA, *Matrimonio e altre situazioni matrimoniali nel diritto romano classico. Matrimonium iustum – matrimonium iniustum*, Naples 2012, p. 92. That marriages contracted without conubium were still recognised as marriages is underlined in G. 1.78: *cum qua ei conubium non sit, uxorem duxerit civis Romanus*; and G. 1.80.

35 Th. REINACH, 'Un code fiscal de l'Égypte romaine : le Gnomon de l'idiologue', *Nouvelle revue historique de droit français et étranger* 44 (1920), pp. 5–136, pp. 28–29; W. UXKULL-GYLLENBAND, *Der Gnomon des Idios Logos. II. Der Kommentar*, Berlin 1934 (= *BGU* V.1), p. 51. More recently Anna Dolganov interpreted the paragraph as a proof that Romans could legally marry only Romans: A. DOLGANOV, 'Imperialism and social engineering: Augustan social legislation

cally. Angelo Segré postulated reading of the passage according to the text preserved on the papyrus, without the negation, which opinion was followed by *i.a.* Salvatore Riccobono and Joseph Mélèze Modrzejewski,[36] and suggested that the passage should be read together with the two following sections: § 53 which specifies that an Egyptian who married a veteran remained Egyptian (*BGU* V 1210, ll. 140–141), and § 54 which explains that the daughter of a Roman veteran could not inherit from her Egyptian mother (*BGU* V 1210, ll. 138–139).[37] The passage should thus be understood as relating to veterans, specifically that Roman veterans could marry *peregrinae*, as they had been granted *conubium* at their *missio honesta*.

An even more likely interpretation was offered a century ago by Paul Meyer, who proposed that the passage constitutes a reference to *matrimonium iniustum*.[38] It seems probable that § 52 has an even broader meaning. The paragraph says simply: 'it is lawful for Romans to marry Egyptians'. This broader understanding is supported both within the *Gnomon* and by a few additional sources discussed later. Such marriages raised further legal questions about the *status civitatis* of peregrine spouses married with *conubium* (§ 53) or succession after them (§ 54). Thus, what we find in the *Gnomon* is the general rule followed by specific regulations for problems that might arise on account of it.

Paragraphs 39 and 46 also shed some light on the status of unions between people of different status. They refer to the children of mixed unions contracted in ignorance: in § 39, the marriage remains without *conubium* and children follow the lesser status, while in § 46 not only are the children given the higher *status civitatis*, but the entire marriage becomes legitimate thanks to a successful *probatio*, which we discuss later in this section.

in the *Gnomon of the Idios Logos*', [in:] K. Harter-Uibopuu & T. Kruse (eds.), *Studien zum „Gnomon des Idios Logos": Beiträge zum Dritten Wiener Kolloquium zur antiken Rechtsgeschichte*, forthcoming.

36 S. Riccobono, *FIRA* I, Firenze 1941, pp. 469–478; idem, *Gnomon dell'idios logos*, Palermo 1950; J. Mélèze-Modrzejewski, 'Gnomon de l'idiologue', [in:] P.F. Girard & F. Senn (eds.), *Les lois des Romains*, Naples 1977, pp. 520–557.

37 A. Segré, 'A proposito di peregrini che prestavano servizio nelle legioni romane', *Aegyptus* 9 (1928), pp. 303–308, p. 304.

38 P. Meyer, *Juristische Papyri. Erklärung von Urkunden zur Einführung in die juristische Papyruskunde*, Berlin 1920, p. 328.

BGU V 1210, ll. 111–112: λθ. Ῥωμαίου ἢ Ῥωμαίας κατ᾽ ἄγνοιαν συνελθόντων ἢ ἀστοῖς ⟨ἢ⟩ Αἰγ̣υ̣π̣τ̣ίοις τὰ τέκνα ⟨τῷ⟩ ἥγτονι (l. ἥττονι) γένει ἀκολουθεῖ.

39. If, as a result of ignorance, Romans of either sex are united with *astoi* or Egyptians, their children will follow the lesser status.

BGU V 1210, ll. 128–129: μ[ς]. Ῥ̣ωμαίοις καὶ ἀστο̣ῖ̣ς κατ᾽ ἄ[γνοι]αν Αἰγυπ[τί]αις συνελθοῦσι⟦αις⟧ συνεχω|ρήθη μετὰ τοῦ ἀ̣νευθύ̣ν̣[ους] ε̣ἶναι[39] καὶ τ̣[ὰ] τέκνα τῷ̣ πατρικῷ̣ γένει ἀκολουθεῖ.

46. Romans and *astoi* who were united with Egyptian women out of ignorance were allowed not to be held accountable, and their children will follow the paternal status.

In both paragraphs the verb denoting the relationship between the parents is συνέρχομαι ('to marry'), also attested in marriage contracts.[40] There is no obvious semantic distinction between the situations described in the two paragraphs, suggesting that families with parents of unequal *status civitatis*, even without *conubium*, were recognised as families in Egypt. This is further supported by comparison with the paragraph forbidding incestuous couples:

BGU V 1210, ll. 70–72: κγ. οὐκ ἐξὸν Ῥωμαίοις ἀδελφὰς γῆμαι οὐδὲ τηθίδας, ἀδελφῶν | θυγατέρας συνκεχώρηται. Παρδαλᾶς μέντοι ἀδελφῶν συν|ελθόντων \τὰ ὑπάρχοντα/ ἀνέλαβεν.

23. It is not permitted for Romans to marry either their sisters or aunts; they are permitted to marry their niece. Pardalas, indeed, confiscated the property of married siblings.

[39] μετὰ τοῦ ἀ̣νευθύ̣ν̣[ους] ε̣ἶναι: Cherry proposed that the phrase should be interpreted as 'are, in accordance with this (?), not accountable', and μετὰ τοῦ would thus refer to a specific law which legitimated a mixed couple. This interpretation would suggest that a noun constituting the core of this reference had been omitted by the scribe of *BGU* V 1210 or one of the earlier versions: D. Cherry, 'The Minician law: marriage and the Roman citizenship', *Phoenix* 44.3 (1990), pp. 244–266, p. 261. Bagnall did not agree with Cherry and interpreted the phrase as a straightforward prepositional phrase with an articular infinitive as the object – 'along with being free from liability': R.S. Bagnall, 'Egypt and the *lex Minicia*', *The Journal of Juristic Papyrology* 23 (1993), pp. 25–28, p. 26. This is also how the passage is understood by Reinach, Riccobono and Modrzejewski: Reinach, 'Code fiscal' (cit. n. 35), pp. 27–28; Riccobono, *Gnomon* (cit. n. 36), p. 49; Mélèze-Modrzejewski, 'Gnomon' (cit. n. 36), pp. 520–557.

[40] *LSJ*, *WB*, *s.v.* 'συνέρχομαι'. Reinach, however, suggested the verb to be understood as qualifying a relationship as 'cohabitation' in contrary to γαμέω denoting marriage: Reinach, 'Code fiscal' (cit. n. 35), p. 27.

The difference in approach is clear. While incestuous unions are both forbidden and punished by law, the only problem resulting from mixed marriages is the *status civitatis* of the children. We recall from Chapter 2 that the children of close relatives were considered to be essentially fatherless. Paragraphs 39 and 46 make it apparent that children born of mixed unions were recognised as having two parents althought following the status of the lesser parent instead of the paternal one.

2.2. *Children of Romans and non-Romans*

In regard to children born of 'mixed unions', it was the combination of *status civitatis* and *conubium* that determined which status the children obtained. Consequently, some marriages between Romans and non-Romans produced legitimate offspring, who were both Roman citizens and subjects to the *potestas* of their fathers as well as *heredes sui* of the latter.[41] Other legitimate unions on the contrary produced children who were recognised as marital but peregrine. The *status civitatis* of children born to 'mixed' couples with *conubium* depended on whether the Roman partner was male or female. If the husband was Roman, the children became Romans according to the rule expressed by Gaius: *cum enim conubium id efficiat, ut liberi patris condicionem sequantur* (G. 1.56). If the mother was Roman, the children became *peregrini* according to the same rule.

Different rules applied to children of parents without *conubium*. If the father was a Roman, the children followed the status of their mother under the rule of *ius gentium* which specified that *inter quos non est conubium, qui nascitur, iure gentium matris condicioni accedit* (G. 1.78). The issue became more complicated if it was the mother who was a Roman citizen. According to *ius gentium* the children should follow her status, which would mean acquiring Roman citizenship.[42] In late republican times,[43] however, the introduc-

[41] E. Volterra, 'La nozione giuridica del *conubium*', [in:] *Studi in memoria di Emilio Albertario*, vol. II, Milan 1950, pp. 348–384, p. 362.

[42] Cherry, 'The Minician law' (cit. n. 39), p. 247.

[43] The date when the *lex* was given was not preserved. In the literature, there is also no consent in regard to its date, *e.g.* Roselaar proposes to date the *lex Minicia* before 90 BC, while

tion of the *lex Minicia* ruled that children should always follow the status of a lesser parent (G. 1.78). As a result, the children of a Roman mother with no *conubium* towards her peregrine partner became *peregrini,* exactly in the same manner as the children of a Roman woman and her legally-wedded peregrine husband. This solution, however, was at odds with the system of status acquisition: a child not recognised as legal offspring of their father followed his status nevertheless. It was perhaps for this reason that Hadrian decided that any marriage between a Roman female and peregrine would produce offspring of the father recognised as *iustus/iusta* (G. 1.77).

Concluding, the position of *legitimus* is problematic, as in Roman terms only those under the *potestas* of their fathers were their *legitimi*, so *legitimus* was a son born to a Roman who had a *conubium* towards his peregrine wife. Yet, as mentioned, also a marriage between a Roman woman and peregrine man produced *iusti filii*. In theory whether children were *iusti* should depend on father's community and be regulated casuistically. The sources, however, suggest that this problem was not left to the discretion of particular communities of non-Romans, but regulated according to one rule of Roman *ius gentium*.

The already quoted §§ 39 and 46 prove that the problems discussed by Gaius were known in Egypt too. The paragraphs are, however, somehow problematic, as seem to contradict each other. In § 39 the *Gnomon* says that the children of a Roman man or woman who lived together with *astoi* or Egyptians due to ignorance should follow the lesser status (*BGU* V 1210, ll. 111–112). Paragraph 46 states that Romans and *astoi* who married an Egyptian due to ignorance were not considered accountable, and that their children would follow their status, not that of the Egyptian mother. The two paragraphs do not overlap exactly, but both attempt to regulate situations in which a Roman man produces children with an Egyptian woman. The paragraphs differ in their solutions: in § 39 the offspring should follow the lesser status, while in § 46 they are granted Roman citizenship.

David Cherry attempted to resolve the inconsistency by suggesting that ἄγνοια referred to *ignorantia iuris* in § 39 and to *ignorantia facti* in § 46,[44] or

Cherry to later date between the Social War and beginning of Principate. See Roselaar, 'The concept of *conubium*' (cit. n. 30), p. 111; Cherry, 'The Minician law' (cit. n. 39), p. 248.

[44] Both cases seem to refer to the ignorance of the status of the partner: L. Winkel, *Error iuris nocet. Rechtsirrtum als Problem der Rechtsordnung*, vol. I: *Rechtsirrtum in der griechischen*

that the application of the *lex Minicia* would not have been very strict in the provinces.[45] Roger Bagnall, however, suggested that this interpretation was unlikely, and proposed that § 39 refers to the ruling of the *lex Minicia*, while § 46 cites an unknown *senatus consultum* also referred to by Gaius.[46] This understanding seems well-based in the text of the *Institutes*:

> G. 1.67: Item si civis Romanus Latinam aut peregrinam uxorem duxerit per ignorantiam, cum eam civem Romanam esse crederet, et filium procreaverit, hic non est in potestate eius, quia ne quidem civis Romanus est, sed aut Latinus aut peregrinus, id est eius condicionis, cuius et mater fuerit, quia non aliter quisque ad patris condicionem accedit, quam si inter patrem et matrem eius conubium sit. Sed ex senatus consulto permittitur causam erroris probare, et ita uxor quoque et filius ad civitatem Romanam perveniunt, et ex eo tempore incipit filius in potestate patris esse. Idem iuris est, si eam per ignorantiam uxorem duxerit, quae dediticiorum numero est, nisi quod uxor non fit civis Romana.
>
> Again, if a Roman citizen takes a Latin or a peregrine wife in a mistaken belief that she is a Roman citizen and begets a son, that son is not in his *potestas*: for he is not even a citizen, but either a Latin or a peregrine according to his mother's status, because, except if there be *conubium* between the father and the mother, a child does not take its father's status. But by a senatusconsult the father is allowed to prove a case of mistake, and thereupon both the wife and the son attain to Roman citizenship, and thenceforth the son is subject to his father's *potestas*. The law is the same if by mistake he marries a wife who is in the class of *dediticii*, except that the wife does not become a Roman citizen.[47]

The text of Gaius provides two rules: the *lex generalis* (1) and *lex specialis* (2). (1) If a Roman man (or a female – G. 1.68) married a peregrine or Latin, believing their partner to be a Roman, the children of such a union would not fall under the power of their father and would not be Roman; they would follow the status of their mother on the grounds that there was no *conubium* between

Philosophie und im römischen Recht bis Justinian [= *Studia Amstelodamensia ad epigraphicam, ius antiquum et papyrologicam pertinentia* XXV], Zupthen 1985, p. 130.

[45] Cherry, 'The Minician law' (cit. n. 39), pp. 261–162.

[46] Bagnall, 'Egypt and the *lex Minicia*' (cit. n. 39).

[47] Tr. F. de Zulueta in: *The Institutes of Gaius. Part I. Text with Critical Notes and Translation*, Oxford 1946.

the parents. (2) If a Roman who married a peregrine or Latin woman (and a Roman woman who married a Latin or peregrine respectively: G. 1.68) could prove the cause of his mistake, his children were recognised as Romans *alieni iuris* and citizenship was granted to the wife. The general rule was still binding even after the *senatus consultum*. It was not the mistake itself, but the *probatio* which gave the children the higher status. Not every *probatio* had to be successful, and not every couple wanted to undertake it.

In § 46 of the *Gnomon* we find the expression *ἀν̣ευθύν̣[ους] ε̣ἶναι*, which David Cherry translated as 'not accountable',[48] Roger Bagnall as 'free from liability',[49] Théodore Reinach as 'exempté de toute peine', and Józef Modrzejewski as '(obtenue) ... leur acquittement'. The French translations seem better as they refer to the fact that either a partner was free of guilt (in their choice of a 'wrong' partner: Reinach) or that the union was granted *conubium* (Modrzejewski).[50] The expression *ἀν̣ευθύν̣[ους] ε̣ἶναι* refers to the *probatio*, as suggested by Reinach.[51]

The discussion in paragraph 39 of the *Gnomon* concerning the status of children born to Romans and *astoi* or Egyptians raises the question of whether any distinction was made between marrying a local citizen and marrying a simple Egyptian. The paragraph suggests that there was not in so far as the children did not become Romans regardless of who the second parent was. A similar conclusion can be drawn from the Gaian passage discussing the *lex Minicia*. In G. 1.79, Gaius says that *peregrinorum nomen* encompasses not only foreign nations and peoples, but also Latins of independent towns.[52] If we apply an *argumentum a fortiori* to the *lex Minicia* and the acquisition of status by children of 'mixed unions', it would seem clear that *astoi* were simply peregrines along with all other groups of non-Romans.[53] When

[48] Cherry, 'The Minician law' (cit. n. 39), p. 261.

[49] Bagnall, 'Egypt and the *lex Minicia*' (cit. n. 39), p. 25.

[50] Mélèze-Modrzejewski, 'Gnomon' (cit. n. 36), p. 539.

[51] Reinach, 'Code fiscal' (cit. n. 35), p. 28.

[52] B. Sirks, rev. of P.J. du Plessis (ed.), *New Frontiers: Law and Society in the Roman World*, Edinburgh 2013, *Tijdschrift voor Rechtsgeschiedenis* 82 (2014), pp. 171–177, p. 173, n. 2.

[53] From the letter of Pliny it seems that outside of the province even officials might have perceived the difference between Egyptians and Egyptian *astoi* irrelevant (*Ep.* 10.6).

it came to the acquisition of Roman citizenship, it did not matter to which category of peregrines the lesser parent belonged.

The children of such unions, however, could become either simply peregrines or *peregrini cives*, which could be interpreted directly from § 39 saying: τὰ τέκνα ⟨τῷ⟩ ἥγτονι (l. ἥττονι) γένει ἀκολουθεῖ. The same confirm papyri discussed below. *Astoi* unlike *Aigyptioi* did not pay the poll-tax and were eligible for other privileges. It is also known that an Egyptian who wished to acquire the Roman citizenship first had to have a local citizenship; in addition to prestige, a Roman might also have preferred to marry an *astos* or *aste* (rather than a simple Egyptian) so as not to deprive their children of future opportunities.

Therefore, it could be no surprise that Romans indeed married *peregrini cives*. Families consisting of Romans and citizens of Antinoopolis are attested in the papyri due to the large number of veterans who lived there.[54] Yet, this phenomenon was not confined to Antinoopolis, and the sources provide examples of both Roman men and Roman women marrying other *astoi* (*infra*, pp. 202–206).

While Romans with Egyptian wives and children are not rare in the sources, such cases are almost always problematic due to the difficulty of distinguishing whether the families are those of soldiers (and thus legally inexistent), or genuine examples of mixed unions. The tendency in scholarly literature is to identify such cases as belonging to the military milieu, even if there is no evidence to suggest that the father and/or husband served in the army. This tendency is understandable, due in part to Youtie's widely-adopted suggestion that the fatherless of Egypt were mostly children of Roman soldiers, but also because families involving soldiers and veterans are relatively numerous in the papyri, well-studied and easily distinguishable. In many cases, however, the Roman partners' profession is impossible to identify with any certainty.

[54] In *P. Oxy.* XIV 1719 *descr.*, Zoilos and Sosia, and in and *SB* X 10257 only Zoilos were labelled citizens of Antinoopolis, and children of Zoilos, Antinoopolite, and Roman mother, Aelia Primigeneia *alias* Praemestina. On the identity of Zoilos, the father, see H. Cadell, 'P. Caire IFAO Inv. 45, P. Oxy. XIV 1719 et les privilèges des Antinoïtes', *Chronique d'Égypte* 40 (1965), pp. 357–363; N. Lewis, 'Νοήματα λέγοντος', *The Bulletin of the American Society of Papyrologists* 6 (1969), pp. 20–26, pp. 20–21.

That proper identification of children and their parents could be more difficult than it seems is illustrated by an early Roman papyrus, *P. Ryl.* II 150 (Euhemeria, AD 50), a complaint about an abuse addressed to the chief of the police, by a man named Sophos using a Roman filiation, ll. 2–3: *παρὰ Σόφου Μάρκου Σα|τορνίλου*.[55] The editors understood Marcus Saturnilus to be the father of Sophos, which would make him the son of a Roman and his Egyptian spouse, which seems an opinion well-grounded in identification methods.[56] Yet Fritz Mitthof identified Marcus Saturnilus with Marcus Aponius Saturninus,[57] a wealthy man mentioned in the Roman historiography[58] and holder of imperial *ousia* in Egypt; this identification should cause us to question whether Sophos was indeed Saturninus' son.[59]

In one of the papyri published in volume XXIII of the *Corpus Papyrorum Raineri*, Marcus Aponius Saturninus is represented by Marcus Aponius Hypnos (*CPR* XXIII 2 [Arsinoite nome, AD 38–41], ll. 2–3 & 7–8). In this case, Marcus Aponius Hypnos declares that Marcus Aponius Saturninus was his *patronus* (l. 9)[60] and describes himself as the *procurator* of his ex-master (ll. 2 & 7: *ἐπίτροπος*). It is possible that Hypnos was the principal procurator of land in the Arsinoite nome for Marcus Aponius Saturninus, while the administration of particular properties was entrusted to slaves.[61] *P. Ryl.* II 150 is early – it is dated to AD 50 – and, as we pointed out earlier, in pre-Roman Greek inscriptions slaves were usually labelled with an identification cluster consisting of their own name plus the owner's name

[55] TAUBENSCHLAG, *Law of Greco-Roman Egypt* (cit. n. 10), p. 106.

[56] See translation in *P. Ryl.* II, p. 149; this interpretation was kept in: A. BRYEN, *Violence in Roman Egypt. A Study in Legal Interpretation*, Philadelphia 2013, p. 220.

[57] F. MITTHOF, 'Korr. Tyche 446', *Tyche* 17 (2002), p. 252.

[58] Suet., *Aug.* 38; Joseph., *AJ.* 19.264, hardly the same person as the M. Aponius Saturninus, Asian proconsul, but likely his father: R.D. MILNS, 'The career of M. Aponius Saturninus', *Historia* 22 (1973), pp. 284–294, p. 293; F. MITTHOF, *CPR* XXIII, p. 17.

[59] G.M. PARÁSSOGLOU, 'New documents on the imperial estates in Egypt', *The Bulletin of the American Society of Papyrologists* 12 (1975), pp. 85–92, p. 90, n. 3; list of papyri where he was mentioned in F. MITTHOF, *CPR* XXIII, p. 16.

[60] The additional proof is that Marcus Aponius Hypnos had the *praenomen* and *nomen* of Marcus Aponius Saturninus as well as *cognomen* typically used as slave name: F. MITTHOF, *CPR* XXIII, p. 15.

[61] F. MITTHOF, *CPR* XXIII, p. 17.

in genitive, but without the term δοῦλος; this makes it difficult to distinguish filiation from a mark of slavery. All of which suggests that Sophos could have been a slave belonging to the *familia* of Marcus Aponius Saturninus involved in the administration of his master's estate in Euhemeria.[62] Were it not for the publication of *CPR* XXIII 2 and the analysis provided by Mitthof, Sophos would have continued to be identified as the son of a Roman married *sine conubio* to an Egyptian woman. The case should illustrate just how difficult it can be to identify the children of 'mixed unions' with any certainty without the help of additional information.

Another case providing various interpretations is *BGU* XI 2020 (Arsinoite nome, AD 124). The text is a declaration of four children submitted by their mother. The four registered children – Apollinarios, Valerius, Gemellus and Gemella – had only single names, but of Roman appearance, except for Apollinarius. Their father Valerius Apollinarius could have been a Roman, but even this is not certain as it was not only Romans who used Roman *nomina*. In this case, the father is described using only *duo nomina* which may suggest that he might have been an *auxiliaris*.[63] Neither the identity of the mother nor the officials to whom the document was addressed has been preserved.

If the father had indeed been a soldier, the children would have been considered fatherless. Military service, however, was a part of one's personal description (as was being a veteran), and at no point does the text mention that Valerius Apollinarius belonged to the army. If the text had been prepared for the children of an auxiliary soldier, its aim would have been to safeguard their rights and allow them to be granted Roman citizenship together with their father at his *missio honesta*, as it is dated still before AD 140. In order to achieve this aim, the document would need to prove two things:

1. that the children were of an auxiliary soldier;
2. that they were born during his military service.

[62] F. Mitthof, *CPR* XXIII, p. 17.

[63] C. Sanchez-Moreno Ellart, 'ὑπομνήματα ἐπιγεννήσεως: The Greco-Egyptian birth returns in Roman Egypt and the case of *P. Petaus* 1–2', *Archiv für Papyrusforschung* 56 (2010), pp. 91–129, p. 112.

In other words, mention that the father sevred in the army would be crucial. One example of such a *testatio* – *P. Diog.* 1, discussed in Chapter One – contains both, and was moreover prepared by the father himself. For soldiers who were not allowed to marry, the presumption of legitimacy did not work, so a *testatio* submitted by the mother would have been of little value at the *missio honesta*. Furthermore, the text does not contain the signatures of witnesses, a crucial element of this type of deed.[64] The onomastics offer further evidence against interpreting the text as the registration of Roman children: in which we would expect to find the proper *tria nomina* (or *duo* for the girl) and filiation. The same evidence would appear to contradict the argument of Carlos Sanchez-Moreno Ellart, who suggested that the text might have been a declaration of a veteran's children intended as a further proof for the *epikrisis*,[65] which would mean that Valerius Apollinarius had been married to his children's mother *cum conubio* granted at his *missio honesta*. In such a case, however, a regular *professio* would have been submitted.

If Valerius Apollinarius was indeed a Roman, the document would be an illustration of a relationship between a Roman and an Egyptian woman which was deprived of the *conubium* and thus produced peregrine children. If the mother belonged to one of the privileged classes of Egyptians, she might have wanted to register her children into the same group; in this case, a father of higher rank would not have been an obstacle, as the evidence discussed in this chapter suggests that in such cases children were entitled to follow the privileged Egyptian rank.[66] Another explanation, suggested by Andrea Jördens, is that the document concerned some matter of private law, *e.g.* succession, and had nothing to do with any claim for privileged civic or fiscal status.[67]

[64] J.G. Wolf, 'Documents in Roman practice', [in:] D. Johnston (ed.), *The Cambridge Companion to Roman Law*, Cambridge 2015, pp. 61–84, pp. 63–64.

[65] Sanchez-Moreno Ellart, 'ὑπομνήματα ἐπιγεννήσεως' (cit. n. 63), p. 113.

[66] Neither the age of the registered children, 4, 5 and 6 years, because children could be registered a few years after they were born. See N. Kruit, 'Age reckoning in Hellenistic Egypt: the evidence of declarations of birth, excerpts from the ephebe registers, and census returns', [in:] A. Verhoogt & S.P. Vleeming (eds.), *The Two Faces of Graeco-Roman Egypt* [= *Papyrologica Lugduno-Batava* XXX], Leiden – Boston – Cologne 1998, pp. 37–58, pp. 37–39.

[67] As suggested by A. Jördens, commentary to *P. Bingen* 105.

Rafał Taubenschlag pointed out that attestations of Roman females married to Egyptians are more numerous than Roman men who married local women,[68] contrary to what we might expect (*i.e.* men of higher status marrying into formally lower strata of society).[69] One such case is *P. Ryl.* II 153, a local will of a wealthy man from Hermopolis Megale (AD 169), which names both the testator's wife, Claudia Leontis, and his son, Hellanikos.[70] Unfortunately the identity of the testator himself is not known to us due to the fragmentary state of preservation of the papyrus; we know only that he was the winner of athletic games. His family was not Roman, nor did they enjoy local citizenship, yet it is likely that they belonged to the metropolite group.[71] If onomastics are any indication, Claudia Leontis was Roman, which would make her son, Hellanikos, the child of a 'mixed union'. The fact that Hellanikos was named as successor to most of his his father's extensive estate, suggests that he was recognised as a lawful child of his father. The text is dated to the reign of Antoninus Pius, thus after Hadrian's decision that such children were always *iusti filii* of their fathers (G. 1.77).

2.3. *Astoi*

2.3.1. Children born to *astoi* and Egyptians

The rule of *deterioris parentis condicio* also applied to children born of *astoi*, although not to citizens of Antinoopolis, who enjoyed the privilege of *epigamia* with anyone (as we will discuss later in the present chapter). The rule worked in both directions: offspring of *astoi* and Romans became *astoi*, while those born to couples consisting of a local citizen and an Egyptian followed the status of the latter.

[68] TAUBENSCHLAG, *Law of Greco-Roman Egypt* (cit. n. 10), p. 106, n. 15.

[69] Dura Europos could be taken as a point of reference, as mixed unions are attested only to the contrary. See GRASSI, 'Matrimoni misti e onomastica' (cit. n. 13).

[70] On the family, see: P. VAN MINNEN & P.J. SIJPESTEIJN, 'Three London papyri from Hermopolis', *Zeitschrift für Papyrologie und Epigraphik* 88 (1991), pp. 151–156.

[71] VAN MINNEN & SIJPESTEIJN, 'Three London papyri' (cit. n. 70), p. 154.

An *aste* marrying an Egyptian did not suffer any consequences, and her children although Egypians were even entitled to inherit not only from the father to whose community they legally belonged, but also from her.

BGU V 1210, ll. 109–110: *λη. οἱ ἐξ ἀστῆς καὶ Αἰγυπτίου γενόμενοι μένουσι μὲν Αἰγύπτιοι, [ἀ]μφοτέρους δὲ κληρονομοῦσι τοὺς γονεῖς.*

38. Any individuals born to an *aste* and an Egyptian will remain Egyptian, but can inherit from both parents.

The same applied to children born to an *astos* and Egyptian female: the children became Egyptians, but belonged to the family of their father. Paragraph 45, however, mentions the *post mortem* confiscation of the property belonging to *astoi* who married Egyptians.

BGU V 1210, ll. 123–127: *με. ἐὰν ἀστὸς Αἰγυπτίαν γαμ̣[ῇ κ]αὶ τελευτήσῃ ἄτ[ε]κ̣νος, ὁ φίσκος τὰ | ἐπίκτητα αὐτοῦ ἀναλαμ[βά]νει, ἐὰν δὲ τέκνα̣ ἔχῃ, τὸ δίμοιρον | ἀναλαμβάνει. ἐὰν δὲ ἦν [πρ]οτετεκνὼς* (l. *[πρ]οτετεκνω[κὼ]ς*) *ἐ̣ξ ἀ̣στῆς καὶ ἔχῃ τέκνα γ | ἢ καὶ πλείονα, τούτοις χ[ω]ρεῖ καὶ τὰ ἐπίκτητα, ἐὰν δὲ δύο [τὸ] τέταρτον | ἢ τὸ πέμπτον, ἐὰν δὲ ἓν [τὸ] ἥμ̣ισυ.*

45. If an *astos* marries an Egyptian woman and dies childless, the fisc will confiscate any property he acquired after this marriage; if he has children, the fisc will take two-thirds. If he had previously had children with an *aste*, and those children numbered three or more, the property acquired after the marriage goes to them, if there are two children, they receive one-fourth or one-fifth, if one, a half.

Although *astoi* were more restricted than *astai* in chosing their spouses, the paragraph is not as severe as it might seem, as the confiscation applied only to property acquired after marrying an Egyptian, τὰ ἐπίκτητα, while the rest was subject to regular succession.[72] The texts also specify that parts of these acquisitions postdating the marriage were to be inherited by the children. Importantly, it was not only the rights of children begotten to peers that were safeguarded, but also those of the offspring born to an Egyptian, which marriage was the reason that property was confiscated

[72] *LSJ*, *WB*, *s.v.* 'ἐπικτάομαι'; F. Montanari, *The Brill Dictionary of Ancient Greek*, M. Goh & C. Schroeder (Eng. eds.), Leiden 2015, *s.v.* 'ἐπίκτησις'; Reinach, 'Code fiscal' (cit. n. 35), p. 30.

at all. The children of citizens and partners of lower status were therefore permitted intestate succession from their father, which would imply that they belonged to his family not only in social, but also in legal terms.

The rule is further illustrated in a few other paragraphs of the *Gnomon*:

BGU V 1210, l. 132: [μ]η. ἀστοὶ γήμαντες Νησ̣ι̣ώ̣τ̣[ιδα]ς ὅμοιοί εἰσι τοῖς Αἰγυπτίοις συνελθοῦσι.

48. *Astoi* who married female islanders are considered similar to those who married Egyptians.

Νησιώτιδες in § 48 had to be female inhabitants of some hard to identify islands, their status had to be of *peregrinae*, but not of Egypt, as the paragraph equates them with Egyptian females,[73] meaning that their children followed the maternal status, and *astoi* were punished with the confiscation of some property after death.

In § 57, the status of children born to men of Paraitonion is discussed.

l. 148: νζ. Παρ̣α̣ιτον[ίω]ν̣ τῶν συνερχομέν[ω]ν γυναιξὶν ἀλ̣λ̣[ο]φύλ̣[ο]ις ἢ Αἰ̣[γ]υ̣πτία[ις] τὰ τέκνα τῷ ἥττον̣ι̣ [γέ]νε[ι] ἀκολουθε[ῖ].

57. The children of Paraetonians who marry foreign women or Egyptians shall follow the lesser status.

Paraitonion was a port-city located around 300 kilometers from Alexandria. Although it is not usually listed among the *poleis* of Egypt in modern scholarship, Théodore Reinach,[74] followed a century later by Thomas Kruse, suggested that the men of Paraitonion were recognised as citizens of the *poleis* at least in the context of the *Gnomon*.[75] The idea seems justified. First, children born to men of Paraitonion who married either Egyptians or women described as *allophylai*[76] acquired the status of their mothers. Second, the paragraph offers, as justification, a Greek translation of

[73] Reinach, 'Code fiscal' (cit. n. 35), pp. 31–32.

[74] Reinach, 'Code fiscal' (cit. n. 35), p. 35.

[75] T. Kruse, 'The labeling of strangers and aliens in Roman Egypt', [in:] M. Nowak, A. Łajtar & J. Urbanik (eds.), *Tell Me Who You Are. Labelling Status in the Graeco-Roman World*, Warsaw 2018, pp. 129–146, pp. 139–140.

[76] The expression γυναιξὶν ἀλ̣λ̣[ο]φύλ̣[ο]ις has been interpreted by Kruse as foreign women, constituting a synonym to *xenos*: Kruse, 'The labeling of strangers' (cit. n. 75), p. 140.

the rule *deterioris condicionem sequitur* – τῷ ἥττονι̣ [γέ]νε[ι] ἀκολουθε[ῖ]. This would suggest that the men of Paraitonion had to be of higher status than *peregrini Aegyptii*. If they were not Romans, they must have been *peregrini cives*, as the *Gnomon* does not distinguish between fiscal categories of *peregrini Aegyptii*. The paragraph does not mention any sanctions imposed on men of Paraitonion for marrying women of lower status, which could be why the group is treated separately.

Marriages between *astoi* and *Aigyptioi* are also attested outside of the *Gnomon*. One early example is an agreement addressed to the *archidikastes*, in which Ammonarion and Ophelous,[77] her daughter, are said to have been repaid by relatives of the deceased husband and father (*P. Oxy.* II 268 = *M. Chr.* 299 [Oxyrhynchos, AD 57]).[78] Ammonarion restituted her dowry and Ophelous was given money as repayment for her share in her father's inheritance. The description of both women is as follows, ll. 2– 3: παρὰ Ἀμμωναρί[ο]υ τῆς Ἀμμω[νί]ου τοῦ Διονυσίου, ὡς ἐν [Πτο]λεμαίδι τῆς Ἑρμίου χρηματί[ζ]ει, ἀ[σ]τῆς (BL I 320 *corr. ex* α[ὐ]τῆς) καὶ τῆς ταύτης | [θ]υ̣[γ]ατρὸς Ὠφε[λοῦτ]ος τῆς Ἡρακλᾶτος τῶν ἀπ' Ὀξυρύγχων πόλεως. Although the mother is described as a citizen of Ptolemais Hermiou, her daughter lacks this distinction, suggesting that she had acquired the Egyptian status of her father. Indeed both the father (in patronym) and the daughter are described ἀπ' Ὀξυρύγχων πόλεως, which suggests that they might have belonged to the metropolite class.

Another example comes from the archive of Ptolemaios son of Diodoros, a wealthy man who held some royal and catoicic land, and owned some private estate in the Arsinoite nome.[79] In a census return submitted by his sister Sambathion for the year AD 145, *P. Wisc.* I 36 (Theadelphia, AD 147) = 145-Ar-24, Ptolemaios and his family are listed as members of the household.

P. Wisc. I 36, ll. 10–18: ἀπογράφομαι εἰς τὴν τοῦ | διεληλυθότος θ (ἔτους) Ἀντωνίνου Καίσαρος τοῦ κυρίου | κ̣α̣τ' οἰ̣κίαν ἀ̣π̣ογραφὴν ἐπὶ τῆς προκιμένης

[77] See K. Czajkowski, 'The limits of legal pluralism in the Roman Empire', *The Journal of Legal History* 40.2 (2019), pp. 110–129, p. 126.

[78] Mélèze-Modrzejewski, 'Dryton le crétois' (cit. n. 6), p. 359, n. 29.

[79] TM Arch id: 325; R. Smolders, 'Ptolemaios son of Diodoros'.

(l. προκειμένης) | κώμης Θ̣ε̣α̣δελφείας τὸν προγεγραμμένον μου | ὁμ̣οπάτριο̣ν κ̣αὶ ὁμομήτριον ἀδελφὸν Πτολεμαῖον | (ἐτῶν) λε κ[α]ὶ τ̣ὸ̣ν̣ τούτου υἱὸν γενάμενον αὐτῷ̣ | ἐκ̣ τῆς συνο̣ύ̣σης \καὶ προο̣ύσης/ αὐτῷ̣ γυναικὸς Ἀνουβιαίνης | τ̣ῆς καὶ Ἀχι̣λ̣ίδος (l. Ἀχιλλίδος) ἀ̣σ̣τῆς Διόσκορον τ̣ὸ̣ν καὶ Ἥρ̣ω|ν̣α̣ (ἐτῶν) γ̣[80].

For the census of the previous 9th year of Antoninus Caesar, the lord, (held) in the above mentioned village of Theadelphia, I declare my above-written paternal and maternal brother, Ptolemaios, 35 years old, and his son Dioskoros *alias* Heron, 3 (?) years old, born to him of his cohabitant and pre-existing wife, Anoubiaine *alias* Achillis, an *aste*.

The wife is described as *aste*, while Ptolemaios and his son, Dioskoros, are labelled neither as *peregrini cives* nor even privileged Egyptians. If descriptions provided by the document are reliable, the son would have followed the paternal status, thus that of the lesser parent.

It is clear that children born of unions between *astoi* and common peregrines were perceived as the children of their fathers not only at the social level, but also at the legal one. Although the rule by which children followed the status of an Egyptian parent is similar to the Roman rule, it may not necessarily have been the same. Yet the idea that status acquisition in the *poleis* imitated the Roman model is apparent in cases in which parents contracted a union by mistake, which are known from §§ 39 *&* 46 of the *Gnomon*. It is not very likely that the matter was regulated in the same *senatus consultum* discussed by Gaius (1.67 and 68),[81] as citizenship in the Egyptian *poleis* did not belong to *ius civile*. Paragraph 46, however, proves that the rules applied to mixed unions were exactly the same for Romans and *astoi*.

2.3.2. Children born to *astoi* and Romans

A further argument that the acquisition of status by the offspring of mixed unions in the *poleis* was regulated according to the Roman model comes from § 39, which notes that a child of a Roman who had a partner of lesser status, became either Egyptian or *astos*, not simply peregrine, τὰ τέκνα ⟨τῷ⟩ ἥγτονι (l. ἥττονι) γένει ἀκολουθεῖ. This would imply that *astoi* had to accept

[80] Or [ι]γ, *BL* X, p. 114.

[81] As suggested by Bagnall, 'Egypt and the *lex Minicia*' (cit. n. 39), p. 27.

the children of Romans among their number. A similar picture emerges from the case studies, *e.g.* a daughter of a Roman and an *aste* is attested in a census return submitted by a certain Sarapion on behalf of Isidora *alias* Harpokratiaine, *BGU* XIII 2223 (Ptolemais Euergetis, AD 175) = 173-Ar-12:

ll. 2–5: *ὑπάρχει τῇ φροντιζο|μένῃ ὑπ' ἐμοῦ Ἰσιδώρᾳ τῇ καὶ | Ἁρποκρατ̣ι̣α̣ίνῃ θυγατρὶ Γαίου Ἰου|λίου Γ[εμ]ε̣λ̣λ̣ου*[82] *ἀστῇ* (...)

There belongs to represented by me Isidora *alias* Harpokratiaine daughter of Caius Iulius Gemellus, *aste* ...

Although Isidora *alias* Harpokratiaine was recognised as both a Roman and *aste* by William Brashear, the first editor of the text,[83] the former status seems unlikely[84] as she has neither *duo nomina* nor the description *Ῥωμαία*. She is, on the other hand, described with the term *aste*, suggesting that she was a citizen of one of the four *poleis*,[85] although her property, declared in *BGU* XIII 2223, was located in the Sekneptyneiou quarter in Ptolemais Euergetis. Her father does indeed seem to have been a Roman, as his *tria nomina* suggest. This would mean that Isidora *alias* Harpokratiaine's mother belonged to the citizen body of one of the *poleis* and transferred her status to the daughter, which would further suggest that she was married to Caius Iulius Gemellus without *conubium*.

The case is, however, problematic, as the *status civitatis* of Isidora *alias* Harpokratiaine would have been the same if her father had been a slave or soldier at the moment of her birth: in such a case she would follow the maternal status in the same way as a fatherless person. Soldiers also married *astai*, especially if they had been *astoi* themselves before their recruitment; this was the case for Octavius Valens in *P. Catt.* who, as an Alexandrian, had married an Alexandrian woman before joining the army (*supra*,

[82] *BL* VIII, p. 55: *Γ[. .]λ̣λ̣ . ου ed. princ.*

[83] See introduction to *BGU* XIII 2223.

[84] R.S. Bagnall & B.W. Frier, *The Demography of Roman Egypt* [= *Cambridge Studies in Population, Economy and Society in Past Time*], Cambridge 2006^2, p. 252, does not mention the possibility that she might be a Roman. Neither does Horsley who included the text under no. 28 in the first volume of *New Documents Illustrating Early Christianity*.

[85] Delia, *Alexandrian Citizenship* (cit. n. 25), pp. 20–21.

pp. 145–147). The marriage was neither 'mixed' nor imperfect, but merely interrupted by Octavius Valens' enrolment in the army, as a result of which all his children were born legally fatherless. Although there is nothing in *BGU* XIII 2223 to suggest a similar scenario, both the labels and the lack thereof can be misleading in Graeco-Roman papyri. In the already discussed *BGU* VII 1662 (AD 182), Kyrilla is described as *aste*, and her father appears with a proper *tria nomina*; it is only through external evidence that we discover she was born to a soldier before his *missio honesta*.

In *P. Tebt.* II 316 = *W. Chr.* 148, it is the mother who was Roman, while the father was an Alexandrian.[86] In the document, several men declare that they had been enrolled as *epheboi* in Alexandria. One of the men whose declaration has survived (*P. Tebt.* II 316, col. III, ll. 30–71), is Sarapion son of Sarapion son of Apollonios, man ascribed to both *phyle* and deme of Alexandria. In addition he claimed to have been enrolled among the Alexandrian ephebes in AD 82 or 83, that the registration was legitimate and that the proper documents had been issued.

The description of Sarapion's mother is interesting, ll. 55–56: *καὶ εἰμὶ μητρὸς Ῥω|μανίας Βερνίκης*. If *Ῥωμανία* is, as assumed by Diana Delia and Bernard Legras, *nomen gentilicium*,[87] it would mean that having a Roman mother was not an obstacle to becoming an Alexandrian citizen. According to Legras, it is an example of double citizenship, in which the mother was both Roman and Alexandrian.[88] This seems doubtful for the simple reason that if she had been an Alexandrian, and if her Alexandrian designation was essential for the status of the child, she would have been labelled as Alexandrian in the document. On the other hand, for double citizenship the father would have to be also a Roman. Instead the mother is described only with her *duo nomina*. Unlike other entries from the same text no maternal grandfather is indicated (ll. 13–14 & 87–88); it mattered

[86] DELIA, *Alexandrian Citizenship* (cit. n. 25), p. 54.

[87] *Gens Romania* is well-attested in epigraphic sources from Rome and Italy. In Egypt, a male form Romanius is attested in *I. Portes du désert* 56, col. II, l. 39. It is in a position of a gentile name, while a person bearing it is a soldier and non-Roman of the origin: C(aius) Romanius C(aii) f(ilius) Fab(ia tribu) Ber(ytensis).

[88] B. LEGRAS, *Néotês : recherches sur les jeunes grecs dans l'Égypte ptolémaïque et romaine*, Geneva 1999, p. 160: 'Le fait qu'une mère soit Romaine ne nous surprendra pas, car nous savons que la double citoyenneté, alexandrine et romaine, était possible'.

only that she was a Roman, which means that an Alexandrian could produce Alexandrian children with a Roman wife regardless of whether she was an Alexandrian or not.

One document that deals with dual citizenship was published recently in the seventeenth volume of *Papiri della Società italiana*. It is a request for the registration of Lucius Calpurnius Caius as an Alexandrian ephebe (*PSI* XVII 1691 [Oxyrhynchos, AD 205]). The application was submitted by a family friend, as the candidate's mother had died, and his father, Lucius Calpurnius Firmus, was away on official business and could not submit the application himself. The status of the parents is indicated in the text.

1. Lucius Calpurnius Firmus, the father, was a prominent citizen of Alexandria, former *kosmetes*, *eutheniarchos* and *antarchidikastes* of Alexandria, and a Roman.[89] Alan Bowman suggested that the family might have originated from an equestrian commander of an auxiliary unit, and would thus have been Romans granted with Alexandrian citizenship.[90] The publication of *PSI* XVII 1691 appears to confirm Bowman's reconstruction: in ll. 9–10, the text says: τῶν [πεπολιτο]|γραφημένων κατὰ πρόσταγμα, which means that Lucius Calpurnius Firmus had been made a citizen by a *prostagma*. The phrase probably refers to Alexandrian citizenship, as it follows the listing of his Alexandrian dignities. It suggests that Alexandrian citizenship would have been quite recent within the family and secondary to the Roman one: it may be that the acquisition of Alexandrian citizenship allowed a Roman high official to assume important dignities within the city's administrative *apparatus*.[91]

[89] A. Bowman, 'Aurelius Horion and the Calpurnii: Elite families in third century Oxyrhynchus', [in:] T. Gagos & R.S. Bagnall (eds.), *Essay and Texts in Honor of J. David Thomas* [= *American Studies in Papyrology* XLII], Exeter 2001, pp. 11–17, p. 12; G. Messeri, *PSI* XVII, p. 172.

[90] Bowman, 'Aurelius Horion' (cit. n. 89), p. 16, n. 19.

[91] Yet, another interpretation is possible: the prominent Alexandrian family would have been granted with the Roman citizenship. It is less likely, but still possible, as the noun πρόσταγμα had a vast meaning in the early Roman period, including *edictum* of magistrates: J. Modrzejewski, 'The πρόσταγμα in the papyri', *The Journal of Juristic Papyrology* 5–6 (1951–1952), pp. 187–206, pp. 201–203. Yet, it could mean also imperial constitutions, which meaning of the πρόσταγμα Woldemar Uxkull-Gyllenband proved for the paragraph 37 of the *Gnomon of idios logos* (Uxkull-Gyllenband, *Der Gnomon* [cit. n. 35], p. 49), followed by *i.a.* Riccobono, *Gnomon* (cit. n. 36), pp. 172–173, yet see *e.g.* Reinach, 'Code fiscal' (cit.

2. Tyrannia Bassa, mother, was a Roman, l. 14: *Τυραννίας Βάσσης Σπουρίου θυγατρὸς Ῥωμαίας*. As she is described as neither Alexandrian nor *aste*, we have no grounds to assume she was an Alexandrian citizen.

There can be no doubt that the child was a legitimate Roman citizen born of two Roman parents, but the text also illustrates the application of *condicio deterioris parentis* acquisition in regard to the Alexandrian citizenship. It is difficult, however, to understand why the rule was applied. Did Alexandrians had *epigamia* towards Romans? Or was the Roman rule enforced on Alexandrians, because the children of Roman-Alexandrian unions had to acquire the status of either of their parents and were not entitled to the Roman one? The second scenario seems more likely.

The text is dated to AD 205, thus after Hadrian had introduced the rule that any child of a Roman woman and a peregrine should be considered lawful; however *P. Tebt.* II 316 was composed only in AD 99, while the enrolment of Sarapion to the Alexandrian *ephebeia* occurred even earlier, in AD 82 or 83. It would seem that accession to the Alexandrian *ephebeia* and the acquisition of citizenship was regulated according to Roman custom from the beginning of the Roman rule in Egypt, and the laws of Alexandria and other *poleis* were adjusted to the Roman model. Furthermore, these examples suggest that the Roman concept of *status civitatis* acquisition was based not on the simple dichotomy of Roman and non-Roman, but on the assignment of people to particular civic groups.

2.3.3. Children born to *astoi* from Egypt and *astoi* from other provinces

The *Gnomon* discusses the consequences of marrying not only simple *peregrini*, but also peers of other *poleis* which paragraphs might be references

n. 35), p. 116, or J. Mélèze Modrzejewski, 'Gnomon' (cit. n. 36), p. 536. As a matter of fact, the Roman citizenship was granted by the emperor, and from the already discussed correspondence between Pliny and Trajan it is known that the emperor could give Alexandrian citizenship to individuals too. The editor of *PSI* XVII 1691, Gabriella Messeri, pointed out another possible interpretation of *τῶν [πεπολιτο]|γραφημένων κατὰ πρόσταγμα*: it could refer to general scrutiny of Alexandrians which would have resulted with a new list: G. Messeri, *PSI* XVII, p. 172.

to Hellenistic rules. § 13 mentions the general rule applicable to female citizens and *xenoi*.

> *BGU* V 1210, l. 48: ιγ. τὰ ἐξ ἀστῆς καὶ ξένου γενόμενα τέκνα ξένα γείνεται καὶ | οὐ κληρονομεῖ τὴν μητέρα.
>
> 13. Children born of an *aste* and foreigner become foreigners and they do not inherit from their mother.

In regard to status acquisition, the children of *astai* and *xenoi* are in the same position as those begotten by *astai* and Egyptians: they followed the status of their father. Their situation, however, was worse in regard to succession, as they were entitled to inherit only from a foreign father. The passage may help us to determine how the term *xenos* was understood in the *Gnomon*. If two citizens of different *poleis* married legally due to the *epigamia* which existed between their cities, the child usually belonged to the paternal community, *metroxenos*, and only rarely to the maternal one, *patroxenos*.[92] If a child of two *astoi* of different *poleis* followed the paternal status, they were allowed to inherit according to the laws of the community where their father belonged, but could no longer inherit in the maternal one.[93] This was certainly the case in classical and Hellenistic Athens, where non-citizens could not own the land, *etc.*[94] It is therefore possible that *xenos* might have had a narrower meaning in the *Gnomon* than Thomas Kruse suggested: instead of simply a foreigner, stranger, or 'non-citizen of the state in question',[95] it may have referred to a citizen, but from outside of Egypt.

This understanding is supported to some extent by § 51, which illustrates that cases of intermarriages outside of Egypt did not escape the attention of those who compiled the *Gnomon*.

> *BGU* V 1210, l. 136: [ν]α. Σύρου καὶ ἀστῆς υἱὸς ἔγημ[εν Αἰγ]υπτίαν καὶ κατεκρίθη ὡρισμένον κεφάλαιον.

[92] Ogden points only to Siphnos and Thasos as relatively certain Hellenistic examples of *patroxenia*: Ogden, *Greek Bastardy* (cit. n. 2), p. 283.

[93] Ogden, *Greek Bastardy* (cit. n. 2), p. 7.

[94] G. Oliver, 'Foreign names, inter-marriage and citizenship in Hellenistic Athens', [in:] R.W.V. Catling & F. Marchand (eds.) with the assistance of M. Sasanow, *Onomatologos: Studies in Greek Personal Names presented to Elaine Matthews*, Oxford 2010, pp. 155–169, p. 160.

[95] Ogden, *Greek Bastardy* (cit. n. 2), p. 18.

51. The son of a Syrian and *aste* married an Egyptian and was sentenced to pay a prescribed sum.

The passage may refer to an individual case decided by the curator of the *idios logos*. It is problematic because one of the spouses is described as 'son of a Syrian and *aste*', which is not an indication of *status civitatis*. We must therefore ask to which category the 'son of a Syrian and *aste*' would have belonged. Certainly, he would not have been an Egyptian (or equivalent status), as his marriage of an Egyptian resulted in negative consequences for him; this would suggest that his status was higher. According to § 13, as the child of an *aste* and a *xenos* he should have followed the status of his father and become Syrian. It has been suggested that the 'Syrian' in the passage might have been from one of the Syrian *poleis*,[96] and it would appear that the man born of an *aste* and a Syrian must have had a status similar to *astos*, as we may deduce from the penalty imposed on him for marrying an Egyptian (§ 45) even though he was not from Egypt.

2.3.4. Freedmen of Alexandrians: special case

An exception to the rules saying that local citizens could marry individuals of lower status but their children followed the lesser status can be found in § 49.

BGU V 1210, l. 133: [μ]θ. ἀπελευθέροις Ἀλεξαν[δρέω]ν οὐκ ἐξὸν Αἰγυπτίαν γῆμαι.

49. Freedmen of Alexandrians are not permitted to marry an Egyptian women.

Indeed, § 49 differs from the other paragraphs quoted in this section, in which mixed marriages are generally recognised; it bears closer resemblance to § 23 (on incest among Romans), and § 110 (on the ownership of property and marital capability of *vicarii*). Paragraphs 23, 49 and 110 are all phrased in a way that includes direct prohibition: οὐκ ἐξόν. In § 23 it says (*BGU* V 1210, l. 70): οὐκ ἐξὸν Ῥωμαίοις ἀδελφὰς γῆμαι οὐδὲ τηθίδας, 'it is not permitted for Romans to marry either sisters or aunts'; § 110 says (l. 242):

[96] Riccobono, *Gnomon* (cit. n. 36), p. 186.

[οὐ]κ ἐ̣ξὸν οὐικαρίοις κτᾶσ̣θα̣ί̣ [τι ουδὲ ἐλ]ε̣υ̣θέρας (*BL* II, p. 30)[97] γαμε[ῖ]ν, 'it is not permitted for *vicarii*[98] to either acquire anything or marry free women'.

There is no doubt that slaves and incestuous couples were forbidden from marrying in any way, or that such unions would not produce any legal effects whatsoever, and that any children of such unions would follow the status of their mothers, as legally they had no fathers. The same formulation in § 49 implies that Alexandrian freedmen married to Egyptians would be subject to similar consequences, *i.e.* the nullity of their marriage. This suggests that the children of such unions would have been recognised as legally fatherless, and would therefore have followed the *status civitatis* of their mothers.

The paragraph following (§ 50) specifies that the property of freedwomen of *astoi* would be confiscated if they had children with Egyptians.

> *BGU* V 1210, ll. 134–135: [ν]. ἀπελευθέρας ἀστοῦ τετ̣[εκν]ω̣μένης ἐξ Αἰγυπτίου Νωρβᾶνος τὰ ὑπάρχοντα ἀνέλαβεν, Ῥοῦφ̣ο̣ς̣ [δὲ] τ̣οῖς τέκνοις ἔδωκε.
>
> 50. Norbanus confiscated the property of the freedwoman of an *astos* who bore a child of an Egyptian, but Rufus gave it to her children.

We can interpret this rule as the sanction applicable to the prohibition expressed in the previous paragraph: marriage with Egyptians was forbidden, and if it did happen (and if it produced offspring), a financial penalty would follow. The references in § 49, however, are to the male freedmen of Alexandrians, while § 50 refers to the freedwomen of all *astoi*.

It is possible, although not very likely, that this prohibition should be read together with § 45,[99] and that all *astoi* of both sexes and their

[97] *Ed. princ.* [ουδὲ ἀπὲλ]ε̣υ̣θέρας, the correction was proposed in Th. Reinach, 'Un code fiscal de l'Égypte romaine : Le Gnomon de l'idiologue', *Nouvelle revue historique de droit français et étranger* 43 (1919), pp. 583–636. Some editors kept the original reading: Mélèze Modrzejewski, 'Gnomon' (cit. n. 36), p. 48.

[98] Obviously the term had to apply not to usual slaves in the service or *peculium* of other slaves, but slaves belonging to *familia Caesaris* and involved in the administration of the province: Riccobono, *Gnomon* (cit. n. 36), pp. 249–250. See P.R.C. Weaver, '*Vicarius* and *vicarianus* in the *familia Caesaris*', *The Journal of Roman Studies* 54 (1964), pp. 117–128.

[99] W. Schubart, 'Rom und die Ägypter nach dem Gnomon des Idios Logos', *Zeitschrift für Ägyptische Sprache und Altertumskunde* 56 (1920), pp. 80–95, p. 86.

freedmen were forbidden to marry Egyptians. If they did, the penalty was imposed. The paragraphs quoted above, 49 and 50, would thus refer only to specific cases emerging from the general prohibition for which exceptions might have been developed. (We should also note that the sanction mentioned in § 50 depended on the individual decision of the official or on an edict from the prefect of Egypt.[100]) Such an interpretetation, however, seems implausible, especially in light of the other paragraphs discussing mixed unions involving *astoi* (*e.g.* §§ 38, 39 or 46) which mention no such prohibition, but rather to the contrary.

Furthermore, Wilhelm Schubart suggested that § 50 of the *Gnomon* forbidding freedmen of Alexandrians to marry Egyptians applied to all Alexandrians.[101] Unlike the other *astoi*, Alexandrians would have not been allowed to marry Egyptians. Elizabeth Meyer followed Schubart's opinion, and supported her argument additionaly with Diana Delia's list of sources for the Alexandrian *ephebeia* in which the mothers, if known, are always *astai* (once Roman, *P. Tebt.* II 316: *supra*, pp. 203–204).[102] This does not, however, prove that Alexandrians could not marry Egyptians, but only that their children could not belong to the Alexandrian *ephebeia*. If an Alexandrian married an Egyptian woman, their offspring would have followed the maternal status according to the rule of the lesser parent and could have not been admitted to the Alexandrian *ephebeia*; we would not, therefore, expect to find children of Alexandrians and Egyptians among documents pertaining to the *ephebeia*.

[100] Unfortunatelly, Norbanus and Rufus could be both curators of *idios logos*. Norbanus Ptolemaeus and C. Seppius Rufus are known from the papyri as curators of the private fisc, while two men of the *cognomen* Rufus were prefects: M. Mettius Rufus (AD 89–91/2), M. Junius Rufus (AD 94–98). It has been also discussed whether Norbanus Ptolemaeus did not acquire the office of Egypt eventually; see A. Jördens, 'Noch einmal: Norbanus *praefectus Aegypti?*', *Zeitschrift für Papyrologie und Epigraphik* 163 (2007), pp. 195–199. M. Metius Rufus is well-attested in source material not only by name, but also by his decrees, as the tariff of Coptos; see A. Jördens, *Statthalterliche Verwaltung in der römischen Kaiserzeit. Studien zum praefectus Aegypti* [= *Historia – Einzelschriften* CLXXV], Stuttgart 2009, pp. 384–387 & 528.

[101] W. Schubart, 'Rom und die Ägypter' (cit. n. 99), p. 86.

[102] Delia, *Alexandrian Citizenship* (cit. n. 25), pp. 143–146; E. Meyer, 'Freed and Astoi in the Gnomon of the Idios Logos and in Roman Egypt', [in:] K. Harter-Uibopuu & T. Kruse (eds.), *Studien zum „Gnomon des Idios Logos": Beiträge zum Dritten Wiener Kolloquium zur antiken Rechtsgeschichte*, forthcoming.

None of the interpretations of §§ 49–50 seem wholly convincing, and we should perhaps take the paragraphs at face value as a prohibition binding only freedmen of *astoi* or even specifically those freed by Alexandrians. It is, nonetheless, difficult to understand the rationale behind such a ruling. While the *lex Iulia et Papia* forbade members of the senatorial order from marrying freed persons and actors (D. 23.2.44: Paul. *ad leg. Iul. et Pap.* 1), the prohibition here is roughly the opposite. It is tempting to look to Hellenistic times for an explanation of this ban. Some of the rules included in the *Gnomon* do indeed refer to pre-Roman times (*e.g.* § 13 and § 51), but the ban cannot be Hellenistic in origin if we accept the Meyer's well-supported argument that freedmen were accepted among *astoi* only in the Roman period.

A deed belonging to the archive of Aphrodisios son of Philippos and descendants (*SB* IV 7393 [Arsinoite nome, AD 161 or after]) is especially interesting in the context of the marital ban discussed above.[103] In the document, Philippos son of Aphrodisios, ***katoikos***, requests that an ***archidikastes*** should register a ***cheirographon*** concerning a sale on the part of Philippos' wife Nike, a freedwoman of Phanias son of Phanias, Alexandrian, *ἡ γυνή μου Νείκη | ἀπελẹ[υθέ]ρ̣[α Φανίο(?)]υ Φανίου τοῦ Ἀλεξά̣[νδρου] | Εἰρηνοφυ̣[λακε]ί̣ου τοῦ καὶ Ἀλθαιέως* (ll. 6–8). Aphrodisios II was certainly one of the ***katoikoi***[104] and he is described thus in the text (ll. 2–5).

The text attests a marriage identical to those prohibited in the *Gnomon*. While we may offer several explanations for such a marriage, none is entirely satisfactory:

1. The couple was simply married despite the prohibition.

2. Freedwomen were not subject to the ban, despite being punished with confiscation if the union with an Egyptian resulted in children. The punishment for ignoring the marital ban in § 50, might already have been lifted by the first century, and could thus have been abandoned by *desuetudo* in the second.

[103] See R. SMOLDERS, 'Aphrodisios son of Philippos and descendants', [in:] K. VANDORPE, W. CLARYSSE & H. VERRETH (eds.), *Graeco-Roman Archives from the Fayum* [= *Collectanea Hellenistica – KVAB* VI], Leuven – Paris – Bristol, CT 2015, pp. 60–64.

[104] SMOLDERS, 'Aphrodisios son of Philippos' (cit. n. 103), p. 61.

3. *Aigyptioi* in §§ 49 and 50 did not include privileged Egyptians.
4. Philippos was not an Egyptian, but belonged to *peregrini cives*.

The first three interpretations are equally possible, but impossible to prove, although the fourth can be excluded. Indeed, Ruben Smolders suggested that Aphrodisios II, the father of Philippos II, would have obtained citizenship of Antinoopolis before AD 139.[105] Smolders based his observation on *P. Ryl.* II 324 *descr*. On the images of *P. Ryl.* II 324[106] and 332[107] *descrr.* (Theadelphia, AD 139) provided by the University of Manchester, the description Ἀντινοεύς[108] is visible after the name and filiation. Yet, in documents mentioning Philippos II, the son of Aphrodisios II, he is labelled not as a citizen of Antinoopolis, but only as *katoikos*. The documents not only postdate the mentioned texts, but they even include one census return.[109] Although it is difficult to explain the discrepancy between the description of Aphrodisios II in these two contracts and the rest of the archive, it does not appear that our Philippos, Nike's husband, was a citizen of Antinoopolis. It is not therefore possible to explain the legal standing of the couple with reference to § 49 or § 50. It may be that the prohibition was simply ignored or abandoned. Thus the text does not contribute much to our understing of the rules on unions between Alexandrian freedmen and Egyptians.

[105] SMOLDERS, 'Aphrodisios son of Philippos' (cit. n. 103), p. 61.

[106] https://luna.manchester.ac.uk/luna/servlet/detail/ManchesterDev-93-3-23692-100434:Agreement-of-Deposit?qvq=q:metadata_schema%3D12987&mi=0&trs=1.

[107] https://luna.manchester.ac.uk/luna/servlet/detail/ManchesterDev-93-3-23680-100442:Loan?qvq=q:metadata_schema%3D12991&mi=0&trs=1.

[108] Ἀντινωει in *P. Ryl.* II 332, l. 11.

[109] *PSI* V 458 (Theadelphia, AD 155), l. 1: Φιλίππωι Ἀ[φροδισίου]; *P. Ryl.* II 98 a (Theadelphia, AD 154), l. 1: Φιλ̣ί̣π̣[πῳ Ἀφροδισίου (?)] (in both texts he plays the role of the superintendent of pastures of Theadelphia and is requested for the hunting permission); *P. Meyer* 8 (Arsinoite nome, AD 151), ll. 2–3: παρὰ Φιλίππου καὶ Χαριτίου ἀμφοτέρω̣ν Ἀφροδισίου τοῦ Φι̣[λίππου κατοίκου] | τῶν ἐν τῷ Ἀρσινοΐτῃ ἀνδρῶν Ἑλλήνων ϛυοε (a party petitioning *epistrategos* about his and his sister's maternal inheritance); *SB* XXII 15336 (Ptolemais Euergetis, AD 133), l. 10: τέκνα Φίλιππον (ἐτῶν) ϛ ἄση(μον) μὴ ἀναγεγρα(μμένον) (a child declared in a census return); and *BGU* IX 1896 (Theadelphia, AD 166), l. 342, as payer of *oktodrachmia* tax: R. SMOLDERS, '*SB* XXII 15336 and the interpretation of *BGU* IX 1897', *Zeitschrift für Papyrologie und Epigraphik* 148 (2004), pp. 239–240.

2.3.5. Antinoopolis: special case

Unlike other *astoi* citizens of Antinoopolis were not only allowed to marry Egyptians, but also to transfer their status to children born in such unions. *Epigamia* towards Egyptians is attested in *W. Chr.* 27 (Antinoopolis, after AD 161), a fragment of proceedings from the city's *boule*. In ll. 17–24, Lucius Apollinarios, a member of the council, informs us:

> *ἡ ἐπι|γαμία ἐδόθη ἡμεῖν* (l. *ἡμῖν*) *πρὸς* | *Αἰγυπ[τί]ου[ς] κατ' ἐξαίρετον* | *ὑπὸ τοῦ θεοῦ Ἀδριανοῦ, ἥν|περ {ου} οὐκ ἔχουσι Ναυκρα⟦τι⟧|τεῖται, ὧν τοῖς νόμοις χρώ|μεθα, καὶ τὰ περὶ τῆς ἐπιγα|μίας πάλιν ἀναγεινώσκω* (l. *ἀναγιγνώσκω*).
>
> The *epigamia* with Egyptians was granted to us as an extraordinary measure by the deified Hadrian, which citizens of Naukratis, whose laws we use, do not have. And now let me read again the clauses concerning *epigamia.*

Citizens of Antinoopolis could marry Egyptians with no adverse effect on the status of their children; citizens of Naukratis and other *poleis* did not enjoy this privilege, as suggested in both the above fragment and the *Gnomon of idios logos*. Therefore the rule of *deterioris parentis condicio* had no application in Antinoopolis. Men could thus produce new citizens with women of the privileged groups,[110] as well as those from the fiscally unprivileged ones.[111]

It is visible in how deeds connected to status acquisition were framed. When children acquired paternal status, maternal status would not have

[110] *E.g.* in *Pap. Lugd. Bat.* VI 48 (AD 202/3), belonging to the archive of Philosarapis son of Lysimachos *alias* Didymos, a census return by five citizens concerning their property in Ptolemais Euergetis. Two families resided in the declared property:

1. Neilos, his wife Eudaimonis, and their daughter Helene: The family belonged to the metropolite order: the father is labelled as *ἀπὸ τῆς μητροπόλεως* (ll. 12–16), the mother as registered with him in the Tameion quarter (ll. 14–15), while their daughter Helene was married to Philosarapis (perhaps one of the declarants), a citizen of Antinoopolis (ll. 15–16).
2. Sarapias *ἀπὸ τῆς μητροπόλεως* and her daughter Tyrannis *alias* Isidora, *Ἀντινοείς*, whose father was one of the declarants, Philantinoos *alias* Herodes, a citizen of Antinoopolis (ll. 16–20).

[111] As Marcus Lucretius Diogenes II who married Ammonarion, a woman described only with her patronym, metronym and domicil, and had two children with her, Aurelia Kopria and Herennas, about whom there could be no doubt that they were citizens of Antinoopolis, because they were described so, *e.g.* in *P. Diog.* 3 = *P. Turner* 30 (Antinoopolis, AD 209; and copy: *P. Diog.* 4) and *P. Diog.* 19 (AD 226). See P. SCHUBERT, *Philadelphie : Un village égyptien en mutation entre le IIe et le IIIe siècle ap. J.-C.*, Basel 2007, pp. 62–65.

mattered, if children were recognised by a father. An early *aparche* belonging to the archive of Philosarapis son of Lysimachos *alias* Didymos is an example of such document, in which the mother was not even listed. Crucial for children's status is that the father belonged to Antinoopolis:

> *Pap. Lugd. Bat.* VI 30 (Antinoopolis, AD 133), ll. 1 – 7: [πεπολιτογραφημέ]νων[112] ἐντ[ὸ]ς τῆς ὡρισμένης προθεσμίας ὑπομν[ή]μα̣τα τῆι βουλῆι | δεδωκό[τ]ω̣ν̣, ὕστερο[ν] δὲ παραστησάντων τοὺς παῖδα̣ς· | Ἡρακλείδη[ς] ὁ καὶ Οὐαλέρ̣ιος Ἡρακλείδου τοῦ Μάρωνος Ἀντινο(εύς), ἄποικ(ος) Ἀρσι(νοΐτου) | ἀνδρῶν Ἑ̣[λ]λήνων, ὡ̣ς̣ (ἐτῶν) νζ, | ὑπὲρ̣ [υ]ἱῶν β· | Λυσιμάχ[ο]υ τοῦ καὶ Διδύμου ἐ[τ]ῶν ἑπτά, | Φιλοσαρά̣πιδος ἐνιαυτοῦ ἑνός.
>
> From the list of new citizens (?) who, within the regulated period, handed in memorials to the senate and afterwards presented their sons: Herakleides also called Valerius, son of Herakleides, son of Maron, Antinoopolite, settler from the Greek men in the Arsinoite nome, aged about 57 years, for two sons: Lysimachos also called Didymos, seven years old, Philosarapis, one year old.[113]

The document is early, Herakleides *alias* Valerius was granted with the Antinoopolite citizenship not even three years after the city was founded. The pattern might be similar to the acquisition of Roman citizenship by peregrines: they obtained it together with their children as the privilege was granted (G. 1.92–94). Yet also a later *aparche* belonging to the same archive and made for Herakleides *alias* Valerius son Lysimachos alias Didymos in AD 159 (*Pap. Lugd. Bat.* VI 34 [Antinoopolis, AD 151]) does not list the mother. Examples from outside this archive are also known: the mothers are omitted in both in *P. Diog.* 2 *&* 4, copies of *aparchai* made for Marcus Lucretius Diogenes and his son Herennas.[114] This suggests that naming the mother was not even necessary, it might have been enough for the citizenship that one citizen declared the child as his own.

The same was suggested in regard to the Antinoopolite *ephebeia*. Kent Rigsby and Jean Bingen put forward that it would have been sufficient to

[112] [ἀνδρῶν Ἑλλή]νων in: H.I. BELL, 'Diplomata antinoitica', *Aegyptus* 13 (1933), pp. 514–528, p. 523.

[113] Tr. BELL, 'Diplomata antinoitica' (cit. n. 112), p. 524.

[114] Full list of children registrations including those from Antinoopolis, see SANCHEZ-MORENO ELLART, 'ὑπομνήματα ἐπιγεννήσεως' (cit. n. 63), pp. 92–93.

have one Antinoopolite parent to become an ephebe. They based this opinion on the ephebial registers discussed above, where the descriptions of the boys provided no ancestry beyond the basic patronym or metronym.[115] Unfortunately, none of the surviving ephebial registrations was submitted by a sole mother.[116] Those submitted by fathers contain more familial details than the *aparchai* – including the metronym and both papponyms – but still no information on the status of parents, siblings or the father's tribe and deme. While they contain less information than analogous documents from other locations, the brevity of description does not suggest that random individuals could be admitted to the Antinoopolite *ephebeia*, but rather that the rules of admission were less rigid than anywhere else.[117]

That children of citizens of Antinoopolis who married Egyptian women were admitted to the citizenship needs no further proof.[118] However, it was initially proposed that *epigamia* applied only to male citizens of Antinoopolis. Yet the publication of *Pap. Lugd. Bat.* II 2 (Antinoopolis, AD 247/8) cast doubt on this opinion.[119] The text is an Antinoopolite *aparche* by Aurelia Sarapias

[115] Discussion summarised on pp. 173–175.

[116] LEGRAS, *Néotês* (cit. n. 88), pp. 162–163: *Pap. Lugd. Bat.* VI 32 = *SB* V 7605; *SB* XVI 12744; *SB* IV 7427 + XIV 11476; *PSI* III 199; *P. Diog.* 8.

[117] LEGRAS, *Néotês* (cit. n. 88), p. 168: *e.g.* it could be even doubted that only sons of former ephebes were admitted to *ephebeia.*

[118] The text which does not fit the described pattern is *P. Bagnall* 3 = *Ch. L. A.* XLVII 1442 (Oxyrhynchos, AD 239), a petition for *bonorum possessio*, in which a mother is described as a citizen of Antinoopolis, while the description of the son is followed by *ab Oxurugch(itarum) civit*[*a*]*t*[*e*] (l. 2). Yet it is uncertain whether this description applied to the petitioner himself or to another person in genitive whose identity and relation to the petitioner is unknown due to the fragmentary state of preservation. *CPL* 216 = *SB* I 1010 = *Ch. L. A.* XI 486 (Antinoopolis, AD 249) and its Greek copy, *SB* VI 9298, is another request for *bonorum possessio* dated to the same period. It was submitted on behalf a boy of Antinoopolis for the *bonorum possessio* from his Oxyrhynchite mother. The document mentions *edictum* in which *bonorum possessio* was to be given to children. The scholars debated whether it was the provincial edict of the prefect or the one by the praetor: *e.g.* J. MÉLÈZE-MODRZEJEWSKI, *Loi et coutume dans l'Égypte grecque et romaine* [= *The Journal of Juristic Papyrology Supplement* XXI], Warsaw 2014, pp. 286–292; J.L. ALONSO, 'Juristic papyrology and Roman law', [in:] P.J. du PLESSIS, C. ANDO & K. TUORI (eds.), *The Oxford Handbook of Roman Law and Society*, Oxford 2016, pp. 56–69, pp. 59–60.

[119] H. BRAUNERT, 'Griechische und römische Komponenten im Stadtrecht von Antinoopolis', *The Journal of Juristic Papyrology* 14 (1962), pp. 73–88, p. 77.

and her husband Aurelius Theodoros *alias* Herakleios, for their son. As Aurelius Theodoros is described as a council member of Herakleopolis, it was the mother who transferred her citizenship to the boy. We notice, however, that the request was submitted by both parents – the verb ἐπιδέδωκα follows the descriptions of the two (ll. 4 *&* 6) – and that it was the father who attested the identity of the boy (l. 8: γνωστεύω). The text suggests that a 'mixed couple' in which only a woman possessed the citizenship of Antinoopolis could register a child as a citizen. The case is, however, specific, because the father, Aurelius Theodoros, belonged to the metropolite order, and the document is dated after AD 200 when *metroplies* obtained their *boulai*.

Horst Braunert, commenting on *Pap. Lugd. Bat.* II 2, noted that the rule granting children the status of their mothers may have been grounded in Roman municipal laws and further identified the *epigamia* given to Antinoopolites as *ius conubii*.[120] The privilege of maternal status acquisition in regard to *municipia* is expressed in a fragment of Ulpian's *Commentary on the edict*.

> D. 50.1.1.2 (Ulp. *ad ed.* 2): Qui ex duobus igitur Campanis parentibus natus est, Campanus est. Sed si ex patre Campano, matre Puteolana, aeque municeps Campanus est, nisi forte privilegio aliquo materna origo censeatur: tunc enim maternae originis erit municeps. (...)
>
> Consequently, the one who was born to two parents from Campania is Campanian. Yet, if (he is born) of the father from Campania and mother from Puteolanum, he is a citizen of Campania as well, unless he was granted with any special privilege of the maternal origine: then he will be a citizen of a *municipium* of the mother.

At the end of the passage, Ulpian analyses the scope of the right, mentioning that certain authorities considered this privilege applicable only to children born out of wedlock. Yet, Celsus, whose opinion Ulpian follows, did not approve of this interpretation: the privilege should not be given to *vulgo quaesiti* (who followed the maternal status in any case):

[120] Braunert, 'Griechische und römische Komponenten (cit. n. 119), p. 77; accepted by F. Strum, 'Ha conferito Adriano uno statuto personale speciale agli Antinoiti?', *Iura* 43 (1992), pp. 83–97, pp. 87–89: A wider comparison between *conubium* and *epigamia* including Antinoopolite *epigamia*, see Volterra, '*Conubium*' (cit. n. 41), pp. 305–320, who concluded that *conubium* was the institution common to Latin and Italian polulations and to Greek cities (p. 317).

Quod beneficium ad volgo quaesitos solos pertinere quidam putant. Quorum sententiam Celsus non probat: neque enim debuisse caveri, ut volgo quaesitus matris condicionem sequeretur (quam enim aliam originem hic habet?): sed ad eos, qui ex diversarum civitatium parentibus orirentur.

Some think that this privilege relates only to *vulgo quaesiti*. Celsus does not approve their opinion: for it would not have been necessary that *vulgo quaesitus* follows the maternal condition (for what other origin could this person have?). But (the grant relates) to those persons, who are born of parents from different communities.

Ulpian explains that certain Italian *municipia* allowed a child born to a mother and father belonging to two different *municipia* to become a *municeps* of the mother's community. Ulpian recognised this as a privilege, *nisi forte privilegio aliquo materna origo censeatur*, both in Italian *municipia* and in communities outside of Italy – Ilion, Delphi and Pontus – which were in fact political entities of different status. Ilion and Delphi were both Roman *poleis*, while 'Pontus' encompassed all cities in this province to whom Pompey had granted the privilege.[121]

In the case of *municipia* it is clear that the privilege was reserved specifically for marriages between two peers of different *origo*.[122] The privilege given by Pompey to the cities of Pontus was recognised as binding for marriages between female citizens of Pontic cities and male citizens of other cities, including those outside of the province (*e.g.* in a neighbouring Hellenistic kingdom). The privilege may, therefore, be recognised as protective for the new Pontic cities and complementary to Pompey's prohibition of dual citizenship.[123] Hadrian may have had similar aims with regard to Antinoopolis, and his special rules may have been designed both to populate the city and safeguard its elites. Yet, Antinoopolis was not listed in Ulpian's text.

Three further texts – *SB* XVI 12290 = VIII 9897 a = VI 9312 a + b, ll. 1–2 (Tebtynis, AD 161), *Pap. Lugd. Bat.* VI 42 (Antinoopolis, AD 180), l. 25, and *SB* XXII 15469 (Karanis, AD 204), l. 3 – describe Egyptians who had married

[121] A.J. MARSHALL, 'Pompey's organization of Bithynia-Pontus: Two neglected texts', *The Journal of Roman Studies* 58 (1968), pp. 103–109, p. 108.

[122] On the *origo*, see D. NÖRR, 'Origo Studien zur Orts-, Stadt- und Reichszugehörigkeit in der Antike', *Tijdschrift voor Rechtsgeschie* 31 (1963), pp. 525–600.

[123] MARSHALL, 'Pompey's organization' (cit. n. 121), pp. 108–109.

female citizens of Antinoopolis as having been granted the right to do so, τὴν ἐπιγαμ̣ίαν πρὸς Ἀντινοΐδα ἔχειν, and they are crucial for our understanding of this privilege.

The privilege must therefore have worked as it did in Hellenistic times: men of a certain community were given privilege to marry women of another and the ability to transfer their status to the children of such unions (*metroxenoi*).[124] *Epigamia* could result from treaties between cities, but could be also granted by the state to an individual alien. In the latter case, an alien could marry a female citizen of the community and his children would acquire the wife's citizenship (*patroxenoi*).[125] This would explain why citizens of Antinoopolis of both sexes were never described as holders of *epigamia*: as men could produce Antinoopolite children with Egyptians under the general terms of the privilege, there was no need to mention that they possessed the *epigamia*, while women were not holders of the right. The effect was different from Roman *conubium*, which was granted to a Roman woman towards her peregrine husband, and did not provide children with Roman citizenship.[126]

Men seem to have to obtain the *epigamia* in order to marry a woman of Antinoopolis. The question remains whether the privilege was automatically granted to anyone who married a female citizen of Antinoopolis, or if it was connected to an application procedure which could result in rejection. If the latter, we must further ask if the right could be obtained by anyone, or if it was reserved solely for men belonging to privileged groups, as suggested by Bernard Abraham van Groningen[127] and accepted by Józef Mélèze Modrzejewski.[128]

[124] Ogden, *Greek Bastardy* (cit. n. 2), pp. 291–292.

[125] Ogden, *Greek Bastardy* (cit. n. 2), p. 292. See J. Vélissaropoulos-Karakostas, 'Les nothoi' (cit. n. 4), pp. 259–260.

[126] *Conubium* attributed to both men and women, see Volterra, '*Conubium*' (cit. n. 41), p. 301.

[127] See commentary to *P. Fam. Tebt.* 42: van Groningen even claimed that it was restricted only to the metropolite group. Yet, Arsinoite *katoikoi* constituted a significant number of Antinoopolis citizen body; see M. Malouta, 'Antinoite citizenship under Hadrian and Antoninus Pius. A prosopographical study of the first thirty years of Antinoopolis', *The Bulletin of the American Society of Papyrologists* 46 (2009), pp. 81–96. Thus it is not likely that they would not be given the privilege.

[128] J. Mélèze-Modrzejewski, 'Dryton le crétois' (cit. n. 6), p. 357, n. 19.

In *SB* XVI 12290[129] a petitioner, who had both *epigamia* and their domicile in Antinoopolis, was assigned to the liturgy in Tebtynis. The document contains a copy of the reply from the *epistrategos*, which states that the petitioner, as the father of an Antinoopolite, should not be burdened with the liturgy outside of Antinoopolis. The petitioner himself mentions that he paid his ἐπικεφάλια in Antinoopolis (ll. 7–8).

P. Fam. Tebt. 42 supplements our knowledge significantly. This piece of official correspondence states that some men from division of Polemon had the *epigamia*. The subjects of the letter had been called upon to pay their ἐπικεφάλια in both their old *idia* and Antinoopolis, despite only being obliged to pay it in the polis. As in *SB* XVI 12290, the rate of *laographia* is not mentioned, although those men are described at the bottom of the document, ll. 35–41. The identification cluster consists of 'person – patronym – (metronym – papponym) – domicil of either Tebtynis or Narmouthis'. On the basis of Egyptian onomastics Montevecchi recognised them as unprivileged Egyptians;[130] this however, is not necessarily correct, as people with Egyptians names are attested among privileged groups. More convincing is the domicile, which suggests that those men had not been registered in any quarters of Ptolemais Euergetis. A similar description applied to a holder of *epigamia* in *SB* XXII 15469, ll. 14–16: ἔστι [δὲ·] | *Πτολεμαῖς ὁ καὶ Κ̣* [- *ca.* ? - *Πτολε*]|*μαίου ἀπὸ Καρ*[*ανίδος*].

An interesting contribution to the discussion on Antinoopolite citizenship appears in the already discussed archive of Gemellus Horion. In the census return belonging to this archive, *P. Mich.* VI 370, ll. 7–14 (quoted in Chapter 3, pp. 162–163), two children, Caia Apolinaria and Gemellus Horion, declared by their mother Tasoucharion, are described as Antinoopolite citizens; their names appear without filiation although their father, Caius Apolinarius Niger, one of the owners of the archive, was known. If the filiation was omitted for no legal reason, but rather because their father had died and their descriptions were long enough to allow precise identification, we could perhaps find an analogy in *P. Diog.* 29, where Aurelia Kopria is described

[129] On the controversies concerning the date, see N. Lewis, 'A restudy of *SB* VIII 9897', *Archiv für Papyrusforschung* 28 (1982), pp. 31–38, pp. 33–36.

[130] O. Montevecchi, 'Adriano e la fondazione di Antinoopolis', *Latomus* 209 (1990), pp. 183–195, pp. 186 & 192.

with only a metronym despite having a legitimate father. If the filiation was absent because Apolinaria and Horion's status depended on their mother, then the case would have been analogous to the ephebic lists.

The father of the two children listed in the census, Caius Apolinarius Niger, was the son of a veteran and citizen of Antinoopolis, Caius Iulius Niger. It has been pointed out, that Caius Apolinarius Niger, unlike his brother Caius Iulius Longinus,[131] was born before his father's *missio honesta*, and for this reason was not a Roman.[132] Indeed, in this period the children of ordinary auxiliary soldiers were no longer granted citizenship at their fathers' discharge;[133] in legal sense the children of soldiers belonged to the category of fatherless individuals and could be compared to children born of free mothers and slave fathers. Caius Apolinarius Niger's *gentilicium* offers another clue regarding his status.[134] It is not of the *gens Iulia*, to which his father belonged, nor is it a *gentilicium* but rather Greek name. Caius Apolinarius Niger did not pretend to be a Roman, but rather tried to underline the connection to his Roman father by creating false *tria nomina*.

The fact that Caius Apolinarius Niger was not a Roman did not preclude becoming a citizen of Antinoopolis. Indeed, Caius Apolinarius Niger, is attested with the description of *Ἀντινοεύς* in *P. Mich.* VI 364 (Arsinoites, AD 179), a declaration concerning land acquisition: in line 4, the declarant calls himself *Γάιος Ἀπολινάριος Νίγερ Ἀντινοεύς*. If this description is correct – and there is no reason to distrust it, especially given that the declaration was addressed to tax authorities – it should mean that his mother, Ptolemais, was a citizen of Antinoopolis. Although she is mentioned only by name in her younger son's ephebic registration (*SB* IV 7427, l. 7 [Karanis, AD 180–230]), this is not proof that she was not a citizen, as the maternal status was not mentioned in such documents, unless the child's status depended on the mother. We can, of course, imagine that a boy belonging to a veteran's family could have obtained citizenship of Antinoopolis as an individual grant. Yet, we cannot prove it.

[131] Whose *epikrisis* among ephebes copy was preserved, *SB* IV 7427.

[132] I. Bieżuńska-Małowist, 'La famille du vétéran romain C. Iulius Niger de Karanis', *Eos* 49 (1957), pp. 155–164, p. 159. Yet, the basis for dating his birth is not solid.

[133] The privilege was abolished half a century earlier by Antoninus Pius, see *supra*, p. 124.

[134] Bieżuńska-Małowist, 'La famille' (cit. n. 132), p. 158.

2.4. *Privileged Egyptians*

The above sections suggest that the Romans imposed the rule of *deterioris parentis condicio* onto all 'mixed unions' in Egypt, not only for unions involving Romans, but also for those between other status groups.[135] Legal similarities in different situations, however, should not always be taken at face value, as similar phenomena often arise independently from different legal realities. *E.g.* from the paragraphs concerning status acquisition in the *Gnomon* it seems that some discussed above rules concerning the acquisition of the status by children of *astoi* had to be Hellenistic, even if later adjusted by the Romans.[136]

We could confirm whether or not the rule of following the lesser parent's status was universal in Roman Egypt by examining how it worked in regard to the privileged *katoikoi*'s and metropolite and gymnasial groups. Peter van Minnen's studies illustrate that they also followed the *deterioris parentis conditio* rule,[137] even though the orders were not *status civitatis*, but rather special categories of *peregrini Aegyptii*. The rule is expressed in a decision by the *strategos* of the Hermopolite nome, dated to the first century.

> *SB* V 8038 (Hermopolis, 1st c. AD):[138] *Ἀντώνιος Πτολεμαῖος στρατηγὸς Ἑρμοπολ(ίτου). | οἱ ἀπὸ τῆς μητροπόλεως εἰς τοὺς τεσσαρεσκαιδεκα|ετεῖς προσβαίνοντες ἀφήλικες ἐν̣ [ὀκταδράχμοι(?)]ς | καὶ ἀπὸ τάγματος τοῦ γυμνασίου ἐ[πεὶ ὀφείλουσι] ἐ|πικρίνεσθαι εἰ ἐξ ἀμφοτέρων γονέω[ν τὸ μητροπ]ο|λιτικὸν γένος σῴζουσι, οἱ δ' ἐκ τοῦ γυμ[νασίου, εἰ] ἀ|π' αὐτοῦ τοῦ τάγματός εἰσι, πρὸς τὴν [ἐπίκρισιν (?)] | τούτων ἀναγκαι[ό]τατο̣ν̣ ἔ̣[σ]τ̣αι καὶ α[... ὑπ'] ἀν|δρῶν ἀξιοχρέων γενέσθαι ἐτῶν ο .[...]*

[135] Salvatore Riccobono was of the opinion that the *lex Minicia* applied: V. ARANGIO-RUIZ, 'Un *liber mandatorum* da Augusto ad Antonino Pio', *Atene e Roma* 3 (1922), pp. 216–223, p. 218.

[136] C. FISCHER-BOVET, 'Official identity and ethnicity: comparing Ptolemaic and Early Roman Egypt', *Journal of Egyptian History* 11 (2018), pp. 208–242, pp. 228–229.

[137] P. VAN MINNEN, '*Αἱ ἀπὸ γυμνασίου*: Greek women and the Greek elite in the metropoleis of Roman Egypt', [in:] H. MELAERTS & L MOOREN (eds.), *Le rôle et le statut de la femme en Égypte hellénistique, romaine et byzantine : acts du colloque international, Bruxelles – Leuven, 27–29 novembre 1997* [= *Studia Hellenistica* XXXVII], Paris 2002, pp. 337–353.

[138] With corrections in J. BINGEN, 'Les papyrus de la Fondation Égyptologique Reine Elisabeth. XIV. Déclarations pour l'épicrisis', *Chronique d'Égypte* 31 (1956), pp. 109–117, p. 109, n. 1.

> Antonius Ptolemaios, *strategos* of the Hermopolites: Minors among those payers of eight drachmae from the *metropolis* entering the fourteen-year old group as well as those from the gymnasial order ought to be determined by *epikrisis* whether they retain the metropolite descent from both parents, while those from the gymnasion whether they are from the same order; for their scrutiny, it shall be indispensable … by trustworthy men …

Although the binding of the preserved text being a decision of the *epistrategos* was perhaps limited to the time when he hold his office and to the Hermopolite nome,[139] deeds of scrutiny from other nomes confirm that the same rule was applied throughout the province. For applications to the metropolite groups, one had to prove they keep the metropolite descent from both parents.[140] The same was enough in the case of *katoikoi*, to become *katoikos* a boy would have to demonstrate both parents to be of this rank.[141] Scrutiny to the gymnasial class, however, required a more extensive proof of ancestry: on the paternal side ancestors had to be listed from the year AD 4/5, when the order was established, while maternal ancestors had to be established as far back as the second half of the first century:[142] AD 72/3 in Oxyrhynchos[143] and AD 64/5

[139] BINGEN, 'Les papyrus de la Fondation Égyptologique Reine Elisabeth. XIV' (cit. n. 138), p. 109, n. 1.

[140] See *e.g.* *P. Oxy*. III 478 = *W. Chr.* 218, ll. 10–12: ἐξ ἀμ|φ[οτ]έρων γονέων μητροπο|λειτῶν (l. μητροπο|λιτῶν) (δωδεκαδράχμων) εἰσί; or *P. Oxy*. II 258 = *W. Chr*. 216, ll. 7–9; *P. Oxy*. VII 1028, ll. 12–14; *P. Oxy*. LXVII 4585, ll. 4–6; *PSI* X 1109, l. 10; *P. Wisc*. I 17 R, ll. 4–5.

[141] O. MONTEVECCHI, 'Nerone a una polis e ai 6475', *Aegyptus* 50 (1970), pp. 5–33, p. 24.
In *P. Erl.* 22 (Ptolemais Euergetis, AD 160/1), an *epikrisis* document, information regarding where the candidate's father had been registered before he died (ll. 11–15) and the identity of his maternal grandparents (ll. 16–20) were included as evidence that both parents had belonged to the *katoikoi.* The same in *P. Fay.* 27 (AD 175) or *SB* XX 14111 = *P. Fay.* 319 *descr.* (after AD 161) providing as a proof census declarations regarding the status of a candidate: O. MONTEVECCHI, 'Epikrisis e dichiarazioni di censimento di cateci arsinoiti', *Aegyptus* 70 (1990), pp. 27–31, p. 31.

[142] On patterns of applications to gymnasial and metropolite groups in Oxyrhynchos, see U. YIFTACH-FIRANKO, 'A gymnasial registration report from Oxyrhynchus', *The Bulletin of the American Society of Papyrologists* 47 (2010), pp. 45–65, pp. 52–53.

[143] It was predated by one earlier scrutiny in mid-50s of the first century: O. MONTEVECCHI, 'L'*epikrisis* dei Greco-Egizi', [in:] *Proceedings of the XIV International Congress of Papyrologists, Oxford, 24—31 July 1974* [= *Graeco-Roman Memoirs* LXI], London 1975, pp. 227–232, p. 229. Detailed analysis of this general *epikrisis* in: P.J. SIJPESTEIJN, 'Some remarks on the *epikrisis*

in Hermopolis.[144] (These were the dates of the general scrutinies for gymnasia members in these *metropoleis* and the moment at which the rules of admission had been re-defined.)

2.4.1. Gymnasial class: special case

The need for such a long ancestry proof in the gymnasial class is discernible. Basing on the observation that maternal relatives are listed only as far back as the time of general scrutinies Peter van Minnen concluded that they would have not mattered before them. In early Roman times the admission to the gymnasial order would have been based on paternal status, and only between the 50s[145] and 70s of the first century was the order closed to children of gymnasial fathers and non-gymnasial mothers.[146] Yanne Broux developed the argument further: as it was only the gymnasial applications that changed during this period, the change must have applied only to the gymnasial group; the metropolite status was based on the same rules from the very beginning of its existence, thus from the time of Augustus.[147] This means that the Romans, in creating fiscally privileged groups among the Egyptians, would have included the *metropolitai* within their own framework of status, while the gymnasial order would have been initially left free to apply its own principles most probably originating in the Ptolemaic structure of the gymnasia.

This reconstruction seems convincing. The problematic part is, however, the assumption that before general scrutinies only the paternal sta-

of οἱ ἀπὸ γυμνασίου in Oxyrhynchus', *The Bulletin of the American Society of Papyrologists* 13 (1976), pp. 181–190, pp. 181–185.

144 van Minnen, 'Αἱ ἀπὸ γυμνασίου' (cit. n. 137), p. 345. For Hermopolis Megale, see T. Kruse, 'Bevölkerungskontrolle, Statuszugang und Archivpraxis im römischen Ägypten', [in:] M. Faraguna (ed.), *Archives and Archival Documents in Ancient Societies: Legal Documents in Ancient Societies IV, Trieste, 30 September – 1 October 2011*, Trieste 2013, pp. 307–332, p. 323.

145 In the Arsinoite for *katoikoi* in AD 54/5: van Minnen, 'Αἱ ἀπὸ γυμνασίου' (cit. n. 137), p. 345; D. Canducci, 'I 6475 cateci greci dell'Arsinoite', *Aegyptus* 70 (1990), pp. 211–255, pp. 228–229.

146 See pp. 173–177.

147 Y. Broux, 'Creating a new local elite. The establishment of the metropolitan orders of Roman Egypt', *Archiv für Papyrusforschung* 59.1 (2013), pp. 143–153, pp. 148–152.

tus was decisive for gymnasium. Indeed, van Minnen observed that the Hermopolite corn dole applications predating AD 64/5 based on gymnasion or *ephebeia*[148] make few references to the membership of mothers in the gymnasial order.[149] This observation certainly supports van Minnen's reconstruction.

In support of his theory, van Minnen discussed *P. Flor.* I 79 = *W. Chr.* 145 (AD 60),[150] an application to the Hermopolite *ephebeia*. The document describes the candidate's mother as *ἐλευθέρας ἐ[ξ ἐ]λευθέρων | γονέων* (ll. 23–24), which, in van Minnen's opinion, proves that the mother's freeborn status was sufficient.[151] The woman, however, is also labelled as *Ἑρμοπολῖτις* (ll. 6 & 23), literraly 'citizen of Hermopolis',[152] which could simply indicate that the woman was from Hermopolis. It could also mean that the mother in question was a member of the metropolite group; and as freedmen were admitted to this group but excluded from the gymnasion, a metropolite woman marrying a member of the gymnasion would have needed to include a declaration of freeborn status so that her children could join the gymnasial group.[153]

[148] See M. NOWAK, 'Get your free corn: The fatherless in the corn-dole archive from Oxyrhynchos', [in:] *Tell Me Who You Are* (cit. n. 75), pp. 215–218.

[149] VAN MINNEN, '*Aἱ ἀπὸ γυμνασίου*' (cit. n. 137), p. 346.

[150] The document belonged to a bigger group of texts discovered in one location and to one family archive; see G. MESSERI & R. PINTAUDI, 'Spigolature VI', *Zeitschrift für Papyrologie und Epigraphik* 129 (2000), pp. 265–273; G. MESSERI, 'P.Flor. III 324 recto/verso e la famiglia del kôm Kâssûm', *Aegyptus* 89 (2009), pp. 239–251, pp. 245–251.

[151] VAN MINNEN, '*Aἱ ἀπὸ γυμνασίου*' (cit. n. 137), p. 346. The view is shared by Y. BROUX, *Double Names and Elite Strategy in Roman Egypt* [= *Studia Hellenistica* LIV], Leuven 2015, pp. 197–198.

[152] LEGRAS, *Néotês* (cit. n. 88), p. 171; see also FISCHER-BOVET, 'Official identity and ethnicity' (cit. n. 136), p. 232.

[153] Another case similar to *P. Flor.* I 79 is *P. Lond.* II 260–261, pp. 42–61 = *SPP* IV, pp. 58–83 (Ptolemais Euergetis, AD 73): the father was, however, ***katoikos***, the mother belonged to the metropolite group, ll. 646–649: *ἄλλος ὁμοίως σ̣η̣μ̣α̣ν̣θ(εὶς) εἶναι υἱὸς κα[το]ίκ() οὗ οἱ γονεῖς̣ | οὐκ εἰσεὶ* (l. *εἰσὶ*) *ἐν ἀπογρα(φῇ)* [*θ*] (*ἔτους*) *Νέρωνος διὰ τὸ τὸν πατέρα ἐν τοῖς | ἐπ' ἴδους* (l. *εἴδους*) *ἐπ[ι]κεκρ[ίσθ(αι)] τῶι α* (*ἔτει*) *Οὐεσπασιανοῦ νικοτελε̣ί̣α̣ις | ἡ δὲ μήτηρ ἐστὶν ἐ̣ν̣γ(ενὴς) μητροπ(όλεως)* (*BL* V, p. 51: *μητροπ(ολῖτις)*) – 'Similarly another who is declared to be a son of *katoikos*, whose parents are not on the list of the 9th year of Nero, because his father has been scrutinised among those in the class in the 1st year of Vespasian as a celebrated victor; the mother being native of the metropolis'.

A parallel to *P. Flor.* I 79 is *P. Ryl.* II 101 a, b *&* c (b = *P. Heid.* IV 342), dated to AD 63, an application for the *eiskrisis* of Dioskoros son of Anoubion, in which the mother is described as the daughter of a man ἀπὸ γυμνασίου (fr. A, ll. 5–6): τὸν υἱόν μου Διόσκορον μητρ[ὸ]ς Ἀντιγό|[νης τῆς] Ὡρίωνος πατρὸς ἀπὸ γυμνα[σ]ίου.[154] If the mother did not matter, we would expect her to be mentioned by name only, or to be absent as in some of the applications submitted by citizens of Antinoopolis.[155] On the other hand, it could be an information without legal significance.

Finally, it is generally accepted that the gymnasial order imitated the Hellenistic polis. As we discussed above, it seems that children of Egyptian women were not accepted as citizens of *poleis*. (The exception is Antinoopolis whose citizens could marry whomever they wished and produce children who followed their status. Yet this analogy could not be used for the gymnasial class for two reasons: first, it comes over 150 years after the creation of the gymnasial rank, and second, Antinoopolis did not differentiate between male and female citizens when it came to the transfer of Antinoopolite status to children, which we discussed in earlier in this chapter.) In other words, there is no good analogy on which the paternal status acquisition in the gymnasial group could be based.

For the above reasons we may wish to modify van Minnen's model. The rules of admission to οἱ ἀπὸ γυμνασίου might have been based on double descent from the beginning, but the application pattern changed after the general scrutiny in order to eliminate status usurpations.[156] The fact that measures against marrying into fiscally privileged groups were taken only gradually and on a nome by nome basis would suggest that the general scrutinies were an enforcement rather than an establishment of a new law. The rule of dou-

The boy in question was inserted into the list of sons of those who were scrutinised to the group of lower *laographia* payers in the first year of Vespasian's reign (ll. 632–636). Unfortunately, the case cannot be taken as an example of regular practice as the father had been granted the status of *katoikos* in honour of his victory.

[154] LEGRAS, *Néotês* (cit. n. 88), p. 171.

[155] See pp. 213–214.

[156] Some credentials, however, do not fit the model: G. RUFFINI, 'Genealogy and the gymnasium', *The Bulletin of the American Society of Papyrologists* 43 (2006), pp. 71–99, pp. 75–78. *E.g. PSI* V 457 discussed in Chapter 2 does not mention the mother's side at all. Another interesting case is *P. Amh.* II 75; see KRUSE, 'Bevölkerungskontrolle' (cit. n. 144), pp. 319–323.

ble descent may thus have regulated admission to *οἱ ἀπὸ γυμνασίου* from the beginning, but circumvented would have needed a stronger enforcement.

Yet even after this correction, the gymnasial group does not fit the Roman model perfectly. As mentioned in the previous chapter, we cannot find even one fatherless individual in the group. The same applies to freedmen, although the sources are not entirely consistent on this subject (*P. Oxy.* I 171 = *SB* XXII 15353 discussed in Chapter 3). Furthermore, in the Oxyrhynchite gymnasial applications after AD 72/3 we find a declaration that a child was not adoptive, but *γνήσιος*, as well as an oath that a boy who was to join *οἱ ἀπὸ τοῦ γυμνασίου* was by no means adopted. Even if the lack of the fatherless and freedmen could be explained by statistics, the clear non-admission of adoptive children in Oxyrhynchos is stricking.

There can be no doubt that the Oxyrhynchite applications use *γνήσιος* to mean not only 'legitimate', but also 'blood of my blood', which is explained in the oath formula, as in *P. Oxy.* X 1266, ll. 32–34 (Oxyrhynchos, AD 98): *εἶναι δ' ἐμοῦ καὶ τῆς | Θερμουθίου φύσ̣[ει υἱὸν τὸ]ν̣ Πλου|τίωνα καὶ μὴ θέ[σει]*.[157] This meaning is further confirmed in two registrations from the late-third century of children to the *γραφῇ ἀφηλίκων* in Oxyrhynchos (*P. Oxy.* XLIII 3136 *&* XLIV 3183, discussed in detail in Chapter 1). In other words, the sources from Oxyrhynchos suggest that parents could only scrutinise their children into the gymnasial group, if the children had been indeed born to them.

The declaration that a child is *γνήσιος* occurs once outside the Oxyrhynchite nome, in the above-discussed *P. Flor.* I 79, l. 21: *εἶναί μου υ[ἱ]ὸν γν[ή]σιο[ν] τὸν προκείμε(νον)*, which pre-dates the general scrutiny of the gymnasial class. It is not certain, however, whether this refers to the same requirement as that in the Oxyrhynchite documents, as the word itself had multiple meanings. Etymologically, *γνήσιος* refers to the same race, but as Ogden writes, 'it is not the simple complement, the equal and opposite of *nothos*, for it also functions as the complement of such terms as *poietos*, adopted, in which case it means "of the blood"'.[158] The word could therefore refer to a child born within a marriage, or simply a legitimate child.

[157] And *P. Oxy.* II 257 = *W. Chr.* 147, ll. 40–44 (Oxyrhynchos, AD 94/5); *SB* XIV 11271, ll. 6–8 (Oxyrhynchos, AD 117); *P. Oxy.* XVIII 2186, l. 10 (Oxyrhynchos, AD 260); *PSI* V 457, ll. 19–21 (Oxyrhynchos, AD 268); *P. Mich.* XIV 676, ll. 20–22 (Oxyrhynchos, AD 272).

[158] OGDEN, *Greek Bastardy* (cit. n. 2), p. 17.

Unfortunately, the other scrutiny documents from the Hermopolite nome do not clarify the meaning of *γνήσιος* in *P. Flor.* I 79. Although they post-date the general scrutiny, they do not contain a similar declaration that a child was *γνήσιος* of their parents, nor do we find an oath comparable to that found in the Oxyrhynchite deeds. *P. Amh.* II 75 (Hermopolis, AD 161–168) and *P. Stras.* IV 288 (Hermopolis, AD 156/7) are too fragmentary, as is *P. Ryl.* II 102 (Hermopolis, after AD 145/6) which preserves only the credentials; *SB* IV 7440, ll. 1–23 (Hermopolis, AD 133), although well-preserved, does not contain the label *γνήσιος*. Furthermore, the oaths seem to be concerned only with establishing that the provided information was accurate.

The term *γνήσιος* appears in other papyri and inscriptions, where it is used not only to describe the legitimacy of a child, but also a wife as lawfully wedded, a friend as real and sincere, or a citizen as legitimate and lawful.[159] The sources we have do not allow us to claim that *P. Flor.* I 79 attests to the same exclusion that appears in the Oxyrhynchite applications. We could therefore not be certain whether the limitation was imposed AD 4/5 or later, nor whether it applied throughout Egypt or only in the Oxyrhynchite nome.

As we mentioned above, it is impossible to explain such a constraint in terms of Greek and Roman adoption concepts. In Roman law, an adopted child had exactly the same position as one begotten within *iustae nuptiae* (G. 1.97). The constraint does not fit the 'Greek' model either. In the Greek world, as far as we know, an adopted child was registered in the adopter's deme and phratry.[160] The exclusion of adopted children from *οἱ ἀπὸ γυμνασίου* would thus be surprising, although not wholly without precedent.[161] It is perhaps possible to explain this phenomenon in terms of

[159] Cf. *WB*, *s.v.* '*γνήσιος*'.

[160] The adoption has been reconstructed for late classical Athens and it has been proved that inscription into adopter's phratry and deme was an indispesible element of the adoption, no matter what form it took. It was the inscription in the phratry and deme that made the adoption legally binding and was the very essence of the whole procedure: L. RUBINSTEIN, *Adoption in IV. Century Athens* [= *Opuscula Graecolatina* XXXIV], Copenhagen 1993, pp. 34–44. It seems that the ways of performing adoption and its principles continued in the Hellenistic times in Atehns: L. RUBINSTEIN, L. BJERTRUP, M.H. HANSEN, T.H. NIELSEN & T. VESTERGAARD, 'Adoption in Hellenistic and Roman Athens', *Classica et Mediaevalia* 42 (1991), pp. 139–151, with further literature.

[161] On the motivated financially exclusion of children born out of wedlock and adopted children from the ceremony honouring orphans at the city of Dionysia, see N.W. SLATER, 'The-

the ease with which the adoption could be performed in Graeco-Roman Egypt. It was informal, often oral and, perhaps even possible by declaration in the census return (or birth declaration, if submitted); perhaps most importantly, it was revocable and did not respect barriers of status.[162] It would not, therefore, have been difficult to 'smuggle' Egyptians into the order, and such persons could then return to their original family. Practical reasons may have prevailed over legal principles. The Roman administration was aware of the inconveniences which adoption might cause if performed in the local way. The subject is addressed in §§ 41 and 107 of the *Gnomon of idios logos*, *BGU* V 1210, ll. 115–116 and 238–239.[163]

Peter van Minnen's observation remains valid in its crucial points: the gymnasial group seems to be framed on the model more restrictive than the basic 'Roman' one as it excluded freedmen and fatherless persons which is discussed in detail in Chapter 3, and at some point the gymnasial order must have been infiltrated by payers of full *laographia* through intermarriages (and adoptions).[164] This provoked closing the order even more which resulted in restraining it to only children of persons who belonged to gymnasial families from generations. Finally, the model of status acquisition is far from the Roman model, but still explainable with the needs of Roman fisc.

2.4.2. Application of *deterioris parentis condicio* rule in unions between privileged Egyptians and persons of higher status

As we have already demonstrated, there can be little doubt that children born to 'mixed unions' by *katoikoi* and *metropolitai* followed the status of the lesser parent. This worked in both directions: if one parent married a simple Egyptian, the children became payers of full *laographia*, but the children born to a

ozotides on adopted sons (Lysias fr. 6)', *Scholia: Studies in Classical Antiquity* 2 (1993), pp. 81–85. But, this exclusion does not seem to have been accepted later, S. Armani & A. Damet, 'Un toit, des lois. Les politiques familiales dans les mondes anciens', *Cahiers « Mondes anciens »* 10 (2018), online publication https://journals.openedition.org/mondesanciens/2059.

[162] See A. Kacprzak & M. Nowak, 'Foundlings in the Greco-Roman world: Status and the (im)possibility of adoption', *Tijdschrift voor Rechtsgeschiedenis* 86 (2018), pp. 13–54.

[163] See Kacprzak & Nowak, 'Foundlings' (cit. n. 162).

[164] van Minnen, '*Αἱ ἀπὸ γυμνασίου*' (cit. n. 137), p. 341.

member of the Egyptian privileged classes and either Romans or a *astoi* were allowed to retain the privileged status. This observation is important to our overall view of the rules regulating status acquisition in Roman Egypt.

In social terms, it should come as no surprise that privileged groups of Egyptians had close contact with Romans, especially as Romans living in the *chora* were integrated into local communities. It may be that this integration extended into marital practices. There are a few instances of Romans marrying *katoikoi* in the Antinoopolite milieu, but such 'exogamy' could certainly have been more widespread, *e.g.* in *BGU* XI 2093 (AD 125), a registration of land acquisition submitted by Charmia, daughter of Sarapion the Younger belonging to the group of *katoikoi*. [165]

> *BGU* XI 2093, ll. 5–10: [παρὰ] Χαρμί[α]ς̣ τ̣ῆ̣ς Σαραπίωνος νεω̣[τέρου | Σαρ]απίωνος κατοίκ(ου) ἀναγραφο[μένης | ἐπ'] ἀμφόδ[ο]υ̣ Φρεμεὶ μετὰ̣ κυρίου [τοῦ ἀν|δρὸ]ς̣ Μάρκ[ου] Λογγίνου Ῥούφου. ἀ[πογράφο|μαι] πρώτ[ως] ἃ παρακεχ[ώρημαι | παρὰ] Μ̣ά̣ρ̣κου Λογγίνου Σατορ[νείλου].
>
> From Charmia, daughter of Sarapion the Younger, the son of Sarapion *katoikos*, registered in the quarter of Phremei with her husband, Marcus Longinus Rufus, acting as her *kyrios*: I register for the first time the ... which were ceded to me by Marcus Longinus Saturnilus.

If the reconstruction is correct, not only was Charmia married to Marcus Longinus Rufus (ll. 7–8), but she also bought the declared property from another Roman, Marcus Longinus Saturninus (l. 10). Unfortunately, the text does not mention any children.

An example of a higher-rank Egyptian fathered by a Roman comes from a late-second-century document listing candidates for *epimeleia* of the renovation of the *exedra* of the Great Gymnasium in Ptolemais Euergetis (*P. Berl. Leihg.* II 42 [2nd c. AD]). Among the men in the text, all of whom belonged to the fiscally privileged groups, we find two Alexandrian citizens (ll. 5 & 9). We also find a man named Sempronius with the patronym Pontius Licin-

[165] Paul Schubert provides many such examples in his monograph of Philadelphia: SCHUBERT, *Philadelphie* (cit. n. 111).

Daniela Canducci observed that names of Latin origin are reasonably well-attested among the *katoikoi*, although, as she noted, onomastics offer the suggestion of familial bonds between Romans and the privileged group, they cannot be taken as proof: D. CANDUCCI, 'I 6475 cateci greci dell'Arsinoite. Prosopografia', *Aegyptus* 71 (1991), pp. 121–216, p. 214.

nius Celer (*P. Berl. Leihg.* II 42 a, ll. 11–12): *Σεμπρώνιος υἱὸς Ποντίου Λικιννίου Κέλερος (τάλαντον) α* | *⟦γενόμ(ενος) ὁρμοφύλαξ ιε (ἔτει) ο[ἰ]κ(ῶν) ἐν ῥύμ(η̣) μ̣ε̣γ̣ά̣λ̣(η) χρυσοχό(ων)⟧*. Sempronius was the son of a Roman,[166] although not Roman himself, and belonged to either the ***katoikoi*** or ***metropolitai***.

A female example of Roman citizen married to a fiscally privileged Egyptian is Claudia Leontis discussed already in this chapter. Furthermore, the illustration that marrying a Roman may be attractive to privileged groups, even if potential husbands were soldiers, come from *SB* XXII 15704, a deed concerning debt, but which includes census returns for two families, one of which belonged to the metropolite class. One member of the family, Apronius discussed in Chapter 2, was fathered by a soldier – not necesarily a Roman, but a man with prospects – while his daughter married Marcus Valerius Rufus, a Roman centurion.[167]

A number of documents attest marriages between elites of ***poleis*** and ***metropoleis***. The effect seems similar, children could be registered in the class of the lesser parent. One document which attests to the marriage of a female citizen of Alexandria and a man *ἀπὸ γυμνασίου* is *P. Coll. Youtie* II 67 (AD 260/1),[168] a confirmation that a dowry was returned after the husband's death.[169] The party confirming receipt of the dowry is Aurelia Dioskouriaina daughter of Dioskourides, a former eutheniarch and member of the Alexandrian *boule* (ll. 1–3). The dowry had been provided by Aurelia Diosk-

[166] The way how the patronym is styled already expresses the higher standing of the father: D. HAGEDORN, 'Zur Verwendung von *υἱός* und *θυγάτηρ* vor dem Vatersnamen in Urkunden römischer Zeit', ***Zeitschrift für Papyrologie und Epigraphik*** 80 (1990), pp. 277–282.

[167] See stemma in: P.J. SIJPESTEIJN, 'Settlement of a debt and extracts from census registers', ***Zeitschrift für Papyrologie und Epigraphik*** 98 (1993), pp. 283–291, p. 287.

It is not certain whether centurions were allowed to marry or were subject to the same ban as other soldiers: P.M. ALLISON. 'Soldiers' families in the early Roman Empire', [in:] B. RAWSON (ed.), *A Companion to Families in the Greek and Roman Worlds*, Malden 2011, pp. 161–182. Certainly, they still received the grant of Roman citizenship for their children after AD 140, so long as they were begotten in stable unions and it could be proved that they were indeed the children of an officer: W. ECK & P. WEIß, 'Die Sonderregelungen für Soldatenkinder seit Antoninus Pius. Ein niederpannonisches Militärdiplom vom 11. Aug. 146', ***Zeitschrift für Papyrologie und Epigraphik*** 135 (2001), pp. 195–208.

[168] BROUX, *Double Names* (cit. n. 151), p. 218.

[169] On the construction of this dowry, see H.J. WOLFF, 'Neue juristische Urkunden', *Zeitschrift der Savigny-Stiftung für Rechtsgeschichte RA* 96 (1976), pp. 258–271, pp. 261–264.

Table 1

Status acquisition by children born to 'mixed unions' in Roman Egypt (no mistake about partner's status)

father / mother	Roman *cum conubio*	Roman *sine conubio*	*astos*	Antinoopolite citizen	Egyptian	privileged Egyptian
Roman *cum conubio*	paternal status	–	paternal status	paternal status & Antinoopolite citizenship (?)	paternal status	paternal status
Roman *sine conubio*	–	maternal status	lesser parent's status	Antinoopolite citizenship	lesser parent's status	lesser parent's status
aste	paternal status	lesser parent's status	paternal status	Antinoopolite citizenship	lesser parent's status	lesser parent's status
Antinoopolite citizen	paternal status & Antinoopolite citizenship (?)	lesser parent's status	Antinoopolite citizenship (?)	Paternal status	Antinoopolite citizenship (?)	Antinoopolite citizenship
Egyptian	paternal status	lesser parent's status	lesser parent's status	Antinoopolite citizenship	paternal status	lesser parent's status
privileged Egyptian	paternal status	lesser parent's status	lesser parent's status	Antinoopolite citizenship	lesser parent's status	paternal status

ouriaina's husband, Aurelius Spartiates *alias* Chairemon, for their common daughter, Aurelia Apollonarion. The important detail is that Aurelius Spartiates was a former gymnasiarch and a member of the Oxyrhynchite council (ll. 12–13). Their daughter, Aurelia Apollonarion, had been married to another member of gymnasial elite of Oxyrhynchos. Five years later, in *PSI* XII 1249, the same Aurelia Dioskouriaina appears together with her son Sarapion *alias* Apollonianos:[170]

> ll. 1–7: *Αὐρήλιοι Σαραπίων ὁ καὶ Ἀπολλωνι|ανὸς γυμνασίαρχος βουλευτὴς τῆς | Ὀξυρυγχειτῶν πόλεως καὶ ἡ μήτηρ | Διοσκουρίαινα ἡ καὶ Σαβεῖνα | θυγάτηρ Διοσκουρίδου εὐθηνιαρ|χήσαντος τῆς λαμπροτάτης πόλεως | τῶν Ἀλεξανδρέων.*
>
> Aurelii Sarapion *alias* Apollonianos, gymnasiarch and *bouleutes* of Oxyrhynchos, and his mother, Dioskouriaina *alias* Sabina daughter of Dioskourides, former eutheniarch of the most glorious city of Alexandria.

Although the text is dated after AD 200, when *metropoleis* obtained *boulai*, there is no proof that the discussed groups became peers to *astoi*. *Metropolitai* are attested still in the corn dole archive of Oxyrhynchos in the reign of Claudius II and Aurelian and the gymnasial group even longer until the end of the third century; the archive also suggests that the distinction between *metropolitai* and the gymnasial class survived.[171] Citizens of the *metropoleis* were not labelled as *astoi* after AD 200.[172]

3. CONSEQUENCES OF THE STATUS

3.1. *Cases involving a Roman parent*

Being born to parents of unequal *status civitatis* could have serious consequences for succession; it is this problem to which the majority of pas-

[170] J. Rowlandson, *Landowners and Tenants in Roman Egypt. The Social Relations of Agriculture in the Oxyrhynchite Nome*, Oxford 1996, p. 112.

[171] van Minnen, '*Αἱ ἀπὸ γυμνασίου*' (cit. n. 137), p. 343. On the classes of people admitted to the *doreion*, see Nowak, 'Get your free corn' (cit. n. 148), with further literature.

[172] van Minnen, '*Αἱ ἀπὸ γυμνασίου*' (cit. n. 137), p. 343.

sages concerning mixed families in the *Gnomon* refer. This should come as no surprise: the curator of the private fisc was, *inter alia*, responsible for *bona vacantia*, and a knowledge of who inherited from whom would have been very much at the center of his professional interests.[173]

The rules for Romans were clear: only children under *patria potestas* of their fathers (or paternal grandfathers) – either by birth or by adoption – could become *sui heredes*.[174] Children who were not subjects to the *potestas* of their fathers had no right to intestate succession, with the exception of emancipated sons allowed to *bonorum possessio* in the edict. Children born out of wedlock did not belong to any class of successors recognised under civil or praetorian law;[175] they were neither *agnati* nor *consanguinei*.[176] Maternal succession was different due to the *senatus consultum Orfitianum*, which admitted all children indiscriminately to intestate succession in the group of *legitimi*; we shall discuss this in greater detail in the final chapter of this work.

The rules for children born to unions of unequal status, however, were not uniform and depended on both *conubium* and the *status civitatis* of the parents. Children of Roman fathers who had *conubium* towards their non-Roman spouses were born under the *potestas* of their fathers, and entitled to inherit from them in the class of *sui heredes*. Such cases must have been reasonably frequent, as veterans were granted *conubium* towards their peregrine partners almost automatically after their *missio honesta*. Yet the offspring of such marriages could not inherit from their peregrine mothers, as confirmed in the *Gnomon of idios logos*:

173 See P.R. SWARNEY, *The Ptolemaic and Roman Idios Logos* [= *American Studies in Papyrology* VIII], Toronto 1970; L. CAPPONI, *Augustan Egypt: the Creation of a Roman Province* [= *Studies in Classics* XIII], London 2005, pp. 32–34.

174 P. VOCI, *Diritto ereditario romano, vol. II. Parte speciale. Successione ab intesttato, successione testamentaria*, Milan 1963², pp. 5 & 9.

175 VOCI, *Diritto ereditario romano* (cit. n. 174), pp. 13–14.

176 D. 38.8.4 (Ulp. *Reg.* 6): *Si spurius intestato decesserit, iure consanguinitatis aut adgnationis hereditas eius ad nullum pertinet, quia consanguinitatis itemque adgnationis iura a patre oriuntur* (...).

Children born out of *matrimonium* could be compared to those who had become *sui iuris* before their *pater familias* died. The praetorian edict provided them with claims for *bonorum possessio*. What mattered was that, unlike *spurii*, they were under the *potestas* at some point of their lives; see VOCI, *Diritto ereditario romano* (cit. n. 174), pp. 10–12.

BGU V 1210, ll. 140–141: νδ. θυγατρὶ μ[ι]σσικίου Ῥωμαίᾳ γεν[ομ]ένῃ Οὖρσος οὐκ [ἐπέτρε]ψε | κληρον[ομ]ῆσαι τὴν μητέραν (l. μητέρα) Αἰγ[υπ]τίαν οὖσαν.

54. Ursus did not permit the daughter of a veteran dismissed with honours to inherit from her Egyptian mother after the daughter became Roman.

The paragraph informs us that Ursus, possibly Lucius Iulius Ursus the Flavian prefect of Egypt in AD 84,[177] denied maternal inheritance to the daughter of a veteran discharged with honours. As we have already mentioned, veterans were granted citizenship at their *missio honesta*, as well as citizenship for their children (but this privilege was limited in AD 140), and *conubium* towards their current and future peregrine wives.

Interestingly, *P. Oxy.* LV 3798, an acknowledgment of a loan repayment dated to AD 144, provides testimony to the contrary. In the document, two Romans, Caius Veturius Gemellus and his sister Lucia Veturia *alias* Thermouthion, acknowledge that they have received the capital and interests of a loan which their mother had made to a certain Epimachos. They also declare that they accepted it because their mother had died intestate, leaving them as her only heirs (ll. 23–27: τὸ δὲ κεφάλαιον δανεισθέν σοι | ὑπὸ τῆς μητ[ρ]ὸς ἡμῶν Ἀ[ρ]τέμει|τος ἧς τελευτησάσης ἀδιαθέτου, | προφερόμεθα εἶναι αὐτῆς μό|να τέκνα καὶ κληρονόμα, 'the sum lent to you by our mother Artemeis who died intestate, we declare to be her only children and heirs'). The father is described as a veteran, and the mother is Artemis daughter of Eudaimon:

ll. 1–9: Γάϊος [Οὐετούριος] Γέμε[λλος καὶ Λου]|κία Οὐε[τουρία] ἡ καὶ Θερμ[ούθ]ι[ον] | ἀμφότεροι Γ[αΐ]ου Οὐετουρίου Γεμέλ|λου οὐετραν[οῦ] ἐνκεχαραγμένου | σὺν τῇ ἑαυτ[ῶ]ν μετηλλαχυίῃ | μητρὶ Ἀρτέμειτι Εὐδαίμονος | τοῦ Εὐδαίμονος μητρὸς Θερμου|θίου περιούσῃ εἰς τὴν ἐπὶ Ῥώμης | χαλκῆν στήλην.

Caius Veturius Gemellus and Lucia Veturia *alias* Thermouthion both children of Caius Veturius Gemellus, a veteran, engraved on the bronze military stele in Rome together with their deceased mother Artemis daughter of Eudaimon, the son of Eudaimon, her mother being Thermouthion, when she was still alive.

[177] On the career and chronology of this prefect, see R.S. BAGNALL, A. BÜLOW-JACOBSEN & H. CUVIGNY, 'Security and water on the Eastern Desert roads: the prefect Iulius Ursus and the construction of *praesidia* under Vespasian', *Journal of Roman Archaeology* 14 (2001), pp. 325–333.

The description mentions that the father had been inscribed on the stele in Rome, meaning he had been discharged with honours from the army; the mother is listed as περιούσῃ on the same stele in the *area Capitolina*. She was mentioned for *conubium* not citizenship, as peregrine wives of veterans were not granted citizenship when their husbands were discharged.[178]

Furthermore, the onomastic evidence supports the idea that the mother remained a *peregrina*, as she is described as Artemis daughter of Eudaimon, *etc.*[179] Caius Veturius Gemellus and Lucia Veturia *alias* Thermouthion both bear proper Roman *nomina*, and have the *nomen* of their father; the son also has both the paternal *praenomen* and *cognomen*. Yet after AD 140 children of *auxiliares* were no longer granted citizenship, and if Caius Veturius Gemellus was released from the army after this date his children would not have been Romans. The document is dated to AD 144, but John Rea notes that Caius Veturius Gemellus, the father, had enlisted in AD 103 (*P. Oxy.* VII 1022 = *Ch. L. A.* III 215 = *W. Chr.* 453 = *Sel. Pap.* II 421) and was already a veteran by AD 143 (*P. Oxy.* VII 1035).[180] The usual length of service in *auxilia* was twenty-six years, and it is therefore highly probable that Gemellus's term of service would have ended in late 20s or early 30s of the second century. Although discharges were sometimes delayed, a term of forty years seems improbable.[181]

Unfortunately, there is nothing in the text to offer any further hint regarding the status of the siblings. They accepted the repayment on their own behalf, which implies that they were not under the *potestas* of their father; yet, this would imply only that they had been born before their father's *missio honesta*, which we already know thanks to *P. Oxy.* VII 1035.[182] As it is highly likely that the siblings were Romans, not *peregrini*, they claimed the inheritance unlawfully from their mother, which Ann Ellis

[178] This is the prevailing opinion in the scholarly literature; see S.E. PHANG, *The Marriage of Roman Soldiers (13 BC – AD 235): Law and Family in the Imperial Army* [= *Columbia Studies in the Classical Tradition* XXIV], Leiden – Boston – Cologne 2001, p. 58; R. FRIEDL, *Der Konkubinat im kaiserzeitlichen Rom. Von Augustus bis Septimius Severus* [= *Historia – Einzelschriften* XCVIII], Stuttgart 1996, pp. 259–261.

[179] For such special cases, see PHANG, *Marriage of Roman Soldiers* (cit. n. 178), p. 58, n. 13.

[180] See Introduction to *P. Oxy.* LV 3798.

[181] See Introduction to *P. Oxy.* LV 3798.

[182] See Introduction to *P. Oxy.* LV 3798.

Hanson has already suggested in her review of volume LV of *The Oxyrhynchus Papyri*,[183] and which is exactly against the ruling of § 54.

The restrictions in Roman law extended beyond intestate succession, as *peregrini* had no *testamenti factio passiva* in Roman wills and *vice versa*.[184] The rule is expressed directly by Gaius (G. 2.110): *cum alioquin peregrine quidem ratione civili prohibeantur capere hereditatem legataque, Latini vero per legem Iuniam* – 'though in general peregrines are prohibited from taking an inheritance or legacies by the principles of civil law, and Latins by the *lex Iunia*'.[185] Wills in the Roman empire were made separately by different civic groups (*Tit. Ulp.* 20.14).[186] In other words, a Roman parent could not appoint his peregrine children as heirs in his testament, while a peregrine parent could not provide Roman children with succession in a will made *secundum leges civitatis suae*.

Yet, we should not believe that there were no attempts to circumvent these rules. One such example is *BGU* II 448 = *M. Chr.* 310 (AD 151–154), which Hans Kreller interpreted as indirect proof that people from different status groups could inherit from one another in the Hellenistic period.[187] The document, dated to the 150s, is a petition to the prefect, Lucius Munatius Felix (AD 150–154),[188] from Sempronius Serenus who describes himself as a veteran and citizen of Antinoopolis. He addresses the prefect in regard to a will made by his parents, Ptolemaios and Thermouthis, landholders in Karanis and obviously Egyptians. The petitioner's parents made a will which was kept by the *strategos* of the Arsinoite nome.

The petition suggests that the succession did not go smoothly, as the veteran had to ask the prefect to force the *strategos* to open the will; sadly the document does not explain why the governor of the nome refused to open

[183] A.E. Hanson, rev. of *The Oxyrhynchus Papyri*, vol. LV, ed. J. Rea, London 1988, *Gnomon* 62.3 (1990), pp. 273–275, p. 274.

[184] M. Amelotti, *Il testamento romano attraverso la prassi documentale. I: Le forme classiche di testamento*, Florence 1966, p. 121.

[185] Tr. de Zulueta.

[186] M. Lauria, '*Ο γνώμων τοῦ ἰδιοῦ λόγου*. Retractatio', *Studia et documenta historiae et iuris* 49 (1983), pp. 1–17, p. 11.

[187] H. Kreller, *Erbrechtliche Untersuchungen auf Grund der graeco-ägyptischen Papyrusurkunden*, Leipzig – Berlin 1919, p. 312.

[188] M. Nuti, 'Le attività e le attestazioni di un prefetto d'Egitto: Lucius Munatius Felix', *Papyrotheke* 1 (2010), pp. 67–77, p. 68.

or enforce the will. The text nonetheless offers proof of the troubles which could arise in a multi-status society. While the petitioner acquired a higher *status civitatis* as a reward for his service to the Empire, his parents remained Egyptians. Obviously, the parents wanted their son to inherit their belongings and the son considered this to be the right thing. We cannot assume that the prefect ordered the *strategos* to open (or enforce) the will; it seems unlikely that Sempronius Serenus ultimately acquired the estate of his parents. The text does not mention Hellenistic *testamenti factio passiva*, but simply testifies to the problem of this particular family, which makes the case similar to *P. Oxy.* LV 3798 and to *VBP* IV 72 discussed in Chapter 2.

That the succession after those who did not belong to the same *civitas* was problematic is further confirmed by the fact that *fideicommissa* were eventually forbidden between *peregrini* and Romans. *Fideicommissum* was an informal request from a testator to their heir to transmit parts of their inheritance – singular goods, or rights such as freedom – to a third person; it would thus have been a perfect way to safeguard succession for children who did not share the *status civitatis* of their parents. The ban appears both in the *Gnomon* and the *Institutes* of Gaius.

BGU V 1210, ll. 56–58: ιη. τὰ\ς/ κατὰ πίστιν γεινομένας κληρονομίας ὑπὸ Ἑλλήνω̣ν̣ \εἰς/ ⟦ὑπὸ⟧ Ῥω|μαίους ἢ ὑπὸ Ῥωμαίων \εἰς/ Ἕλληνας ὁ θεὸς Οὐεσπασιανὸς̣ [ἀ]νέλαβεν. | οἱ μέντοι τὰς πίστεις ἐξωμολογησάμενοι (l. ἐξομολογησάμενοι) τὸ ἥμισ[υ ε]ι̣λήφασι.

18. The divine Vespasian confiscated inheritances left as trusts by Greeks for Romans, and by Romans for Greeks. Yet those who confessed that they had accepted such trusts were permitted to keep half.

G. 2.285: Ut ecce peregrini poterant fideicommissa capere, et fere haec fuit origo fideicommissorum. sed postea id prohibitum est, et nunc ex oratione divi Hadriani senatus consultum factum est, ut ea fideicommissa fisco vindicarentur.

Thus peregrines could take under *fideicommissa* – indeed, this was probably the origin of *fideicommissa* – but later this was forbidden, and now on the proposition of the divine Hadrian a *senatus consultum* has enacted that such *fideicommissa* should be claimed for the fisc.[189]

[189] Tr. de Zulueta with minor modifications.

The two texts ascribe the ban to two different emperors, Vespasian and Hadrian respectively. Woldemar Uxkull-Gyllenband attempted to explain this discrepancy by suggesting that the *senatus consultum* referred to in the *Institutes* would not have been applied in Egypt.[190] Ulrike Babusiaux, however, pointed out that the two prohibitions had a different focus: the *Gnomon* comments on universal *fideicommissa* as they appear in the *senatus consultum Pegasianum* from the reign of Vespasian, while the passage from Gaius is discussed in the context of a comparison between *legata* and *fideicommissa*, and would thus have applied to singular *fideicommissa*. Babusiaux also argued that the passage from the *Gnomon* is a *testimonium* of a preventive measure against the circumvention of *testamenti factio*.[191] This would imply that singular *fideicommissa* for peregrines were allowed at least until Hadrian (although they also continued to happen even after Hadrian).

In his monograph on testamentary law and practice, Mario Amelotti discussed two Roman wills containing dispositions for peregrines. One of them is discussed in Chapter 3, *BGU* VII 1662 (AD 182), a *homologia* issued by Kyrilla for Longinia Nemesilla to confirm that Kyrilla had received money owned to her for a bequest left to her by Marcus Valerius Turbo, her father. Importantly, she was an *aste*, while her father was a Roman veteran. The text is important to our understanding of succession in 'mixed' families.

Rafał Taubenschlag suggested that the will of Marcus Valerius Turbo occuring in *BGU* VII 1662 was an example of *testamentum militis*.[192] However, this seems hardly plausible: if the descriptions in the papyri are to be trusted, Marcus Valerius Turbo was no longer a soldier by AD 176. It seems unlikely that he would have died within a year of his discharge, which was the length of time for which a *testamentum militis* remained valid.[193] Furthermore, *BGU* VII 1662 clearly specifies διαθήκη Ῥωμαϊκή, which would

[190] Uxkull-Gyllenband, *Der Gnomon* (cit. n. 35), p. 33.

[191] U. Babusiaux, 'Römisches Erbrecht im Gnomon des Idios Logos', *Zeitschrift der Savigny-Stiftung für Rechtsgeschichte RA* 135 (2018), pp. 108–177, pp. 142–143.

[192] Taubenschlag, *Law of Greco-Roman Egypt* (cit. n. 10), p. 200, n. 40; accepted in H.-A. Rupprecht, *Studien zur Quittung im Recht der gräco-ägyptischen Papyri* [= *Münchener Beiträge zur Papyrusforschung und antiken Rechtsgeschichte* LVII], Munich 1972, p. 53.

[193] On the meaning of τοῖς ἐν στρατείᾳ καὶ ἀπὸ στρατείας οὖσι, see p. 121, n. 68.

imply a regular Roman *testamentum*. Although the text postdates Hadrian, it contains a bequest for a peregrine by her Roman father.

Amelotti doubted whether such dispositions were enforceable[194] and offered *FIRA* III 65 = *BGU* I 327 = *M. Chr.* 61 as proof that dispositions made for non-Romans had no legal binding.[195] The text dated to AD 176 is a petition addressed to the *dikaiodotes* acting as a prefect, Caius Caecilius Salvianus, brought by Aitete Phrontis against Caius Longinus Kastor.[196] According to the document, Caius Fabullius Macer made a will[197] in which he appointed Caius Longinus Kastor as his heir, but left 2000 drachmae and an outer cloak to Aitete Phrontis, which Caius Longinus Kastor kept. If Aitete Phrontis sought justice from the *iuridicus*, she must have been convinced that she was entitled to the bequest. The text does not prove whether or not the disposition was valid, it illustrates only that a veteran bequeathed some modest property to a peregrine woman and that the woman believed the bequest to be lawfully hers.

In *P. Ryl.* II 153, a will from Hermopolis Magna discussed above, we find evidence of a similar model, but to the opposite way: a peregrine left a bequest to a Roman. Unfortunately, the text is not complete and it is not known how generous the testator was towards his wife. We do know that she was granted the right to dwell in the property inherited by Hellanikos, the testator's son, as well as the services of slaves for life.

Another example comes from a text belonging to the archive of (Caii) Iulii Sabinus and Apollinarios, *P. Mich.* IX 549, dated to the early second century (AD 117/8). The document contains a copy of a will composed for Sambathion, in which she lists her nephew, Caius Iulius Sabinus, and his son, Caius Iulius Apollinarios, in the context of testamentary dispositions.

194 AMELOTTI, *Il testamento romano* (cit. n. 184), p. 121: 'Pertanto, se la legataria non romana nominate nel testamento di Valerio Turbone vienne soddisfata, è solo per generosità o inesperienza degli eredi'.

195 AMELOTTI, *Il testamento romano* (cit. n. 184), p. 121.

196 A veteran known from from *BGU* I 326 = *M. Chr.* 316 = *Sel. Pap.* I 85 = *FIRA* III 50 = *Jur. Pap.* 25, Roman will widely discussed in the scholarly literature; see M. NOWAK, *Wills in the Roman Empire: A Documentary Approach* [= *The Journal of Juristic Papyrology Supplement* XXIII], Warsaw 2015, *passim*.

197 The will was considered to be *testamentum militis* in: KRELLER, *Erbrechtliche Untersuchungen* (cit. n. 187), p. 312.

It seems certain that Caius Iulius Sabinus, a veteran, had already been discharged from the army when the will was composed.[198] The family was metropolite, and Sambathion's brother, Caius Iulius Sabinus, had acquired Roman citizenship and was recruited to the army as a legionary soldier.[199] The family became Egypto-Roman, which, as we have seen, did not discourage relatives from bequeathing property to family members of unequal *status civitatis*. Unfortunately, the text is too fragmentary to determine what exactly was left to Caius Iulius Sabinus and his son in Sambathion's will, or whether the bequest became a cause for controversy. A letter from Caius Iulius Sabinus sent from Alexandria mentions a legal issue for which he went there (*P. Mich.* VIII 493), but there is not enough information in the text to connect it with Sambathions's will.

The sources do not ultimately provide us with a coherent picture, yet it seems certain that universal succession by family members with *status civitatis* other than *de cuius* was eventually prohibited. There is, however, no question that people attempted to circumvent this prohibition. However, singular dispositions in the form of *fideicommissa* were generally accepted. They are also attested in the papyri. Yet we must also take into account an enigmatic passage from Pausanias who, in the eighth book of his *Periegesis*, makes reference to a law ascribed to Antoninus Pius.

> Paus. 8.43.5: ὁ δὲ βασιλεὺς ὑπελίπετο οὗτος καὶ ἄλλο τοιόνδε ἐς μνήμην. ὅσοις τῶν ὑπηκόων πολίταις ὑπῆρχεν εἶναι Ῥωμαίων, οἱ δὲ παῖδες ἐτέλουν σφίσιν ἐς τὸ Ἑλληνικόν, τούτοις ἐλείπετο ἢ κατανεῖμαι τὰ χρήματα ἐς οὐ προσήκοντας ἢ ἐπαυξῆσαι τὸν βασιλέως πλοῦτον κατὰ νόμον δή τινα: Ἀντωνῖνος δὲ ἐφῆκε καὶ τούτοις διδόναι σφᾶς παισὶ τὸν κλῆρον, ὁ προτιμήσας φανῆναι φιλάνθρωπος ἢ ὠφέλιμον ἐς χρήματα φυλάξαι νόμον. τοῦτον Εὐσεβῆ τὸν βασιλέα ἐκάλεσαν οἱ Ῥωμαῖοι, διότι τῇ ἐς τὸ θεῖον τιμῇ μάλιστα ἐφαίνετο χρώμενος.

[198] The edition provides the description, l. 10: Ἰουλίου Σαβείνου τῶν ἀπὸ λε[γιῶνος ὡς δὲ] πρὸ τῆς στρατει(ᾶς), but according to the archive's description by Graham Claytor and Birgit Feucht, the editors of the forthcoming 22nd volume of the *Michigan Papyri* read τῶν ἀπολελ̣[υμένων] instead of τῶν ἀπὸ λε[γιῶνος]: G. Claytor & B. Feucht, '(Gaii) Iulii Sabinus and Apollinarius', [in:] K. Vandorpe, W. Clarysse & H. Verreth (eds.), *Graeco-Roman Archives from the Fayum* [= *Collectanea Hellenistica – KVAB* VI], Leuven – Paris – Bristol, CT 2015, pp. 186-198, p. 188 n.

[199] His career is described in: Claytor & Feucht, '(Gaii) Iulii' (cit. n. 198), pp. 187–188.

> But there is also another memorial of himself left by this emperor. There was a certain law whereby provincials who were themselves of Roman citizenship, while their children were considered of Greek nationality, were forced either to leave their property to strangers or let it increase the wealth of the emperor. Antoninus permitted all such to give to the children their heritage, choosing rather to show himself benevolent than to retain a law that swelled his riches. This emperor the Romans called Pius, because he showed himself to be a most religious man.[200]

David Johnston suggested that Antoninus Pius might have abolished the prohibition introduced by Hadrian (G. 2.285: quoted above), which would mean that the law to which Pausanias refers would have been general and applied to all inhabitants of the Empire.[201] Lise Arends Olsen also interpreted the passage as having applied to all children born of marriages between peregrines and Romans concluded *iure gentium*, which would suggest that, after Antoninus Pius, the offspring of mixed unions had full *testamenti factio passiva* in wills of their parents.[202] Valerio Marotta understood the ruling referred to by Pausanias as having applied only to local citizens of Greek *poleis*, suggesting it was issued to ameliorate the situation of children born to local citizens of whom only one was a Roman citizen, as well as to equate the Greek elites with the western ones which enjoyed *ius Latii*.[203] David Cherry and Arnaud Besson, on the other hand, interpreted the rule as applying only to Arcadia.[204]

As the ruling of Antoninus Pius is not mentioned in other sources it is impossible to determine its geographical scope, nor is it even possible

[200] Pausanias, *Description of Greece*, with an English translation by W.H.S. Jones, vol. IV, Cambridge, MA 1935.

[201] D. Johnston, *The Roman Law of Trusts*, Oxford 1988, p. 39.

[202] L. Arends Olsen, *La femme et l'enfant dans les unions illégitimes à Rome. L'évolution du droit jusqu'au début de l'Empire*, Bern 1999, pp. 208–209.

[203] V. Marotta, 'I diritti degli stranieri', [in:] A. Giardina & F. Pesando (eds.), *Roma caput mundi. Una città tra dominio e integrazione*, Milan 2012, pp. 201–209, p. 203; idem, 'Doppia cittadinanza e pluralità degli ordinamenti. La Tabula Banasitana e le linee 7–9 del Papiro di Giessen 40 col I', *Archivio giuridico Filippo Serafini* 236 (2016), pp. 461–491, pp. 481–482.

[204] Cherry, 'The Minician law' (cit. n. 39), p. 260; A. Besson, 'Fifty years before the Antonine Constitution: Access to Roman citizenship and exclusive rights', [in:] L. Cecchet & A. Busetto (eds.), *Citizens in the Graeco-Roman World*, Leiden 2017, pp. 199–220, p. 213.

to state whether Pausanias was referring to a law issued by the imperial chancellery or *senatus consultum*, or simply to a particular imperial privilege granted to a certain group of people. The latter seems most likely because the law is not repeated besides Pausanias.

3.2. *Cases involving a citizen parent*

The paragraphs of the *Gnomon* concerning the succession between persons of different *status civitatis*, yet which do not involve Roman citizens, do not appear to be based on any general rule similar to Roman one. Although the Romans imposed their rules for status acquisition on the *peregrini*, they did not interfere with succession.[205] Unfortunately, the *Gnomon* existed in a certain social and functional context that would have been clear for its users, but is less so for scholars. The meaning of many paragraphs remains mysterious, if their interpretation cannot be supported by other sources.

Certainly, the laws of the Egyptian *poleis* were more restrictive in regard to testamentary freedom than Roman law. In § 15 for instance, we find the general rule prohibiting *astai* from disposing of their property *mortis causa*.

> *BGU* V 1210, l. 50: ιε. οὐκ ἐξὸν ἀπελευθέραις ἀστῶν διατίθεσθαι ὥσπερ οὐ[δ]ὲ ἀσταῖς.
>
> 15. It is not permitted for the freedwomen of *astoi* to make a will, just as it is not lawful for *astai*.

Indeed, none of the surviving wills from Graeco-Roman Egypt were composed by a testatrix described as a citizen.[206] Although the restriction of § 15 makes little sense in terms of classical Roman law, it was standard in the law of classical Athens that a will originating in an adoption could

[205] J.L. Alonso, 'The status of peregrine law in Egypt: "Customary law" and legal pluralism in the Roman Empire', *The Journal of Juristic Papyrology* 43 (2013), pp. 351–404, pp. 352–356.

[206] Taubenschlag, *Law of Greco-Roman Egypt* (cit. n. 10), p. 201. New local wills have been published since Taubenschlag, but still none composed by an *aste.*

None of those wills was composed by a male local citizen either, but a few paragraphs from the *Gnomon* refer to restrictions on making wills by either Alexandrians or *astoi* in general (§§ 5, 6 *&* 45), which would confirm that they had *testamenti factio activa.*

not be made by a woman.[207] If the laws of Alexandria were indeed based on those of classical Athens, as the earlier scholarly literature suggested, the passages in the *Gnomon* may simply have been a direct borrowing – or, to use Watson's terminology, a 'transplant'[208] – from the law of Athens.[209]

The interpretation, however, is not quite so simple. It now seems clear that the passages from the *Gnomon* which mention *astoi* and *astai* refer to the entire *status civitatis*, not merely to Alexandrians, and would thus have applied also to those *peregrini cives* whose laws were based on laws of other *poleis*.[210] Furthermore, recent literature has found fewer connections between the laws of Athens and Alexandria than the earlier literature claimed.[211] Consequently, the restriction should not be interpreted as having been specific to Alexandria, nor perhaps did it have its direct origin in Athens. It is possible that women were not permitted to make wills in the Hellenistic world, or that their *testamenti factio activa* was highly limited. There are no Hellenistic Greek wills from Egypt made by women, and examples of wills from the rest of the Hellenistic world made by women are rare.[212]

The lack of *testamenti factio activa* would certainly have influenced the reality of 'mixed families', as the succession from mothers, daughters and sisters would only have been possible according to the order set by law. The quoted rule, however, was not focused on the hereditary rights of children born to 'mixed families'; children born to *astai* and Egyptians could inherit from their mothers in intestate succession, as confirmed in § 38 of the *Gnomon* (*BGU* V 1210, ll. 109–110). Similarly, the children of *astoi* and Egyptians could inherit from their fathers, albeit with some restrictions of an obviously penal origin (*BGU* V 1210, ll. 123–127). There was no

[207] A.R.W. Harrison, *The Law of Athens. Family and Property*, Oxford 1968, pp. 149–155.

[208] A. Watson, *Legal Transplants: An Approach to Comparative Law*, Edinburgh 1974.

[209] Reinach, 'Code fiscal' (cit. n. 35), p. 75; Riccobono, *Gnomon* (cit. n. 36), p. 129.

[210] Summary of scholarly discussion of the terms in the *Gnomon*; see Delia, *Alexandrian Citizenship* (cit. n. 25), pp. 8–9.

[211] On this problem, see J. Mélèze Modrzejewski, *Loi et coutume* (cit. n. 118), pp. 122–142, with further literature.

[212] B. Legras, 'Les testaments grecs dans le droit hellénistique : la question des héritières et des testatrices', [in:] E. Cantarella (ed.), *Symposion 2005. Vorträge zur griechischen und hellenistischen Rechtsgeschichte (Salerno, 14.–18. September 2005)*, pp. 293–306, pp. 299–303.

general rule applicable to 'mixed families', and their succession was regulated casuistically, as illustrated in §§ 11–13.

BGU V 1210, ll. 44–48: *ια. γυνὴ Κρηνέα τέκνον οὐ κληρ[ο]νομεῖ.*
ιβ. τὰ ἐκ Κρηνέας καὶ ξένου γενόμενα τέκνα τοὺς γονεῖς ἀμφο|τέ[ρ]ους κληρονομεῖ.

11. A Krenea cannot inherit from her child.
12. Children born of a Krenea and *xenos* inherit from both parents.

The word *Κρηνέα*, which occurs in § 12, is an unidentified toponym. As the precise meaning of Krenea remains obscure, it is difficult to comment on this passage. Salvatore Riccobono suggested that it refers to a particular case decided by one of curators of the private fisc concerning an inhabitant of the area around Alexandria where the *idios logos* operated.[213] The paragraph may also express the Alexandria-centric perspective of the *Gnomon*.[214] Theodor Reinach suggested that Krene was a district (?) along the west coast of the Delta close to the border with Cyrenaica. He further interpreted Kreneoi to be *peregrini in genere*, thus a group of the same status as *Aigyptioi*.[215] Thomas Kruse, in turn, interpreted Krenea to be 'a woman enjoying the privileged citizenship of a polis'.[216]

The two paragraphs are followed immediately by § 13 (discussed above), which states that children born of *aste* and *xenos* became *xenoi* and could not inherit from their mothers (*BGU* V 1210, ll. 47–48). The sequence of paragraphs suggests that Kruse's interpretation is correct: Krenea could have been a woman with a status comparable to *aste*, as it was necessary to explain the ramifications of her union with a *xenos* in the *Gnomon*. If she is treated separately, it may be due to the exceptional regulations surrounding her succession. The lack of reciprocity underlined in § 11, would suggest that children would normally have inherited only from their *xenos*

[213] Riccobono, *Gnomon* (cit. n. 36), p. 126.

[214] M. Thoma, 'Women's role in domestic economy of Roman Egypt. The contribution of the *Gnomon of idios logos* (*BGU* V 1210)', [in:] R. Berg (ed.), *The Material Sides of Marriage. Women and Domestic Economies in Antiquity* [= *Acta Instituti Romani Finlandiae* XLIII], Rome 2016, pp. 145–151, p. 149.

[215] Reinach, 'Code fiscal' (cit. n. 35), p. 34.

[216] Kruse, 'Labeling of strangers' (cit. n. 75), p. 140.

father; the fact that the children of Krenea were allowed intestate succession from their mother was an exception to the rule. If this exception had not been introduced, the children of Krenea would not have had any hereditary rights from their mother, as was the case for the children of *aste* and *xenos*.

The paragraphs of the *Gnomon* discussed here illustrate that the imposition of the Roman status acquisition model on *astoi* did not interfere with the local laws of succession. It remains only to ask whether children born of Egyptians and Egyptians entitled to a partial poll-tax exemption could inherit from both parents. The answer would seem to be yes, as the former group did not constitute a separate *status civitatis*, and would not therefore have interfered with succession. After all, both full laographia payers and members of the gymnasial class were *peregrini Aegyptii*. The problem, however, is that membership in one of those groups could also have repercussions in private law as well, as we have already illustrated.

CONCLUSIONS

There are two conclusions to be drawn from this chapter. First, it is highly likely that 'mixed unions' were neither discouraged nor penalised in Egypt. As far as Roman authorities were concerned, such unions were considered marriages; evidence for this claim can be found in the language applied to such unions in the *Gnomon* as well as the frequency with which such unions appear in the legal practice of the province. Second, the offspring of such unions were neither described nor recognised as ἀπάτορες or *spurii*. This is illustrated not only in the descriptions applied to such children, but also by the fact that they did not acquire the status of their mothers in the same way as those who had no fathers either in the social or legal senses, but rather acquired the status of the lesser parent. These conclusions offer further evidence that the Romans did indeed impose their own rules and standards of status acquisition onto the various groups in Egypt.

CHAPTER FIVE

CONSTANTINE'S LAWS ON NATURALES

IN THE PREVIOUS CHAPTERS we examined how, in Roman Egypt, there existed three categories of individuals born out of *iustum matrimonium*. The first consisted of those who were actually fatherless; as they had no father in either the legal or social sense. In the second category were individuals whose fathers were recognised at a social level, but whose filial bond with their fathers could not be recognised under Roman law; the children of soldiers and slaves are the most obvious members of this group. Certainly, the former group had to disappear when the ban on soldiers marriages was abolished. The third and final group consisted of individuals born of so-called 'mixed unions'; they could be recognised both legally and socially as marital children, but usually did not have the standing of *legitimi* as defined by Roman law. This latter group must have decreased after the *constitutio Antoniniana*, although they did not disappear entirely, as the privileged metropolite and gymnasial groups survived for at least a century afterwards, and there must have been marriages contracted with partners from outside of the Empire.

The standing and classification of children born outside of *matrimonium iustum* changed considerably in the early fourth century. Constantine's laws introduced two categories of out-of-wed lock children, *naturales* born in informal unions, whose inheritance rights were significantly diminished, and others. These reforms, which effectively defined perceptions of illegitimacy that have remained a part of European history ever since, will be described and explained in the following chapter.

1. CONSTANTINE'S LAWS – THE CONTENT

At the end of his reign, the emperor Constantine issued at least three constitutions which included provisions restricting the inheritance rights of children born out of wedlock. These laws were included in the *Theodosian Code* under the title *De naturalibus filiis et matribus eorum*. The first constitution did not survive, and the second survived only as a fragment; only No. 3 provides us with a fully preserved extract of Constantine's law.

Let us begin with the partially preserved No. 2.

> *C.Th.* 4.6.2: [...]ri fecit vel si ipsorum nomine comparavit, totum legitima suboles recipiat. Quod si non sint filii legitimi nec frater consanguineus aut soror aut pater, totum fisci viribus vindicetur. Itaque Liciniani etiam filio, qui per rescriptum sanctissimum dignitatis culmen ascendit, omnis substantia auferatur et secundum hanc legem fisco adiudicetur, ipso verberato compedibus vinciendo, ad suae originis primordia redigendo. Lect. iii K. Mai. Carthagine Nepotiano et Facundo conss.
>
> ... or if he has bought (something) on their behalf (for them?), legitimate children recover all of it. But if there are no legitimate children or brother by blood (and law) or (such a) sister or father, all of it shall be vindicated by the power of fisc. Accordingly, the entire substance of Licinianus' son, who has climbed to the summit of dignity via an imperial rescript, is taken too and (it is) adjudged to the fisc according to this law, as he himself has been beaten, chained and reduced to his status by birth. (The law was) read in Carthage 3 days before the Kalends of May in the consulship of Nepotianus and Facundus (29 April 336).

While the prohibition or limitation introduced in the law has not survived, it must have either excluded or restricted the hereditary rights of illegitimate children. The second part refers to the son of Licinianus who may have been born to a free woman, but perhaps to a slave.[1] The latter is suggested by the passage saying that he was reduced to his original status, *ad suae originis primordia redigendo*. He must, at some point, have been elevated to the position of *legitimus per rescriptum principis*, thus by *adroga-*

[1] J. Evans-Grubbs, *Law and Family in Late Antiquity. The Emperor Constantine's Marriage Legislation*, Oxford 1995, p. 285.

tio,[2] which at the time was possible only through *rescriptum principis*.[3] After acquiring the status of *legitimus* he became a senator and, when Licinianus died, he inherited his father's estate; it is this paternal inheritance that would have been the object of the confiscation mentioned in the constitution. Certainly, the constitution was intended to reverse the effects of the adoption and to prohibit such practices in general.

The third constitution is addressed to Gregorius, *praefectus praetorio*.[4]

> *C.Th.* 4.6.3 = C. 5.27.1[5]: IDEM A. AD GREGORIUM. Senatores seu perfectissimos, vel quos [in civ]itatibus duumviralitas vel quinquennalitas vel fla[monii] vel sacerdotii provinciae ornamenta condecorant, pla[cet m]aculam subire infamiae et peregrinos a Romanis legibus [fieri, s]i ex ancilla vel ancillae filia vel liberta vel libertae [filia], sive Romana facta seu Latina, vel scaenica {vel scaenicae} filia, vel ex ta[bern]aria vel ex tabernari filia vel humili vel abiecta vel leno[nis ve]l harenarii filia vel quae mercimoniis publicis praefuit, [suscep]tos filios in numero legitimorum habere voluerint [aut pr]oprio iudicio aut nostri praerogativa rescribti, ita ut, [quidq]uid talibus liberis pater donaverit, sive illos legitimos [seu natur]ales dixerit, totum retractum legitimae subo[li redda]tur aut fratri aut sorori aut patri aut matri. Sed et [uxori t]ali quodcumque datum quolibet genere fuerit vel empti[one c]onlatum, etiam hoc retractum reddi praecipimus: ip[sas et]iam, quarum venenis inficiuntur animi perditorum, [si qui]d quaeritur vel commendatum dicitur, quod his redd[end]um est, quibus iussimus, aut fisco nostro, tormentis {subici} iubemus. Sive itaque per ipsum donatum est qui pater [dicitu]r vel per alium sive per suppositam personam sive [ab eo e]mptum vel ab alio sive ipsorum nomine comparatum, [stati]m retractum reddatur quibus iussimus, aut, si non exis[tunt, f]isci viribus vindicetur. Quod si existentes et in praesen[tia re]rum constituti agere noluerint pacto vel iureiu[rand]o exclusi, totum sine mora fiscus invadat. Quibus tacen[tibus et] dissimulantibus a defensione fiscali duum mensuum [temp]ora limitentur, intra quae si non retraxerint vel [propter] retra[hendum] rectorem provinciae interpellaverint, quidquid ta[libus fil]iis vel uxoribus liberalitas inpura contulerit, fiscus nos[ter inv]adat, donatas vel commendatas res

[2] M. Sargenti, *Il diritto privato nella legislazione di Costantino. Persone e famiglia*, Milan 1938, p. 136.

[3] A. Arjava, *Women and Law in Late Antiquity*, Oxford 1996, p. 211.

[4] M. Bianchini, *Caso concreto e lex generalis: per lo studio della tecnica e della politica normativa da Costantino a Teodosio II*, Milan 1979, p. 21.

[5] Omits the last sentence.

[sub po]ena quadrupli severa quaestione perquirens. Liciniani autem filius, qui fugiens comprehensus est, compe[dibus vinct]us ad gynaecei Carthaginis ministerium deputetur. L[ecta XII] K. Aug. Carthagine Nepotiano et Facundo conss.

The same Augustus to Gregorius. It is Our pleasure that Senators or persons of the rank of Most Perfect or those adorned with the honors of the duumvirate or the quinquennalitate in the municipalities or with the honor of flamen or of the civil priesthood of a province shall suffer the brand of infamy and shall become foreigners in the eyes of the Roman law, if by their own judgment or by the prerogative of Our rescript they should wish to consider as legitimate the children born to them of a slave woman, a daughter of a slave woman, a freedwoman, a daughter of a freedwoman, whether made a Roman or a Latin, a woman of the stage, a daughter of a woman of the stage, a mistress of a tavern, a daughter of a tavern keeper, a low and degraded woman, the daughter of a procurer or of a gladiator or a woman who has charge of wares for sale to the public. Thus if a father should give anything to such children, whether he calls them legitimate or natural, all such property shall be taken from them and restored to his legitimate offspring, or to his brother or sister or father or mother.

Also if any property of any kind should be given in any way to such a wife or bestowed upon her pursuant to a purchase, We command that such property also shall be taken from her and returned. We also order that if anything that is to be restored to those persons to whom We have so ordered or to Our fisc should be sought or should be said to have been entrusted to such women by whose venomous charms the minds of these ruined men are infected, these women shall be subjected to examination under torture. Whether, therefore, the gift is made by the person himself who is called the father or through another or through suborned person, or whether the property is bought by such a father or by another or in the name of the mother or children themselves, it shall be immediately taken away and restored to those persons to whom We have so ordered, or if there are no such persons, such property shall be vindicated to the account of the fisc.

But if there should be such persons and they should be living but unwilling to bring suit, because they are prevented by a pact or by an oath, the fisc shall immediately confiscate the entire estate. If such persons should remain silent and should dissimulate, they have a time limit of two months in which to exclude the claim of the fisc. If within this time they have not recovered such property or if they have not applied to the governor of the province for that purpose, Our fisc shall confiscate the property which by an impure liberality was given to such children or wives and shall seek out by means of a severe examination under torture and the threat of a fourfold penalty everything that was given or entrusted to them.

Moreover, the son of Licinianus, who escaped but had been apprehended, shall be bound in fetters and consigned to service in the imperial weaving establishment in Carthage.

Read on the twelfth day before the Kalends of August at Carthage in the year of the consulship of Nepotianus and Facundus.[6]

The constitution discusses two issues relating to children born out of wedlock: the first is the *adrogatio* or *legitimatio* of children born of *iustae nuptiae* to men of high rank – including high-ranking officials (senators, *perfectissimi*) or Imperial administrators (civic priests of imperial cult, those in charge of the games)[7] – and their low-born life partners; the second is the succession of children born to such couples. Such children could never become legitimate, and any father who would attempt to adopt or legitimise them risked *infamia* or *capitis deminutio media*, thus the loss of his Roman citizenship.

It is perhaps more surprising that these children were excluded from testamentary succession after their fathers. If their father left something to them (and/or their mother), it would fall instead to his legitimate offspring or immediate *legitimi*. If these children received anything from their father against the prohibition, either the father's legitimate children or his siblings were allowed to make a claim within two months; if they failed to do so, the fisc could claim the estate.[8] The last part of the constitution refers again to the son of Licinianus, who having been caught trying to avoid the consequences of the previous law, was condemned and sent to the imperial weaving mills.

The partial state of preservation of *C.Th.* 4.6.1–3 makes it difficult to reconstruct their content. While the last constitution forbade the adoption of *naturales* and curtailed their hereditary rights, the text is concerned

[6] *The Theodosian Code and Novels and the Sirmondian Constitutions*, tr. C. PHARR, Princeton 1952, with slight modifications.

[7] BIANCHINI, *Caso concreto e lex generalis* (cit. n. 4), p. 32.

[8] Interestingly, the law prohibiting elites from bequeathing their property to extramarital children was not only biding, but also circumvented. Examples of which in ARJAVA, *Women and Law* (cit. n. 3), pp. 214–215.

only with the children of men of high-rank. The incomplete *C.Th.* 4.6.2 might have contained a *lex generalis* – to which *C.Th.* 4.6.3 was an exception – that limited or ruled out dispositions made by fathers for their extramarital children.[9] As a *lex specialis C.Th.* 4.6.3, might have included the additional punishments of *infamia* and *capitis diminutio media* for fathers of high-rank.[10] Yet it is also possible that the lost text of *C.Th.* 4.6.1 was the *lex generalis*,[11] in which case *C.Th.* 4.6.2 would have been the *lex specialis* covering one particular aspect of succession and/or adoption.[12]

The idea that Constantine's regulation on the succession of *naturales* was wider than what has been preserved in the Codex can be inferred from the following constitution, addressed by Valentinian I to Ampelius, *praefectus Urbi* in AD 371.[13] The text refers to the laws of Constantine.

> *C.Th.* 4.6.4: (...) Placuit man[entibus] ceteris, quae de naturalibus liberis Constantinianis legibus c[auta] sunt, haec tantummodo temperare (...).
>
> All provisions set forth by the laws of Constantine with reference to natural children will remain valid, subject only to the following modification (...).[14]

We should note that the emperor granted to all *filii naturales* the right to acquire 1/12 of the paternal estate in testamentary succession, if there were legitimate children, and 1/4 if there were none. The constitution, which does not address any specific group of fathers, was a general rule;

[9] This is the view of *e.g.* BIANCHINI, *Caso concreto e lex generalis* (cit. n. 4), p. 21.

[10] BIANCHINI, *Caso concreto e lex generalis* (cit. n. 4), p. 28.

[11] Yet, it has been also suggested that *C.Th.* 4.6.1 might have contained the concession for *legitimatio per subsequens matrimonium* (*infra*, p. 302): G. LUCHETTI, *La legittimazione dei figli naturali nelle fonti tardo imperiali e giustinianee*, Milan 1990, p. 183.

[12] Sargenti noted that the phrase *etiam filio, qui per rescriptum sanctissimum dignitatis culmen ascendit, omnis substantia auferatur et secundum hanc legem fisco adiudicetur* in *C.Th.* 4.6.2 implies that steps against Licinianus' son would have been taken according to an earlier law. Hence, the prohibition regarding *testamenti factio passiva* of children born out of wedlock had to predate *C.Th.* 4.6.2: M. SARGENTI, *Studi sul diritto del tardo impero*, Padua 1986, p. 41.

[13] BIANCHINI, *Caso concreto e lex generalis* (cit. n. 4), p. 35.

[14] Tr. J. TATE, 'Inheritance rights of nonmarital children in late Roman law', *Roman Legal Tradition* 4 (2008), pp. 1–36, p. 11.

it even refers to ***naturales*** born *ex consortio cuiuslibet mulieris*.[15] Constantine must therefore, as Joshua Tate suggested, have ruled out *testamenti factio passiva* for all children born of non-marital unions,[16] or restricted it so severely that children born out of wedlock were entitled to less than 1/12 or 1/4 of the paternal estate. The former seems more likely. Yet regardless of whether Constantine excluded illegitimate children from succession after their fathers or merely limited their hereditary rights, the question of why he did so is intriguing.

It has been suggested that the specific case of Licinianus' son was the impetus behind the constitutions preserved in *C.Th.* 4.6.2–3. Although some of the earlier literature identified Licinianus as Licinius, Constantine's imperial rival, the evidence to support such a claim is lacking.[17] Even if the laws were issued as a reaction to particular events or individuals, there must have been more general grounds for taking such harsh steps against testamentary freedom, one of very basic freedoms in Roman law.[18] The laws of Constantine remained in force until the time of Justinian and shaped legal thinking about illegitimacy in the following centuries. While subsequent constitutions either softened the rules or restricted them, full *testamenti factio passiva* was never restored to children born out of wedlock.[19]

2. THE FATHERLESS SINCE CONSTANTINE

The first question we must ask is whether attitudes changed only towards children begotten in unions lacking the quality of formal marriage, or

[15] See LUCHETTI, *Legittimazione dei figli naturali* (cit. n. 11), p. 24.

[16] TATE, 'Inheritance rights' (cit. n. 14), p. 11.

[17] See BIANCHINI, *Caso concreto e lex generalis* (cit. n. 4), p. 29, n. 34; EVANS GRUBBS, *Law and Family* (cit. n. 1), pp. 285–286; T. McGINN, 'The social policy of emperor Constantine in Codex Theodosianus 4.6.3', *Tijdschrift voor Rechtsgeschiedenis* 67 (1999), pp. 57–73, pp. 62–63. Yet, it has been accepted in that besides his son born of Constantine's own sister, Constantia, and executed by his own uncle, Licinius had another elder son by a slave woman. See Zosime, *Histoire nouvelle*, vol. II (livres I–II), ed. & tr. F. PASCHOUD, Geneva 1971, p. 212.

[18] TATE, 'Inheritance rights' (cit. n. 14), p. 6.

[19] The in-depth reconstruction of the sequence and content of constitutions issued in regard to the succession of extramarital children in: TATE, 'Inheritance rights' (cit. n. 14), pp. 1–36.

wider. If this was the case, it would suggest that Constantine's primary aim was to restrict concubinage, rather than to stigmatise children born out of wedlock.

On the one hand, it is obvious that the restrictions introduced by Constantine affected only the children of informal unions. Fatherless individuals do not appear in constitutions concerning the limitations of paternal inheritance, as they had no fathers from whom they could inherit. On the other hand, it has been long accepted that Constantine provided the term *naturalis* with a new meaning and, in doing so, introduced an actual division between the children of informal unions and other types of children born out of wedlock.[20] The term *liberi naturales* assumed the more specific meaning of a child born of a permanent union of which at least one partner was free. Children excluded from the category of *naturales* included those conceived out of any union (*i.e.* fatherless), and those born of forbidden unions, such as incestuous ones or ones consisting of a free woman and a slave.[21] *Naturales filii* or φυσικοὶ παῖδες, therefore, constituted a sub-category of bastards, *spurii*, νόθοι, *vulgo concepti*, or ἀπὸ πορνείας τεχθέντες. In later Roman society, belonging to the category of *spurii* was no longer neutral, but shameful, unwelcome and inconvenient. The question remains whether this was intended by Constantine, or if it was merely a side-effect of his campaign against informal unions.

An increasing negativity on the subject of bastardy is visible in sources post-dating Constantine. This is illustrated in the Gaian passage on *incestum*. The text is summarised in the *Epitome Gai*, included in the *Institutes* of Justinian, and paraphrased by Theophilus. In reading the three passages together, one may observe how birth out of wedlock evolved from a more-or-less neutral fact to a moral opprobrium. The second-century passage from Gaius (G. 1.64, *supra*, pp. 50–52), says that *spurii filii* were those who had no father because the father was uncertain: *quales sunt ii, quos mater*

[20] H.J. Wolff, 'The background of the postclassical legislation on illegitimacy', *Seminar (Jurist)* 3 (1945), pp. 21–45, p. 37.

[21] Luchetti, however, argued and demonstrated that attempts to connect the term with more specific meaning pointing out to the type of the union that produced the offspring should fail: Luchetti, *Legittimazione dei figli naturali* (cit. n. 11), pp. 14–64. The only constitution using the term in more restrictive sense should be the law given by Valentinian III, *C.Th.* 4.6.7: *ibidem*, p. 29.

vulgo concepit: nam et hi patrem habere non intelleguntur, cum is etiam incertus sit; unde solent spurii filii appellari vel a Graeca voce quasi σποράδην *concepti vel quasi sine patre filii*. A passage from the roughly contemporary *Tituli ex corpore Ulpiani* is even more neutral.[22]

> *Tit. Ulp.* 5.7: Si quis eam quam non licet uxorem duxerit, incestum matrimonium contrahit: ideoque liberi in potestate eius non fiunt, sed quasi vulgo concepti spurii sunt.
>
> If a man marries a woman whom it is not allowed (to marry), he contracts an incestuous marriage, for this reason children are not under his power, but they are *spurii* as if casually conceived.

Both texts inform us simply that the children of incestuous couples were not in *postestas*, and were thus considered *spurii*, as if conceived casually and therefore without father. The description of illegitimacy refers to the fact that the conception occurred outside of marriage.

The text of the *Epitome Gai* (*Ep. Gai* 4.8), omits the section on *patria potestas* – of essential importance to the Gaian text – and explains that children born of incestuous marriages had no relation to their fathers, but only to their mothers. As in Gaius, the *Epitome* classifies the children of incest as *spurii*, but the explanation differs significantly from the original: *et tamquam si de adulterio concepti fuerint, computantur; qui spurii appellantur, hoc est sine patre filii* – 'they are considered just as if conceived in adultery, they are named *spurii*, that is sons without fathers'. The author of the *Epitome* perceived *spurii* as having been conceived in *adulterium*; it is interesting to note how the idea of casual conception in Gaius has been transformed into something licentious and illegal. While it is certainly not a reference to *adulterium* in the strict sense – it is closer to the Christian *porneia* or the extended sense of *adulterium* known from late classical and late antique Roman legal sources – it is nonetheless presented as a stigmatising and highly shameful deed. Gian Gualberto Archi pointed out that the *Epitome* does not represent an accurate paraphrase of the Gaian *Institutes*; rather it has changed the meaning of the original text to reflect the state of law and society at the time it was

[22] Repeated in *Coll. leg.* 6.2.1.4.

composed.[23] The conflation of illegitimacy with debauchery may therefore have represented contemporary perceptions of the phenomenon.

Although the *Institutes* of Justinian repeat the Gaian definition (I. 1.10.12), the *Paraphrasis* of Theophilus goes to even greater lengths than the *Epitome* to stigmatise illegitimate children:

> Theoph., *Par*. 1.10.12: (...) *λέγει γὰρ τοὺς ἐκ τοιαύτης συναφείας τικτομένους ὑπεξουσίους μὴ γίνεσθαι τῷ πατρί· καὶ οὓς ἡ φύσις ἐδωρήσατο, ὁ νόμος ἀγνοεῖ, ὡς μὴ κατὰ τὴν αὐτοῦ τεχθέντας προαίρεσιν. ἀλλ' ὅσον ἀνήκει εἰς τὴν τοῦ πατρὸς ὑπεξουσιότητα τοιοῦτοί εἰσιν ὁποίους εἶναι συμβαίνει τοὺς ἀπὸ πορνείας συλληφθέντας. καὶ γὰρ οὐδε οὗτοι πατέρα ἔχειν νοοῦνται, ὁπότε ἄδηλος οὗτος ἐστι διὰ τὸ πλῆθος τῶν μιγνυμένων· ἀλλ' εἰώθασι τούτους* spurius *καλεῖν, ἢ ἀπὸ Ἑλληνικῆς φωνῆς* quasi *σποράδην* concepti, *οιᾶ σποράδην συλληφθέντες, ἢ* quasi sine patre filii, *ἐπειδὴ παῖδές εἰσιν ἀπάτορες.*
>
> For it says that those begotten of such a union do not become subject to the parental power; *i.e.*, those who were the gift of nature, yet the law does not recognize, as they were born not in accordance with its scope. But with respect to the paternal power, they have such qualities as those who happen to have been conceived out of *porneia*; for neither they are considered to have father, since he is uncertain due to the multitude of those who had intercourse (with their mother), but usually they are called *spurii*, either from the Greek language as having been conceived here and there (*quasi σποράδην concepti*), or as having been *sine patre filii*, because they are fatherless children.

For Theophilus, persons were *spurii* due to the licentious deeds of their mother, who had slept with many men – *διὰ τὸ πλῆθος τῶν μιγνυμένων* – and could not recognise the father. *Spurii* were, therefore, born as a result of *porneia*, understood here not as sex for money, but as promiscuous conduct. Theophilus even added a sentence to explain the content of the *Institutes*: *Γυνή τις πορνευθεῖσα παῖδα ἔσχεν. οὐχ ἕξουσιν οὗτοι πρός τινα* **legitima** *δίκαια, κτλ.*

While the *terminus ante quem* of the *Epitome* is AD 506, it is normally dated to the second half of the fifth century;[24] it thus postdates the con-

[23] G.G. Archi, *L'Epitome Gai. Studio sul tardo diritto romano in Occidente* [= *Antiqua* LXI], Naples 1991², pp. 141–148 in regard to the title 4.

[24] S. Schiavo, 'Aspetti processuali nell'Epitome Gai', [in:] G. Bassanelli Sommariva & S. Tarozzi (eds.), *Ravenna capitale. Giudizi, giudici e norme processuali in occidente nei secoli IV–VIII*, vol. II, Santarcangelo di Romagna 2015, pp. 49–94, p. 52.

stitutions of Constantine by over a century, and the *Institutes* by around two hundred years. There is, alas, no definition of *spurii* written between the age of Gaius and the *Tituli* and the composition of the *Epitome*, a time chronologically closer to the reign of Constantine.

Yet there are indications that the legislative attitude towards the fatherlessness had started to change in the time of Constantine. Another constitution of Constantine, issued in AD 326 or AD 329,[25] is an *edictum* addressed *ad populum* against unions of free women and their own slaves (*C.Th.* 9.9.1 = C. 9.11.1). There can be no doubt that this law was directed at the unions and not their offspring, as it was the partners who were severely punished for being together.[26] The law seems somewhat surprising: according to the sources, in the time before Constantine it was only unions between a free woman and a slave belonging to another master that could (but did not always) result in unwelcome consequences for the woman.[27] It would appear that unions with a woman's own slave remained unpunished until Constantine's law.[28] The extraordinary language of the constitution has led some to interpret the text as referring specifically to adulterous affairs between a woman and her slave, whom she might even buy directly for this purpose.[29] But Judith Evans Grubbs proposed that the text should be taken at face value, as it was not included in the title on adulteries, but under the separate title *De mulieribus, quae se servis propriis iunxerunt*. It should thus be interpreted as having applied to all types of union between mistresses and their slaves.[30]

[25] On the date, see A. BANFI, 'Commistioni improprie: a proposito della legislazione costantiniana circa le unioni fra donne libere e schiavi', *Index* 40 (2012), pp. 475–493, pp. 475–477.

[26] On the punishment, see ARJAVA, *Women and Law* (cit. n. 3), pp. 226–227; BANFI, 'Commistioni improprie' (cit. n. 25), pp. 480–484.

[27] See J. EVANS-GRUBBS, '"Marriage more shameful than adultery": Slave-mistress relationships, mixed marriages, and late Roman law', *Phoenix* 47.2 (1993), pp. 125–154.

[28] EVANS GRUBBS, '"Marriage more shameful than adultery"' (cit. n. 27), p. 128; G. RIZZELLI, *Lex Iulia de adulteriis. Studi sulla disciplina di adulterium, lenocinium, stuprum*, Lecce 1997, pp. 228–229.

[29] *E.g.* B. BIONDI, 'Vicende postclassiche del *S.C. Claudiano*. Contributo alla formazione della prassi giuridica postclassica', *Iura* 3 (1952), pp. 142–154, p. 144; T. YUGE, 'Die Gesetze im Codex Theodosianus über die eheliche Bindung von freien Frauen mit Sklaven', *Klio* 64 (1982), pp. 145–150, p. 148.

[30] EVANS GRUBBS, '"Marriage more shameful than adultery"' (cit. n. 27), pp. 145–147, with earlier literature.

As for the children born of such unions, the law says:

C.Th. 9.9.1.2: Filii etiam, quos ex hac coniunctione habuerit, exuti omnibus dignitatis insignibus, in nuda maneant libertate, neque per se neque per interpositam personam quolibet titulo voluntatis accepturi aliquid ex facultatibus mulieris.

Children, whom she had from such a union, deprived of all signs of dignity, remain only with sole freedom being able to receive nothing of the woman's resources either through her or any interposed person under any deed.

Constantine maintained the rule that children of free women and their slave partners were *spurii* who acquired the maternal status, and were therefore free; the phrase *exuti omnibus dignitatis insignibus* should thus be interpreted as a rhetorical element indicating the shameful character of the circumstances in which such children were begotten.[31] Yet, the law did deprive children of *testamenti factio passiva* with regard to their mothers' property. It was a severe step and, similar to the rulings preserved in *C.Th.* 4.6.2 *&* 3, children were prohibited from inheriting from their mothers, as succession from their fathers was already impossible. Taken together, the rulings of *C.Th.* 9.9.1 and *C.Th.* 4.6.1–3 suggest that Constantine was not only attempting to prevent people from living in non-marital unions, but to push children born outside the normal family structure beyond the margins of respectable society. Such radical changes in law rarely happened without social backing.

3. DISAPPEARANCE OF THE FATHERLESS FROM PAPYRI

The idea that changes in the legislative approach to illegitimacy were connected to changes in the social perception of fatherlessness is supported by the chronological distribution of the terms ἀπάτωρ and χρηματίζων

[31] Banfi suggested that the law might have been issued as a reaction to a particular situation involving a female partner of high social status. Yet, the text does not provide information allowing to prove or disprove such a hypothesis: Banfi, 'Commistioni improprie' (cit. n. 25), p. 489. See p. 307, n. 217.

μητρός in Egypt. The disappearance of these descriptive terms predates the constitutions of Constantine by a few decades:[32] the latest precisely dated texts come from AD 271/2 (*P. Oxy.* XL 2936, ll. 8 and 36 = nos. 179 and 180)[33] or AD 279–282 (*PSI* V 456 = no. 192),[34] thus closer to the reign of Diocletian.

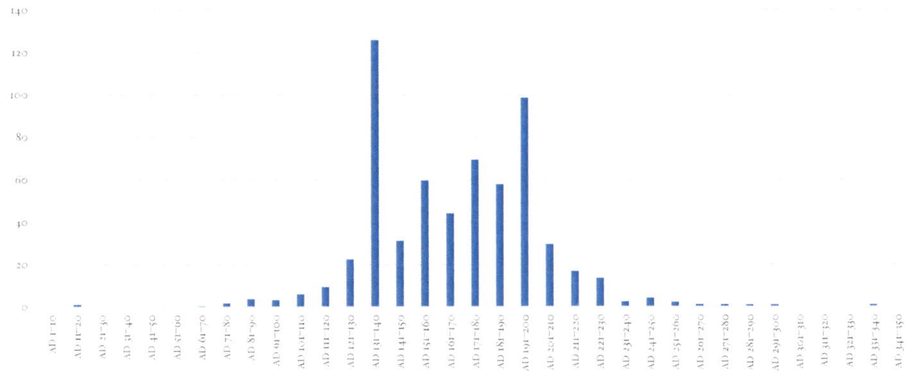

Fig. 1. Ἀπάτορες in absolute numbers

[32] Although two attestations of the term ἀπάτωρ postdate Constantine, they are little credible. In *P. NYU* I 12 = *Sel. Pap.* II 319, col. I, l. 19, dated to AD 336–337 account of tax collection, the edition provides the reading: Ἀτοῦς ἀπάτ[ωρ] (τάλαντα) β. In *P. Ryl.* IV 714, sixth-century account from Hermopolis, ἀπάτωρ occurs in line 3: δ(ιὰ) Φλ(αυίου) Ἡγεμμς (l. Ἡγεμ(όνος)) ἀπάτορ(ος) σί(του) (ἀρτάβαι) ν δ´ η. The reconstruction ἀπάτ[ωρ] seems unlikely, but still possible: The text comes from the Arsinoite where the term was applied, but it postdates last precisely dated attestation of the term (*P. Ryl.* I 12) for over 80 years. It seems, therefore, that a better reconstruction would be simply Ἀτοῦς Απατ[] (τάλαντα) β. It is, however, also uncertain because other entries in this account do not refer to filiations. *P. Ryl.* IV 714 seems simply too late. Yet, if ἀπάτωρ indeed makes an element of personal description in this text, we should not assume that the meaning of the description is the same as in the second and third centuries.

[33] M. Malouta, 'Fatherlessness and formal identification in Roman Egypt', [in:] S.R. Huebner & D.M. Ratzan (eds.), *Growing up Fatherless in Antiquity*, Cambridge 2009, pp. 120–138, p. 133. Nos. 179 & 180 according to www.romanbastards.wpia.uw.edu.pl.

[34] No. 192; χρη(ματίζοντος) μη(τρός) in l. 7 is reconstructed: this reconstruction is possible, yet not certain, as the patronym could have been short and μητρός abbreviated with a single *mu*, or, if we are indeed dealing with a fatherless man, the lacuna could be also reconstructed with μητρός written in full.

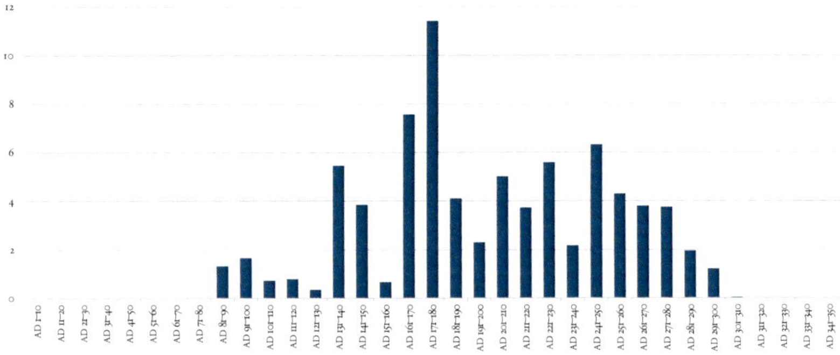

Fig. 2. *Χρηματίζοντες μητρός* in absolute numbers

The difficulties in interpreting these charts should be addressed from the outset. The first shows a significant disproportion between the number of ἀπάτορες attested in the second and third centuries. Indeed, ἀπάτωρ appears over five hundred times in the second century, but only just over fifty times in the third century, a ratio of nearly 10:1.[35] This disproportion could lead one to suspect that the term was in fact limited to the second century. If this was the case, the decrease of the term would have predated Constantine by over a century, which would not allow us to make any connection between the two phenomena.

Our interpretation, however, should not be based on raw numbers, as many of the second-century attestations come from a small handful of sources. The *Charta Borgiana* dated to AD 193 contains 68 ἀπάτορες (*SB* I 5124 + Litinas, *Pap. Congr.* XXIII, pp. 399–405), the administrative archive of Theadelphia has 170, and there are 43 in the Karanis tax roll. In the third century, most attestations come from separate and unrelated documents (the one exception is the archive of the *sitologoi* from Soknopaiou Nesos), which perhaps illustrates only the distribution within texts from the Arsinoite archives.[36] If we subtract the *Charta Borgiana*, the

[35] After www.romanbastards.wpia.uw.edu.pl. The numbers could be checked directly there, because the database is being kept up to date.

[36] See the list of archives ordered chronologically with the indication of their origins in: O. Montevecchi, *La papirologia*, Milan 1988^{2}, pp. 250–261. For the exact numbers of papyri preserved in the Arsinoite archives in the second and third centuries numbers of texts provided for

administrative archive of Theadelphia, and the Karanis tax roll, the number of second-century attestations is nearly half as much.

The disproportion between second- and third-century attestations of *ἀπάτωρ* could also be attributed to the general pattern of papyrus distribution in the Arsinoite nome. Myrto Malouta noticed and addressed this problem: after examining the patterns of chronological and geographical distribution proposed by Wolfgang Habermann,[37] she concluded that the number of texts containing *ἀπάτορες* follows the pattern applicable to all papyri. In other words, texts from the second-century Arsinoites are far more numerous than the papyri found in this nome from the third century, and we would thus expect to find more second-century documents containing *ἀπάτωρ*.[38] If we adjust the number of attested *ἀπάτορες* to the general distribution proportions between the second and third centuries the disproportion becomes considerably lower than 10:1. In regard to *χρηματίζοντες μητρός* Malouta also noted that, third-century instances of *χρηματίζοντες μητρός* outnumber those in the second century and the proportion of the Oxyrhynchite third-century attestations is considerably higher.[39]

The problem with these estimates is that they are not precise enough. In order to determine the relative proportion of *ἀπάτωρ* and *χρηματίζων μητρός* in the second and third centuries, one would have to compare these numbers with the number of all persons described with patronyms during the same period and in the same nomes. This task, however, would require the identification of all people with patronyms from the Oxyrhynchite and Arsinoite nomes between the late first and late third centuries, as well as checking those individuals against the various editions to eliminate multiple attestations of a single person. In addition to the problems of imprecise chronology found in the majority of published documentary texts, one would also have to exclude cases such as *Πτολεμαῖος υἱὸς μη(τρὸς) Ταπεθ(έως)* (discussed in Chapter 1, p. 78). In the absence of

each archive in: K. Vandorpe, W. Clarysse & H. Verreth (eds.), *Graeco-Roman Archives from the Fayum* [= *Collectanea Hellenistica – KVAB* VI], Leuven – Paris – Bristol, CT 2015.

37 W. Habermann, 'Zur chronologischen Verteilung der papyrologischen Zeugnisse', *Zeitschrift für Papyrologie und Epigraphik* 122 (1999), pp. 144–160.

38 Malouta, 'Fatherlessness' (cit. n. 33), pp. 133–134.

39 Malouta, 'Fatherlessness' (cit. n. 33), p. 134.

such an extensive study, the surviving evidence should at least allow us to suggest that, between the late first and late third centuries, both ἀπάτωρ and χρηματίζων μητρός were used with more or less the same frequency, but disappeared completely shortly thereafter.

The terms disappeared from the papyri roughly fifty years before the laws of Constantine. It is a long span, but not so long as to exclude a connection between the disappearance of the terms and changes in the popular perception of illegitimacy that would lead to changes in the law some five decades later. Before testing this hypothesis, however, it is worth stressing that neither ἀπάτωρ nor χρηματίζων μητρός were formal labels,[40] rather practical means of description that were used in different contexts, but strongly connected to taxation. The disappearance might therefore have been connected to technical or administrative phenomena, as was the case of *sp()f()*, which fell out of use at the end of the second century in the Roman Empire.[41] This occurred around the same time that the *praenomina*, which had been the basis for Roman patronyms, including *sp()f()*, in republican and early imperial times, disappeared from Latin inscriptions.[42] The disappearance of *sp()f()* should thus be viewed as the result of wider onomastic change.[43] Perhaps a similar process may also explain why the terms for fatherlessness fell into disuse in Egypt.

[40] M. Nowak, 'Ways of describing illegitimate children vs. their legal situation', *Zeitschrift für Papyrologie und Epigraphik* 193 (2015), pp. 207–219.

[41] Yanne Broux identified 612 individuals described with the false filiation *spurii filii*: the term is attested already in the sources from the beginning of the third century BC, but it became popular in the imperial period. The peak of its popularity was in the first quarter of the first century, after that it declined gradually. At the beginning of the third century it is attested poorly and finally ceases from inscriptions completely by mid-third century. On the specific analysis, see Y. Broux, 'Ancient profiles exploited. First results of Named Entity Recognition applied to Latin inscriptions', [in:] M. Nowak, A. Łajtar & J. Urbanik (eds.), *Tell Me Who You Are. Labelling Status in the Graeco-Roman World*, Warsaw 2018, pp. 11–33.

[42] Already in the first century Latin authors started omitting *praenomina*, in inscriptions the same trend is visible only since the second century, after which the *praenomina* disappeared almost completely. The dying out of *praenomina* was earlier among lower classes of Roman society, while senators born in Italy used the traditional Roman nomenclature until the mid-fourth century: H. Thylander, *Étude sur l'épigraphie latine: date des inscriptions – noms et dénomination latine – noms et origine des personnes*, Lund 1952, pp. 77–81.

[43] Yet, in Roman Egypt also the term *spurius* and its Greek counterpart disappeared in the same period as *sp()f()* and both labels ἀπάτωρ and χρηματίζων μητρός.

Yanne Broux suggested that ἀπάτωρ and χρηματίζων μητρός was significant for taxation and facilitated division of individuals among fiscal groups.[44] Thus, the disappearance of these groups could be the reason why the discussed terms disappeared too. Yet, the chronology does not support such an interpretation fully: as demonstrated above, the regular use of these terms postdates the creation of the fiscal groups (ascribed to the era of Augustus) by almost a century. Moreover, applications to the gymnasial group continued to be submitted until the end of the third century,[45] while the last χρηματίζοντες μητρός appear in the 270s. If the 'fatherless' label facilitated the exclusion of individuals from the gymnasial group, we would expect the term to disappear after the group, not before it. To the mertopolite and ketoikoi's groups fatherless individuals were admitted (*supra*, pp. 166–172).

The terminological change may also have been connected more broadly to taxes; certainly there were other changes in third-century Egypt which might have affected the application of such labels. At some point after (and, to some extent, because of) the universal grant of Roman citizenship both the poll-tax and census disappeared. Yet this seems no more plausible an explanation for the disuse of the labels of fatherlessness. The term χρηματίζων μητρός remained in use[46] after the poll-tax and census ceased in AD 257/8.[47] In addition, the labels were not used exclusively in the census, or even in κατ' ἄνδρα reports: in the second and third centuries χρηματίζων μητρός appears mostly in private contexts (see Chapter 1); and while ἀπάτορες were indeed numerous in κατ' ἄνδρα reports, the description was undoubtedly more widely applied. Both terms were used as practical substitutes for filiation, and were thus useful in different types of documents. We would expect them to survive the end of census just as patronyms did.

[44] Y. Broux, 'Re: Apatores. Identification issues and loss of status in Roman Egypt', *Zeitschrift für Papyrologie und Epigraphik* 2015 (194), pp. 212–214.

[45] P. van Minnen, '*Aἱ ἀπὸ γυμνασίου*: Greek women and the Greek elite in the metropoleis of Roman Egypt', [in:] H. Melaerts & L Mooren (eds.), *Le rôle et le statut de la femme en* Égypte *hellénistique, romaine et byzantine : acts du colloque international, Bruxelles – Leuven, 27–29 novembre 1997* [= *Studia Hellenistica* XXXVII], Paris 2002, pp. 337–353, p. 343.

[46] See in Statistics on www.romanbastards.wpia.uw.edu.pl.

[47] D. Rathbone, 'Egypt, Augustus and Roman taxation', *Cahiers Glotz* 4 (1993), pp. 81–112, p. 87; R.S. Bagnall & B.W. Frier, *The Demography of Roman Egypt* [= *Cambridge Studies in Population, Economy and Society in Past Time*], Cambridge 2006², p. 9.

4. CHRISTIAN INFLUENCE

To investigate whether the disappearance of the discussed terms was connected to the laws of Constantine it is necessary to have a closer look at other possible backgrounds of his legislation. The question of what inspired Constantine's constitutions has been discussed by a few historians of Roman law. In earlier scholarship, Christianity was recognised as a primary inspiration. Some scholars assumed a direct Christian influence, while others proposed that the less-direct impact of Christian ideas on social life found its way eventually into imperial legislation.[48] The disappearance of our two terms may thus reflect a substantial change in the popular perception of bastardy: if the state of being fatherless had become shameful and unwelcome under the influence of Christianity, people would have stopped applying the labels to themselves. Constantine's restrictive and unprecedented laws against extramarital children may simply have been a reflection of prevalent social attitudes in his time.

Sexuality was indeed an important topic in Christian writings from the very beginning. Paul of Tarsus was the first author to put forth a Christian vision for sexuality, suggesting in his *Letters*, that marriage was a remedy for desire and promiscuity (1 Cor. 7.2–10).[49] He identified *πορνεία* – referring in this case to all types of illicit sexual acts[50] – as one of the factors preventing Christians from achieving holiness and sanctification (1 Thess. 4.3–4).[51] He castigates the Corinthians for having a sexual sinner among them (1 Cor. 5.9–

[48] See, *e.g.*, C. Dupont, *Les constitutions de Constantin et le droit privé au début du IVe siècle : les personnes* [= *Studia iuridica Bari* XVII], Bari 1937, p. 191; B. Biondi, *Il diritto romano cristiano*. vol. III: *La famiglia, rapporti patrimoniali, diritto pubblico*, Milan 1954, pp. 130 & 193; C. van de Wiel, 'Les différentes formes de cohabitation hors justes noces et les dénominations diverses des enfants qui en sont nés dans le droit romain, canonique, civil et byzantin jusqu'au treizième siècle', *Revue internationale des droits de l'Antiquité* 39 (1992), pp. 327–358, pp. 240–241; S.A. Cristaldi, 'Unioni non matrimoniali a Roma', [in:] F. Romeo (ed.), *Le relazioni affettive non matrimoniali*, Rome 2014, pp. 143–200, p. 180, with further literature.

[49] P. Karavites, *Evil, Freedom, and the Road to Perfection in Clement of Alexandria* [= *Supplements to Vigiliae Christianae* XLIII], Leiden – Boston – Cologne 1999, p. 90.

[50] A study on changing notion of the term *πορνεία* in Christian and pre-Christian writings in: K. Harper, '*Porneia*: The making of a Christian sexual norm', *Journal of Biblical Literature* 131.2 (2012), pp. 363–383.

[51] Harper, '*Porneia*' (cit. n. 50).

11) and lists πόρνοι and μοιχοί, men 'with a lascivious lack of self-control' and 'men who corrupt respectable women', among those who would not enter Kingdom of Heaven (1 Cor. 6.9–10).[52] For Paul, the human body was not neutral, but a temple of the Holy Spirit belonging to the Lord,[53] and marriage was a way of managing desire safely.[54] Paul thus condemns even those extramarital sexual acts which were tolerated in Greek and Roman culture.[55] He goes even further in his expectations of sexual purity, condemning not merely extramarital sex, but also divorce and re-marriage.[56]

The opinions of Paul were developed further throughout the second and third centuries by virtually all Christian thinkers who turned their attention to matters of sexuality. While marital sex for procreation was accepted among the majority of Christians, other sexual deeds were recognised as morally bad and even adulterous (Clem. *Strom.* 3.171). In addition to the condemnation of extramarital sex, divorce and re-marriage, Christian sexual ethics placed a very high value on the idea of chastity.

Texts stigmatising birth out of wedlock exist in the earliest corpus of Christian writing, at least at a linguistic level. The earliest attestation comes from chapter 8 in the Gospel of John in which Jesus tells the Jews: 'If you were Abraham's children, you would do the works of Abraham. But now you seek to kill Me, a Man who has told you the truth which I heard from God. Abraham did not do this. You do the deeds of your father'. The Jews replied to Jesus (Jn. 8.41.2): Ἡμεῖς ἐκ πορνείας οὐ γεγεννήμεθα· ἕνα πατέρα ἔχομεν τὸν θεόν.

A similar associations between adultery and birth out of wedlock is present in a passage from the early-second-century *Dialogue with Trypho* by Justin the Martyr. The expression ἀπὸ πορνείας was used to explain that Jesus was not conceived outside of marriage.

> Justinus Martyr, *Dialogus cum Triphone* 78.3.4: καὶ Ἰωσὴφ δέ, ὁ τὴν Μαρίαν μεμνηστευμένος, βουληθεὶς πρότερον ἐκβαλεῖν τὴν μνηστὴν αὐτῷ Μαριάμ, νομίζων ἐγκυμονεῖν αὐτὴν ἀπὸ συνουσίας ἀνδρός, τοῦτ' ἔστιν ἀπὸ πορνείας,

[52] Harper, '*Porneia*' (cit. n. 50), pp. 377–378.

[53] P. Brown, *The Body and Society: Men, Women, and Sexual Renunciation in Early Christianity*, New York 1988, p. 51.

[54] Brown, *Body and Society* (cit. n. 53), p. 55.

[55] Harper, '*Porneia*' (cit. n. 50), p. 378.

[56] Brown, *Body and Society* (cit. n. 53), p. 57.

δι᾽ ὁράματος κεκέλευστο μὴ ἐκβαλεῖν τὴν γυναῖκα αὐτοῦ, εἰπόντος αὐτῷ τοῦ φανέντος ἀγγέλου ὅτι ἐκ πνεύματος ἁγίου ὃ ἔχει κατὰ γαστρός ἐστι.

And Joseph, who was promised Maria, at first had wanted to cast away his fiancée Maria, believing that she became pregnant by an intercourse with a man, that is in fornication, but was ordered by a dream vision not to cast away his wife, because the angel who appeared before him told him that the unborn which she had inside her womb was coming from the Holy Spirit.

The phrase *τοῦτ᾽ ἔστιν ἀπὸ πορνείας* could, however, refer to any type of physical intercourse as it is followed by *ἀπὸ συνουσίας ἀνδρός*; it might also have been used because Joseph suspected that Maria had become pregnant by another man despite being promised to him. It could also be an allusion to conception out of wedlock.

Antti Arjava noted that bishops of the fourth century stressed that individuals born out of wedlock should not be appointed as heirs,[57] as in Ambrose's *On Abraham*, 19: *ne huiusmodi suscipiant liberos, quos haeredes habere non possint*. Such writings, however, postdate the constitutions of Constantine, and while they may express the earlier opinions of Christian authors, they may simply have been inspired by the laws themselves. Certainly, they do not hint as to how widespread such attitudes were among Christians.

There can be no doubt that early Christian writings were concerned with sexuality, and were specifically not in favour of children being born out of wedlock. Yet we cannot simply assume a Christian influence either on Constantine's laws or on the social perception of illegitimacy. The important question, as Peter Brown pointed out, is whether or not the ideology of these writings found their way into the everyday life of the Empire during the second and third centuries.[58] More specifically we must ask how quickly these ideas spread in Egypt, a province in which the disappearance of labels referring to fatherlessness can be traced in the sources.

The spread of Christian ideas is undoubtedly connected to spread of Christians. We must therefore investigate whether Christians were numerous enough before Constantine that they could have influenced popular perception of social phenomena such as illegitimacy. Non-literary papyri

[57] Arjava, *Women and Law* (cit. n. 3), p. 215, sources listed in n. 88.

[58] Brown, *Body and Society* (cit. n. 53), p. 132.

and inscriptions from the first two centuries AD do not contain many clear references to Christianity. Attempts have nonetheless been made to estimate the number of Christians and the pace with which Christianity spread in second- and third-century Egypt. One method based on onomastics was developed by Roger Bagnall in 1982.[59] He investigated the frequency of Christian names and concluded that Christians became the majority in Egypt in around AD 320–325 and constituted around 80% of Egyptian population by AD 350. Yet in 1987, he published an article correcting the date of one of the documents on which he had based his earlier calculation; by moving the date of *CPR* V 26 from AD 388 to AD 448 he proposed new estimates for the percentage of Christians among the population of Egypt: 15.3% in 280, 20.4% in AD 313 and 315, 56.1% in AD 393 and 88.4% in AD 428.[60]

In 2013, Willy Clarysse and Mark Depauw offered a new estimate based on a quantitative approach and a larger corpus of evidence, including several hundred thousand names collected on the platform Trismegistos and entries recognised as personal names in *DDbDP*;[61] they also revised the selection of names classified by Bagnall as Christian.[62] The results indicated that Christian names became popular in Egypt in the fourth and fifth centuries, but that the process was slower than Bagnall had initially proposed,[63] with *ca.* 20% at the beginning of Constantine's rule, around 80% in the time of Theodosius, and nearly 100% by the time of the council of Chalcedon.[64] In both studies, the results for the second and early third centuries remain the same: below 5%.

[59] R.S. BAGNALL, 'Religious conversion and onomastic change in early Byzantine Egypt', *The Bulletin of the American Society of Papyrologists* 19 (1982), pp. 105–124. See also the discussion in: E. WIPSZYCKA, 'La valeur de l'onomastique pour l'histoire de la christianisation de l'Égypte. À propos d'une étude de R.S. Bagnall', *Zeitschrift für Papyrologie und Epigraphik* 62 (1986), pp. 173–181; and R.S. BAGNALL, 'Conversion and onomastics: A replay', *Zeitschrift für Papyrologie und Epigraphik* 69 (1987), pp. 243–250.

[60] BAGNALL, 'Conversion and onomastics' (cit. n. 59), pp. 248–249.

[61] W. CLARYSSE & M. DEPAUW, 'How Christian was fourth century Egypt? Onomastic perspectives on conversion', *Vigiliae Christianae* 67.4 (2013), pp. 407–435.

[62] CLARYSSE & DEPAUW, 'How Christian was fourth century Egypt?' (cit. n. 61), pp. 414–421.

[63] CLARYSSE & DEPAUW, 'How Christian was fourth century Egypt?' (cit. n. 61), pp. 421–425.

[64] CLARYSSE & DEPAUW, 'How Christian was fourth century Egypt?' (cit. n. 61), p. 434.

More precise numbers for the early stages of Christianity were provided by Roger Bagnall in his study of early Christian books. His calculations were based on a model previously proposed by Rodney Stark, who assumed a growth rate of 3.4% per year, starting with around 1000 Christians in AD 40 and becoming the majority among Romans by the end of the fourth century.[65] Bagnall, assuming an Egyptian population of 5.5 million, provided the following numbers: 753 Christians in AD 100 (0.014% of all inhabitants of Egypt), 1,746 (0.032%) in AD 125, 4,047 (0.074%) in AD 150, 9,382 (0.17%) in AD 175, 21,747 (0.395%) in AD 200, 50,409 (0.917%) in AD 225 and 116,849 (2.12%) in AD 250.[66] Combining these numbers with the previous studies, we can suggest that the percentage of Christians escalated more quickly between AD 250 and the time of Constantine, rising from *ca.* 2% to 20% in the span of just over half a century. Yet, in relative numbers Christians were still the minority.

On the basis of these estimates, we cannot reasonably claim that Christianity would have had much impact on popular attitudes toward sex or legal practices in the late-second and early-third centuries.[67] Even if the numbers had been higher, it would not have translated into an immediate and profound change of attitudes and perceptions. The process of Christianisation was long and multi-faceted,[68] and the pace with which Christian thought spread among Egyptians in the third century does not suggest that attitudes toward children born out of wedlock would have been influenced by Pauline letters or later writings. In fact, the sources suggest that very different sexual attitudes developed within Roman society in the decades before Constantine, as we shall see below.

[65] R. STARK, *The Rise of Christianity: A Sociologist Reconsiders History*, Princeton 1996 (after R.S. BAGNALL, *Early Christian Books in Egypt*, Princeton 2009, pp. 18–19).

[66] BAGNALL, *Early Christian Books* (cit. n. 65), pp. 18–20, with his methodological reservations.

[67] Such assumptions were made by previous generations of students of Roman law, *e.g.* F. MAROI, 'Intorno all'adozione degli espositi nell'Egitto romano', [in:] *Raccolta di scritti in onore di Giacomo Lumbroso (1844–1925)*, Milan 1925, pp. 377–406, who claimed that the reason for introducing rules preserved in *the Gnomon of idios logos* (§ 41 & 107) was to prevent Christians from adopting foundlings and raising them according to their faith; or A. TOSO, 'Emilio Papiniano e le influenze cristiane nell'evoluzione del diritto romano classico', [in:] *Acta Congressus iuridici internationalis: VII saeculo a Decretalibus Gregorii IX et XIV a Codice Iustiniano promulgatis. Romae, 12–17 Novembris 1934*, Rome 1935, pp. 21–35.

[68] The anthropologic approach to Christianizing, see in: D. FRANKFURTER, *Christianizing Egypt: Syncretism and Local Worlds in Late Antiquity*, Princeton – London 2018.

Christian attitudes towards sexuality were a product of their times, and scholars have also identified strong Jewish influences on them[69] and stoic inspirations;[70] it is possible that the ideas presented in early Christian writings were common to the Mediterranean region in both pagan and Christian mentalities,[71] and we should not necessarily interpret negative late antique attitudes towards human sexuality as specifically Christian.

Finally, it is worth stressing that even the early Church fathers did not postulate Christian ideas of family life to be incorporated in Roman law. In one of Jerome's letters we find the statement *aliae sunt leges Caesarum, aliae Christi. Aliud Papinianus, aliud Paulus noster praecipit* (*ep.* 77 *ad Oceanum de morte Fabiolae*, 3), suggesting a discrepancy between Roman law (*apud illos*) and the New Testament (*apud nos*) in regard to the measures taken against men and women who engage in illicit acts.[72]

5. MARRIAGE NOTION EXTENDED

If changes in the social perception of illegitimacy did not come from Christianity, we must turn our attention to other sources. In Roman jurisprudence of the late-second and early-third centuries we find an extensive discussion on the *lex Iulia de adulteriis* and its extension to include cases not recognised as *adulterium* in the original *lex*, specifically deeds of infidelity committed by unmarried women. The sources, however, also attest an amelioration of the legal position of children born out of wedlock in the second century. Both of these trends can be confirmed in non-legal sources pertaining to every-day life. At first glance the trends seem contradictory, but a closer look at this development in late classical jurisprudence may shed some light on the constitutions of Constantine quoted above.

[69] Brown, *Body and Society* (cit. n. 53), pp. 34–64 and *passim*.

[70] Brown, *Body and Society* (cit. n. 53), p. 31.

[71] Evans Grubbs, *Law and Family* (cit. n. 1), pp. 321–342.

[72] J. Urbanik, 'La repressione constantiniana dei divorzi: La libertà dei matrimoni trafitta con una forcina', [in:] *Fides. Humanitas. Ius. Studii in onore di Luigi Labruna*, vol. VIII, Naples 2007, pp. 5705–5726, p. 5722.

5.1. *Late classical jurisprudence on the lex Iulia de adulteriis coercendis*

Sources for late-second- and third-century classical jurisprudence contain some discussion on the *lex Iulia de adulteriis coercendis*, an Augustan marriage law introduced as *plebiscitum* and designed to repress certain forms of sexual relations, especially adultery. As a result of this discussion, the notion of adultery was extended to include deeds not covered under the original *lex Iulia*.[73] The law and its extensions were investigated in detail by Giunio Rizzelli in his book on the *lex Iulia de adulteriis*.[74]

The primary difficulty in dealing with the *lex Iulia* is that the content of the original law remains uncertain.[75] The majority of fragments from which the law was reconstructed are preserved in the *Digest* of Justinian (title 4, book 48), a compilation of jurisprudential works postdating the original law by several centuries, and often altered by the interventions of compilers. Fortunately we possess other sources which preserve references both to the original *lex Iulia* and its later classical interpretations. One of them is the fourth book of *Collatio Mosaicarum et Romanarum legum*, which repeats some of the prescriptions preserved in the *Digest* and sometimes refers to the same fragments (as D. 48.5.14.3 and *Coll.* 4.6.1)[76]. As with the *Digest*, the *Collatio* postdates the discussions it preserves and encompasses only a tiny part of Roman classical jurisprudence on the *lex Iulia de adulteriis coercendis*; the passages have, moreover, been selected carefully according to the needs of the compilers. However, the information preserved in both sources is often in agreement, and can be corroborated by other sources, such as the *Pauli Sententiae* and the imperial laws preserved in the *Theodosian* and *Justinianian Codes*, as well as literature (including Cassius Dio) and the occasionally papyrus, such as *P. Aktenbuch* from the fourth century.

[73] Treggiari suggested that such an extension of the *lex Iulia de adulteriis* was possible because the *lex* was formulated loosely: S. Treggiari, *Roman Marriage. Iusti Coniuges from the Time of Cicero to the Time of Ulpian*, Oxford 1991, p. 279.

[74] Rizzelli, *Lex Iulia de adulteriis* (cit. n. 28).

[75] See reconstruction proposed in: Treggiari, *Roman Marriage* (cit. n. 73), pp. 278–287.

[76] See Rizzelli, *Lex Iulia de adulteriis* (cit. n. 28), pp. 203–206.

While it is difficult to distinguish the original text of the *lex Iulia de adulteriis coercendis* from the later additions, we can trace with reasonable certainty the interpretative tendencies and extensions of the *lex Iulia* that developed in later Principate. We may note especially that the definition of *adulterium*, originally extramarital intercourse with a woman who was legally wedded, has been extended to deeds committed with and by some women who were not legally wedded wives:[77]

1. a woman with whom marriage had not been lawfully contracted, *iniusta uxor* (D. 48.5.14.1: Ulp. *de adult.* 2, referring to Africanus; *Coll.* 4.5.1: Papinian);[78]
2. a woman in an incestuous or *nefas* relationships (D. 48.5.14.4: Ulp. *de adult.* 2);[79]
3. a fiancée (*Coll.* 4.6.1: Paulus; D. 48.5.14.3 and 8: Ulp. *de adult.* 2; D. 48.5.12.7: Pap. *lib. sing. de adult.*[80]);[81]
4. a concubine who was married by her partner after having a sexual relationship with another man (D. 48.5.14.6: Ulp. *de adult.* 2);
5. a daughter who married without paternal consent, and obtained it only afterwards, *i.e.* after having engaged in a sexual relationship with another man (D. 48.5.14.6: Ulp. *de adult.* 2);

[77] C. Fayer, *La familia romana. Aspetti giuridici ed antiquari*, vol. III: *Concubinato, divorzio, adulterio*, Rome 2005, pp. 311–326.

[78] The fragment of Papinian's *liber responsorum* preserved in *Collatio* refers also to a marriage contracted with a *peregrina* without *conubium*, while Ulpian when referring to Africanus already after the *constitutio Antoniniana* perhaps had in his mind only marriages contracted against other prohibitions, as reference to *peregrina* would not be practical. See V. Sanna, *Matrimonio e altre situazioni matrimoniali nel diritto romano classico. Matrimonium iustum – matrimonium iniustum*, Naples 2012, pp. 143–150. According to Volterra in this case the accusation concerned *stuprum*: E. Volterra, 'La nozione giuridica del *conubium*', [in:] E. Volterra, *Scritti giuridici*, vol. II, Naples 1992, pp. 277–320 (reprinted from: *Studi in memoria di Emilio Albertario*, vol. II, Milan 1950, pp. 348–384), pp. 300–301.

[79] Fayer, *La familia romana.* III (cit. n. 77), p. 314.

[80] This case concerned a fiancé who wanted to use *accusatio* against his fiancée whose father gave her into marriage to another man. Obviously, the jurist did not recognise this situation as *adulterium*, consequently, no accusation was given: H. Ankum, 'La *sponsa adultera* : problèmes concernant l'*accusatio adulterii* en droit romain classique', [in:] *Estudios de derecho romano en honor de Alvaro d'Ors*, vol. I, Navarra 1987, pp. 161–198, pp. 191–192; Rizzelli, *Lex Iulia de adulteriis* (cit. n. 28), pp. 193–194.

[81] Fayer, *La familia romana.* III (cit. n. 77), pp. 315–323.

6. an under-age girl who was taken as a wife and became one after coming of age, but had had sex with another man while still under-age (D. 48.5.14.8: Ulp. *de adult.* 2; D. 48.5.39.4: Pap. *quaest.* 36);

7. a wife who had been held captive and, having regained her freedom, returned to Rome and revived her dissolved marriage (D. 48.5.14.7: Ulp. *de adult.* 2[82]).[83]

The question was whether women belonging to the categories listed above should be accused of adultery. The answer, generally speaking, was yes, but only to some extent: they could be accused *iure extranei*, an accusation available to anyone, but privileged *accusatio ex iure mariti vel patris* was usually denied in such cases.[84] The difference between these two types of accusation lay not only in the person entitled to bring it[85] – the latter could only be brought forth by a lawful spouse or father – but also in its content.[86]

[82] This passage was perhaps the most controversial one, as it raises two significant problems: 1. a woman taken as a captive was a slave who could not commit adultery (D. 48.5.6 pr.); 2. a marriage of a captive was automatically dissolved. Therefore, it was considered as interpolated. See E. Volterra, 'In tema di *accusatio adulterii*', [in:] *Studi in onore di Pietro Bonfante*, vol. II, Milan 1930, pp. 109–126, pp. 122–126, whose opinion was held by quite a few scholars, see Fayer, *La familia romana.* III (cit. n. 77), p. 324, with further literature in n. 429. Rizzelli recognised the discussed passage as classical: it concerns cases in which a husband wanted to accuse his wife for deeds committed before marriage; a married woman was taken into captivity, she lost her Roman citizenship and became a slave, her marriage was automatically dissolved, she regained her freedom, came back to her husband contracting with him a new marriage. Therefore, the case discussed in D. 48.5.14.7 is not different than D. 48.5.14.6 & 8: Rizzelli, *Lex Iulia de adulteriis* (cit. n. 28), pp. 206–212.

[83] All referred cases discussed thoroughly in: Rizzelli, *Lex Iulia de adulteriis* (cit. n. 28), pp. 171–212.

[84] Rizzelli, *Lex Iulia de adulteriis* (cit. n. 28), p. 185. On the accusation, see Ankum, 'La *sponsa adultera*' (cit. n. 80), pp. 166–175. Some scholars claimed that this privileged accusation was granted to a husband of *uxor quae volgaris fuerit* (D. 48.5.14.2: Ulp. *de adult.*), which most likely signifies a woman married against the prohibitions of the *lex Iulia et Papia*. For the discussion and literature, see Sanna, *Matrimonio e altre situazioni matrimoniali* (cit. n. 78), pp. 150–153.

[85] Yet, both fathers and husbands could bring this special accusation only within a definite period, *i.e.* up to sixty days after the marriage with an adulteress was dissolved, during this period no one else could bring an accusation (D. 48.5.15(14).2: Scaev. *reg.*; D. 48.5.4.1: Ulp. *disp.*). Having this time passed, they could bring an ordinary *accusatio* (*iure extranei*). See Fayer, *La famiglia romana.* III (cit. n. 77), pp. 271–272.

[86] See Fayer, *La famiglia romana.* III (cit. n. 77), pp. 270–311.

At some point in the second century, jurists started extending *accusatio adulterii* to misconducts which were not technically *adulterium* as defined under the Augustan *lex Iulia*. They resembled adultery in so far as they were committed by women in heterosexual, monogamous and stable relationships,[87] yet they were still covered only under ordinary public accusations.

That the debates on the definition of adultery must have preceded the sources discussed above is confirmed by a passage of Paulus preserved in the *Collatio* which mentions a rescript given by the emperors Septimius Severus and Caracalla refusing *accusatio ex iure mariti* to a betrayed fiancé.

> *Coll.* 4.6.1: In uxorem adulterium vindicatur iure mariti, non etiam sponsam. Severus quoque Antoninus ita rescripserunt.
>
> The adultery is vindicated *iure mariti* against the wife, but not against fiancée. As Severus and Antoninus have decided in the rescript.

This text, taken together with other fragments devoted to similar matters (*Coll.* 4.6.1; D. 48.5.14.3 and 8; D. 48.5.12.7), would seem to imply that the question of whether or not a fiancé should be allowed to accuse his fiancée of adultery using the privileged procedural means of *accusatio ex iure mariti*, had been discussed before. A commentary on the same law ascribed to Ulpian illustrates how betrothal had been assimilated into the idea of marriage.

> D. 48.5.14.3 (Ulp. *de adult.* 2): Divi Severus et Antoninus rescripserunt etiam in sponsa hoc idem vindicandum, quia neque matrimonium qualecumque nec spem matrimonii violare permittitur.
>
> Deified Severus and Antoninus have decided in the rescript that also the same should be vindicated against fiancée, as it is permitted to dishonour neither any sort of marriage, nor the hope for marriage.

This assimilation must have predated the constitution itself, and the passage from Paulus preserved in the *Collatio* should thus be interpreted as a softer solution to the problem at hand: a fiancé could bring forth an

[87] Rizzelli, *Lex Iulia de adulteriis* (cit. n. 28), p. 186.
In some cases the resemblance to marriage was further strengthen by its later conclusion (D. 48.5.14.6–8).

accusation but, despite some opinions in favour of granting him *accusatio ex iure mariti*, he was only permitted *iure extranei*.

We know from the passage of Ulpian preserved in the *Digest*, that Sextus Caecilius Africanus, a jurist of the first half of the second century, had already proposed *accusatio adulterii* for unions which did not meet the requirements for *matrimonium iustum*, including concubinage and unions between people of unequal *status civitatis* without *conubium*.[88]

> D. 48.5.14.1 (Ulp. *de adult.* 2): Plane sive iusta uxor fuit sive iniusta, accusationem instituere vir poterit: nam et Sextus Caecilius ait, haec lex ad omnia matrimonia pertinet, et illud Homericum adfert: nec enim soli, inquit, Atridae uxores suas amant. *οὐ μόνοι φιλέουσ' ἀλόχους μερόπων ἀνθρώπων Ἀτρεῖδαι.*
>
> Clearly no matter whether the wife is *iusta* or *iniusta*, her husband is allowed to bring the accusation: for even Sextus Caecilius claims, this law pertains to all marriages, and he adduces the following quotation from Homer. He says: for not only sons of Atreus love their wives. Do they then alone of mortal men love their wives, these sons of Atreus?[89]

The passage illustrates that, by the early second century, some already believed that *adulterium* should be applied to situations outside *iustum matrimonium*. It is likely that the definition of *adulterium* was expanded gradually to include many of the situations listed above, which makes it even more difficult to date the changes precisely. The discussion itself does not prove that the extension of *adulterium* was universally accepted; this would have come later. Although some fragments refer to imperial laws which granted *accusatio adulterii* against unfaithful, unwedded women

[88] The most accepted definition of *matrimonium iniustum* coined by Volterra describes it by the opposition to *matrimonium iustum*. It would have been, therefore, a union which did not fulfill at least one of condition necessary for *matrimonium iustum* – invalid marriage, factual union: *e.g.* E. Volterra, '*Iniustum matrimonium*', [in:] *Studi in onore di Gaetano Scherillo*, vol. II, Milan 1972, pp. 441–470, or idem, 'Precisazioni in tema di matrimonio classico', *Bullettino dell'Istituto di diritto romano "Vittorio Scialoja"* 78 (1975), pp. 245–270. The literature discussing the difference between *matrimonium iustum* and *iniustum* is abundant. The recent comprehensive study has been published by Maria Virginia Sanna: Sanna, *Matrimonio e altre situazioni matrimoniali* (cit. n. 78), with further literature.

[89] Translation of *Il.* 9.340–341 from Homer, *Iliad*, tr. A.T. Murray, revis. W.F. Wyatt [= *Loeb Classical Library* CLXX], Leipzig 1924.

(D. 48.5.14.8; D. 48.5.14.3; *Coll.* 4.6.1),[90] we cannot determine whether the solutions proposed by the emperors were new, or if they simply reflected opinions elaborated earlier. Most of the fragments are dated to the Severan period, although some refer to earlier jurisprudence, such as Ulpian's mention of Africanus, an early-second-century jurist (D. 48.5.14.1).[91] In the absence of any further evidence, we may suggest that the situations listed above become assimilated into the broader definition of adultery in or before the early second century, but that *accusatio adulterii* was granted only in the Severan period.

We cannot be sure if the cases described above were penalised as *stuprum* in the original *lex Iulia* – and whether the changes discussed by the Severan jurists should thus be interpreted as the new definition of an extant crime (recognised as *stuprum* and presumably punished in a more favourable manner)[92] – or if the expanded laws were intended to penalise acts which had not been forbidden in the original *lex*. The sources refer only to the moment when the solution was elaborated, but not to the previous state; we may, as Rizzelli observed, interpret this as evidence that such cases went unpunished at least before the second century.[93]

As Rizzelli claimed, the original definition of *stuprum* could not have been very broad.[94] His most important arguments are:

[90] Ankum, 'La *sponsa adultera*' (cit. n. 80), p. 189, claimed that although *accusatio iure extranei* against an infidel fiancée and her lover was granted by Septimius Severus and Caracalla, before a fiancé could accuse his fiancée of *stuprum*. Yet, Rizzelli, *Lex Iulia de adulteriis* (cit. n. 28), p. 205, noticed that such an assumption is not supported by the sources. See also J. Mélèze Modrzejewski, 'La fiancée adultère à propos de la pratique matrimoniale du judaisme hellénisé à la lumière du dossier du politeuma juif d'Hérakléopolis (144/3 – 133/2 avant n.è.)', [in:] Z. Służewska & J. Urbanik, *Marriage: Ideal – Law – Practice. Proceedings of a Conference Held in Memory of Henryk Kupiszewski in Warsaw on the 24th of April 2004* [= *The Journal of Juristic Papyrology Supplement* V], Warsaw 2005, pp. 141–160.

[91] As Rizzelli, *Lex Iulia de adulteriis* (cit. n. 28), p. 187, has rightly pointed out, the passage illustrates that Africanus was not the first one who posed a question whether *iniusta uxor* could be persecuted for adultery (*nam et Sextus Caecilius ait*), therefore, the accusation *iure extranei* in such cases had to be well-based at the beginning of the third century.

[92] Ankum, 'La *sponsa adultera*' (cit. n. 80), pp. 165–166.

[93] Rizzelli, *Lex Iulia de adulteriis* (cit. n. 28), pp. 216–217.

[94] The literature on *stuprum*, see in: Fayer, *La familia romana*. III (cit. n. 77), p. 216, n. 110.

1. The evidence for persecution of *stuprum* in the Augustan period is non-existent.[95] The sources do not refer to either an *accusatio stupri* or to penalties imposed on those who were found guilty of this crime.[96]

2. In the second century, the marriage of a tutor and his *pupilla* was penalised (in the *senatus consultum ad orationem divi Marci et Commodi*: D. 48.5.7 pr.). Interestingly, this union was recognised as adultery, even though it did not violate the idea of marriage or even any stable union resembling marriage. The same conclusion applies to the much later prohibition of marriages between Christians and Jews (*T.Ch.* 3.7.2 = *C.Th.* 9.7.5 = C. 1.9.6).[97]

3. The *lex Iulia de adulteriis coercendis* provided a point of reference for the creation of new sexual offences in regard to homosexual male relations, probably ignored in the original *lex Iulia*, but which contradict late classical and postclassical sources ascribed to this law – P.S. 2.26.12 and I. 4.18.4.[98] This suggests that jurists could add new offences easily to the *lex Iulia*.

4. Not all cases of extramarital sex were added to the *lex Iulia*. According to the discussed in Chapter 1 *senatus consultum Claudianum*, sex between a free woman and a slave was penalised by the woman being reduced to slavery unless the slave's master approved the union (G. 1.160, P.S. 2.21a.1). The rule was intended to protect property, rather than to prevent unmarried free women from having sex with slaves.[99] Sexual relationships with one's own slave were not penalised until Constantine (*C.Th.* 9.7.2).[100]

5. The *senatus consultum Tertulianum* allowed women to include illegitimate children when making up the number necessary to obtain *ius trium*

[95] Rizzelli's conclusions are further supported by Antti Arjava's studies, who noticed that information on the penalty on *stuprum* in classical period does not appear in the source material and even legal sources are inconsistent in regard thereto, as the penalty in P.S. 5.22.5 does not agree with P.S. 5.4.14 and *Coll.* 5.2.2: ARJAVA, *Women and Law* (cit. n. 3), p. 219.

[96] RIZZELLI, *Lex Iulia de adulteriis* (cit. n. 28), pp. 211–212.

[97] RIZZELLI, *Lex Iulia de adulteriis* (cit. n. 28), pp. 213–215.

[98] RIZZELLI, *Lex Iulia de adulteriis* (cit. n. 28), pp. 220–222; E. CANTARELLA, *Secondo natura. La bisessualita nel mondo antico*, Milan 2016, pp. 182–186.

[99] See, *i.a.*, B. SIRKS,'Der Zweck des *Senatus Consultum Claudianum* von 52 n. Chr.', *Zeitschrift der Savigny-Stiftung für Rechtsgeschichte RA* 122 (2005), pp. 138–149, pp. 145–149; A. KACPRZAK, '*Servus ex libera natus*. Überlegungen zum *senatusconsultum Claudianum*', [in:] D. FEICHTINGER & I. FISCHER (eds.), *Sexualität und Sklaverei* [= *Alter Orient und Altes Testament* CDLVI], pp. 63–82.

[100] RIZZELLI, *Lex Iulia de adulteriis* (cit. n. 28), pp. 226–231.

liberorum (D. 38.17.2.1: Ulp. *Sab.* 13). If all extramarital relationships were penalised, such provisions would be unlikely, as it is difficult to imagine that the result of a criminal offence could be used to obtain privilege in private law.[101]

6. When Constantine limited the right to bring *accusatio adulterii* to *proximae necessariaeque personae*, he did not make the same provisions for *accusatio stupri*, nor did he even mention it (*C.Th.* 9.7.2).[102]

Rizzelli's arguments suggest that *stuprum*, in its broadest sense, developed only in the course of the third century; it seems unlikely that the original *lex Iulia de adulteriis coercendis* penalised anything other than extramarital sex (as well as perhaps intercourse with virgins and with widows, to whom prohibition would have applied for only a short period after the death of their husband).[103] Yet, it is certain that both the imperial chancellery and jurists in late Principate extended the provisions of the original law to a significant degree. The question is to what extent these expanded provisions may have contributed to the social perceptions reflected in Constantine's laws on *naturales*. Yet before turning to this question, we must first examine other changes in Roman law pertaining to informal families in the classical period.

5.2. *Illegitimate children in the second-century jurisprudence*

Around the same time that the *lex Iulia* was being expanded, a series of privileges was granted to children born out of wedlock. The children of soldiers were given new rights concerning succession from fathers, while a series of enactments also strengthened the position of children regarding succession from their mothers, including children born out of wedlock.

At the beginning of his reign Hadrian issued a privilege allowing the children of soldiers to request *bonorum possessio* from their fathers in the class *unde cognati*, which is discussed in Chapter 2 (*infra*, p. 122).

[101] Rizzelli, *Lex Iulia de adulteriis* (cit. n. 28), p. 231.

[102] Rizzelli, *Lex Iulia de adulteriis* (cit. n. 28), p. 215.

[103] Rizzelli, *Lex Iulia de adulteriis* (cit. n. 28), pp. 262–267.

The *senatus consultum Tertullianum*, also dated to the reign of Hadrian, took further steps to improve the standing of informal families, allowing mothers with three or four children to claim *bonorum possessio unde legitimi* in the group of civil heirs. In practice they were still preceded by their grandchildren, their own (ex-)husbands, and sons.[104] It was nonetheless an improvement, as they had only previously been allowed to petition for *bonorum possessio* in the group *unde cognati*. Mothers were admitted regardless of whether or not the children had been conceived within marriage. A passage from Ulpian suggests that the enactment of the *senatus consultum Tertullianum* raised little controversy in the third century:

> D. 38.17.2 pr.–1 (Ulp. *Sab.* 13): Sive ingenua sit mater sive libertina, habebit Tertullianum commodum. 1. Filium autem vel filiam accipere debemus, sive iuste sint procreati vel vulgo quaesiti: idque in vulgo quaesitis et Iulianus libro quinquagesimo nono digestorum scripsit.
>
> No matter whether a mother is free-born or freed, she shall have a benefit of the Tertullian senate decree. 1. As a son or daughter we should, however, understand those who were begotten either legitimately or casually. And this Julian wrote about children begotten casually in the fifty-ninth book of the *digesta*.

Ulpian seems to have accepted Julian's definition without hesitation.[105] The rule granting mothers *bonorum possessio* from their *vulgo quaesiti* is repeated once in Justinian's *Institutes* (3.3.7).

In practical terms, mothers could petition *bonorum possessio* for the inheritance of their extramarital children, and if the children were childless there would be no one else who would qualify as *unde legitimi*. If the woman had grandchildren, she was preceded by them, regardless of the group under which they decided to claim *bonorum possessio*. The one exception was the mother of an extramarital son, who had his own extramarital offspring. In this case, according to the *senatus consultum Tertullianum*, the mother would be in a better position if she claimed *bonorum possessio unde legitimi*.

[104] P. Voci, *Diritto ereditario romano*, vol. II: *Parte speciale. Successione ab intesttato, successione testamentaria*, Milan 1963², pp. 18–21.

[105] M. Meinhart, *Die Senatusconsulta Tertullianum und Orfitianum in ihrer Bedeutung für das klassische römische Erbrecht*, Graz – Vienna – Cologne 1967, p. 41.

It was not only the mother who could inherit from her illegitimate offspring, but *spurii* siblings were also allowed to petition *bonorum possessio* from one another. This is expressed in the sixth book of Ulpian's *Regulae* D. 38.8.4, which states that no one is entitled to *hereditas* after *spurii* by *ius consanguinitatis* or *adgnationis*, as both of these derive from the *pater familias*, whom *spurii* do not have. He then states that a mother and maternal brother could petition *bonorum possessio* from a brother as next of kin, *proximitatis autem nomine*. While the fragment was preserved in the *Digest* under the title *Unde cognati* (38.8), it was, as Otto Lenel observed, originally a part of a commentary on *legitima hereditas*.[106] In this case the *bonorum possessio* appears to come from the edict itself.

The *senatus consultum* also informs us that *vulgo quaesiti* counted for *ius trium liberorum*. If this had not been the case, as mentioned in the previous section, it would not have been possible to admit their mothers to *bonorum possessio unde legitimi*. Whether counting extramarital children counted for *ius trium liberorum* since the time of Augustus or only after the *senatus consultum Tertullianum* is unclear.

While all children had the right to inherit from their mother, unless their mother was *in manu*, they could apply for *bonorum possessio* only in the group *unde cognati*; unless the mother had made a will appointing her children as heirs, their chances for maternal inheritance were meagre.[107] A fragment from Gaius' commentary on the provincial edict confirms that children born out of wedlock were also allowed to claim *bonorum possessio unde cognati* of *bona materna* (D. 38.16.8 pr.: G. *ed. prov.* 16). That this right is expressed separately suggests that it might have been granted to extramarital offspring only later; if this is correct, it is reasonable to assume that it happened at the reign of Hadrian.[108] This would suggest that the admission, and the *senatus consultum* itself, belonged to series of second-century

[106] O. Lenel, *Palingenesia iuris civilis. Iuris consultorum reliquiae quae Iustiniani Digestis continentur ceteraque iurisprudentiae civilis fragmenta minora secundum auctores et libros*, Leipzig 1889 (reprint: Graz 1960), col. 1015.

[107] Voci, *Diritto ereditario*. II (cit. n. 104), p. 22.

[108] Meinhart argued that *vulgo quaesiti* were discussed as entitled to claim *bonorum possessio unde cognati* already in Julian's *digesta*: Meinhart, *Die Senatusconsulta* (cit. n. 105), pp. 41–43.

legal measures designed to acknowledge the blood-ties between family members who were not agnates.[109]

A significant change in maternal succession was enacted in AD 178 as part of the *senatus consultum Orfitianum*. This *senatus consultum* admitted children to intestate succession from their mothers, regardless of whether they were conceived in a single marriage or different ones (D. 38.17.4: Modest. *reg.* 9) and regardless of whether they were under the power of their fathers, emancipated or given into adoption.[110] Children were placed into the class *unde legitimi*, and thus became civil heirs, which was the first class of women's heirs, since women, unable to hold *patria potestas*, had no *sui heredes*. Children preceded *agnates*, including maternal grandfathers[111] or the mother's patrons (*Tit. Ulp.* 26.7); under the *senatus consultum Orfitianum* they were the first to inherit from their mothers, and the previous order was respected so long as none of children petitioned *bonorum possessio* (D. 38.17.1.9: Ulp. *Sab.* 12).[112]

Some groups of people recognised as socially stigmatised were excluded from the original text of the *senatus consultum*, notably *rei capitalis damnatus* and *bestiarius* (D. 38.17.1.6: Ulp. *Sab.* 12).[113] The sources discussing the *senatus consultum*, however, leave us in no doubt that children born out of wedlock were not excluded from succession, but were rather included in the group *unde legitimi* (D. 38.17.1.2: Ulp. *Sab.* 12; P.S. 4.10.1, I. 3.4.3.). This was an obvious amelioration of their standing as previously, under the system built on agnatic relations, they had had few chances to inherit from anyone, except in a will.[114]

Ulpian, who also participated in the discussion on the extension of *adulterium*, informs us that, under the *senatus consultum Orfitianum*, *vulgo quaesiti* should be admitted to succession after their mothers.

[109] Treggiari, *Roman Marriage* (cit. n. 73), p. 31.

[110] Voci, *Diritto ereditario*. II (cit. n. 104), p. 22.

[111] Voci, *Diritto ereditario*. II (cit. n. 104), p. 24. See the discussion in: Meinhart, *Die Senatusconsulta* (cit. n. 105), pp. 297–302.

[112] See J. Gardner, *Family and Familia in Roman Law and Life*, Oxford 1999, p. 231.

[113] Prostitutes and pimps might have been excluded too: T. McGinn, *Prostitution, Sexuality, and the Law in Ancient Rome*, Oxford 2003, pp. 111–112.

[114] Meinhart, *Die Senatusconsulta* (cit. n. 105), p. 39.

D. 38.17.1.2: Sed et vulgo quaesiti admittuntur ad matris legitimam hereditatem.

Also children begotten casually are admitted to the legitimate succession after their mothers.

For Ulpian, *vulgo quaesiti* referred to all children begotten out of wedlock, not only to children born of quasi marital relations.[115] The rule is repeated in *Pauli Sententiae* (4.10.1) and Justinian's *Institutes* (3.4.3). Exceptions to the *senatus consultum* appeared only in the time of Constantine (in *C.Th.* 9.9.1, discussed above), which excluded children born of a free mother and her slave from succession after the mother.[116]

One of the preserved fragments of Ulpian includes the rule allowing *spurii* to bring *querella inofficiosi testamenti* against their mother's will, D.5.2.29.1 (Ulp. *opinio.* 5): *De inofficioso testamento matris spurii quoque filii dicere possunt* – 'Also sons of Spurius are entitled to bring an action regarding undutiful will of their mother'. It would seem that the obligation of the mother to leave *portio debita* to her children predates the *senatus consultum Orfitianum*.[117] The *senatus consultum*, however, changed the situation so that both legitimate children and those born out of wedlock, as *bonorum possessores unde legi-*

[115] Luchetti, *Legittimazione dei figli naturali* (cit. n. 11), p. 12.

[116] The next limitation was introduced only later in a constitution of Justinian (C. 6.57.5 pr.–1). The prohibition of transferring property to *spurii*, if there were legitimate children, is probably an invention of Justinian pertaining only to a *mulier illustris*, a woman of the senatorial rank, of whom Justinian expected a special level of chastity: Meinhart, *Die Senatusconsulta* (cit. n. 105), pp. 141–142. The question remains whether the prohibition applied to all children produced out of *iustae nuptiae* or only those of unions recognised as illicit under Byzantine law, *nefariae* or incestuous; the latter appears to be confirmed by the second part of the constitution (C. 6.57.5.2) which points out that children begotten in *concubinatus* are admitted to the maternal inheritance together with legitimate children. The interpretation could be restricted even further, as the prohibition was imposed on children born to *mulier illustris*, thus women married to men of senatorial rank: A. Chastagnol, 'Les femmes dans l'ordre sénatorial : titulature et rang social à Rome', *Revue historique* 262 (1979), pp. 3–28, pp. 27–28. It could signify that the prohibition applied to children born to married women, but conceived outside of their marriages. Although such a narrow interpretation is uncertain, it is nonetheless possible. Yet, the law itself suggests that only Justinian questioned the equality of legitimate and illegitimate children in succession *ab intestato*.

[117] Voci, *Diritto ereditario*. II (cit. n. 104), pp. 671–672.

timi, were always entitled to the maternal inheritance and could thus bring *querella inofficiosi testamenti* if skipped by their mother in her will.

5.3. *Conclusion*

At some point during the second and third centuries, both the jurists and the imperial chancellery started to introduce measures to equalise the situations of formal and informal families. Male partners obtained a means of prosecuting the infidelity of their life partners, which could suggest that such deeds had started to be perceived as similar to marital infidelity. This in turn suggests that legitimate marriages and informal but stable monogamous unions would not have been so different in terms of social perception. Jurists also provided the children of such unions with some safeguards concerning their hereditary rights: for maternal inheritance, extramarital children were given the same legal provisions as those available to legitimate children. This could suggest that the distinction between formal and informal families had become blurred. As the cases discussed in previous chapters demonstrate, this tendency in the second- and third-century Roman law could have been a reaction to the needs of society. In Egypt at least, there does not appear to have been any difference between children begotten in legitimate unions and by unwedded parents, even those who were forbidden from marrying one another.

5.4. *The lex Iulia de adulteriis in legal practice*

Echoes of the *lex Iulia de adulteriis* can be found in sources pertaining to every-day life, but the evidence of its application is problematic.[118] If the Augustan law on adulteries had not been applied in any widespread way, it would be difficult to explain the extensive jurisprudential discussion summarised above. Yet evidence for adultery trials is meagre. Some cases are preserved in Tacitus and Suetonius, but they concern the higher strata

[118] Arjava, *Women and Law* (cit. n. 3), pp. 219–220.

of the society.[119] Other Roman writers noted cases in which adultery was punished as exceptional.[120] Papyrological attestations of the prosecution of adultery or other sexual misconducts are rare and late.[121]

The low number of papyrological attestations could be accidental, but it might also be due to the fact that deeds of sexual misconducts were managed within financial and contractual frameworks which left little space for public prosecution. In Greek marriage contracts from the early Hellenistic period in Egypt it was not uncommon to have prohibitions against having sexual intercourse with another man, bringing shame on a husband by committing deeds that generally bring shame on husbands, or ruining the common household.[122] In early Greek contracts, a wife who violated these contractual provisions ran the risk of losing her dowry. As the sanction was financial and enforced in private law, it was not subject to public accusation.

Hans Julius Wolff recognised the imposition of financial liability on spouses as a Greek import.[123] Yet he also noticed that Hellenistic marriage contracts composed in Greek must have been influenced by Egyptian law.[124] In pre-Hellenistic and Hellenistic marital deeds written in Egyptian scripts, we find similar clauses stipulating financial liability in the case of infidelity and other mistreatments. As a rule, a wife was free to divorce her husband, and a husband was free to divorce his wife, but such actions could be subject to private compensation, paid either in money or goods, and imposed mostly on husbands.[125] Pieter Pestman pointed out that in

[119] See the list of adultery prosecutions in: TREGGIARI, *Roman Marriage* (cit. n. 73), pp. 509–510.

[120] Cassius Dio reported 3000 accusations of the *lex Iulia de adulteriis* in the reign of Septimius Severus (Dio 67.12.1; 77.16.4; 78.16.4): ARJAVA, *Women and Law* (cit. n. 3), p. 194.

[121] J. BEAUCAMP, *Le statut de la femme à Byzance (4ᵉ–7ᵉ siècle)*, vol. II: *Les pratiques sociales*, Paris 1992, pp. 79–82.

[122] U. YIFTACH-FIRANKO, *Marriage and Marital Arrangements: A History of the Greek Marriage Document in Egypt. 4th Century* BCE – *4th Century* CE [= *Münchener Beiträge zur Papyrusforschung und antiken Rechtsgeschichte* XCIII], Munich 2003, p. 191.

[123] H.J. WOLFF, *Written and Unwritten Marriages in Hellenistic and Postclassical Roman Law* [= *American Philological Association Philological Monographs* IX], Haverford, PA 1939, p. 77.

[124] WOLFF, *Written and Unwritten Marriages* (cit. n. 123), p. 33.

[125] P.W. PESTMAN, *Marriage and Matrimonial Property in Ancient Egypt: A Contribution to Establishing the Legal Position of the Woman*, Leiden 1961, pp. 155–160.

some Egyptian documents from before the Hellenistic period we find stipulations allowing a husband to repudiate his wife without any financial consequences if the repudiation was the result of her adultery.[126] Sandra Lippert noted that pre-Demotic marital agreements contained a clause that the woman would forfeit her dowry and compensation in the event of her infidelity. Such clauses are no longer present in Demotic settlements, perhaps because the liability of the wife was already enforced *ex lege* and there would have been no need to include it in the marriage contract.[127]

The idea that adultery was traditionally covered under private contracts is further supported by a group of temple oaths. One example is *PSI* I 64 (Oxyrhynchos, 2nd–1st c. BC), a Greek oath taken by Thais towards her husband. Thais declared that she had not been with another man in the female way, had not prepared love charms, put poisons into her partner's food and drinks, and had not conspired with anyone against him (ll. 18–22).[128] The document does not mention a dowry, but it does attest a loan which the woman owed to her spouse. The aim of this loan was to prevent her from leaving her husband without just cause; if she did, the money would go to her husband.[129] The document seems to demonstrate that the aim of the marital agreement, arranged after some turbulence between the spouses, was to prevent similar events from occurring in future. This can be deduced from the detailed and atypical prohibitions imposed upon the wife.[130] In this instance, the marital problems were solved without the involvement of authorities, despite the wife's infidelity and other misconducts. Demotic oaths taken by wives prove the same point: in Egyptian legal practice, a husband with doubts about his wife's fidelity could oblige her to take an oath that she had not had sexual relations with anyone else during their marriage. Temple oaths regarding infidelity and embezzlement of the husband's property were standard features

[126] PESTMAN, *Marriage and Matrimonial Property* (cit. n. 125), p. 56.

[127] S. LIPPERT, *Einführung in die altägyptische Rechtsgeschichte* [= *Einführungen und Quellentexte zur Ägyptologie* V], Münster 2012², pp. 123–124 & 167.

[128] YIFTACH-FIRANKO, *Marriage and Marital Arrangements* (cit. n. 122), pp. 192–193.

[129] YIFTACH-FIRANKO, *Marriage and Marital Arrangements* (cit. n. 122), pp. 193–194.

[130] YIFTACH-FIRANKO, *Marriage and Marital Arrangements* (cit. n. 122), pp. 194–195.

of divorce proceedings:[131] if the wife refused to take an oath, she was considered guilty of adultery[132] which, as we know from marriage contracts, would result in financial consequences. Yet, if she took the oath, the accusation was considered false and the husband was liable for a penalty.[133]

Although the sanctions imposed on spouses started to vanish during the late Ptolemaic period – they are absent from the second-century BC *P. Gen.* I 21[134] – they reappear in agreements from late Hellenistic and Roman periods.[135] In Greek Alexandrian marriage *synchoreseis* dated to the reign of Augustus, prohibitions are present as a regular provision.[136] This may explain why the *lex Iulia de adulteriis* had no real application in Egyptian social life. The Julian law was directed primarily against adulteries committed by Roman women, and it is difficult to believe that it would have been implemented in a society in which such accusations were left to individuals especially that there were no officials to bring such cases to the courtroom. There are, moreover, no sources to support the idea that the *lex Iulia* was applied widely in Roman Egypt. Cases of sexual misconduct were managed within the family and limited to marital infidelity.

There is, however, one source which suggests that wives and informal partners were treated equally when it came to the prosecution of infidel-

[131] U. KAPLONY-HECKEL, *Die demotischen Tempeleide*, Wiesbaden 1963, nos. 1, 5, 6, 7, 8, 9, 10, 11, 12, 13 (?), 14. This reference as well as the problem are known to me thanks to Sandra Lippert.

[132] PESTMAN, *Marriage and Matrimonial Property* (cit. n. 125), p. 56.

[133] PESTMAN, *Marriage and Matrimonial Property* (cit. n. 125), p. 56.

[134] YIFTACH-FIRANKO, *Marriage and Marital Arrangements* (cit. n. 122), p. 201.

[135] Collected by YIFTACH-FIRANKO, *Marriage and Marital Arrangements* (cit. n. 122), pp. 312–317: *P. Tebt.* I 104 = *M. Chr.* 285 = *Sel. Pap.* I 2 = *C. Pap. Hengstl* 72 (92 BC), ll. 27–30; *P. Freib.* III 30 (Philadelphia, 179 BC), ll. 19–20; *P. Münch.* III 62 (provenance unknown, 2nd c. BC), ll. 9–13; *P. Giss.* 2 = *C. Ptol. Sklav.* I 55 (Krokodilopolis, 173 BC), ll. 27–28; *P. Tebt.* III.2 974 (Tebtynis, 2nd c. BC), ll. 9–10; Alexandria: *BGU* IV 1050 = *M. Chr.* 286 = *Jur. Pap.* 19 (Augustean period), ll. 19–23; 1051 (Augustean period), ll. 28–31; 1052 (13 BC), ll. 22–29; 1098 (19–15 BC), ll. 32–39; 1101 (Augustean period), ll. 14–17; *SB* XXIV 16073 (12 BC), l. 29; Roman Oxyrhynchos: *P. Oxy.* II 372 = *SB* XXVIII 17045 (AD 74/5), ll. 11–13; III 497 (2nd c. AD), ll. 3–4; 604 (2nd c. AD), ll. 9–10. See also I. ARNAOUTOGLOU, 'Marital disputes in Greco-Roman Egypt', *The Journal of Juristic Papyrology* 25 (1995), pp. 11–28, p. 18, n. 10.

[136] ARNAOUTOGLOU, 'Marital disputes' (cit. n. 135), p. 18.

BGU IV 1050 (11–10 BC), ll. 23–24; 1051 (30 BC – AD 14), ll. 32–35; 1052 (14–13 BC), ll. 29–33; 1098 (19–15 BC), ll. 39–40; 1101 (13 BC), ll. 17–18.

ity. It consists of two abstracts of court proceedings belonging to a papyrus codex published as *BGU* IV 1024–1027 (re-published as *P. Aktenbuch*)[137] and dated to the second half of the fourth century.[138] The codex consists of various texts – seven abstracts of court proceedings, receipts for the *annona militaris*, lists, magic texts, and an official note from Flavius Domitius Asclepiades, *praeses Thebaidis* – written in five different hands.[139]

The abstracts of process proceedings were all written in the same hand,[140] and are based on a common pattern: a short description of the case 'against someone who...' followed by the decision of the *hegemon* – most probably the prefect – who seems to have possessed *ius gladii* and could condemn citizens *in metallum*;[141] the latter begin with 'the hegemon said' and are given in *oratio recta*. Each of the recorded cases are related to some form of moral turpitude and social scandal: the exhumation of a human body, the marriage of a soldier to both a mother and a daughter, the theft of someone's jewellery from his head, and the killing of a prostitute by a member of the Alexandrian council. The two cases of interest to us are also anecdotal, they concern one man who killed his wife after catching her with a lover (p. 3, ll. 11–30) and another who killed his lover having caught her with another man (p. 4, l. 18 – p. 5, l. 7).

The case of the unfaithful wife killed by her husband is not fully preserved and the decision of the *hegemon* does not survive. James Keenan observed that the case refers to a problem discussed in the Roman legal sources,[142] the *ius occidendi* of a betrayed husband who has caught his wife *in flagrante*. Under Roman law, the husband's right of *ius occidendi* was lim-

[137] G. Poethke, S. Prignitz & V. Vaelske (eds.), *Das Aktenbuch des Aurelios Philammon. Prozeßberichte, Annona Militaris und Magie in BGU IV 1024–1027* [= *Archiv für Papyrusforschung Beiheft* 34], Berlin 2012.

[138] See *P. Aktenbuch*, pp. 10–11.

[139] The physical description and reconstruction of the physical appearance of the code in: *P. Aktenbuch*, pp. 3–8.

[140] *P. Aktenbuch*, pp. 17–18.

[141] D. 1.18.6.8 (Ulp. *opinio.* 1): P. Garnsey, 'The criminal jurisdiction of governors', *The Journal of Roman Studies* 58.1–2 (1968), pp. 51–59, p. 51.

[142] J. Keenan, 'Roman criminal law in a Berlin papyrus codex (*BGU* IV 1024–1027)', *Archiv für Papyrusforschung* 35 (1989), pp. 15–23, p. 18.

ited to killing his wife's lover – although not his wife (*Coll.* 4.10.1: Pap.)[143] – and even then only if the lover was caught in the husband's own house and belonged to a certain category of person.[144] If any of these conditions were not met, the husband was prosecuted for a regular homicide.[145] Yet in the imperial interpretation of the *lex Iulia* – from the period between Antoninus Pius and Alexander Severus, thus chronologically parallel to the passages on accusing non-wives with *accusatio adulterii* discussed above – there is a tendency to be more lenient in punishing husbands who transgressed the limits of *ius occidendi*, as the husband's anger was justified and sane (*iustus dolor*, *honestus calor*). This applied not only to killing a lover, but also a wife (D. 48.5.39.8: Pap. *quaest.* 36; 48.8.1.5: Marcel. *inst.* 14; 29.5.3.3: Ulp. *ad ed.* 50; *Coll.* 4.12.4: Paul.; 4.10.1: Pap.).[146]

The case of the man who killed his lover (φίλη) because he loved her too much (p. 4, l. 18 – p. 5, l. 7) seems to refer to the same discussion. The man killed his mistress with a sword after finding her with another man because he could not restrain his anger or passion (ὀργή). He escaped, but eventually returned to his lover's grave to mourn her. The *hegemon* declared the man *ad metallum*, claiming the murder had been committed under the influence of strong passion and anger. Both the punishment and its justification resemble the imperial interpretation of the *lex Iulia*. In the passage ascribed to Papinian referring to a ruling of Marcus Aurelius and Commodus (D. 48.5.39.8), the husband, *cum sit difficillimum iustum dolorem temperare*, should be punished, but it is sufficient *si humilis loci sit, in opus perpetuum eum tradi, si qui honestior, in insulam relegari*.[147] The cases discussed in Roman jurisprudence naturally concerned the killing of *legitima uxor*. However if we interpret the text in *P. Aktenbuch* in light of the previously discussed passages illustrating the assimilation of marriage and marriage-like rela-

[143] Fayer, *La familia romana.* III (cit. n. 77), p. 246.

[144] Slaves, freedmen belonging to either the husband's or wife's or her immediate agnates' family, men condemned in public prosecution, actors, dancers, singers, gladiators and *bestiarii*, prostitutes, pimps. See sources in: Fayer, *La familia romana.* III (cit. n. 77), pp. 248–249.

[145] For other conditions which justified *ius occidendi*, see Fayer, *La familia romana.* III (cit. n. 77), p. 250.

[146] Rizzelli, *Lex Iulia de adulteriis* (cit. n. 28), pp. 12–13.

[147] See also D. 48.8.1.5, *Coll.* 4.10.1.

tions in terms of prosecuting female infidelity, it makes perfect sense. Whoever the author of these texts may have been, they were clearly at least aware of the discussion concerning the notion of *adulterium*, and the imperial lenience towards husbands who abused *ius occidendi*. The final case in the codex, concerning the killing of a prostitute, was dated by Nikoletta Kanavou and Amphilochios Papathomas (p. 6, l. 3 – p. 8, l. 21) to the early third century.[148] If the other cases were written around the same time and copied to the codex only later, it would make them contemporary with the discussion on the *lex Iulia de adulteriis*.

The question is whether these two cases offer any clues regarding the application of the *lex Iulia de adulteriis coercendis*; sadly it seems clear that they had nothing to do with actual court proceedings.[149] This was argued by Kanavou and Papathomas who compared the cases to the accounts of trials found in Greek novels[150] and other literary works, including rhetoric.[151] The anecdotal subjects, narration of emotions, literary *topoi*, and lack of any reference to real laws suggest that the cases belong to this type of literature. As such they were unrelated to the administration of justice, but served perhaps as amusement and may also have been used in the education of future or active rhetors.[152] This, however, makes the cases in *P. Aktenbuch* even more important as evidence, as it suggests that the jurisprudential discussion on adultery had found its way into popular literature. While the sources attesting the extended definition of *adulterium* to non-marital infidelity are absent, it is clear that the notion of marriage itself was not strict in Roman Egypt. We will return to this point at the end of this chapter.

[148] N. Kanavou & A. Papathomas, 'An Alexandrian murder case revisited (*P. Philammon* = *BGU* IV 1024, pp. 6.3–8.21)', *Zeitschrift für Papyrologie und Epigraphik* 200 (2016), pp. 453–469, p. 458.

[149] Yet, scholars interpreted them as a quasi-literary sources, 'salomonische Sentenzen', belonging to the chancellery of the *praeses Thebaidis* serving him as an aid in his justice-related tasks, *i.e.* when he acted as a judge, or even real-life cases. On the interpretations, see *P. Aktenbuch*, pp. 21–22 and *passim*.

[150] Kanavou & Papathomas, 'An Alexandrian murder case' (cit. n. 148), pp. 461–465.

[151] Kanavou & Papathomas, 'An Alexandrian murder case' (cit. n. 148), pp. 464–466.

[152] Kanavou & Papathomas, 'An Alexandrian murder case' (cit. n. 148), p. 467.

5.5. *Extramarital children in legal practice*

The papyrological evidence for children born out of wedlock is more satisfying than that concerning the *lex Iulia de adulteriis*. The papyri attest that the privileges acquired by children born out of wedlock were applied in legal practice, but they also demonstrate that neither children of stable non-marital unions, nor those labelled openly as fatherless, suffered from any social stigma until late third century, the point at which they disappeared from the papyrological record.

In the papyri, we find some attestations of the hereditary right given by Roman emperors to offspring born out of wedlock. One example is a petition dated to AD 225 concerning the appointment of a tutor (preserved in three copies: A and B published as *P. Harr.* I 68, C published as *P. Diog.* 18). Marcus Lucretius Diogenes, Roman citizen, petitioned the *strategos* to appoint him as a guardian for his two nephews, the infant sons of his deceased sister. According to the text, the applicant's sister, Octavia Lucretia, died intestate leaving her three sons Marci Aurelii Iulias, Lucretius and Rufus as heirs.

> ll. 7–9: *τ̣[ῷ] δι̣[ε]λ̣ηλυθότι μ̣ηνὶ Φαῶφι̣ ἡ ἀδε̣λ̣φή μου Ὀκτ̣αου|ία̣ Λο̣υ̣κρητία ⟨ἐτελεύτησεν⟩ ἀδιάθετος ἐπὶ κληρονόμοις τρισὶν υἱοῖς ἐκ διαφόρ[ων] γ̣ά[μ]ων, Μάρκοις Αὐρηλίοις Ἰου̣λιᾷ̣ καὶ̣ Λουκρη|τ̣ί̣ῳ κ̣α̣ὶ̣ Ῥούφῳ̣ ἀφῆλιξι.*
>
> In the past month Phaophi, my sister, Octavia Lucretia, died without a will (leaving) as heirs three sons of different unions – Marci Aurelii Iulias, and Lucretius and Rufus – minors.

When the petition was issued one of the boys, Marcus Aurelius Iulias, was already under the power of his father and had thus acquired his share of the inheritance.[153] The other two had no legal representatives: one was 'fatherless' and another had lost his father, *P. Diog.* 18, ll. 10–11: *ὁ μὲ[ν] Λ̣ο̣υκρ̣ήτιος ἀπάτωρ̣ τυγχάν̣⟨ε⟩ι, τοῦ δὲ Ῥούφου ὁ πα̣τ̣ὴρ̣ ἐτελεύτησεν.* Marcus Aurelius Iulias was undoubtedly born in *iustae nuptiae*, otherwise he could not have been

[153] ll. 9–10: *ὁ μὲν οὖν εἷς αὐτῶν Ἰουλιᾶς ὑποχείριος ὢν [τ]ῷ̣ ἰ̣δ̣ίῳ̣ πατρὶ Μάρκ[ῳ̣] Αὐ̣ρηλίῳ̣ Ἥρωνι ἀπίληφεν* (l. *ἀπείληφεν*) | *τὸ̣ ἐ̣π̣ι̣βάλλον αὐτῷ̣ μέρος ⟨τῶν⟩ ἀπολελιμμένων* (l. *ἀπολελειμμένων*). – one of them, Iulias being under the power of his father, Marcus Aurelius Heron, received a part of the things left belonging to him.

under *patria potestas*. The status of Lucretius and Rufus is more problematic. Lucretius is described as ἀπάτωρ, although the description is used here not as substitute for the filiation, but as a *terminus technicus*. As illustrated in Chapter 1 of this book, ἀπάτωρ could be used as the counterpart of *spurius* or *spurii filius* in the context of Roman law. The description could therefore mean that Lucretius was either genuinely fatherless, or that he had been fathered by a man who could not legally be a father, *e.g.* a slave, or the informal Roman partner of his mother. The actual status of Lucretius would not have mattered for the petition, and the world ἀπάτωρ would only have been included to explain why the boy needed a guardian. If ἀπάτωρ was applied here in its broadest meaning, it would imply that Rufus, who is described neither as ἀπάτωρ nor with a similar label, was born of *iustae nuptiae*, which terminated at the death of his father.

The onomastics, however, are disturbing. All three boys were named Marcus Aurelius, which would imply that Lucretius and perhaps Rufus had the *nomina* of their step-father. Lucretius, as ἀπάτωρ, should have taken his after his mother, while Rufus should have been named after his father. His father, of course, might also have been named Marcus Aurelius: after the *constitutio Antoniniana* the name was given to many new Romans of higher standing in Egypt, while others simply became Aurelius without *praenomen*.[154] Yet if this was not the case, all three boys would have had the *gentilicium* of their mother's husband, Marcus Aurelius Heron, which would suggest that Rufus was also extramarital: his father might not have wanted to (or been able to) be associated with his son by giving him his names, even if the relationship was known. Octavia Lucretia may thus have had three sons arising from three different situations: Lucretius was casually conceived, Rufus with an informal partner, and finally Iulias with her formal husband. The three sons are, however, described ἐκ διαφόρ[ων] γ̣ά[μ]ων. If there is no differentiation in the type of union it may be because, as Herbert Youtie noted when commenting on the text, there was no clear distinction between marriage and non-marital unions in Egypt.[155]

[154] D. Hagedorn, 'Marci Aurelii in Ägypten nach der Constitutio Antoniniana', *The Bulletin of the American Society of Papyrologists* 16 (1979), pp. 47–59.

[155] H. Youtie, 'Ἀπάτορες. Law vs. custom in Roman Egypt', [in:] J. Bingen, G. Cambier & G. Nachtergael (eds.), *Le monde grec : pensée, littérature, histoire, documents. Hommages à*

This petition could be viewed as evidence that the *senatus consultum Orfitianum* worked for children born out of wedlock in Egypt,[156] even if they applied together with legitimate children. Yet, the text does not mention the grounds for which the sons were entitled to inherit from their mother. As mentioned earlier in this chapter, extramarital children had the right to petition the possession of maternal property in the group *unde cognati* at least since the time of Hadrian. Yet it is possible that people were convinced that children could acquire the inheritance of their mother, regardless of the circumstances of their conception, as this was simply the way things worked in the province.

Indeed, for peregrines in Egypt the ruling of the *senatus consultum Orfitianum* was hardly a novel concept. If cases where succession is not restricted by the artificial concept of kinship, as it was in Roman law, children are usually their mothers' heirs before anyone else. This is how succession worked in Egypt:[157] children were first to inherit from their mothers regardless of whether or not they were born out of wedlock. That the rule applied to fatherless individuals is confirmed in *PSI* XV 1532 (Oxyrhynchos, AD 100–117), which was discussed in detail in Chapter 1. The text states that a man acquired inheritance from his brother, Thonis, who is described, ll. 13–15: χ[ρη]|ματίζοντος μητρ̣[ὸς] | τῆς αὐτῆς. The document illustrates that siblings of the same mother were entitled to inherit from one another, even if one or both of them were born out of wedlock. The papyrus offers strong grounds for an argument *a fortiori*: if extramarital siblings born of the same mother were entitled to intestate succession after one another, and if children were primary heirs of their mothers, it is more than likely that fatherless children were first to succeed their mothers.

Claire Préaux, Brussels 1975, pp. 723–740 [reprinted in: *Scriptiunculae posteriores*, vol. I, Bonn 1981, pp. 17–35], p. 728.

The problem is further developed at the end of this chapter.

[156] An example of the actual application for the *bonorum possessio* according to the *senatus consultum Orfitianum* is *SB* I 1010 + *SB* VI 9298 = *Jur. Pap.* 27 = *FIRA* III 61 = *CPL* 216 = *Ch. L. A.* XI 486; perhaps *P. Oxy.* VIII 1114 = *Sel. Pap.* II 326 = *Ch. L. A.* III 216 = *FIRA* III 63 = *CPL* 217; *P. Bagnall* 3 = *Ch. L. A.* XLVII 1442 *descr.* See E. Volterra, 'Il senatoconsulto Orfiziano e la sua applicazione in documenti egiziani del III secolo d.C.', [in:] *Atti dell'XI Congresso Internazionale di Papirologia, Milano, 2–8 settembre 1965*, Milan 1966, pp. 551–585.

[157] H. Kreller, *Erbrechtliche Untersuchungen auf Grund der graeco-ägyptischen Papyrusurkunden*, Leipzig – Berlin 1919, p. 142; R. Taubenschlag, *The Law of Greco-Roman Egypt in the Light of the Papyri. 332 BC – 640 AD*, Warsaw 1955², p. 184.

This is further supported by the rules in the *Gnomon of idios logos*, discussed in the previous chapter, which illustrate the strong (although not absolute) tendency to provide children with the maternal inheritance, even if they were not entitled to the maternal status. In these circumstances, the *senatus consultum Orfitianum* would cover only social practice. It does not need to be proved that the privileges provided for the children of soldiers were applied in Egypt, as Hadrian's decree that the children of soldiers should be classified *unde cognati* has survived in the papyri (*supra*, p. 122).

In documents dated to late second and first half of the third century, people described as ἀπάτωρ and χρηματίζων μητρός are attested as holding functions such as *presbyteroi*,[158] *archephodoi*,[159] tax collectors,[160] *etc.*,[161] which suggests a relatively high social and financial standing. This is in line with the jurisprudential sources, which note that *spurii* should not be excluded from *ordo decurionis*, and could be admitted as members of local councils selected from along the *honestiores*, the local elites.[162] This is confirmed by two passages preserved in the *Digest* – one ascribed to Ulpian, the other to Papinian. The former, D. 50.2.3.2 (Ulp. *de off. procons.* 3), says: *Spurios posse in ordinem allegi nulla dubitatio est*, 'there is no doubt that *spurii* could be selected to the order'. Ulpian then explains that if they were in competition with legitimate offspring, the latter should take precedence. He quotes as his source a rescript by the emperors Marcus Aurelius and Lucius Verus.[163]

[158] *SB* XIV 11932, l. 4 = no. 680 (Kanopias, AD 143–208); *P. Oxy*. XVII 2121, l. 13 = no. 683 (Athenas Kome, AD 175–210); *P. Fay.* 39, ll. 5–6 = no. 567 (Theadelphia, AD 183); *P. Gen.* I² 41, ll. 2–3 = no. 676 (Philadelphia, AD 223); Soknopaiou Nesos, 3rd c. AD: *SPP* XXII 52, l. 9 = no. 671; *P. Lond.* II 199, p. 158, l. 3 = no. 657.

[159] *P. Oxy.* I 80, ll. 9–11 = no. 196 (Senokomeis, AD 238–244); *SB* XVI 12494, ll. 4–5 = no. 399 (Seryphis, AD 222–225).

[160] Oxyrhynchos: *P. Oxy.* XLIII 3097, ll. 4–5 = no. 186 (AD 224–225); III 514 = no. 387, l. 1 (AD 190–191); *SPP* XXII 6, l. 3 = no. 675 (Karanis, AD 204–205); *P. Ryl.* II 91, l. 6 = no. 484 (Euhemeria, AD 200–225); *P. Louvre* I 46, ll. 28, 49, 71, 84 = no. 690 (Soknopaiou Nesos, AD 220).

[161] Malouta collected all occupations and liturgical professions held by the fatherless: MALOUTA, 'Fatherlessness' (cit. n. 33), pp. 126–128.

[162] C. GIZEWSKI & J.B. CAMPBELL, 'Decurio, Decuriones', [in:] H. CANCIK & H. SCHNEIDER (eds.), *Brill's New Pauly*, doi:http://dx.doi.org/10.1163/1574-9347_bnp_e312510.

[163] S. CORCORAN, 'The sins of the fathers. A neglected constitution of Diocletian on incest', *The Journal of Legal History* 21.2 (2000), pp. 1–34, p. 6.

D. 50.2.3.2 (Ulp. *de off. procons.* 3): Spurios posse in ordinem allegi nulla dubitatio est: sed si habeat competitorem legitime quaesitum, praeferri eum oportet, divi fratres Lolliano Avito Bithyniae praesidi rescripserunt. Cessantibus vero his etiam spurii ad decurionatum et re et vita honesta recipientur: quod utique non sordi erit ordini, cum ex utilitate eius sit semper ordinem plenum habere.

There is no doubt that *spurii* could be selected for the order, but deified brothers responded to Lollianus Avitus, *praeses* of Bithynia, in a rescript: if he had a legitimately conceived competitor, he should be preferred. If those, however, neglect, *spurii* of honest conduct and life will be admitted: so that it will not spoil the order, for it is for its welfare to have the order always full.

The text of Papinian goes even further, explaining that the rule applied also to those born as a result of incest.

D. 50.2.6 pr. (Pap. *resp.* 1): Spurii decuriones fiunt: et ideo fieri poterit ex incesto quoque natus: non enim impedienda est dignitas eius qui nihil admisit.

Spurii become decurions; and the same shall be possible even for someone born of incest, as a dignity of this who committed nothing should not be hindered.

It is worth noting that these passages ascribed to Papinian and Ulpian would have been composed before the rank of *decurio* had become little more than a burden. Ulpian refers to an even earlier source for his opinion, a rescript of Marcus Aurelius and Lucius Verus (AD 161–169).

Perhaps the greatest proof that fatherless individuals were not stigmatised is the fact that not only did they hold offices and play important roles in their communities, but they were openly described – and self-described – as 'fatherless'. This is important to note as neither ἀπάτωρ nor χρηματίζων μητρός were formal descriptions, so using them was a matter of individual choice either by the author of the document or the described individual (*supra*, pp. 258–263). As mentioned in Chapter 1, direct descriptions were used not only in official κατ' ἄνδρα reports, but also in private deeds, such as contracts or petitions.[164] This pattern of application did not change in late second and third centuries, and the terms continued to be used in private documents in the third century. Furthermore, the same person could be described both with a term referring directly to extramarital birth, as well as with other descriptive terms, such as *μητρός*, which did not make explicit reference to their fatherless status; this would offer additional confirmation that the application of labels was a matter of choice, and would not have been recognised as shameful.[165]

[164] A few examples: *BGU* II 663, ll. 3–4: Priskos *ἀπάτωρ* (no. 674) petitioning a strategos *ca.* AD 203; *P. Oxy.* XVII 2131 = *Sel. Pap.* II 290, l. 3: Totoes *χρηματίζων μητρός* (no. 398) proving to be mistakenly appointed for a liturgy in AD 207; *P. Tebt. Wall* 7 = *P. Tebt.* II 440 *descr.* = *SB* XVIII 13788, l. 3: Sarapias *ἀπάτωρ* (no. 437) debtor in a loan deed dated to AD 198–210; *P. Gen.* II 116: Aurelia Germania *χρηματίζουσα μητρός* (no. 193) selling her land in AD 247; *SB* IV 7343, l. 2: Aurelia Gemellina *χρηματίζουσα μητρός* (no. 402) buying a land in the second half of the 3rd c. AD; *P. Oxy. Hels.* 43, ll. 2–3: Aurelius Per[...] *χρηματίζων μητρός* (no. 392) one of debtors in loan acknowledgment dated to the last quarter of the 3rd c. AD.

[165] In *P. Oxy.* IX 1200 (AD 270), a registration of land sale, Aurelia Isidora bought land from Aurelios Moros, then requested that the deed be registered in the Bibliotheke of Hadrian; after notarising the deed, Nanaion the *archidikastes* sent it back to Oxyrhynchos so that it could be registered there as well. The text therefore consists of several chronological layers: the main body written by the seller and sent to the *archidikastes*, the part added by the *archidikastes*' office, and finally the part added in Oxyrhynchos. In the text of the contract (ll. 14–40), the woman is described as *Αὐρηλίᾳ Ἰσιδώρᾳ χρηματιζούσᾳ* (l. *χρηματιζούσῃ*) *μητρὸς Ἀριστῶνος* (l. *Ἀριστῶτος*). The same description is given in the application by Aurelia Isidora to the *archidikastes* for the publication and registration of the contract (ll. 9–13). In lines 5–8 which is a description of the appended deed, we read: *Αὐρηλίῳ Διδύμῳ τῷ καὶ Σαραπίωνι ἱερεῖ ἀρχιδικαστῇ καὶ πρὸς τῇ | ἐπιμελείᾳ τῶν χρηματιστῶν καὶ τῶν ἄλλων κριτηρίων | παρὰ Αὐρηλίας Ἰσιδώρας. τῆς τετελειωμένης δημοσιώσεως ἀντίγρα|φον ὑπόκειται.* – 'To Aurelius Didymos also called Sarapion, priest, *archidikastes* and superintendent of *chrematistai* and other courts from Aurelia Isidora. The copy of the public communication was appended.' The description of the deed was written by a scribe of the office of *archidikastes* and the identification cluster is limited to *nomen* and *cognomen*. Perhaps the scribe chose the shortest way of identifying the buyer, as the full one had already been given in the application and sale contract copied therein. Aurelia Isidora is mentioned once again with her *nomen* and *cognomen* on the *verso* of the document containing the archival description of the text given in Oxyrhynchos: *δημοσιώ(σεως) | προσφώ(νησις) εἰς Αὐρ(ηλίαν) Ἰσιδώραν*. In ll. 57–58, a subscription of Aurelia Isidora written by a third party after the registration had been completed due to Isidora's illiteracy provides the following pattern: *Αὐρηλία Ἰσιδώρα μητρὸς Ἀριστῶτος ἐπήνε⟨γ⟩κα κέ* (l. *καὶ*) *ἔστιν ἐν καταχωρισμῷ*, 'I, Aurelia Isidora of (her) mother Arsistos, have brought it and it is in the register'. The document illustrates how a simple metronym and *χρηματίζων μητρός* were effectively interchangeable.

Individuals described as 'fatherless' are visible not only among the holders of local offices, but also as beneficiaries of privileges. We find ἀπάτορες and χρηματίζοντες μητρός among the citizens of Antinoopolis, such as Aurelia Thermoutharion in *P. Rein.* I 49 = *W. Chr.* 206 dated to AD 215 (no. 320); among the ***metropolitai***, such as Aurelius Epimachos holder of πρακτορεία σιτικῶν μητροπολιτικῶν λημμάτων in *P. Oxy.* XLIII 3097 dated to AD 224–225 (no. 186), or Aurelius Silbanos *phylarchos* in *P. Harr.* I 64 dated to AD 269–270 (no. 195);[166] and among the ***katoikoi***, such as Thermoutharion and her son in *BGU* III 971 dated to after AD 245 (no. 1752), Aurelia Thermoutharion's σπουρίοι children in *P. Flor.* I 5 dated to AD 244–245 (nos. 304 and 305). These orders retained their privileges long after AD 212.[167]

One example of such privileges is the corn dole. Several fatherless individuals are attested in the corn archive from Oxyrhynchos dated to AD 268–271: they occur at least four times either with extended filiation, χρηματίζων μητρός (*P. Oxy.* XL 2936, ll. 8 [= no. 179] and 23 [= no. 180]; 2913, col. II [= no. 178]), or with a sole metronym (*P. Oxy.* XL 2904, ll. 4–5 [= no. 366]); one further case (*P. Oxy.* XL 2912) is uncertain. It is clear that corn was not given out indiscriminately, but only to certain people as a privilege or reward. Although fatherless individuals were not granted the corn as members of the ἐπικριθέντες, the group originally entitled to the σιτηρέσιον, they could apply in the group of ῥεμβοί (as a reward for services to the city), as well as the group of ὁμόλογοι. The latter is perhaps most important, as it seems the group of ὁμόλογοι was created to admit those who belonged to the fiscally privileged metropolite group but were not entitled to the σιτηρέσιον as they did not fulfil the criteria for the gymnasial class; in other words, the group as a means of granting *i.a.* metropolite fatherless with corn.[168] It is difficult to say when this happened, but certainly the group was still extant in the 70s of the third century.

[166] See C. DRECOLL, *Die Liturgien im römischen Kaiserreich des 3. und 4. Jh. n. Chr. Untersuchung über Zugang, Inhalt und wirtschaftliche Bedeutung der öffentlichen Zwangsdienste in Ägypten und anderen Provinzen* [= *Historia – Einzelschriften* CXVI], Stuttgart 1997, pp. 18–19.

[167] VAN MINNEN, '*Aἱ ἀπὸ γυμνασίου*' (cit. n. 45), pp. 342–343.

[168] This explanation of was suggested by John Rea in *P. Oxy.* XL. Further developed in: M. NOWAK, 'Get your free corn: The fatherless in the corn-dole archive from Oxyrhynchos', [in:] *Tell Me Who You Are* (cit. n. 41), pp. 215–228, with further literature.

5.5.1. Illegitimate offspring with fathers in the third century

The evidence discussed above suggests that the situation of the fatherless remained quite good until the late-third century: not only did they obtain certain privileges regarding succession in Roman law, but their social standing was no different from provincials using filiations. Yet, we are only able to draw a connection between the fatherless and illegitimate children of stable unions *a fortiori*. This is because it is difficult to trace children of informal unions in any sources dating from after the second century. The most obvious reason for this is the *constitutio Antoniniana*, which resulted in a reduction of the number of people deprived of *ius conubii*. In other words, almost all free people within the Empire acquired not only citizenship, but also the ability to marry under Roman law. Consequently, an Egyptian woman who had not previously been able to form a legal marriage with a Roman without the special grant of *conubium*, and who could thus not produce legitimate children, became fully Roman after AD 212 and could marry almost any free man in the Empire. The category of children considered illegitimate due to the unequal status of their parents and the lack of *conubium*, would therefore have disappeared almost completely. Certainly, unions between Romans and those from outside of the Empire would still have lacked *conubium*. The scale of the phenomenon, however, would have decreased significantly.

Another group of illegitimate children from stable but non-marital relationships was those belonging to soldiers. There is, however, no way to establish whether they attest to formal or informal families in the sources of the third century. We do not know the exact date when the ban on soldiers marrying was abolished. For a long time most scholars accepted the view that Septimius Severus had lifted the ban in AD 197,[169] an assumption based primarily on a passage from Herodian (3.8.5).[170] In 2011, Werner Eck re-opened the question by publishing a military *diploma* issued for a Syrian

[169] M.A. Speidel, 'Les femmes et la bureaucratie : quelques réflexions sur l'interdiction du mariage dans l'armée romaine', *Cahiers Glotz* 24 (2013), pp. 205–215, p. 206.

[170] See S.E. Phang, *The Marriage of Roman Soldiers (13 BC – AD 235): Law and Family in the Imperial Army* [= *Columbia Studies in the Classical Tradition* XXIV], Leiden – Boston – Cologne 2001, pp. 17–19 & 107–109, with further literature regarding this problem.

veteran released from his service in Egypt, which contains a constitution dated to 205/6 addressed to auxiliary troops in Egypt.[171]

According to the text the privilege of Roman citizenship was granted to children of decurions and centurions serving in the auxiliary troops, so long as they had been born and recognised by their fathers at the time of their service: *praeterea praestiterunt filiis decurionum et centurionum quos ordinati susceperunt cives Romani essent*.[172] The text implies that soldiers granted this privilege could contract *iustum matrimonium* only after the service: *et / conubium cum uxoribus quas tunc habuissent / cum est civitas iis data aut cum iis quas postea / duxissent dumtaxat singulis singulas*.[173] If Septimius Severus had allowed soldiers to marry, then children born after AD 197 during their fathers' service would have been legitimate, and the soldiers themselves would not have needed any special privilege to enter into legal marriage. The passage of Herodian 3.8.5: *γυναξί τε συνοικεῖν*, does not necessarily contradict this, as it could be understood as referring to factual cohabitation. The privilege granted by Septimius Severus may simply have consisted of giving soldiers the freedom to live with their female partners outside of the camp.[174]

If the Syrian *diploma* excludes the possibility that the ban was abolished as early as the end of the second century, it does not provide any hint as to when it might have been lifted. A later Roman source referring to the marriage of soldiers is a rescript by the emperor Gordian addressed to a certain Sulpicia in AD 239 (C. 2.11.15).[175] The text concerns the mourning of a widow, and in its final part it mentions that both a widow and her husband, if he knew that his spouse had been a widow, would be subject to *infamia* if they married before the prescribed time had passed.[176] The edict specifies that

[171] W. Eck, 'Septimius Severus und die Soldaten. Das Problem der Soldatenehe und ein neues Auxiliardiplom', [in:] B. Onken & D. Rohde (eds.), *In omni historia curiosus. Studien zur Geschichte von der Antike bis zur Neuzeit. Festschrift für Helmuth Schneider zum 65. Geburtstag* [= *Philippika* LXVII], Wiesbaden 2011, pp. 63–77.

[172] Eck, 'Septimius Severus' (cit. n. 171), p. 75.

[173] Eck, 'Septimius Severus' (cit. n. 171), pp. 75–76.

[174] Eck, 'Septimius Severus' (cit. n. 171), pp. 76–77.

[175] Phang, *Marriage of Roman Soldiers* (cit. n. 170), p. 108.

[176] On the time of mourning, see A. Kacprzak, 'The widow's duty of mourning and the ancient concept of pregnancy', [in:] E. Hoebenreich & V. Kuhne (eds.), *El Cisne. Derecho romano, biologismo y algomas*, Lecce 2010, pp. 81–98.

the penalty would be imposed, even if the husband was a soldier, *qui sciens eam duxit uxorem, etiam si miles sit*. It is difficult to determine whether this text in fact confirms that soldiers could marry legally, as the husband-soldier seems to be treated as special case. This could be interpreted in two ways:

1. Soldiers could not marry, nor were they allowed to form a union with a widow before the mourning period passed.
2. Soldiers could marry, but they needed to be treated as a special case, because they could be mistaken about the law in general.[177]

If the latter is true, the abolition must have taken place in the first half of the third century. This is supported by other pieces of Roman jurisprudence, notably a ruling that a soldier being a son *in potestate* could not contract a marriage without paternal consent (D. 23.2.35: Pap. *resp.* 6: *Filius familias miles matrimonium sine patris voluntate non contrahit*), or another passage specifying that a dowry should not be counted as a part of *peculium castrense*, if given or promised to a soldier who was *alieni iuris* (D. 49.17.16 pr.: Pap. *resp.* 19).[178] Even a century ago, Jean Lesquier observed the text must have referred to marriage, as there could be no *dos* without *nuptiae*.[179] The texts are ascribed to the *responsa* of Papinian who died in AD 211 or 212.[180] If the fragments were not altered by Tribonian's commision, the abolition probably occurred in the first years of the third century, specifically between AD 205 and 212.[181]

The children of soldiers begotten in mixed unions were certainly not the only families not recognised as legitimate under Roman law. They may not even have constituted the majority. According to Richard Alston, the number of soldiers in Egypt ranged from 23,000 at the beginning of the

[177] See L. Winkel, 'Forms of imposed protection in legal history, especially in Roman law', *Fundamina: A Journal of Legal History* 16.1 (2010), pp. 578–587, pp. 583–585.

[178] Similarly D. 23.2.45 pr. *&* 3 (Ulp. *ad leg. Iul.* 3).

[179] J. Lesquier, 'Le mariage des soldats romains', *Comptes rendus des séances de l'Académie des inscriptions et belles-lettres* 61.4 (1917), pp. 227–236, p. 232.

[180] On Papinian and his works with references to further literature, see M. Peachin, 'Papinian', [in:] R.S. Bagnall *et al.* (eds.), *The Encyclopedia of Ancient History*, online edition, doi:10.1002/9781444338386.wbeah25026.

[181] Lesquier, 'Le mariage' (cit. n. 179), p. 234.

Roman rule, to around 11–12,000 in the second century.[182] Furthermore, we cannot reasonably assume that every soldier kept a concubine and produced children with her during his service in the army.[183] The total number of mixed unions could not have been much higher either, as we saw in the chapter devoted to children born of such unions. Such cases may even be over-represented in the *Gnomon*, which we can explain by the fact that they were regulated casuistically; although marriages contracted by Krenea and *xenos* are regulated in the *Gnomon*, they are otherwise unattested in the Egyptian sources. Yet, children born of soldiers before the marital ban was abolished, and those born of mixed marriages before AD 212, are – with the exception of free–slave unions, rarely attested in Egypt (*supra*, p. 107) – the only ones whose status we can assume with any degree of certainty. Other cases are difficult, as the descriptions do not differentiate between children born of marriages or informal unions. The sources only differentiate between people with a patronym and those without.

Tracing the offspring of these individuals is, therefore, always conjectural, as in the case of Octavia Lucretia's sons discussed at the beginning of this section (*P. Harr.* I 68 + *P. Diog.* 18). We might expect to find such a pattern in *BGU* II 667, a contract drafted in Ptolemais Euergeris ten years after the *constitutio Antoniniana* between Aurelia Thermoutarion, seller, and Aurelius Sokmenis, buyer. The seller, who was still a minor when the contract was drafted, acted with her *kyrios*, guardian, and father, Aurelius Heron, ll. 21–22: *ἀφῆλιξ μετὰ κυρίου καὶ ἐπιτρόπου κατὰ τοὺς ν[όμ]ους τοῦ πατρὸς Αὐρηλίου Ἡρων||[â]* (and l. 3). Since the text is dated after Caracalla's universal grant, the girl, if born of legitimate marriage, should have been under the paternal power of Aurelius Theon – in the same way as one of the three boys in *P. Diog.* 18, l. 9: *Ἰουλιᾶς ὑποχείριος [τ]ῷ ἰ̣δ̣ίῳ πατρί*[184] – and not merely under his guardianship. She would also not have been the owner of the land. The girl therefore must have been *sui iuris*, either because she was born outside of *iustae nuptiae* or because she was eman-

[182] R. ALSTON, *Soldier and Society in Roman Egypt: A Social History*, London – New York 1995, p. 31.

[183] See summary of the problem in: PHANG, *Marriage of Roman Soldiers* (cit. n. 170), pp. 142–196.

[184] And in other texts, see the list in: A. ARJAVA, 'Paternal power in late Antiquity', *The Journal of Roman Studies* 88 (1998), pp. 147–165, p. 156, n. 55.

cipated. Antti Arjava claimed the latter.[185] It seems more likely, however, that she was not *legitima*, as emancipations are attested only occasionally in Egypt, which suggests that the practice was not wide-spread.[186] Moreover, if they were first-generation Roman citizens – perhaps illiterate, and almost certainly inhabitants of a village in the Arsinoite nome – the idea that they would perform *emancipatio* seems quite unconvincing. We might expect to find formal acts involving *mancipatio*[187] in Karanis or Philadelphia, but not in a village such as Phylakitike Nesos. Furthermore, Hans Julius Wolff noted that *emancipatio* was not practiced in Greek speaking parts of the Roman world and that the Roman concept of *emancipatio* itself was not easily comprehensible.[188] It may also be that Aurelia Thermoutharion acted μετὰ κυρίου καὶ ἐπιτρόπου, which had nothing to do with *patria potestas*, but referred rather to a local law in which women in Egypt acted μετὰ κυρίου both before and after AD 212. Or, it was simply the way, how new Romans comprehended (or confused) a concept of *patria potestas*.

6. BACK TO CONSTANTINE – CONCLUSION

The material presented above demonstrates that the division between marriages and stable, monogamous marriage-like unions became less strict during the second and third centuries, both in jurisprudence and imperial law. The process was two-fold. On the one hand, jurists attempted to provide a betrayed male partner with tools comparable to those provided for spouses.[189] On the other hand, the standing of children born out of wedlock became closer to that of marital offspring (albeit within limits: intestate succession after fathers remained excluded).

[185] ARJAVA, 'Paternal power' (cit. n. 184), p. 157.

[186] ARJAVA, 'Paternal power' (cit. n. 184), p. 157: *CPR* VI 78; *CPL* 206 = *FIRA* III 14.

[187] See M. NOWAK, 'Mancipatio and its life in late-Roman law', *The Journal of Juristic Papyrology* 41 (2011), pp. 103–122.

[188] WOLFF, 'The background' (cit. n. 20), pp. 21–45.

[189] Such an interpretation of the sources pertaining to the extension of the *lex Iulia de adulteriis* was suggested already in: WOLFF, 'The background' (cit. n. 20), p. 35.

The observations presented thus far also corroborate the conformity of the legal changes with social practice – at least in Egypt – and suggest that the changes were generally in line with the trend in praetorian law to recognise cognatic bonds.[190] It is therefore probable that such changes occurred as a response to social needs. Sources recording everyday life do not differentiate between marital and extramarital children, either in terms of terminology, descriptions and their standing within the family, or in their perception within society. In other words, there is no identifiable differentiation between formal and informal families in the everyday life of Roman Egypt. This conclusion applies not only to cases which Roman law recognised as marriages and families outside the framework of the Roman institutions, but also to cases, such as those of slaves and active soldiers, in which the fathers were explicitly deprived of the ability to marry.

It may be that some of the Roman restrictions imposed on marriages were incomprehensible to the local population – as in the case of soldiers – which is why they did not comply with them. It should not therefore come as a surprise to find that soldiers treated and described their informal families in the same way as others regarded their legitimate families. While the concept of a marriage which resulted in *patria potestas* and succession was specific to the Roman *ius civile*, it may not necessarily have been well-understood in local laws, and the boundary between marriage and non-marriage may not have been especially well-defined, or even extant, among those in the provinces. This is what we know about Egypt and, as Hans Julius Wolff suggested, it may also have been the case more broadly in the Eastern parts of the Empire, or at least in the Greek cities.

As Sandra Lippert noted in her introduction to the history of Egyptian law, the Egyptian concept of marriage was far less strict and precise than in its Roman or Greek counterparts: adult men and women could, by mutual consent, live openly together which would make them married.[191] In such situations, children born of stable unions, even if the union did not last very long, had the same position as children born of life-long

[190] U. Babusiaux, 'Römisches Erbrecht im Gnomon des Idios Logos', *Zeitschrift der Savigny-Stiftung für Rechtsgeschichte RA* 135 (2018), pp. 108–177, p. 172.

[191] Lippert, *Einführung* (cit. n. 127), p. 119.

relationships. All children were therefore entitled to inherit equally from their fathers,[192] with the exception of the eldest son who was entitled to more.[193] This does not leave much space for the concept of illegitimacy. Wolff pointed out that, in the Greek-speaking part of the Empire, the keeping of concubines even by married men might have been an accepted practice. Such children, at least in some Greek cities, might have had hereditary and public rights similar to legitimate offspring.

Wolff suggested that Constantine's constitutions against *filii naturales* (*C.Th.* 4.6.1–3) were enacted to deal with the practice of keeping concubines instead of (or as well as) wives. The idea was, on the one hand, to provide children already born in informal unions with a chance to became *legitimi*, as Constantine allowed people to legitimise their extramarital children by marrying their mothers (*legitimatio per subsequens matrimonium*).[194] On the other hand, the laws sought to limit the phenomenon of non-marital unions.[195]

This interpretation, while convincing, needs to be developed further: The Roman legal sources extending the definition of marriage in the *lex Iulia de adulteriis*, as well as the privileges granted to children born out of wedlock illustrate that Roman law had already responded to this social practice in an affirmative way. Constantine's response was to reverse the process. His laws were a reaction against informal families, although not directed (at least not initially) against social practices prevalent in the

[192] This is understood from the fact that Egyptian sources do not introduce a division into marital and extramarital children, but also from already Greek marital contracts preventing husbands from producing heirs outside of marriage and securing the succession of common offspring and from humiliating wife by introducing a mistress into the joint household: the husband was not allowed to keep a concubine or a boy-lover, to found a new household without his wife, to have children from another woman and introduce another woman into the common house. A husband disobedient to those prohibitions was liable financially to his wife. *E.g. P. Eleph.* 1, ll. 8–9; *P. Freib.* III 30, ll. 29–30; *P. Münch.* III.1 62, ll. 4–7; *P. Giss.* 2, ll. 19–24; *P. Tebt.* I 104, ll. 19–23; *P. Tebt.* III.2 974, ll. 4–8. Collected by YIFTACH-FIRANKO in: *Marriage and Marital Arrangements* (cit. n. 122), pp. 312–317.

[193] LIPPERT, *Einführung* (cit. n. 127), p. 125.

[194] The concession to to make children legitimate was preserved only indirectly, through the constitution of the emperor Leo, it makes a clear reference that it was Constantine who allowed this form of *legitimatio* (C. 5.27.5). Arjava, however, observed that such a constitution might have a low influence on every-day life of the Empire: ARJAVA, *Women and Law* (cit. n. 3), p. 213.

[195] WOLFF, 'The background' (cit. n. 20), pp. 40–42.

Greek speaking parts of the Roman world. Indeed his constitutions were designed to distinguish the concept of Roman marriage from the types of family which certainly existed within Egyptian legal practice and, as we might infer from the jurisprudential sources, may have been more widespread throughout the Empire. Constantine took similar steps in regard to other institutions of the Roman family law as illustrated in his regulations concerning divorce.[196]

Several scholars have already noted that the 'spirit' of Constantine's laws was traditional, meaning specifically pagan Roman.[197] Antti Arjava summarised Constantine's legislative approach, saying 'when Constantine came to power, he assumed a very traditional Roman upper-class attitude towards illegitimacy'.[198] We could add that his attitudes extended to the ideas of family and marriage; his constitutions refer openly to the ideals found in the laws of Augustus, with their obsessive protection of marriage, and their provisions designed to prevent *commixtio sanguinis* among the Roman elites. In the scholarly literature, it has been noted that the content of *C.Th.* 4.6.3 is both a renewal and extension of the *leges Iuliae* forbidding senators and their descendants to marry freed persons and their offspring.[199] Certainly Constantine attempts to restrict members of the elites[200] from marrying women of much lower standing were similar to those of Augustus.[201]

The difference is that Augustus stipulated that no free men were allowed to marry women held by the public in low esteem, while Constan-

[196] J. URBANIK, 'La repressione constantiniana dei divorzi' (cit. n. 72).

[197] *E.g.* SARGENTI, *Studi sul diritto* (cit. n. 12), pp. 34–46; EVANS GRUBBS, *Law and Family* (cit. n. 1), pp. 317–321; TATE, 'Inheritance rights' (cit. n. 14), p. 8, with further literature.

[198] ARJAVA, *Women and Law* (cit. n. 3), p. 212.

[199] As *C.Th.* deals only with effects of the disobedience to the prohibition, the direct ban had to be given in the lost part of *C.Th.* 4.6.2 or fully lost *C.Th.* 4.6.1: EVANS GRUBBS, *Law and Family* (cit. n. 1), pp. 286–287.

[200] These prohibitions were considered to serve not only to legal, but also to social purposes and help Constantine to re-define imperial elites extending their notions beyond traditional senatorial class: MCGINN, 'The social policy' (cit. n. 17), p. 69.

[201] In Constantine's law the group which was to refrain from such unions was wider than in the *lex Iulia*, as it included also equestrian officials: EVANS GRUBBS, *Law and Family* (cit. n. 1), pp. 290–293; MCGINN, 'The social policy' (cit. n. 17), pp. 57–73, p. 60.

tine wanted only members of the elites to abstain from such unions.[202] Also the sanctions imposed by Constantine referred to Augustus' legislation. In the *leges Iuliae* those who married persons whom it was forbidden to marry were regarded as *caelibes*, thus their *capacitas* to inherit was strongly limited.[203] Thus, both in Augustus' and Constantine's laws the penalty regarded *testamenti factio*.

The laws of Constantine were undoubtedly issued as a response to social practices. Yet his reaction was not prompted by hostile social attitudes towards extramarital children, as there is little evidence in the sources to suggest that such attitudes existed. Rather, he was reacting to the widely accepted social phenomenon of informal families, which had started to sneak into Roman law from around second century. Constantine's laws were not a legal recognition of popular social attitudes, but a negative reaction intended to reverse a common practice.

One could object that this hypothesis does not explain the disappearance of fatherlessness labels in Egypt before Constantine. Indeed, if it was only Constantine who decided to combat informal families, the respective labels would have disappeared after and not before the introduction of his laws. Perhaps they simply disappeared from the papyri because the *constitutio Antoniniana* had brought about so many changes in *status civitatis*, that some of the old labels were no longer useful.

There is, however, another possible explanation: the idea of restoring the traditional Roman concept of marriage, not only in Rome itself but also in provinces, may have predated Constantine. Simon Corcoran pointed out that Diocletian's constitutions relating to family place an emphasis on the Roman way of doing things, *e.g.* in regard to *apokeryxis* (C. 8.46.6), bigamy (C. 5.5.2) or *raptus* (C. 5.1.1; 9.12.3).[204] Diocletian was also the author of laws against incestuous unions. One of them is a rescript addressed most likely to a governor of a province included in the *Codex*

[202] C. Humfress, 'Civil law and social life', [in:] N. Lenski (ed.), *The Cambridge Companion to the Age of Constantine* [= *Cambridge Companions to the Ancient World*], Cambridge 2005, pp. 205–225, p. 206.

[203] On these limitations, see C. Fayer, *La familia romana. Aspetti giuridici ed antiquari. Parte seconda. Sponsalia, matrimonio, dote*, Rome 2005, p. 572; M. Kaser, *Das römische Privatrecht. Erster Abschnitt. Das altrömische, das vorklassische und klassische Recht*, Munich 1971², pp. 320–321.

[204] Corcoran, 'The sins of the fathers' (cit. n. 163), p. 8.

Hermogenianus and preserved in *Coll. leg.* 6.5. The text informs us that incestuous marriages contracted by mistake should not be punished so long as they were broken after the error was discovered.[205] In the Damascus incest edict, preserved in both the *Code* (C. 5.4.17) and the *Collatio* (6.4), we find a strong condemnation of incest and the belief that deeds such as incest could threaten divine favour.[206] Both of these laws could have been propaganda directed at social practices in the East.[207] There is, as Judith Evans Grubbs noted, a similarity in the approaches of Constantine and Diocletian.[208] The text of Damascus edict mentions that incestuous parents could not inherit from their children, although it does not mention whether the hereditary rights of the children were affected. Evans Grubbs has suggested that changes in the legislative approach towards illegitimacy may have originated with Diocletian.[209]

It is tempting to suggest that Diocletian initiated the hostile legislation against illegitimacy, yet it is difficult to verify and the arguments against it are strong. It must be noted that Diocletian's edict against incest was given in Damascus. The Empire, at the time, was at war with Persia, where incest was not only practiced, but part of religious practices.[210] The edict might thus have been propagandistic and political. Furthermore, the mention of succession in the text may have been rhetorical, as it appears without any concrete prohibition: *ut liberorum quos inlicite genuerunt successione arceantur*. It does not specify that testamentary provisions for parents

[205] Corcoran, 'The sins of the fathers' (cit. n. 163), pp. 8–9.

[206] Corcoran, 'The sins of the fathers' (cit. n. 163), p. 9.

Another Diocletian's law against incest could be a constitution preserved in four manuscripts, one of canon law and three *epitome* of the *Codex*, but left outside of Justinian's Code. Corcoran proposed to recognise it as Tetrarchic law. See Corcoran, 'The sins of the fathers' (cit. n. 163). Yet, in the personal communication he said he would date it now later, thus I do not include the fragment as an attestation of Diocletian's constitution.

[207] Corcoran, 'The sins of the fathers' (cit. n. 163), pp. 10–12.

[208] J. Evans-Grubbs, 'Making the private public: Illegitimacy and incest in Roman law', [in:] C. Ando & J. Rüpke (eds.), *Public and Private in Ancient Mediterranean Law and Religion* [= *Religionsgeschichtliche Versuche und Vorarbeiten* LXV], Berlin 2015, pp. 115–141, p. 115.

[209] Evans-Grubbs, 'Making the private public' (cit. n. 208), p. 133.

[210] Corcoran, 'The sins of the fathers' (cit. n. 163), p. 10; P.J. Frandsen, *An Incestuous and Close-Kin Marriage in Ancient Egypt and Persia: Examination of the Evidence* [= *Carsten Niebuhr Institute Publications*], Copenhagen 2009, p. 99.

would be void, but says rather that parents could not inherit from such children because they were illegitimate. As the father was already unable to inherit from his children born out of wedlock in intestate succession, the edict did not really change the position of children born of incest.

It is difficult to determine whether the laws of Diocletian represent the origins of a hostile legislative attitude towards illegitimate children, or if they were merely an attempt to limit incest. The latter hypothesis seems more likely, as no other steps against illegitimacy were taken by Diocletian, and incest, unlike illegitimacy, was unacceptable in Roman eyes.

The conclusions which seem most firm are, therefore:

1. Constantine took steps against both informal families and non-marital unions on a wider scale.
2. The laws issued by the emperor were reactions to legal changes which took place during the second and third centuries.
3. The laws of Constantine should be classified as social engineering, meaning they were aimed specifically at changing the social reality.
4. The constitutions referred to the traditional pagan Roman family pattern, especially to the Julian marital laws.

Even if the content of Constantine's laws was inspired by the traditional Roman concept of marriage, which seems to be the most probable scenario, we must nonetheless ask why Constantine – whose mother Helena was recognised in Byzantine historiography as the daughter of innkeeper[211] – decided to fight against non-marital unions. Although it is not the intention of this book to explain the psychological aspects of Constantine's legal decisions, a few details from his life may be related to his laws against illegitimacy.

C.Th. 4.6.2–3, and presumably *C.Th.* 4.6.1, are late, dated to the very end of Constantine's life. Ten years earlier, Constantine had experienced a serious family tragedy. According to later historiography, he condemned both his first-born son, Crispus, and his wife Fausta to death (*Epitome de*

[211] S.N.C. Lieu, 'Constantine in legendary literature', [in:] *Companion to the Age of Constantine* (cit. n. 202), pp. 298–325, pp. 308–309.

Caesaribus 41.11–12; Phot. *HE* 2.4; Sid. Apoll. *Epist.* 5.8.2; Zosim. *HN* 2.29.2; *Passion of Artemisia* 45; Zonar. *Epit.* 13.2.38–41).[212] Crispus and Fausta were also condemned to *damnatio memoriae*.[213] The sources differ in their explanation of this tragedy, but all of them mention that Fausta accused Crispus falsely of rape. Constantine reacted by condemning him to death, but when he discovered that the accusation was false he made his wife follow Crispus' fate. Whether the story is real or the cover for a political purge is uncertain.[214] Something very serious must have happened if Constantine condemned his beloved son – victor over Licinius, Caesar, and potential Augustus – to death or, as David Woods suggested, to exile.[215] Fausta was not only the daughter, sister and wife of Roman emperors, but the mother of at least five of Constantine's children. Such a tragedy must have left traces.

It is worth noting that Crispus was thought to be the son of a low-born life companion whom Constantine had left in order to marry Fausta. Zosimos described Crispus as *ἐκ παλλακῆς αὐτῷ γεγονότα Μινερβίνης ὄνομα* (2.20.2). The mother's position of concubine and her lower social standing could explain why the sources remained silent about her, although Timothy Barnes suggested that she might have been related to Diocletian, from whom Constantine wanted to distance himself.[216]

Certainly, the laws discussed in this chapter should not be interpreted as Constantine's reaction of to the supposed seduction of his wife by his own son for the simple reason that they were issued ten years after the tragic events.[217] These events might nonetheless have shaped Constantine's personal attitudes towards family and children born out of wedlock. If Crispus' mother was indeed a concubine, the laws may have been intended to prevent the possibility of an illegitimate son being accepted

[212] D. Woods, 'On the death of the empress Fausta', *Greece & Rome* 45.1 (1998), pp. 70–86, pp. 71–72.

[213] E. Varner, *Monumenta Graeca et Romana: Mutilation and Transformation: Damnatio Memoriae and Roman Imperial Portraiture*, Leiden – Boston 2004, p. 221.

[214] Varner, *Monumenta Graeca et Romana* (cit. n. 213), p. 222.

[215] Woods, 'Death of the empress Fausta' (cit. n. 212), p. 80.

[216] T. Barnes, *Constantine: Dynasty, Religion and Power in the Later Roman Empire*, Oxford 2010.

[217] Yuge suggested that these events might have been an inspiration for *C.Th.* 9.9.1, which seems unlikely, because Crispus was free-born: Yuge, 'Die Gesetze' (cit. n. 29), p. 148.

and promoted, as had happened with Crispus. Such a move would have had also an additional advantage, that is reducing the number of competitors for power.

Finally, it is worth stating that Christianity should not be dismissed as a factor in the laws: even if society was not yet Christianised, Constantine or the *quaestores* responsible for drafting his laws might certainly have been inspired by Christian teachings. The laws were issued at the very end of Constantine's life, and there is no doubt in the scholarly literature that Christianity influenced Constantine's reign. For this reason we cannot exclude that his laws against bastards were inspired by Christian teachings on marriage and sex. There is, alas, no way of knowing whether early Christian teachings wanted children born outside of formal marriage to be stigmatised and excluded from succession after their fathers, nor the extent to which Constantine was influenced by Christian teachings.

BIBLIOGRAPHY

G. Alföldy, 'Epigraphica Hispanica V. Inschriften aus Jérica und Umgebung', *Zeitschrift für Papyrologie und Epigraphik* 54 (1984), pp. 221–245.

P.M. Allison, 'Soldiers' families in the early Roman Empire', [in:] B. Rawson (ed.), *A Companion to Families in the Greek and Roman Worlds*, Malden 2011, pp. 161–182.

J.L. Alonso, 'The *bibliotheke enkteseon* and the alienation of real securities in Roman Egypt', *The Journal of Juristic Papyrology* 40 (2010), pp. 11–54.

J.L. Alonso, 'The status of peregrine law in Egypt: "customary law" and legal pluralism in the Roman Empire', *The Journal of Juristic Papyrology* 43 (2013) = *Special Issue. Papyrology* AD *2013*, pp. 351–404.

J.L. Alonso, 'Juristic papyrology and Roman law', [in:] P.J. du Plessis, C. Ando & K. Tuori, *The Oxford Handbook of Roman Law and Society*, Oxford 2016, pp. 56–69.

R. Alston, *Soldier and Society in Roman Egypt. A Social History*, London – New York 1995.

M. Amelotti, *Il testamento romano attraverso la prassi documentale*, I: *Le forme classiche di testamento* [= *Studi e testi di papirologia* I], Florence 1966.

H. Ankum, 'La *sponsa adultera*: problèmes concernant l'*accusatio adulterii* en droit romain classique', [in:] *Estudios de derecho romano en honor de Alvaro d'Ors*, vol. I, Navarra 1987, pp. 161–198.

V. Arangio-Ruiz, 'Un *liber mandatorum* da Augusto ad Antonino Pio', *Atene e Roma* 3 (1922), pp. 216–223.

V. Arangio Ruiz, 'Intorno agli *astoi* dell'Egitto greco-romano', *Revue internationale des droits de l'Antiquité* 4 (1950) = *Studi de Visscher*, pp. 7–20.

G.G. Archi, *L'Epitome Gai. Studio sul tardo diritto romano in Occidente* [= *Antiqua* LXI], Naples 1991².

L. Arends Olsen, *La femme et l'enfant dans les unions illégitimes à Rome. L'évolution du droit jusqu' au début de l'Empire*, Bern 1999.

A. Arjava, *Women and Law in Late Antiquity*, Oxford 1996.

A. Arjava, 'Paternal power in late antiquity', *The Journal of Roman Studies* 88 (1998), pp. 147–165.

S. Armani & A. Damet, 'Un toit, des lois. Les politiques familiales dans les mondes anciens', *Cahiers « Mondes anciens »* 10 (2018), online publication https://journals.openedition.org/mondesanciens/2059.

I. Arnaoutoglou, 'Marital disputes in Greco-Roman Egypt, *The Journal of Juristic Papyrology* 25 (1995), pp. 11–28.

R. Astolfi, *La lex Iulia et Papia*, Milan 1996[4].

C. Azzara & S. Gasparri (eds.), *Le leggi dei Longobardi. Storia, memoria e diritto di un popolo germanico*, Milan 1992.

U. Babusiaux, 'Römisches Erbrecht im Gnomon des Idios Logos', *Zeitschrift der Savigny-Stiftung für Rechtsgeschichte RA* 135.1 (2018), pp. 108–177.

R.S. Bagnall, 'Religious conversion and onomastic change in early Byzantine Egypt', *The Bulletin of the American Society of Papyrologists* 19.3–4 (1982), pp. 105–124.

R.S. Bagnall, 'Conversion and onomastics: A replay', *Zeitschrift für Papyrologie und Epigraphik* 69 (1987), pp. 243–250.

R.S. Bagnall, 'Notes on Egyptian census declarations I', *The Bulletin of the American Society of Papyrologists* 27 (1990), pp. 1–14.

R.S. Bagnall, 'Freedmen and freedwomen with fathers?', *The Journal of Juristic Papyrology* 21 (1991), pp. 7–8.

R.S. Bagnall, 'Notes on Egyptian census declarations IV', *The Bulletin of the American Society of Papyrologists* 29 (1992), pp. 101–115.

R.S. Bagnall, 'Egypt and the *lex Minicia*', *The Journal of Juristic Papyrology* 23 (1993), pp. 25–28.

R.S. Bagnall, 'Notes on Egyptian census declarations V', *The Bulletin of the American Society of Papyrologists* 30 (1993), pp. 35–56.

R.S. Bagnall, 'The people of P. Mich. Inv. 5806', *Zeitschrift für Papyrologie und Epigraphik* 105 (1995), pp. 253–255.

R.S. Bagnall, *Early Christian Books in Egypt*, Princeton – Oxford 2009.

R.S. Bagnall, 'Illegitimacy in Roman and late antique Egypt', [in:] T. Derda, A. Łajtar & J. Urbanik (eds.), in collaboration with A. Mirończuk & G. Ochała, *Proceedings of the 27th International Congress of Papyrology, Warsaw 29.07–3.08 2013* [= *The Journal of Juristic Papyrology Supplement* XXVII], Warsaw 2016, vol. I, pp. 5–17.

R.S. Bagnall, A. Bülow-Jacobsen & H. Cuvigny, 'Security and water on the Eastern Desert roads: the prefect Iulius Ursus and the construction of *praesidia* under Vespasian', *Journal of Roman Archaeology* 14.1 (2001), pp. 325–333.

R.S. Bagnall & B.W. Frier, *The Demography of Roman Egypt* [= *Cambridge Studies in Population, Economy and Society in Past Time* XXIII], Cambridge 2006².

J. Bardach, 'Les statuts lituaniens – codifications de l'époque de la Renaissance', [in:] B. Geremek & A. Mączak (eds.), *Poland at the 14th International Congress of Historical Sciences in San Francisco. Studies in Comparative History*, Wrocław – Warsaw – Cracow – Gdańsk 1975, pp. 45–65.

C. Bearzot, 'Né cittadini né stranieri: *apeleutheroi* e *nothoi* in Atene', [in:] M.G. Angeli Bertinelli & A. Donati (eds.), *Il cittadino, lo straniero, il barbaro, fra integrazione ed emarginazione nell'Antichità. Atti del I Incontro internazionale di Storia Antica, Genova, 22–24 maggio 2003* [= *Serta antiqua et mediaevalia* VII], Rome 2005, pp. 77–92.

J. Beaucamp, *Le statut de la femme à Byzance (4ᵉ–7ᵉ siècle)*, II: *Les pratiques sociales* [= *Travaux et mémoires du Centre de recherche d'histoire et civilisation de Byzance. Monographies* VI], Paris 1992.

H.I. Bell, 'Diplomata antinoitica', *Aegyptus* 13 (1933), pp. 514–528.

H.I. Bell, 'A Latin registration of birth', *The Journal of Roman Studies* 27, part 1: *Papers Presented to Sir Henry Stuart Jones* (1937), pp. 30–36.

A. Besson, 'Fifty years before the Antonine Constitution: Access to Roman citizenship and exclusive rights', [in:] L. Cecchet & A. Busetto (eds.), *Citizens in the Graeco-Roman World. Aspects of Citizenship from the Archaic Period to* AD *212* [= *Mnemosyne Supplement* CDVII], Leiden 2017, pp. 199–220.

M. Bianchini, *Caso concreto e "lex generalis": per lo studio della tecnica e della politica normativa da Costantino a Teodosio II*, Milan 1979.

E.J. Bickermann, 'Beiträge zur antiken Urkundengeschichte. I: Der Heimatsvermerk und die staatsrechtliche Stellung der Hellenen im ptolemäischen Ägypten', *Archiv für Papyrusforschung* 8 (1927), pp. 216–239.

E.J. Bickermann, 'Beiträge zur antiken Urkundengeschichte. II: Ἀπογραφή, οἰκογένεια, ἐπίκρισις, Ἀιγύπτιαι', *Archiv für Papyrusforschung* 9 (1930), pp. 24–46.

I. Bieżuńska-Małowist, 'La famille du vétéran romain C. Iulius Niger de Karanis', *Eos* 49 (1957), pp. 155–164.

I. Bieżuńska-Małowist, 'Les affranchis dans les papyrus de l'époque ptolémaïque et romaine', [in:] *Atti dell'XI Congresso Internazionale di Papirologia, Milano 2–8 settembre 1965*, Milan 1966, pp. 433–443.

I. Bieżuńska-Małowist, *L'esclavage dans l'Égypte gréco-romaine. Première partie : période ptolémaïque*, Wrocław – Warsaw – Cracow – Gdańsk 1974.

I. Bieżuńska-Małowist, *L'esclavage dans l'Égypte gréco-romaine. 2. Période romaine* [= *Archiwum Filologiczne* XXX], Wrocław – Warsaw – Cracow – Gdańsk 1977.

J. Bingen, 'Les papyrus de la Fondation Egyptologique Reine Elisabeth. XIV. Déclarations pour l'épicrisis', *Chronique d'Égypte* 31 (1956), pp. 109–117.

B. Biondi, 'Vicende postclassiche del *SC. Claudiano*. Contributo alla formazione della prassi giuridica postclassica', *Iura* 3 (1952), pp. 142–154.

B. Biondi, *Il diritto romano cristiano*, III: *La famiglia, rapporti patrimoniali, diritto pubblico*, Milan 1954.

A.K. Bowman, 'Aurelius Horion and the Calpurnii: Elite families in third century Oxyrhynchus', [in:] T. Gagos & R.S. Bagnall (eds.), *Essays and Texts in Honor of J. David Thomas* [= *American Studies in Papyrology* XLII], Exeter 2001, pp. 11–17.

A.K. Bowman & D. Rathbone, 'Cities and administration in Roman Egypt', *The Journal of Roman Studies* 82 (1992), pp. 107–127.

H. Braunert, 'Griechische und römische Komponenten im Stadtrecht von Antinoopolis', *The Journal of Juristic Papyrology* 14 (1962), pp. 73–88.

Y. Broux, 'Creating a new local elite. The establishment of the metropolitan orders of Roman Egypt', *Archiv für Papyrusforschung* 59.1 (2013), pp. 143–153.

Y. Broux, *Double Names and Elite Strategy in Roman Egypt* [= *Studia Hellenistica* LIV], Leuven – Paris – Bristol, CT 2015.

Y. Broux, 'Re: Apatores. Identification issues and loss of status in Roman Egypt', *Zeitschrift für Papyrologie und Epigraphik* 2015 (194), pp. 212–214.

Y. Broux, 'Ancient profiles exploited. First results of Named Entity Recognition applied to Latin inscriptions', [in:] M. Nowak, A. Łajtar & J. Urbanik (eds.), *Tell Me Who You Are. Labelling Status in the Graeco-Roman World* [= *U schyłku starożytności. Studia źródłoznawcze* XVI], Warsaw 2017, pp. 11–33.

Y. Broux & M. Depauw, 'The maternal line in Greek identification: Signalling social status in Roman Egypt (30 BC – AD 400)', *Historia* 64.4 (2015), pp. 467–478.

P. Brown, *The Body and Society: Men, Women, and Sexual Renunciation in Early Christianity* [= *Lectures on the History of Religions, new series* XIII], New York 1988.

P.A. Brunt, *Italian Manpower, 225 BC – AD 14*, Oxford 1971.

Ch. Bruun, 'Slaves and freed slaves', [in:] Ch. Bruun & J. Edmondson (eds.), *The Oxford Handbook of Roman Epigraphy*, Oxford 2014, pp. 605–626.

W.W. Buckland, *The Roman Law of Slavery. The Condition of the Slave in Private Law from Augustus to Justinian*, Cambridge 1908.

F. Burkhalter, 'Archives locales et archives centrales en Egypte romaine', *Chiron* 20 (1990), pp. 191–216.

I. Buti, *Studi sulla capacità patrimoniale dei servi* [= *Pubblicazioni della Facoltà di Giurisprudenza dell'Università di Camerino* XIII], Naples 1976.

H. Cadell, 'P. Caire IFAO Inv. 45, P. Oxy. XIV 1719 et les privilèges des Antinoïtes', *Chronique d'Égypte* 40 (1965), pp. 357–363.

A. Calderini, *La manomissione e la condizione dei liberti in Grecia*, Milan 1908.

A. Calderini, '*Ἀπάτορες*', *Aegyptus* 33 (1953), pp. 358–369.

G. Camodeca, 'Per una reedizione dell'archivio ercolanese di L. Venidius Ennychus. II.', *Cronache Ercolanesi* 36 (2006), pp. 189–211.

B. Campbell, 'The marriage of soldiers under the Empire', *The Journal of Roman Studies* 68 (1978), pp. 153–166.

J.B. Campbell, *The Emperor and the Roman Army, 31 BC – AD 235*, Oxford 1984.

D. Canducci, 'I 6475 cateci greci dell'Arsinoite', *Aegyptus* 70 (1990), pp. 211–255.

D. Canducci, 'I 6475 cateci greci dell'Arsinoite. Prosopografia', *Aegyptus* 71 (1991), pp. 121–216.

E. Cantarella, *Secondo natura. La bisessualità nel mondo antico*, Milan 2016.

L. Capponi, *Augustan Egypt: the Creation of a Roman Province* [= *Studies in Classics* XIII], London – New York 2005.

C. Castello, *In tema di matrimonio e concubinato nel mondo romano*, Milan 1940.

C. Castello, 'La condizione del concepito da libero e schiava e da libera e schiavo in diritto romano', [in:] V. Arangio-Ruiz (ed.), *Studi in onore di Siro Solazzi*, Naples 1948, pp. 232–250.

A.S. Chankowski, *L'éphébie hellénistique. Étude d'une institution civique dans les cités grecques des îles de la Mer Égée et de l'Asie Mineure* [= *Culture et cité* IV], Paris 2010.

P. Chantraine, *Dictionnaire étymologique de la langue grecque. Histoire des mots*, Paris 1968.

D. Cherry, 'The Minician law: marriage and the Roman citizenship', *Phoenix* 44.3 (1990), pp. 244–266.

Th. Christensen, 'SB XIV 11355 – A reedition. Copy of a census return', *Archiv für Papyrusforschung* 44.1 (1998), pp. 29–37.

W. Clarysse, 'Une famille alexandrine dans la chora', *Chronique d'Égypte* 63 (1988), pp. 137–140.

W. Clarysse, 'Nemesion son of Zoilos', [in:] K. Vandorpe, W. Clarysse & H. Verreth (eds.), *Graeco-Roman Archives from the Fayum* [= *Collectanea Hellenistica – KVAB* VI], Leuven – Paris – Bristol, CT 2015, pp. 256–258.

W. Clarysse & M. Depauw, 'How Christian was fourth century Egypt? Onomastic perspectives on conversion', *Vigiliae Christianae* 67.4 (2013), pp. 407–435.

W. Clarysse & D. J. Thompson, *Counting the People in Hellenistic Egypt. Vol. 2: Historical Studies* [= *Cambridge Classical Studies*], Cambridge 2006.

R. Coles, 'New documentary papyri from the Fayum', *The Journal of Juristic Papyrology* 18 (1974), pp. 177–187.

C. Cosentini, *Studi sui liberti. Contributo allo studio della condizione giuridica dei liberti cittadini*, vol. I, Catania 1948.

P.E. Corbett, *The Roman Law of Marriage*, Oxford 1930.

S. Corcoran, 'The sins of the fathers. A neglected constitution of Diocletian on incest', *The Journal of Legal History* 21.2 (2000), pp. 1–34.

J. Cowey & D. Kah, 'Bemerkungen zu Texten aus *BGU* I–IV. Teil I: Zensusdeklarationen', *Zeitschrift für Papyrologie und Epigraphik* 163 (2007), pp. 147–182.

A. Cowley, *Aramaic Papyri of the Fifth Century BC*, Oxford 1923.

S.A. Cristaldi, 'Unioni non matrimoniali a Roma', [in:] F. Romeo (ed.), *Le relazioni affettive non matrimoniali*, Rome 2014, pp. 143–200.

J.A. Crook, 'Gaius, *Institutes* I 84–86', *The Classical Review* 17.1 (1967), pp. 7–8.

J.A. Crook, *Law and Life of Rome, 90 BC – AD 212* [= *Aspects of Greek and Roman Life*], Ithaca 1984.

É. Cuq, 'Les lois d'Auguste sur les déclarations de naissance', [in:] *Mélanges Paul Fournier*, Paris 1929, pp. 119–133.

K. Czajkowski, 'The limits of legal pluralism in the Roman Empire', *The Journal of Legal History* 40.2 (2019), pp. 110–129.

F. De Decker, 'Etymological and methodological observations on the "PG" and "PG?" vocabulary in Robert Beekes's Etymological Dictionary of Greek: N', *Studia Linguistica Universitatis Iagellonicae Cracoviensis* 133.3 (2016), pp. 149–169.

R. Dekker, *Episcopal Networks and Authority in Late Antique Egypt. Bishops of the Theban Region at Work* [= *Orientalia Lovaniensia Analecta* CCLXIV], Leuven 2018.

D. Delia, *Alexandrian Citizenship during the Roman Principate* [= *American Classical Studies* XXIII], Atlanta, GA 1991.

M. Depauw, 'The use of mothers' names in Ptolemaic documents. A case of Greek-Egyptian influence', *The Journal of Juristic Papyrology* 37 (2007), pp. 21–29.

M. Depauw, 'Do mothers matter? The emergence of metronymics in early Roman Egypt', [in:] T.V. Evans & D.D. Obbink (eds.), *The Language of the Papyri*, Oxford 2010, pp. 120–139.

T. Derda, *Arsinoites Nomos. Administration of the Fayum under Roman Rule* [= *The Journal of Juristic Papyrology Supplement* VII], Warsaw 2006.

L. Desanti, 'Costantino e il matrimonio fra tutore e pupilla', *Bullettino dell'Istituto di diritto romano "Vittorio Scialoja"* 89 (1986), pp. 443–463.

A. Dimopoulou-Piliouni, 'Apeleutheroi: metics or foreigners?', *Dike* 11 (2008), pp. 27–50.

A. Dolganov, 'Imperialism and social engineering. Augustan social legislation in the *Gnomon of the Idios Logos*', [in:] K. Harter-Uibopuu & T. Kruse (eds.), *Studien zum „Gnomon des Idios Logos": Beiträge zum Dritten Wiener Kolloquium zur antiken Rechtsgeschichte* [= *Wiener Kolloquien zur antiken Rechtsgeschichte*], forthcoming.

C. Drecoll, *Die Liturgien im römischen Kaiserreich des 3. und 4. Jh. n. Chr. Untersuchung über Zugang, Inhalt und wirtschaftliche Bedeutung der öffentlichen Zwangsdienste in Ägypten und anderen Provinzen* [= *Historia – Einzelschriften* CXVI], Stuttgart 1997.

C. Dupont, *Les constitutions de Constantin et le droit privé au début du IVe siècle : les personnes* [= *Studia iuridica Bari* XVII], Bari 1937.

R. Duttenhöfer, 'Korrekturen zu Ostraka aus Elephantine / Syene II', *Zeitschrift für Papyrologie und Epigraphik* 157 (2006), pp. 147–158.

M. Ebbott, *Imagining Illegitimacy in Classical Greek Literature*, Lanham – Boulder – New York – Oxford 2003.

W. Eck, 'Die Veränderungen in Konstitutionen und Diplomen unter Antoninus Pius', [in:] M. A. Speidel & H. Lieb (eds.), *Militärdiplome. Die Forschungsbeiträge der Berner Gespräche von 2004* [= *Mavors* XV], Stuttgart 2007, pp. 87–104.

W. ECK, 'Septimius Severus und die Soldaten. Das Problem der Soldatenehe und ein neues Auxiliardiplom', [in:] B. ONKEN & D. ROHDE (eds.), *In omni historia curiosus. Studien zur Geschichte von der Antike bis zur Neuzeit. Festschrift für Helmuth Schneider zum 65. Geburtstag* [= *Philippika* LXVII], Wiesbaden 2011, pp. 63–77.

W. ECK & P. WEIß, 'Die Sonderregelungen für Soldatenkinder seit Antoninus Pius. Ein niederpannonisches Militärdiplom vom 11. Aug. 146', *Zeitschrift für Papyrologie und Epigraphik* 135 (2001), pp. 195–208.

V. EHRENBERG, *L'État grec*, Paris 1976.

K.-L. ELVERS, 'Carvilius', [in:] H. CANCIK & H. SCHNEIDER (eds.), *Der Neue Pauly. Enzyklopädie der Antike*, vol. II, Stuttgart – Weimar 1997, coll. 1000–1001.

K.-L. ELVERS, 'Didius', [in:] *Der Neue Pauly Enzyklopädie der Antike*, vol. III, Stuttgart – Weimar 1997, coll. 540–541.

J. EVANS GRUBBS, '"Marriage more shameful than adultery": Slave-mistress relationships, "mixed marriages", and late Roman law', *Phoenix* 47.2 (1993), pp. 125–154.

J. EVANS GRUBBS, *Law and Family in Late Antiquity. The Emperor Constantine's Marriage Legislation*, Oxford 1995.

J. EVANS GRUBBS, 'Making the private public: Illegitimacy and incest in Roman law', [in:] C. ANDO & J. RÜPKE (eds.), *Public and Private in Ancient Mediterranean Law and Religion* [= *Religionsgeschichtliche Versuche und Vorarbeiten* LXV], Berlin 2015, pp. 115–141.

N. EVERETT, 'Literacy and the law in Lombard government', *Early Medieval Europe* 9 (2000), pp. 93–127.

C. FAYER, *La familia romana. Aspetti giuridici ed antiquari. Parte seconda. Sponsalia, matrimonio, dote*, Rome 2005.

C. FAYER, *La familia romana. Aspetti giuridici ed antiquari. Parte terza. Concubinato, divorzio, adulterio*, Rome 2005.

R. FIORI, 'La struttura del matrimonio romano', *Bullettino dell'Istituto di diritto romano "Vittorio Scialoja"* 105 (2011), pp. 197–233.

C. FISCHER-BOVET, 'Official identity and ethnicity: comparing Ptolemaic and Early Roman Egypt', *Journal of Egyptian History* 11 (2018), pp. 208–242.

J. FRANCE, 'Three papyri from Theadelpheia in Gent', *Zeitschrift für Papyrologie und Epigraphik* 123 (1998), pp. 135–144.

P.J. FRANDSEN, *An Incestuous and Close-Kin Marriage in Ancient Egypt and Persia: An*

Examination of the Evidence [= *Carsten Niebuhr Institute Publications* XXXIV], Copenhagen 2009.

D. Frankfurter, *Christianizing Egypt: Syncretism and Local Worlds in Late Antiquity*, Princeton – Oxford 2018.

The French Civil Code. Literally Translated from the Original and Official Edition, Published at Paris, in 1804, translation attributed to G. Spence, London 1827.

P.M. Fraser, *Ptolemaic Alexandria*, Oxford 1972.

R. Friedl, *Der Konkubinat im kaiserzeitlichen Rom. Von Augustus bis Septimius Severus* [= *Historia – Einzelschriften* XCVIII], Stuttgart 1996.

P. Garnsey, 'The criminal jurisdiction of governors', *The Journal of Roman Studies* 58.1–2 (1968), pp. 51–59.

K. Geens, 'Administrative archive of Theadelpheia', [in:] K. Vandorpe, W. Clarysse & H. Verreth (eds.), *Graeco-Roman Archives from the Fayum* [= *Collectanea Hellenistica – KVAB* VI], Leuven – Paris – Bristol, CT 2015, pp. 34–39.

K. Geens & W. Clarysse, 'Tax collectors from Soknopaiou Nesos', [in:] K. Vandorpe, W. Clarysse & H. Verreth (eds.), *Graeco-Roman Archives from the Fayum* [= *Collectanea Hellenistica – KVAB* VI], Leuven – Paris – Bristol, CT 2015, pp. 383–386.

M. Gibbs, 'Manufacture, trade, and the economy', [in:] Ch. Riggs (ed.), *The Oxford Handbook of Roman Egypt*, Oxford 2012, pp. 38–55.

J.F. Gilliam, 'Notes on Latin texts from Egypt', [in:] J. Bingen, G. Cambier & G. Nachtergael (eds.), *Le monde grec : pensée, littérature, histoire, documents. Hommages à Claire Préaux*, Brussels 1975, pp. 766–774 (reprinted in: J.F. Gilliam, *Roman Army Papers*, Amsterdam 1986, pp. 363–372).

J.F. Gilliam, 'Some Roman elements in Roman Egypt', *Illinois Classical Studies* 3 (1978), pp. 115–131.

C. Gizewski & J.B. Campbell, 'Decurio, Decuriones', [in:] H. Cancik & H. Schneider (eds.), *Brill's New Pauly*, Accessed April 20, 2019. doi: http://dx.doi.org/10.1163/1574-9347_bnp_e312510.

E.S. Golubcova, A.I. Pavlovskaja & T.V. Blavatskaja, *Die Sklaverei in hellenistischen Staaten im 3.–1. Jh. v. Chr.*, Wiesbaden 1972.

J. González & M.H. Crawford, 'The lex Irnitana: A new copy of the Flavian municipal law', *The Journal of Roman Studies* 76 (1986), pp. 147–243.

K. Goudriaan, *Ethnicity in Ptolemaic Egypt* [= *Dutch Monographs on Ancient History and Archaeology* V], Amsterdam 1988.

G.F. Grassi, 'Matrimoni misti e onomastica nella Siria d'età romana: il caso di Dura Europos', [in:] S. Marchesini (ed.), *Atti del Convegno Matrimoni misti: una via per l'integrazione tra i popoli. Mixed Marriages: A Way to Integration among Peoples. Convegno multidisciplinare internazionale (Verona – Trento, 1–2 dicembre 2011)*, Trento 2012, pp. 127–138.

E. Grzybek, 'Die griechische Konkubine und ihre „Mitgift" (*P. Eleph.* 3 und 4)', *Zeitschrift für Papyrologie und Epigraphik* 76 (1989), pp. 206–212.

L.-M. Günther, '*Nothoi* und *nothai* – eine Randgruppe in der hellenistischen Polis? Zur Auswertung der einschlägigen Inschriften Milets', [in:] A. Matthaei & M. Zimmermann (eds.), *Stadtkultur im Hellenismus* [= *Die hellenistische Polis als Lebensform* IV], Heidelberg 2014, pp. 133–147.

W. Habermann, 'Zur chronologischen Verteilung der papyrologischen Zeugnisse', *Zeitschrift für Papyrologie und Epigraphik* 122 (1998), pp. 144–160.

D. Hagedorn, 'Marci Aurelii in Ägypten nach der Constitutio Antoniniana', *The Bulletin of the American Society of Papyrologists* 16 (1979), pp. 47–59.

D. Hagedorn, 'Zur Verwendung von υἱός und θυγάτηρ vor dem Vatersnamen in Urkunden römischer Zeit', *Zeitschrift für Papyrologie und Epigraphik* 80 (1990), pp. 277–282.

A.E. Hanson, rev. of *The Oxyrhynchus Papyri*, vol. LV, ed. J.R. Rea, London 1988, *Gnomon* 62.3 (1990), pp. 273–275.

K. Harper, '*Porneia*: The making of a Christian sexual norm', *Journal of Biblical Literature* 131.2 (2012), pp. 363–383.

A.R.W. Harrison, *The Law of Athens. Family and Property*, Oxford 1968.

E. Herrmann-Otto, *Ex ancilla natus: Untersuchungen zu den „hausgeborenen" Sklaven und Sklavinnen im Westen des Römischen Kaiserreiches* [= *Forschungen zur antiken Sklaverei* XXIV], Mainz 1993.

M. Hirt, 'In search of Junian Latins', *Historia* 67.3 (2018), pp. 288–312.

D.W. Hobson, 'Naming practices in Roman Egypt', *The Bulletin of the American Society of Papyrologists* 26 (1989), pp. 157–174.

T. Honoré, *Law in the Crisis of Empire 379–455 AD: The Theodosian Dynasty and its Quaestors*, Oxford 1998.

S.R. HUEBNER, 'Brother-sister marriage in Roman Egypt: A curiosity of humankind or a widespread family strategy?', *The Journal of Roman Studies* 97 (2007), pp. 21–49.

S.R. HUEBNER, *The Family in Roman Egypt. A Comparative Approach to Intergenerational Solidarity and Conflict*, Cambridge 2013.

C. HUMFRESS, 'Civil law and social life', [in:] N. LENSKI (ed.), *The Cambridge Companion to the Age of Constantine* [= *Cambridge Companions to the Ancient World*], Cambridge 2006, pp. 205–225.

P.E. HUSCHKE, *Gaii Institutionum iuris civilis commentarii quattuor. Separatim ex iurisprudentiae anteiustinianae reliquiarum*, Leipzig 1886.

N. ISTASSE, 'Trois notes sur les affranchis dans les papyrus de l'Égypte romaine', *Chronique d'Égypte* 76 (2001), pp. 202–208.

D. JOHNSTON, *The Roman Law of Trusts*, Oxford 1988.

A. JÖRDENS, 'Noch einmal: Norbanus *praefectus Aegypti*?', *Zeitschrift für Papyrologie und Epigraphik* 163 (2007), pp. 195–199.

A. JÖRDENS, *Statthalterliche Verwaltung in der römischen Kaiserzeit. Studien zum praefectus Aegypti* [= *Historia – Einzelschriften* CLXXV], Stuttgart 2009.

A. JÖRDENS, 'Nochmals zur bibliotheke enkteseon', [in:] G. THÜR (ed.), *Symposion 2009: Vorträge zur griechischen und hellenistischen Rechtsgeschichte (Seggau, 25.–30. August 2009)* [= *Akten der Gesellschaft für griechische und hellenistische Rechtsgeschichte* XXI], Vienna 2010, pp. 277–290.

A. JÖRDENS, 'Öffentliche archive und römische Rechtspolitik', [in:] K. LEMBKE, M. MINAS-NERPEL & S. PFEIFFER (eds.), *Tradition and Transformation: Egypt under Roman Rule. Proceedings of the International Conference, Hildesheim, Roemer- and Pelizaeus-Museum, 3–6 July 2008* [= *Culture and History of the Ancient Near East* XLI], Leiden 2010, pp. 159–179.

A. JÖRDENS, 'Status and citizenship', [in:] C. RIGGS (ed.), *The Oxford Handbook of Roman Egypt*, Oxford 2012, pp. 247–259.

A. JÖRDENS, 'Keine Konkurrenz und dennoch Recht: Zum Umgang Roms mit den lokalen Rechten', [in:] D. LEÃO & G. THÜR (eds.), *Symposion 2015. Vorträge zur griechischen und hellenistischen Rechtsgeschichte (Coimbra, 1–4 September 2015)* [= *Akten der Gesellschaft für griechische und hellenistische Rechtsgeschichte* XXV], Vienna 2016, pp. 237–250.

A. Kacprzak, 'The widow's duty of mourning and the ancient concept of pregnancy', [in:] E. Hoebenreich & V. Kuhne (eds.), *El Cisne. Derecho romano, biologismo y algomas*, Lecce 2010, pp. 81–98.

A. Kacprzak, '*Servus ex libera natus*. Überlegungen zum senatusconsultum Claudianum', [in:] D. Feichtinger & I. Fischer (eds.), *Sexualität und Sklaverei* [= *Alter Orient und Altes Testament* CDLVI], Münster 2018, pp. 63–82.

A. Kacprzak & M. Nowak, 'Foundlings in the Greco-Roman world: Status and the (im)possibility of adoption', *Tijdschrift voor Rechtsgeschiedenis* 86 (2018), pp. 13–54.

I. Kajanto, *The Latin Cognomina* [= *Commentationes Humanarum Litterarum* XXXVI.2], Helsinki 1965.

A. Kakoschke, 'Annotationes Epigraphicae VII. Zu einigen Inschriften aus den römischen Provinzen Germania inferior und Germania superior', *Frankfurter elektronische Rundschau zur Altertumskunde* 34 (2017), pp. 1–29, https://doi.org/10.21248/fera.32.191.

D. Kamen, *Status in Classical Athens*, Princeton – Oxford 2013.

N. Kanavou & A. Papathomas, 'An Alexandrian murder case revisited (*P. Philammon* = *BGU* IV 1024, pp. 6.3–8.21)', *Zeitschrift für Papyrologie und Epigraphik* 200 (2016), pp. 453–469.

U. Kaplony-Heckel, *Die demotischen Tempeleide* [= *Ägyptologische Abhandlungen* VI], Wiesbaden 1963.

P. Karavites, *Evil, Freedom, and the Road to Perfection in Clement of Alexandria* [= *Vigiliae Christianae Supplement* XLIII], Leiden – Boston – Cologne 1999.

M. Kaser, *Das römische Privatrecht, 1: Das altrömische, das vorklassische und klassische Recht. 2. Neubearbeite Auflage* [= *Rechtsgeschichte des Altertums im Rahmen des Handbuchs der Altertumswissenschaft* X.3.3.1], Munich 19712.

J. Keenan, 'Roman criminal law in a Berlin papyrus codex (*BGU* IV 1024–1027)', *Archiv für Papyrusforschung* 35 (1989), pp. 15–23.

J. Kolendo, 'L'esclavage et la vie sexuelle des hommes libres à Rome', *Index* 10 (1981), pp. 288–297.

M. Krawczyk, 'Paternal onomastical legacy vs. illegitimacy in Roman epitaphs', [in:] M. Nowak, A. Łajtar & J. Urbanik (eds.), *Tell Me Who You Are. Labelling Status in the Graeco-Roman World* [= *U schyłku starożytności. Studia źródłoznawcze* XVI], Warsaw 2017, pp. 107–128.

H. Kreller, *Erbrechtliche Untersuchungen auf Grund der graeco-ägyptischen Papyrusurkunden*, Leipzig – Berlin 1919.

T. Kruse, *Der Königliche Schreiber und die Gauverwaltung: Untersuchungen zur Verwaltungsgeschichte Ägyptens in der Zeit von Augustus bis Philippus Arabs (30 v. Chr.–245 n. Chr.)* [= *Archiv für Papyrusforschung und verwandte Gebiete* XI.1–2], vols. I & II, Munich 2002.

T. Kruse, 'Bevölkerungskontrolle, Statuszugang und Archivpraxis im römischen Ägypten', [in:] M. Faraguna (ed.), *Archives and Archival Documents in Ancient Societies: Legal Documents in Ancient Societies, IV. Trieste, 30 September – 1 October 2011*, Trieste 2013, pp. 307–332.

T. Kruse, 'The labeling of strangers and aliens in Roman Egypt', [in:] M. Nowak, A. Łajtar & J. Urbanik (eds.), *Tell Me Who You Are. Labelling Status in the Graeco-Roman World* [= *U schyłku starożytności. Studia źródłoznawcze* XVI], Warsaw 2017, pp. 129–146.

M. Langellotti, 'Occupations and naming trends in first-century Tebtunis and Philadelphia', [in:] M. Nowak, A. Łajtar & J. Urbanik (eds.), *Tell Me Who You Are. Labelling Status in the Graeco-Roman World* [= *U schyłku starożytności. Studia źródłoznawcze* XVI], Warsaw 2017, pp. 147–182.

M. Lauria, '*Ὁ γνώμων τοῦ ἰδιοῦ λόγου*. Retractatio', *Studia et documenta historiae et iuris* 49 (1983), pp. 1–17.

Y. Le Bohec, *The Imperial Roman Army*, tr. R. Bate, London – New York 2000.

A. Leeman-De Ridder, 'Requête concernant une vente de terrains. Papyrus de Leyde', [in:] M. David, B.A. van Groningen & E.M. Meijers (eds.), *Symbolae ad jus et historiam antiquitatis pertinentes Julio Christiano van Oven dedicatae*, Leiden 1946, pp. 122–128.

B. Legras, *Néotês : recherches sur les jeunes Grecs dans l'Egypte ptolémaïque et romaine* [= *Hautes études du monde gréco-romain* XXVI], Geneva 1999.

B. Legras, 'Les testaments grecs dans le droit hellénistique : la question des héritières et des testatrices', [in:] E. Cantarella (ed.), *Symposion 2005. Vorträge zur griechischen und hellenistischen Rechtsgeschichte (Salerno, 14.–18. September 2005) = Comunicazioni sul diritto greco ed ellenistico (Salerno, 14–18 settembre 2005)* [= *Akten der Gesellschaft für griechische und hellenistische Rechtsgeschichte* XIX], Vienna 2007, pp. 293–306.

O. Lenel, *Palingenesia iuris civilis. Iuris consultorum reliquiae quae Iustiniani Digestis continentur ceteraque iurisprudentiae civilis fragmenta minora secundum auctores et libros*, Leipzig 1889 (reprint: Graz 1960).

F. Lerouxel, 'Les femmes sur le marché du crédit en Égypte romaine (30 avant J.-C. – 284 après J.-C.). Une approche néo-institutionnaliste', *Les cahiers du Centre de recherches historiques* 37 (2006), pp. 121–136.

F. Lerouxel, 'The private credit market, the *bibliotheke enkteseon*, and public services in Roman Egypt', *Annales. Histoire, Sciences Sociales* 67.4 (2012), pp. 629–659.

J. Lesquier, 'Le mariage des soldats romains', *Comptes rendus des séances de l'Académie des inscriptions et belles-lettres* 61.4 (1917), pp. 227–236.

J. Lesquier, *L'armée romaine d'Égypte d'Auguste à Dioclétien* [= *Mémoires publiés par les membres de l'Institut français d'archéologie orientale du Caire* XLI], Cairo 1918.

J.-P. Lévy, 'Les actes d'état civil romains', *Revue historique de droit français et étranger* 29 (1952), pp. 449–486.

D. Lewis, 'Slave marriages in the laws of Gortyn: A matter of rights?', *Historia* 62.4 (2013), pp. 390–416.

D. Lewis, 'Notes on slave names, ethnicity, and identity in Classical and Hellenistic Greece', [in:] M. Nowak, A. Łajtar & J. Urbanik (eds.), *Tell Me Who You Are. Labelling Status in the Graeco-Roman World* [= *U schyłku starożytności. Studia źródłoznawcze* XVI], Warsaw 2017, pp. 183–213.

N. Lewis, 'A restudy of SB VIII 9897', *Archiv für Papyrusforschung* 28 (1982), pp. 31–38.

N. Lewis, 'Dryton's wives: two or three?', *Chronique d'Égypte* 57 (1982), pp. 317–321.

N. Lewis, 'Notationes legentis', *The Bulletin of the American Society of Papyrologists* 29 (1992), pp. 127–133.

W.H.M. Liesker & P.J. Sijpesteijn, 'More remarks on some imperial titles in the papyri III', *Zeitschrift für Papyrologie und Epigraphik* 63 (1986), pp. 281–290.

S.N.C. Lieu, 'Constantine in legendary literature', [in:] N. Lenski (ed.), *The Cambridge Companion to the Age of Constantine* [= *Cambridge Companions to the Ancient World*], Cambridge 2005, pp. 298–322.

S. Lippert, *Einführung in die altägyptische Rechtsgeschichte* [= *Einführungen und Quellentexte zur Ägyptologie* V], Münster 20122.

G. Luchetti, *La legittimazione dei figli naturali nelle fonti tardo imperiali e giustinianee*, Milan 1990.

A. Łajtar, *Deir el-Bahari in the Hellenistic and Roman Periods. A Study of an Egyptian Temple Based on Greek Sources* [= *The Journal of Juristic Papyrology Supplement* IV], Warsaw 2006.

M. Malouta, 'The terminology of fatherlessness in Roman Egypt: *ἀπάτωρ* and *χρηματίζων μητρός*', [in:] J. Frösén, T. Purola & E. Salmenkivi (eds.), *Proceedings of the 24th International Congress of Papyrology, Helsinki, 1–7 August, 2004* [= *Commentationes Humanarum Litterarum* CXXII], Helsinki 2007, vol. II, pp. 615–623.

M. Malouta, 'Antinoite citizenship under Hadrian and Antoninus Pius. A prosopographical study of the first thirty years of Antinoopolis', *The Bulletin of the American Society of Papyrologists* 46 (2009), pp. 81–96.

M. Malouta, 'Fatherlessness and formal identification in Roman Egypt', [in:] S.R. Huebner & D.M. Ratzan (eds.), *Growing up Fatherless in Antiquity*, Cambridge 2009, pp. 120–138.

J.C. Mann, 'Name forms of recipients of diplomas', *Zeitschrift für Papyrologie und Epigraphik* 139 (2002), pp. 227–234.

K. Maresch, 'Die Bibliotheke Enkteseon im römischen Ägypten. Überlegungen zur Funktion zentraler Besitzarchive', *Archiv für Papyrusforschung* 48.1 (2002), pp. 233–246.

F. Maroi, 'Intorno all'adozione degli esposti nell'Egitto romano', [in:] *Raccolta di scritti in onore di Giacomo Lumbroso (1844–1925)*, Milan 1925, pp. 377–406.

V. Marotta, 'I diritti degli stranieri', [in:] A. Giardina & F. Pesando (eds.), *Roma caput mundi. Una città tra dominio e integrazione*, Milan 2012, pp. 201–209.

V. Marotta, 'Doppia cittadinanza e pluralità degli ordinamenti. La Tabula Banasitana e le linee 7–9 del Papiro di Giessen 40 col. I', *Archivio giuridico Filippo Serafini* 236 (2016), pp. 461–491.

V. Marotta, 'Egyptians and citizenship from the first century AD to the *constitutio Antoniniana*', [in:] L. Cecchet & A. Busetto (eds.), *Citizens in the Graeco-Roman World. Aspects of Citizenship from the Archaic Period to AD 212* [= *Mnemosyne Supplement* CDVII], Leiden 2017, pp. 172–198.

A.J. Marshall, 'Pompey's organization of Bithynia-Pontus: Two neglected texts', *The Journal of Roman Studies* 58.1–2 (1968), pp. 103–109.

A. Martin, 'En marge de la Charta Borgiana', *Chronique d'Égypte* 75 (2000), pp. 118–125.

A. Martin & R. Pintaudi, 'Le journal fiscal *SB* XXVI 16560 : une réédition', *Aegyptus* 95 (2015), pp. 25–42.

S. McDougall, *Royal Bastards: The Birth of Illegitimacy, 800–1230* [= *Oxford Studies in Medieval European History*], Oxford 2016.

Th. McGinn, *Prostitution, Sexuality, and the Law in Ancient Rome*, Oxford 1998.

Th. McGinn, 'The social policy of emperor Constantine in Codex Theodosianus 4,6,3', *Tijdschrift voor Rechtsgeschiedenis* 67.1–2 (1999), pp. 57–73.

B.H. McLean, *An Introduction to Greek Epigraphy of the Hellenistic and Roman Periods from Alexander the Great down to the Reign of Constantine (323 BC – AD 337)*, Ann Arbor 2002.

M. Meinhart, *Die Senatusconsulta Tertullianum und Orfitianum in ihrer Bedeutung für das klassische römische Erbrecht* [= *Wiener Rechtgeschichtliche Arbeiten* IX], Graz – Vienna – Cologne 1967.

J. Mélèze-Modrzejewski, 'Gnomon de idiologue', [in:] P.F. Girard & F. Senn (eds.), *Les lois des Romains*, Naples 1977, pp. 520–557.

J. Mélèze-Modrzejewski, 'Dryton le crétois et sa famille ou les mariages mixtes dans l'Égypte hellénistique', [in:] *Aux origines de l'Hellénisme, la Crète et la Grèce. Hommage à Henri Van Effenterre présenté par le Centre Gustave Glotz* [= *Publications de la Sorbonne. Histoire ancienne et médiévale* XV], Paris 1984, pp. 353–377.

J. Mélèze-Modrzejewski, 'Bibliographie de papyrologie juridique : 1972–1982 (III.3)', *Archiv für Papyrusforschung* 32 (1986), pp. 97–147.

J. Mélèze-Modrzejewski, 'La fiancée adultère : à propos de la pratique matrimoniale du judaisme hellénisé à la lumière du dossier du politeuma juif d'Hérakléopolis (144/3–133/2 avant n.è.)', [in:] Z. Służewska & J. Urbanik (eds.), *Marriage: Ideal – Law – Practice. Proceedings of a Conference Held in Memory of Henryk Kupiszewski in Warsaw on the 24th of April 2004* [= *The Journal of Juristic Papyrology Supplement* V], Warsaw 2005, pp. 141–160.

J. Mélèze-Modrzejewski, *Droit et justice dans le monde grec et hellénistique* [= *The Journal of Juristic Papyrology Supplement* X], Warsaw 2010.

J. Mélèze-Modrzejewski, *Loi et coutume dans l'Égypte grecque et romaine.* [= *The Journal of Juristic Papyrology Supplement* XXI], Warsaw 2014.

E. Meyer, 'Freed and *astoi* in the *Gnomon of the Idios Logos* and in Roman Egypt', [in:] K. Harter-Uibopuu & T. Kruse (eds.), *Studien zum „Gnomon des Idios Logos": Beiträge zum Dritten Wiener Kolloquium zur antiken Rechtsgeschichte* [= *Wiener Kolloquien zur Antiken Rechtsgeschichte*], forthcoming.

P.M. Meyer, 'Papyrus Cattaoui. II. Kommentar', *Archiv für Papyrusforschung* 3 (1906), pp. 67–105.

P.M. Meyer, *Juristische Papyri. Erklärung von Urkunden zur Einführung in die juristische Papyruskunde*, Berlin 1920.

J.B. Mispoulet, 'Du nom et de la condition de l'enfant naturel romain', *Nouvelle revue historique de droit français et étranger* 9 (1885), pp. 15–63.

J. Modrzejewski, 'The πρόσταγμα in the papyri', *The Journal of Juristic Papyrology* 5–6 (1951–1952), pp. 187–206.

A. Monson, 'Late Ptolemaic capitation taxes and the poll tax in Roman Egypt', *The Bulletin of the American Society of Papyrologists* 51 (2014), pp. 127–160.

F. Montanari, *The Brill Dictionary of Ancient Greek*, M. Goh, C. Schroeder (Eng. ed.), Leiden – Boston 2015.

O. Montevecchi, 'Nerone a una polis e ai 6475', *Aegyptus* 50 (1970), pp. 5–33.

O. Montevecchi, 'L'*epikrisis* dei Greco-Egizi', [in:] P.J. Parsons, J.R. Rea & E.G. Turner (eds.), *Proceedings of the XIV International Congress of Papyrologists, Oxford, 24–31 July 1974* [= *Graeco-Roman Memoirs* LXI], London 1975, pp. 227–232.

O. Montevecchi, 'Endogamia e cittadinanza romana in Egitto', *Aegyptus* 59 (1979), pp. 137–144.

O. Montevecchi, *La papirologia*, Milan 1988².

O. Montevecchi, 'Adriano e la fondazione di Antinoopolis', *Latomus* 209 (1990), pp. 183–195.

O. Montevecchi, 'Epikrisis e dichiarazioni di censimento di cateci arsinoiti', *Aegyptus* 70 (1990), pp. 27–31.

O. Montevecchi, 'PSI V 457. Un caso di endogamia o una semplificazione del formulario?', *Aegyptus* 73 (1993), pp. 49–55.

O. Montevecchi, 'Efebia e ginnasio. In margine a B. Legras, "Néotês"', *Aegyptus* 80 (2000), pp. 133–138.

D. Montserrat, G. Fantoni & P. Robinson, 'Varia descripta Oxyrhynchita', *The Bulletin of the American Society of Papyrologists* 31 (1994), pp. 11–80.

P. Moreau, *Incestus et prohibitae nuptiae : conception romaine de l'inceste et histoire des prohibitions matrimoniales pour cause de parenté dans la Rome antique* [= *Collection d'études anciennes* LXII], Paris 2002.

H. Mouritsen, *The Freedman in the Roman World*, Cambridge – New York 2011.

E. Nardi, 'Sui divieti matrimoniali delle leggi augustee', *Studia et documenta historiae et iuris* 7 (1941), pp. 112–146.

C.A. Nelson, *Status Declarations in Roman Egypt* [= *American Studies in Papyrology* XIX], Amsterdam 1979.

M. Niziołek, 'Meaning of the phrase *liberi naturales* in Roman law sources up to Constantine's reign', *Revue internationale des droits de l'antiquité* 22 (1975), pp. 317–344.

M. Niziołek, *Legal Effects of Concubinage in Reference to Concubine's Offspring in the Light of Imperial Legislation of the Period of Dominate*, Cracow 1980.

M. Nowak, '*Mancipatio* and its life in late-Roman law', *The Journal of Juristic Papyrology* 41 (2011), pp. 103–122.

M. Nowak, 'Ways of describing illegitimate children vs. their legal situation', *Zeitschrift für Papyrologie und Epigraphik* 193 (2015), pp. 207–218.

M. Nowak, *Wills in the Roman Empire: A Documentary Approach* [= *The Journal of Juristic Papyrology Supplement* XXIII], Warsaw 2015.

M. Nowak, 'The fatherless and family structure in Roman Egypt', [in:] D. Leão & G. Thür (eds.), *Symposion 2015. Vorträge zur griechischen und hellenistischen Rechtsgeschichte (Coimbra, 1–4 September 2015)* [= *Akten der Gesellschaft für griechische und hellenistische Rechtsgeschichte* XXV], Vienna 2016, pp. 100–114.

M. Nowak, 'Fatherless among *οἱ ἀπὸ τῆς μητροπόλεως* – a revision', *Zeitschrift für Papyrologie und Epigraphik* 208 (2018), pp. 213–225.

M. Nowak, 'Get your free corn: The fatherless in the corn-dole archive from Oxyrhynchos', [in:] M. Nowak, A. Łajtar & J. Urbanik (eds.), *Tell Me Who You Are. Labelling Status in the Graeco-Roman World* [= *U schyłku starożytności. Studia źródłoznawcze* XVI], Warsaw 2017, pp. 215–228.

D. Nörr, 'Origo Studien zur Orts-, Stadt- und Reichszugehörigkeit in der Antike', *Tijdschrift voor Rechtsgeschie* 31 (1963), pp. 525–600.

T. Nuorluoto, 'Emphasising matrilineal ancestry in a patrilineal system. Maternal name preference in the Roman world', [in:] M. Nowak, A. Łajtar & J. Urbanik (eds.), *Tell Me Who You Are. Labelling Status in the Graeco-Roman World* [= *U schyłku starożytności. Studia źródłoznawcze* XVI], Warsaw 2017, pp. 257–281.

M. Nuti, 'Le attività e le attestazioni di un prefetto d'Egitto: Lucius Munatius Felix', *Papyrotheke* 1 (2010), pp. 67–77.

D. Ogden, *Greek Bastardy in the Classical and Hellenistic Periods*, Oxford 1996.

D. Ogden, *The Crooked Kings of Ancient Greece*, London 1997.

G. Oliver, 'Foreign names, inter-marriage and citizenship in Hellenistic Athens', [in:] R.W.V. Catling & F. Marchand (eds.) with the assistance of

M. Sasanow, *Onomatologos: Studies in Greek Personal Names Presented to Elaine Matthews*, Oxford 2010, pp. 155–169.

J. Partsch, *Griechisches Bürgschaftsrecht*, I: *Das Recht des altgriechischen Gemeindestaats*, Leipzig – Berlin 1909.

C. Patterson, 'Those Athenian bastards', *Classical Antiquity* 9 (1990), pp. 40–73.

M. Peachin, 'Papinian', [in:] R.S. Bagnall *et al.* (eds.), *The Encyclopedia of Ancient History*, 2015, doi:10.1002/9781444338386.wbeah25026.

O.M. Pearl, 'Part of a daybook of payments in kind', *Zeitschrift für Papyrologie und Epigraphik* 10 (1973), pp. 55–62.

P. Perdrizet, 'Copria', *Revue de l'Égypte ancienne* 23 (1921), pp. 85–94.

P.W. Pestman, *Marriage and Matrimonial Property in Ancient Egypt: A Contribution to Establishing the Legal Position of the Woman* [= *Papyrologica Lugduno-Batava* IX], Leiden 1961.

B. Pferdehirt, *Die Rolle des Militärs für den sozialen Aufstieg in der römischen Kaiserzeit* [= *Römisch-Germanisches Zentralmuseum. Monographien* XLIX], Mainz – Bonn 2002.

S.E. Phang, *The Marriage of Roman Soldiers (13 BC – AD 235): Law and Family in the Imperial Army* [= *Columbia Studies in the Classical Tradition* XXIV], Leiden – Boston – Cologne 2001.

A. Piganiol & R. Laurent-Vibert, 'Recherches archéologiques à Ammaedara (Haïdra)', *Mélanges d'archéologie et d'histoire* 32 (1912), pp. 69–229.

G. Plaumann, *Ptolemais in Oberägypten: ein Beitrag zur Geschichte des Hellenismus in Ägypten*, Leipzig 1910.

S.B. Pomeroy, 'Copronyms and the exposure of infants in Egypt', [in:] R.S. Bagnall & W.V. Harris (eds.), *Studies in Roman Law in Memory of A. Arthur Schiller* [= *Columbia Studies in the Classical Tradition* XIII], Leiden 1986, pp. 147–162.

B. Porten, 'Egypt. Elephantine', [in:] R. Westbrook (ed.), *A History of Ancient Near Eastern Law* [= *Handbook of Oriental Studies. Section 1. The Near and Middle East* LXXII], vol. 2, Leiden – Boston 2003, pp. 863–881.

B. Porten & H.Z. Szubin, 'The status of the handmaiden Tamet: A new interpretation of Kraeling 2 (TAD B3.3)', *Israel Law Review* 29.1–2 (1995), pp. 43–64.

J. Quaegebeur, 'Considérations sur le nom propre égyptien Teëphthaphônukhos', *Orientalia Lovaniensia Periodica* 4 (1973), pp. 85–100.

N. Quenouille, 'Eine Sklavenfreilassung aus der Ptolemäerzeit (P.UB Trier S 135-2 und 135-12)', *Archiv für Papyrusforschung* 48.1 (2002), pp. 67–97.

D. Rathbone, 'Egypt, Augustus and Roman taxation', *Cahiers du Centre Gustave Glotz* 4 (1993), pp. 81–112.

B. Rawson, rev. of I. Kajanto, *The Latin Cognomina* [= *Commentationes Humanarum Litterarum* XXXVI.2], Helsinki 1965, *Classical Philology* 63.2 (1968), pp. 154–159.

B. Rawson, '*Spurii* and the Roman view of illegitimacy', *Antichthon* 23 (1989), pp. 10–41.

Th. Reinach, 'Un code fiscal de l'Égypte romaine : le Gnomon de l'Idiologue', *Nouvelle revue historique de droit français et étranger* 43 (1919), pp. 583–636.

Th. Reinach, 'Un code fiscal de l'Égypte romaine : le Gnomon de l'Idiologue', *Nouvelle revue historique de droit français et étranger* 44 (1920), pp. 5–136.

S. Remijsen & W. Clarysse, 'Incest or adoption? Brother-sister marriage in Roman Egypt revisited', *The Journal of Roman Studies* 98 (2008), pp. 53–61.

S. Riccobono, *Gnomon dell'Idios Logos*, Palermo 1950.

K. Rigsby, 'An ephebic inscription from Egypt', *Greek, Roman and Byzantine Studies* 19 (1978), pp. 239–249.

G. Rizzelli, *Lex Iulia de adulteriis. Studi sulla disciplina di adulterium, lenocinium, stuprum*, Lecce 1997.

The Roman Questions of Plutarch: A New Translation, with Introductory Essays & a Running Commentary, ed. H. J. Rose, New York 1974.

S.T. Roselaar, 'The concept of *conubium* in the Roman Republic', [in:] P.J. Du Plessis (ed.), *New Frontiers: Law and Society in the Roman World*, Edinburgh 2013, pp. 102–122.

J. Rowlandson, *Landowners and Tenants in Roman Egypt. The Social Relations of Agriculture in the Oxyrhynchite Nome* [= *Oxford Classical Monographs*], Oxford 1996.

J. Rowlandson, 'Dissing the Egyptians: legal, ethnic and cultural identities in Roman Egypt', [in:] A. Gardner, E. Herring & K. Lomas (eds.), *Creating Ethnicities & Identities in the Roman World* [= *Bulletin of the Institute of Classical Studies Supplement* CXX], London 2013, pp. 213–247.

J. Rowlandson & R. Takahashi, 'Brother-sister marriage and inheritance strategies in Greco-Roman Egypt', *The Journal of Roman Studies* 99 (2009), pp. 104–139.

L. Rubinstein, *Adoption in IV. Century Athens* [= *Opuscula Graecolatina* XXXIV], Copenhagen 1993.

L. Rubinstein, L. Bjertrup, M.H. Hansen, T.H. Nielsen, T. Vestergaard, 'Adoption in Hellenistic and Roman Athens', *Classica et Mediaevalia* 42 (1991), pp. 139–151.

G. Ruffini, 'Genealogy and the gymnasium', *The Bulletin of the American Society of Papyrologists* 43 (2006), pp. 71–99.

H.-A. Rupprecht, *Studien zur Quittung im Recht der gräco-ägyptischen Papyri* [= *Münchener Beiträge zur Papyrusforschung und antiken Rechtsgeschichte* LVII], Munich 1972.

O. Salomies, *Die römischen Vornamen. Studien zur römischen Namengebung* [= *Commentationes Humanarum Litterarum* LXXXII], Helsinki 1987.

B. Salway, 'What's in a name? A survey of Roman onomastic practice from c. 700 BC to AD 700', *The Journal of Roman Studies* 84 (1994), pp. 124–145.

A.E. Samuel, *Ptolemaic Chronology* [= *Münchener Beiträge zur Papyrusforschung und antiken Rechtsgeschichte* XLIII], Munich 1962.

D.H. Samuel, 'Taxation at Socnopaiou Nesos in the early third century', *The Bulletin of the American Society of Papyrologists* 14 (1977), pp. 161–207.

C. Sánchez-Moreno Ellart, 'Notes on some new issues concerning the birth certificates of Roman citizens', *The Journal of Juristic Papyrology* 34 (2004), pp. 107–119.

C. Sánchez-Moreno Ellart , '*Ipsis liberis posterisque eorum.* Die Bedeutung der Geburtsurkunden von Soldaten der Auxiliareinheiten und der Wandel im Formular von *diplomata militaria* im Jahre 140 n. Chr. ausweislich RMD I 39 und RMD IV 266', *Zeitschrift der Savigny-Stiftung für Rechtsgeschichte RA* 125 (2008), pp. 348–374.

C. Sánchez-Moreno Ellart, '*ὑπομνήματα ἐπιγεννήσεως*: The Greco-Egyptian birth returns in Roman Egypt and the case of *P. Petaus* 1–2', *Archiv für Papyrusforschung* 56.1 (2010), pp. 91–129.

V. Sanna, *Matrimonio e altre situazioni matrimoniali nel diritto romano classico. Matrimonium iustum – matrimonium iniustum*, Naples 2012.

M. Sargenti, *Il diritto privato nella legislazione di Costantino. Persone e famiglia*, Milan 1938.

M. Sargenti, *Studi sul diritto del tardo impero* [= *Pubblicazioni della Università di Pavia. Studi nelle scienze giuridiche e sociali* XLVII], Padua 1986.

W. Scheidel, 'Quantifying the sources of slaves in the early Roman Empire', *The Journal of Roman Studies* 87 (1997), pp. 156–169.

W. Scheidel, 'Human mobility in Roman Italy, II: The slave population', *The Journal of Roman Studies* 95 (2005), pp. 64–79.

S. Schiavo, *Il falso documentale tra prevenzione e repressione. Impositio fidei criminaliter agere civiliter agere*, Milan 2007.

S. Schiavo, 'Aspetti processuali nell'Epitome Gai', [in:] G. Bassanelli Sommariva & S. Tarozzi (eds.), *Ravenna capitale. Giudizi, giudici e norme processuali in occidente nei secoli IV–VIII*, vol. II, Santarcangelo di Romagna 2015, pp. 49–94.

W. Schubart, 'Rom und die Ägypter nach dem Gnomon des Idios Logos', *Zeitschrift für Ägyptische Sprache und Altertumskunde* 56 (1920), pp. 80–95.

P. Schubert, *Philadelphie : Un village égyptien en mutation entre le IIe et le IIIe siècle ap. J.-C.* [= *Schweizerische Beiträge zur Altertumswissenschaft* XXXIV], Basel 2007.

F. Schulz, 'Roman registers of births and birth certificates', *The Journal of Roman Studies* 32 (1942), pp. 78–91.

F. Schulz, 'Roman registers of births and birth certificates. Part II', *The Journal of Roman Studies* 33.1–2 (1943), pp. 55–64.

A. Segré, 'A proposito di peregrini che prestavano servizio nelle legioni romane', *Aegyptus* 9 (1928), pp. 303–308.

E. Seidl, *Ptolemäische Rechtsgeschichte* [= *Ägyptologische Forschungen* XXII], Glückstadt 1962².

A.N. Sherwin-White, *The Roman Citizenship*, Oxford 1973².

P.J. Sijpesteijn, 'Some remarks on the *epicrisis* of οἱ ἀπὸ γυμνασίου in Oxyrhynchus', *The Bulletin of the American Society of Papyrologists* 13 (1976), pp. 181–190.

P.J. Sijpesteijn, 'Theognostos *alias* Moros and his family', *Zeitschrift für Papyrologie und Epigraphik* 76 (1989), pp. 213–218.

P.J. Sijpesteijn, 'Short remarks on some papyri, V', *Aegyptus* 71 (1991), pp. 43–51.

M. Silver, *Slave-Wives. Single Women and 'Bastards' in the Ancient Greek World: Law and Economics Perspectives*, Oxford 2018.

B. Sirks, 'Der Zweck des Senatus Consultum Claudianum von 52 n. Chr.', *Zeitschrift der Savigny-Stiftung für Rechtsgeschichte RA* 122 (2005), pp. 138–149.

B. SIRKS, rev. of P.J. du PLESSIS (ed.), *New Frontiers: Law and Society in the Roman World*, Edinburgh 2013, *Tijdschrift voor Rechtsgeschiedenis* 82 (2014), pp. 171–177.

N.W. SLATER, 'Theozotides on adopted sons (Lysias fr. 6)', *Scholia: Studies in Classical Antiquity* 2 (1993), pp. 81–85.

R. SMOLDERS, '*SB* XXII 15336 and the interpretation of *BGU* IX 1897', *Zeitschrift für Papyrologie und Epigraphik* 148 (2004), pp. 239–240.

R. SMOLDERS, 'Aphrodisios son of Philippos and descendants', [in:] K. VANDORPE, W. CLARYSSE & H. VERRETH (eds.), *Graeco-Roman Archives from the Fayum* [= *Collectanea Hellenistica – KVAB* VI], Leuven – Paris – Bristol, CT 2015, pp. 60–64.

R. SMOLDERS, 'Gemellus Horion', [in:] K. VANDORPE, W. CLARYSSE & H. VERRETH (eds.), *Graeco-Roman Archives from the Fayum* [= *Collectanea Hellenistica – KVAB* VI], Leuven – Paris – Bristol, CT 2015, pp. 143–149.

S. SOLAZZI, 'Glosse a Gaio, I', [in:] *Studi in onore di Salvatore Riccobono nel XL anno del suo insegnamento*, vol. I, Palermo 1936, pp. 73–191 (reprinted in: S. SOLAZZI, *Scritti di diritto romano*, vol. VI, Naples 1972, pp. 153–267).

H. SOLIN, *Beiträge zur Kenntnis der griechischen Personennamen in Rom*, vol. I [= *Commentationes Humanarum Litterarum* XLVIII], Helsinki 1971.

H. SOLIN, 'Analecta epigraphica', *Arctos* 41 (2007), pp. 89–115.

H. SOLIN, 'Name', *Reallexikon für Antike und Christentum*, vol. XXV, Stuttgart 2013, coll. 723–795.

M. SOŁEK, '*Origo castris* and the local recruitment policy of the Roman army', *Novensia* 26 (2015), pp. 103–115.

J.D. SOSIN, 'A metic was a metic', *Historia* 65.1 (2016), pp. 2–13.

M.A. SPEIDEL, 'Les femmes et la bureaucratie : quelques réflexions sur l'interdiction du mariage dans l'armée romaine', *Cahiers du Centre Gustave Glotz* 24 (2013), pp. 205–215.

J.F. STAGL, 'Das *testamentum militare* in seiner Eigenschaft als *ius singulare*', *Revista de estudios histórico-jurídicos: Sección derecho romano* 36 (2014), pp. 129–157.

R. STARK, *The Rise of Christianity: A Sociologist Reconsiders History*, Princeton 1996.

R. STEWART, 'Tribus', [in:] R. S. BAGNALL *et al.* (eds.), *The Encyclopedia of Ancient History*, online edition, doi:10.1002/9781444338386.wbeah20132.

A. STORCHI MARINO, 'Restaurazione dei mores e controllo della mobilità sociale a Roma nel I secolo d.C.: il senatusconsultum claudiano *de poena feminarum quae servis coniungerentur*', [in:] F. REDUZZI MEROLA & A. STORCHI MARINO (eds.),

Femmes-esclaves : modèles d'interprétation anthropologique, économique, juridique : atti del 21. Colloquio internazionale GIREA, Lacco Ameno – Ischia, 27–29 ottobre 1994, Naples 1999, pp. 391–426.

R.F. Storrow, 'The phantom children of the Republic: international surrogacy and the new illegitimacy', *American University Journal of Gender Social Policy and Law* 20.3 (2012), pp. 561–609.

J.A. Straus, 'Le statut fiscal des esclaves dans l'Égypte romaine', *Chronique d'Égypte* 48 (1973), pp. 364–369.

J.A. Straus, 'Remarques sur quelques contrats de vente d'esclaves conservés sur papyrus', *Zeitschrift für Papyrologie und Epigraphik* 104 (1994), pp. 227–229.

J.A. Straus, *L'achat et la vente des esclaves dans l'Égypte romaine. Contribution papyrologique à l'étude de l'esclavage dans une province orientale de l'Empire romain* [= *Archiv für Papyrusforschung. Beiheft* XIV], Munich – Leipzig 2004.

A.K. Strong, 'Incest laws and absent taboos in Roman Egypt', (April 27, 2003). Available at SSRN: https://ssrn.com/abstract=1596967 or http://dx.doi.org/10.2139/ssrn.1596967.

F. Strum, 'Ha conferito Adriano uno statuto personale speciale agli Antinoiti?', *Iura* 43 (1992), pp. 83–97.

P.R. Swarney, *The Ptolemaic and Roman Idios Logos* [= *American Studies in Papyrology* VIII], Toronto 1970.

J.C. Tate, 'Inheritance rights of nonmarital children in late Roman law', *Roman Legal Tradition* 4 (2008), pp. 1–36.

R. Taubenschlag, *The Law of Greco-Roman Egypt in the Light of the Papyri, 332 BC – 640 AD*, Warsaw 1955[2].

L.R. Taylor, 'Freedmen and freeborn in the epitaphs of imperial Rome', *The American Journal of Philology* 82.2 (1961), pp. 113–132.

A. Theiner, *Vetera monumenta Poloniae et Lithuaniae gentiumque finitimarum historiam illustrantia maximam partem nondum edita ex tabulariis Vaticanis deprompta collecta ac serie chronologica disposita*, vol. II, Rome 1861.

C. Terreni, 'P. Mich 3.169: Il mistero di Sempronia Gemella', *Studia et documenta historiae et iuris* 62 (1996), pp. 573–582.

M. Thoma, '*Women's role in domestic economy of Roman Egypt.* The contribution of the *Gnomon of Idios Logos* (*BGU* V 1210)', [in:] R. Berg (ed.), *The Material Sides*

of Marriage. Women and Domestic Economies in Antiquity [= *Acta Instituti Romani Finlandiae* XLIII], Rome 2016, pp. 145–151.
H. Thylander, Étude sur l'épigraphie latine*: date des inscriptions – noms et dénomination latine – noms et origine des personnes* [= *Acta Instituti Romani regni Sueciae* V], Lund 1952.
M.N. Tod, 'An ephebic inscription from Memphis', *The Journal of Egyptian Archaeology* 37.1 (1951), pp. 86–99.
A. Toso, 'Emilio Papiniano e le influenze cristiane nell'evoluzione del diritto romano classico', [in:] *Acta Congressus iuridici internationalis VII saeculo a Decretalibus Gregorii IX et XIV a Codice Iustiniano promulgatis. Romae, 12–17 Novembris 1934*, Rome 1935, pp. 21–35.
S. Treggiari, 'Concubinae', *Papers of the British School at Rome* 49 (1981), pp. 59–81.
S. Treggiari, *Roman Marriage. Iusti Coniuges from the Time of Cicero to the Time of Ulpian*, Oxford 1991.

J. Urbanik, 'La repressione constantiniana dei divorzi: La libertà dei matrimoni trafitta con una forcina', [in:] *Fides. Humanitas. Ius. Studii in onore di Luigi Labruna*, vol. VIII, Naples 2007, pp. 5705–5726.
J. Urbanik, 'Dioskoros and the law (on succession): lex Falcidia revisited', [in:] J.-L. Fournet (ed.), *Les archives de Dioscore d'Aphrodité cent ans après leur découverte. Histoire et culture dans l'Égypte byzantine* [= *Études d'archéologie et d'histoire ancienne*], Paris 2008, pp. 117–142.
J. Urbanik, 'On the uselessness of it all: the Roman law of marriage and modern times', *Fundamina* 20.1 = *Editio specialis: Meditationes de iure et historia. Essays in honour of Laurens Winkel* (2014), pp. 937–951.
J. Urbanik, 'Husband and wife', [in:] P.J. du Plessis, C. Ando & K. Tuori, *The Oxford Handbook of Roman Law and Society*, Oxford 2016, pp. 473–486.
W. Uxkull-Gyllenband, *Der Gnomon des Idios Logos*, II: *Der Kommentar*, Berlin 1934 (= *BGU* V.1).

M. Vallet, 'Dryton et la citoyenneté ptolémaïte : statut juridique et stratégies sociales', *Chronique d'Égypte* 88 (2013), pp. 125–146.
B. Van Beek, 'Kronion son of Apion, head of the *grapheion* of Tebtynis', [in:] K. Vandorpe, W. Clarysse & H. Verreth (eds.), *Graeco-Roman Archives*

from the Fayum [= *Collectanea Hellenistica – KVAB* VI], Leuven – Paris – Bristol, CT 2015, pp. 215–221.

C. Van de Wiel, 'Les différentes formes de cohabitation hors justes noces et les dénominations diverses des enfants qui en sont nés dans le droit romain, canonique, civil et byzantin jusqu'au treizième siècle', *Revue internationale des droits de l'Antiquité* 39 (1992), pp. 327–358.

K. Vandorpe, 'Apollonia, a businesswoman in a multicultural society (Pathyris, 2nd–1st centuries BC)', [in:] H. Melaerts & L. Mooren (eds.), *Le rôle et le statut de la femme en Égypte hellénistique, romaine et byzantine : acts du colloque international, Bruxelles – Leuven, 27–29 novembre 1997* [= *Studia Hellenistica* XXXVII], Paris – Leuven – Sterling, VA 2002, pp. 325–336.

K. Vandorpe, 'Zenon son of Agreophon', [in:] K. Vandorpe, W. Clarysse & H. Verreth (eds.), *Graeco-Roman Archives from the Fayum* [= *Collectanea Hellenistica – KVAB* VI], Leuven – Paris – Bristol, CT 2015, pp. 447–455.

K. Vandorpe & S. Van Beselaere, 'Tax rolls of Karanis', [in:] K. Vandorpe, W. Clarysse & H. Verreth (eds.), *Graeco-Roman Archives from the Fayum* [= *Collectanea Hellenistica – KVAB* VI], Leuven – Paris – Bristol, CT 2015, pp. 388–390.

K. Vandorpe & S. Waebens, 'Women and gender in Roman Egypt: the impact of Roman rule', [in:] K. Lembke, M. Minas-Nerpel & S. Pfeiffer (eds.), *Tradition and Transformation: Egypt under Roman Rule. Proceedings of the International Conference, Hildesheim, Römer- und Pelizaeus-Museum, 3–6 July 2008* [= *Culture and History of the Ancient Near East* XLI], Leiden 2010, pp. 415–435.

P. van Minnen, 'House-to-house enquiries. An interdisciplinary approach to Roman Karanis', *Zeitschrift für Papyrologie und Epigraphik* 100 (1994), pp. 227–251.

P. van Minnen, '*Αἱ ἀπὸ γυμνασίου*. "Greek" women and the Greek "elite" in the metropoleis of Roman Egypt', [in:] H. Melaerts & L. Mooren (eds.), *Le rôle et le statut de la femme en Égypte hellénistique, romaine et byzantine : acts du colloque international, Bruxelles – Leuven, 27–29 novembre 1997* [= *Studia Hellenistica* XXXVII], Paris – Leuven – Sterling, VA 2002, pp. 337–353.

P. van Minnen, 'Another copy of *P. Mich.* XVIII 792', *Zeitschrift für Papyrologie und Epigraphik* 191 (2014), pp. 251–252.

M. Varvaro, 'Per la datazione del palinsesto veronese delle *Institutiones* di Gaio (Verona, B. Cap., Cod. XV)', *Scriptorium* 69.1 (2015), pp. 79–103.

J. Vélissaropoulos-Karakostas, 'Les nothoi hellénistiques', [in:] E. Harris

& G. Thür (eds.), *Symposion 2007. Vorträge zur griechischen und hellenistischen Rechtsgeschichte (Durham, 2.–6. September 2007)* [= *Akten der Gesellschaft für griechische und hellenistische Rechtsgeschichte* XX], Vienna 2008, pp. 253–274.

P. Voci, *Diritto ereditario romano*, II: *Parte speciale. Successione ab intesttato, successione testamentaria*, Milan 1963².

E. Volterra, 'In tema di *accusatio adulterii*', [in:] E. Albertario, P. de Francisci & P. Ciapessoni, *Studi in onore di Pietro Bonfante nel XL anno d'insegnamento*, vol. II, Milan 1930, pp. 109–126.

E. Volterra, 'La nozione giuridica del conubium', [in:] *Studi in memoria di Emilio Albertario*, vol. II, Milan 1950, pp. 348–384 (reprinted in: E. Volterra, *Scritti giuridici*, vol. II, Naples 1992, pp. 277–320).

E. Volterra, 'L'acquisto della cittadinanza romana e il matrimonio del peregrino', [in:] *Studi in onore di Enrico Redenti*, vol. II, Milan 1951, pp. 403–442 (reprinted in: *Scritti giuridici*, vol. II, Naples 1992, pp. 257–274).

E. Volterra, 'Manomissione e cittadinanza', [in:] *Studi in onore di U.E. Paoli*, Florence 1956, pp. 695–716.

E. Volterra, 'Manomissioni di schiavi compiute da peregrini', [in:] *Studi in onore di Pietro de Francisci*, vol. IV, Milan 1956, pp. 73–106.

E. Volterra, 'Il senatoconsulto Orfiziano e la sua applicazione in documenti egiziani del III secolo d.C.', [in:] *Atti dell'XI Congresso Internazionale di Papirologia, Milano, 2–8 settembre 1965*, Milan 1966, pp. 551–585.

E. Volterra, 'Iniustum matrimonium', [in:] *Studi in onore di Gaetano Scherillo*, vol. II, Milan 1972, pp. 441–470.

S. Waebens, 'Reflecting the "change in AD 140". The veteran categories of the *epikrisis* documents revisited', *Zeitschrift für Papyrologie und Epigraphik* 180 (2012), pp. 267–277.

A. Watson, *Legal Transplants. An Approach to Comparative Law*, Edinburgh 1974.

P.R.C. Weaver, '*Vicarius* and *vicarianus* in the *familia Caesaris*', *The Journal of Roman Studies* 54 (1964), pp. 117–128.

P.R.C. Weaver, 'Gaius I 84 and the S.C. Claudianum', *The Classical Review* 14.2 (1964), pp. 137–139.

P.R.C. Weaver, *Familia Caesaris. A Social Study of the Emperor's Freedmen and Slaves*, Cambridge 1972.

P. Weiss, 'Die vorbildliche Kaiserehe. Zwei Senatsbeschlüsse beim Tod der älteren und der jüngeren Faustina, neue Paradigmen und die Herausbildung des „antoninischen" Prinzipats', *Chiron* 38 (2008), pp. 1–46.

G. Wesch-Klein, 'Recruits and veterans', [in:] P. Erdkamp (ed.), *A Companion to the Roman Army* [= *Blackwell Companions to the Ancient World*], Malden – Oxford – Victoria 2007, pp. 435–450.

C. Wessely, *Karanis und Soknopaiu Nesos. Studien zur Geschichte antiker Cultur- und Personenverhältnisse*, Milan 1975 (reprint).

J.E.G. Whitehorne, 'The ephebate and the gymnasial class in Roman Egypt', *The Bulletin of the American Society of Papyrologists* 19 (1982), pp. 171–184.

J. Whitehorne, 'Becoming an Alexandrian citizen', *Comunicazioni* 4 (2001), pp. 25–34.

L. Winkel, *Error iuris nocet. Rechtsirrtum als Problem der Rechtsordnung*, vol. I: *Rechtsirrtum in der griechischen Philosophie und im römischen Recht bis Justinian* [= *Studia Amstelodamensia ad epigraphicam, ius antiquum et papyrologicam pertinentia* XXV], Zupthen 1985.

L. Winkel, 'Forms of imposed protection in legal history, especially in Roman law', *Fundamina: A Journal of Legal History* 16.1 (2010), pp. 578–587.

J.K. Winnicki, 'Ein Ptolemäischer offizier in Thebais', *Eos* 60 (1972), pp. 343–353.

E. Wipszycka, 'La valeur de l'onomastique pour l'histoire de la christianisation de l'Égypte. À propos d'une étude de R. S. Bagnall', *Zeitschrift für Papyrologie und Epigraphik* 62 (1986), pp. 173–181.

H.J. Wolff, *Written and Unwritten Marriages in Hellenistic and Postclassical Roman Law* [= *American Philological Association Philological Monographs* IX], Haverford, PA 1939.

H.J. Wolff, 'The background of the postclassical legislation on illegitimacy', *Seminar (Jurist)* 3 (1945), pp. 21–45.

H.J. Wolff, 'Neue juristische Urkunden', *Zeitschrift der Savigny-Stiftung für Rechtsgeschichte RA* 96 (1976), pp. 258–271.

H.J. Wolff, *Das Justizwesen der Ptolemäer*, Munich 1970².

R. Yaron, *Introduction to the Law of the Aramaic Papyri*, Oxford 1961.

U. Yiftach-Firanko, *Marriage and Marital Arrangements: A History of the Greek Marriage Documents in Egypt. 4th Century* BCE *– 4th Century* CE [= *Münchener Beiträge zur Papyrusforschung und antiken Rechtsgeschichte* XCIII], Munich 2003.

U. Yiftach-Firanko, 'A gymnasial registration report from Oxyrhynchus', *The Bulletin of the American Society of Papyrologists* 47 (2010), pp. 45–65.

U. Yiftach, 'Did *BGU* XIV 2367 work?', [in:] M. Depauw & S. Coussement (eds.), *Identifiers and Identification Methods in the Ancient World. Legal Documents in Ancient Societies*, vol. III [= *Orientalia Lovaniensia analecta* CCXXIX], Leuven – Paris – Walpole, MA 2014, pp. 103–118.

U. Yiftach, '*Apator metros*: The rise of a formula in bureaucratic perspective. Response to Maria Nowak', [in:] D. Leão & G. Thür (eds.), *Symposion 2015. Vorträge zur griechischen und hellenistischen Rechtsgeschichte (Coimbra, 1–4 September 2015)* [= *Akten der Gesellschaft für griechische und hellenistische Rechtsgeschichte* XXV], Vienna 2016, pp. 115–120.

M. Youni, 'Transforming Greek practice into Roman law: manumissions in Roman Macedonia', *Tijdschrift voor Rechtsgeschiedenis* 78 (2010), pp. 313–342.

H. Youtie, '*BGU* XI 2018', *Zeitschrift für Papyrologie und Epigraphik* 9 (1972), pp. 133–137.

H. Youtie, 'Ἀπάτορες. Law vs. custom in Roman Egypt', [in:] J. Bingen, G. Cambier & G. Nachtergael (eds.), *Le monde grec: pensée, littérature, histoire, documents. Hommages à Claire Préaux*, Brussels 1975, pp. 723–740 (reprinted in: H. Youtie, *Scriptiunculae Posteriores*, vol. I, Bonn 1981, pp. 17–35).

J. Yoyotte, 'Une étude sur l'anthroponymie gréco-égyptienne du nome prosôpite', *Bulletin de l'Institut français d'archéologie orientale* 55 (1955), pp. 125–140.

T. Yuge, 'Die Gesetze im Codex Theodosianus über die eheliche Bindung von freien Frauen mit Sklaven', *Klio* 64 (1982), pp. 145–150.

R. Ziegler, 'Bemerkungen zur Datierung dokumentarischer Papyri und Ostraka', *Zeitschrift für Papyrologie und Epigraphik* 114 (1996), pp. 157–161.

INDEX

LITERARY SOURCES

ROMAN LAW

PAPYRI AND OSTRACA

INSCRIPTIONS